DATE DUE			

Personal Selling

The Advances in Retailing Series

The Institute of Retail Management (IRM) was established to advance the understanding and practice of retailing by serving as a bridge between the academic community and industry. Two of the principal avenues the IRM uses to achieve this goal are conferences focusing on the latest ideas and research, and publications, including the *Journal of Retailing* and conference proceedings. Thus, the IRM's two most important audiences are academic scholars and practitioners in retailing-related fields.

The Advances in Retailing Series is a point of intersection for the IRM's conference and publication programs. Initiated with valuable input from both retailers and academics, the series presents an enduring collection of up-to-date studies of problems and issues in retailing theory and practice. It is intended to respond to a variety of pervasive needs by: presenting timely assessments of new developments in the field, bringing fresh perspectives from other industries to critical issues in retailing, stimulating further research on challenging issues raised at conferences, and fostering productive communication and cooperation between retailing executives and academic researchers.

We believe that, as a whole, this series effectively addresses these and other needs. We invite comments and suggestions from our readers on how it can best fulfill its purpose.

The books in the Advances in Retailing Series are:

Personal Selling: Theory, Research, and Practice
Edited by Jacob Jacoby and C. Samuel Craig

Managing Human Resources in Retail Organizations
Edited by Arthur P. Brief

Consumer Perception of Merchandise and Store Quality
Edited by Jacob Jacoby and Jerry C. Olson

The Service Encounter
Edited by John A. Czepiel, Michael R. Solomon, and Carol Suprenant

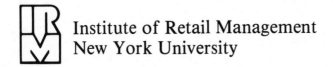 Institute of Retail Management
New York University

Personal Selling

Theory, Research, and Practice

Edited by
Jacob Jacoby
Institute of Retail Management
and Department of Marketing
New York University

C. Samuel Craig
Department of Marketing
New York University

LexingtonBooks
D.C. Heath and Company
Lexington, Massachusetts
Toronto

Library of Congress Cataloging in Publication Data

Main entry under title:
   Personal selling.

   (The Advances in retailing series)
   Papers presented at a conference, co-sponsored by the Institute for
Retail Management and the Association for Consumer Research.
   1. Selling—Congresses. I. Jacoby, Jacob. II. Craig, C. Samuel.
III. New York University. Institute of Retail Management. IV. Association
for Consumer Research (U.S.) V. Series.
HF5438.25.P46   1984   658.8'5   83–48825
ISBN 0–669–07606–6

Published simultaneously in Canada

Printed in the United States of America

International Standard Book Number: 0–669–07606–6

Library of Congress Catalog Card Number: 83–48825

To Fran, a salesperson par excellence
—J.J.

To the memory of my Father
—C.S.C.

Contents

Figures   ix

Tables   xi

Preface   xiii

Chapter 1   **Principles of Automatic Influence**
Robert B. Cialdini   1

Chapter 2   **Attitude Change and Personal Selling: Central and Peripheral Routes to Persuasion**
Richard E. Petty, John T. Cacioppo, and
David Schumann   29

Chapter 3   **Behavioral Influence Applied to Retail Selling Situations: When Actions Speak Louder than Words**   *Jerome B. Kernan* and
Peter H. Reingen   57

Chapter 4   **Some Social Psychological Perspectives on Closing**   *Jacob Jacoby*   73

Chapter 5   **An Attribution Theory Perspective on Using Two-Sided Messages to Increase Seller Credibility**
James M. Hunt, Michael F. Smith, and
Jerome B. Kernan   93

Chapter 6   **Ostensible Demarketing as a Personal Selling Strategy**   *Donald W. Barclay*   109

Chapter 7   **Sales Effectiveness through Adaptation to Situational Demands**   *Barton A. Weitz*   123

Chapter 8   **Bargaining Behavior in Personal Selling and Buying Exchanges**   *Arch G. Woodside*   143

Chapter 9   **Improving the Effectiveness of Salespersons' Time Allocation: A Research Program**
Terry Deutscher and *Adrian B. Ryans*   163

Chapter 10   **Determining Specialized Sales Assignments**
                Using Job Execution and Personal Criteria:
                A Method and Application
                Lawrence M. Lamont, William J. Lundstrom,
                and *William G. Zikmund*   183

Chapter 11   **The Personal Selling Process in the Life**
                Insurance Industry
                Elizabeth J. Johnston-O'Connor,
                Robert J. O'Connor, and *Walter H. Zultowski*   205

Chapter 12   **Consumer Scripts for Insurance Salesperson**
                Behavior in Sales Encounters   *Thomas W. Leigh*
                and *Arno J. Rethans*   223

Chapter 13   **The Job Satisfaction–Job Performance**
                Relationship: A Preliminary Analysis for
                Insurance Salespeople   *Ben M. Enis* and
                George H. Lucas, Jr.   237

Chapter 14   **The Impact of Interpersonal Attraction on**
                Salesperson Effectiveness   *Robert W. Chestnut*
                and *Jacob Jacoby*   261

Chapter 15   **Improving Retail Selling: A Corporate Cultures**
                Perspective   *Ben M. Enis* and
                Lawrence B. Chonko   269

Chapter 16   **Issues in Retail Selling: A Panel Discussion**
                Jay Hundley, Stan Jaffee, Robert Koch,
                Don Merritt, Larry Robinson, and
                Harmon Tobler   285

                About the Contributors   305

                About the Editors   313

                Members of the IRM Industry Councils   315

Figures

2-1   The Elaboration Likelihood Model of
       Attitude Change   33

2-2   Rhetorical Questions and Message Processing   37

2-3   Results of Source-Cue Study   41

2-4   Mock Magazine Ads for Razors   43

2-5   The Impact of an Attractive Source on a Moderately
       Involving Counteradditional Message   48

4-1   Applying the General Communication Model to the
       Sales Process   75

4-2   Generating a Positive Reaction to the Product
       According to the Balance Model, − − + Condition   77

5-1   The Effects of Expectancy Confirmation/
       Disconfirmation   96

6-1   Conceptual Model of Ostensible Demarketing   110

7-1   Adaptive Selling and Sales Effectiveness   129

7-2   Types of Sales Behaviors   133

7-3   Motivation to Engage in Adaptive Selling   137

8-1   The Car Dealers Game: Seller's Role   147

8-2   The Car Dealers Game: Buyer's Role   148

8-3   The Car Dealers Game: Bill of Sale   149

8-4   Framework of Buyer-Seller Exchanges   150

9-1   Schematic Diagram of Research Questions   165

13-1   The Hypothesized Model   239

13-2   The Revised Model   252

15-1   A Personal Selling Model   270

Tables

4-1	Patterns of Like-(Neutral)-Dislike and More Likely-Less Likely to Buy Responses by Sex and Product	75
5-1	Mean Attribute Belief Scores by Expectancy Disconfirmation	98
7-1	Cues for Recognizing Social Styles	134
8-1	Defining Characteristics of Bargaining and Personal Selling and Buying	146
8-2	Average Buyer and Seller Price Strategies and Contract Price	154
8-3	Example of Buyer and Seller Strategies of a Negotiation Resulting in a Price Favorable to the Buyer	156
8-4	Example of Buyer and Seller Strategies of a Negotiation Resulting in a Price Favorable to the Seller	157
9-1	Time Allocation in Sample Callplan Allocations	166
9-2	Factor Expected to Affect Task Performance	168
9-3	Comparison of the Three Research Paradigms	178
10-1	Summary of Personality Variables and Career Anchorage	188
10-2	Clusters of Industrial Salespeople Defined Using Behavioral Dimensions	192
10-3	Means of Personality, Personal Characteristic, Compensation, and Performance Measures by Salesperson Cluster	196
11-1	Consumer Reasons for Buying Insurance	206
11-2	Percent of Respondents Indicating Difficulty with Each of Five Aspects of Life Insurance	207
11-3	Buyers' Evaluations of Agents from Whom They Purchased Coverage	208
11-4	Incidence of Cost Comparison According to Belief in Cost Differences	210

11–5   Sources of Consumer Information   211

11–6   Consumer's Precontact Relationship with Agent   211

11–7   Buyers' Purchase Decisions by Agents'
          Recommendations   215

11–8   Agent Helpfulness as a Determinant of Purchase Rate   215

11–9   Consumer Satisfaction Relative to Purchase Rate   216

11–10   Percent of Policies That Lapsed within Policyowners'
          Ratings of the Quality of Their Agents' Sales
          Presentations   218

12–1   Insurance Script: Close Friend Manipulation   227

12–2   Insurance Script: Casual Acquaintance Manipulation   228

12–3   Interactive Script: Insurance Sales Call   229

13–1   Path Coefficients for Both Tested and Revised Models   246

13–2   Correlations between Variables in the Model   247

13–3   Comparison of Observed Correlations and
          Correlations Reconstructed from Revised Model   250

Preface

". . . more and more shoppers are stalking out of the stores empty-handed because of trouble with sales personnel."

"The biggest problem in retailing today is the sales people."
—Isadore Barmash, the *New York Times*, March 15, 1983

Background

To ensure that the issues the IRM addresses are relevant for the retailing community, a portion of the 1981–1982 academic year was devoted to a series of one-on-one and informal round-table discussions with knowledgeable industry representatives as well as mail surveys of its council members. From this process, the topic of personal selling emerged as a high-priority issue. The prevailing opinion was that there was much to be learned about and improved in the retail sales force. Given a better understanding and implementation of the factors surrounding personal selling, substantial improvements in sales force productivity could be expected.

Accordingly, a conference focusing on the subject of personal selling seemed warranted. The broad purpose was to bring interested academicians from various disciplines together with interested practitioners from various industries to discuss the subject and explore the latest relevant academic research and thinking. In addition to the hoped-for synergy, other objectives were: (1) to provide industry with useful, directly applicable insights; (2) to provide academic researchers with insights from knowledgeable executives so that their research would be relevant; (3) to highlight the practices and problems of industry and, especially, the research that was needed to address these problems; (4) to open opportunities for joint research between retailers and scholars; and (5) through the conference and subsequent proceedings, to interest other academic researchers in the challenging research problems posed by the personal selling process.

Once the rationale and objectives for such a conference were outlined, IRM approached the Association for Consumer Research (ACR) and invited them to become conference co-sponsors. ACR is an international, intersector organization consisting of over one-thousand consumer researchers. The ACR is also interdisciplinary in focus, in that its scholars come from marketing, psychology, economics, sociology, communications, law, home economics backgrounds, and so on. ACR agreed to co-sponsor the conference and provided assistance in reaching a broad range of relevant researchers.

Personal Selling

But just what do we mean by the term *personal selling*? Selling can take many forms. With the phenomenal growth of mail-catalog shopping and the promised emergence of shopping at home via telephone-computer hook-ups, an increasing amount of selling is occurring on an *im*personal level. In contrast, personal selling involves direct—that is, either face-to-face or over the telephone—interaction and communication between two human beings, the buyer and the seller. Direct personal contact between the two parties is not enough, however. To qualify as personal selling, there must be an attempt on the part of the salesperson to exert some influence over the behavior of the buyer; otherwise, personal contact reduces to simple order-taking or clerking. We believe that improvements in personal selling—or in turning clerking into selling—represent one of the most effective means by which retailers can improve employee productivity and, thereby, profitability.

This volume contains chapters on the theory underlying effective personal selling, relevant empirical research on personal selling, and insights from practitioners on selling in a retail environment. Each chapter is an original contribution and represents the substance of what was presented at the conference.

Text Outline

In chapter 1, Cialdini identifies six pervasive influence principles—namely, consistency, reciprocity, social validation, authority, scarcity, and friendship/liking. He discusses each principle in terms of its ability to produce a distinct kind of automatic influence. Next Petty, Cacioppo, and Schumann examine persuasion in the context of personal selling. They propose and present evidence for the view that there are two relatively distinct routes to changing attitudes. The central route involves getting a customer to carefully consider the merits of the product while the peripheral route involves associating the product with a positive cue. This is followed by Kernan and Reingen's chapter which presents a non-traditional view of persuasion wherein people do not require elaborated arguments to justify the advocated behavior. Rather, people behave without first developing a strong set of feelings.

In chapter 4, Jacoby illustrates how behavioral science theory can be used to diagnose problems in closing, suggest appropriate corrective action, and derive new approaches to closing. He also summarizes seventeen basic closing techniques. Hunt, Smith, and Kernan apply attribution theory to personal selling in chapter 5. They present a model dealing with seller credibility and buyer message acceptance along with a discussion of message content and format. Barclay in chapter 6 examines ostensible demarketing (the take-away close) as a personal selling strategy. He relates it to the theories of psychological reactance and innoculation theory.

Next, in chapter 7, Weitz suggests that effective salespeople have a unique ability to size up a sales situation and select an appropriate approach. He goes on to indicate how adaptive selling skills can be developed. In chapter 8, Woodside advances five defining characteristics of seller-buyer exchanges. He also tests twelve hypotheses concerning buyer-seller exchanges. Deutscher and Ryans consider the problem of salesperson time allocation in chapter 9. They identify and organize some of the major factors associated with poor time allocation and suggest a research program for improving how salespeople allocate their time. Lamont, Lundstrom, and Zikmund develop the concept of a personal selling style in chapter 10. They also discuss the need for sales managers to balance the salesperson's selling style with the requirements of the job.

In chapter 11, Johnston-O'Connor, O'Connor, and Zultowski summarize and integrate consumer research on personal selling in the life insurance industry. They look at the variables that influence a successful sale and the persistency of a sale. Leigh and Rethans in chapter 12 demonstrate how personal selling behavior can be examined through the use of cognitive scripts. They present the results of two empirical studies and suggest guidelines for further research using scripts. Chapter 13 by Enis and Lucas proposes and tests a model relating job satisfaction to the job performance of life insurance salespeople. The authors also develop implication for the practice of sales management. In chapter 14, Chestnut and Jacoby report the results of an experiment on the relationship between liking of salesperson and consumer's information acquisition and choice behavior. They also cover the marketing implications of the results.

The concept of corporate culture and the role it plays in retail selling is examined by Enis and Chonko in chapter 15. The authors argue for a more scientific understanding of the retail selling situations, the elements, the process, and the relationships in that situation. Chapter 16 is the transcription of a panel discussion of six leading retail executives on retailing-related personal selling issues.

Acknowledgments

Finally, we would like to offer a note of thanks to the many who assisted in either identifying the need for this conference or who played a major role in bringing this conference to fruition. In particular, in addition to the members of our two councils, we would like to thank Ike Lagnado, Walter Levy, Steven Osterweis, Al Pennington, Marvin Rothenberg, Charles

Turlinsky, and especially Sid Stein of J.C. Penney. We would also like to thank Marvin Jolson, who moderated a discussion on personal selling, and Monte Barber, Phil Langsdorf, and Don Smith who were on the panel. Finally, a great deal of thanks is due to the staff at IRM, especially George Agudow, Tim Cicak, and Linda Nagel.

Personal Selling

1 Principles of Automatic Influence

Robert B. Cialdini

Several years ago, some animal researchers performed a fascinating experiment on the maternal behavior of turkeys. Although female turkeys are normally good and reliable mothers—vigilant, loving, and protective—their method is somewhat odd. Their elaborate mothering responses seem to be triggered by one thing: the unique "cheep-cheep" sound made by turkey chicks. A chick who makes this sound will be fed, tended, warmed, and preened; one who does not may be starved or purposely murdered. Other identifying characteristics of the young (for example, smell, appearance) will be relatively ignored by the mothers in the process.

To demonstrate the singleminded reliance of turkey mothers on the cheep-cheep sound, the researchers arranged the following procedures. With a cord, they brought a stuffed replica of a polecat toward a maternal turkey and her chicks; the protective mother's response was an immediate pecking, clawing onslaught until the cat was withdrawn. On another occasion, the same polecat replica was pulled toward the same turkey mother and chicks but with one difference: A tape recorder playing the distinctive cheep-cheep of turkey young was inserted into the stuffed polecat. This time, the mother not only refrained from attack but received the natural enemy beneath her. As soon as the tape ended, however, she again delivered a furious assault.

When seen in this light, a female turkey seems silly. In robot-like fashion, she appears to be programmed to respond automatically to a single signal, embracing a natural enemy if it goes cheep-cheep and abusing one of her own chicks if it does not. It is clear, however, that turkey mothers are hardly alone in this regard. Practitioners of the relatively new science of ethology—the study of the behavior of animals as it occurs in natural environments—have idenitified such mechanical sequences of action in a broad spectrum of species.

These behavior sequences are termed *fixed action patterns* and often involve entire chains of acts that enroll, as if on tape, in a regular way time after time. For example, in a species whose courtship behavior is on tape, we see intricate courtship rituals enacted in virtually identical form in each appropriate instance.

For students of human behavior (especially interpersonal influence) the most instructive thing about this is the way in which the tapes are activated. For instance, when a male animal acts to defend its territory, he usually does so in a pattern of vigilance, threat, and, if necessary, aggressive

1

behaviors. Of course, he usually does so in response to the intrusion of another male species member into the territory. However, there is something nonintuitive about the signal that cues the territorial defense pattern. It is not just the rival male that is the trigger; it is some particular feature of him. The trigger feature (also known as the *sign stimulus* or the *releaser*) is usually one small part of the intruder; sometimes, a mere shade of color will suffice. For instance, ethologists have done experiments in which a clump of red breastfeathers is clipped to a tree limb in a male robin's territory. The result is that the feathers invariably draw a vigorous attack from the bird. At the same time, it will not bother a life-like model of a male robin that is anatomically correct in every detail except for the color of its breastfeathers (Lack 1943).

Lest we think too poorly of the lower animals' vulnerability to trigger features that can spur them to behave in quite inappropriate ways, we must first understand that the fixed action patterns of these animals usually work very well for them. By responding maternally to the singular cheep-cheep sound of turkey young, for example, the mother bird will nearly always decide correctly when and when not to be motherly. It takes a scientist to make her tape-like response seem ridiculous. Second, we must realize that humans also have so-called behavior tapes. Like those of the lower animals, these tapes normally are decidedly efficient, allowing us to unroll correct sequences of action after we register just one instructive feature of the environment. But we too can be fooled into playing our tapes at the wrong times.[1]

Ellen Langer and her associates researched the phenomenon of "mindlessness"; their work provides one illustration of the frequent automaticity of human responding (*cf.* Langer 1978). In their most dramatic demonstration, Langer, Blank, and Chanowitz (1977) showed how the concept of mindless action could be linked to the compliance process. The researchers reasoned that people are more likely to comply with a request when they have been given a reason to justify the request. Support for this rather unexciting prediction was obtained by Langer and her group when they provided individuals waiting in line to use a library copy machine with both a small request, "Excuse me, I have five pages. May I use the Xerox machine?" and a reason for the request, "because I'm in a rush." The percentage of people who complied with the request under these circumstances was very high: 94 percent gave up their places. Compare the effectiveness of this request-plus-reason procedure with that of a request only: "Excuse me, I have five pages. May I use the Xerox machine?" Here only 60 percent of those asked complied.

Had the experiment included only these two procedures, we would probably conclude that the large difference in the effectiveness of the two procedures was due to the additional information provided by the reason, "because I'm in a rush." But the effects of a third experimental procedure challenges this interpretation. The third procedure followed the request with what Langer called a "placebic" reason, that is, a phrase that sounded like a reason (since it began with the word "because") but merely restated the obvious: "Excuse me, I have five pages. May I use the Xerox machine because I have to make some copies?" Once again, the success rate (93 percent) was very high. Although no genuine reason carrying new information had been provided, the word "because" cued Langer's subjects to behave as if there had. Just as the cheep-cheep sound of turkey chicks triggered an automatic mothering response from maternal turkeys, even when it came from a polecat, so it seems that the word "because" triggered an automatic compliance response from Langer's human subjects, even when they were given no real reason to comply.

The Search for Shortcuts

This evidence certainly does not suggest that all, or even most, human action has an automatic, mindless character. Research by Langer (1978) and others shows that there are many situations in which we decide and behave in a mindful fashion. In such instances, we do not react to a sole piece of information—even if it is highly diagnostic—but we try to process the environment fully to take into account all of the relevant information. Under the proper conditions (i.e., when we have the time, energy, capacity, and incentive), a considered analysis of the available information is always preferred.

However, the form and pace of modern life deprives us largely of the proper conditions for mindful analysis. We currently live in what is unquestionably the most complex and rapidly changing stimulus environment that has ever existed on this planet. Thus we are faced with a tremendous amount of information to assimilate and organize. Rather than processing it all carefully, we frequently must resort to shortcuts or *heuristics*—rules of thumb that, while not perfect, usually direct us correctly. In a way, we do not have much choice but to use our heuristics more than ever as the stimulation that saturates daily life becomes increasingly intricate and variable. Without these rules, we would become immobilized as the time for action sped by and away.

The most general information-processing shortcut is the one mentioned earlier; to use it, one needs only to be alert to a single feature of information that is normally associated with an entire and influential stimulus array. Once that single, highly representative feature (for example, cheep-cheep or because) is registered, it can cue the behavior pattern (for example, mothering or enhanced compliance) that is appropriate to the larger array (for example, a healthy turkey chick or a legitimate reason). The advantage of this shortcut approach is, of course, its economy. Provided that the single trigger feature is highly correlated with the presence of the larger array, appropriate responding will typically occur while valuable information-processing time and capacity can be saved for the crush of other decisions in the day. On the other hand, the disadvantage of the shortcut approach is its vulnerability to error. Since even the best trigger features are imperfectly correlated with the presence of the larger array, sometimes they will stimulate the wrong response. Under these conditions, in which a full analysis of all the relevant information would have counseled differently, we find turkeys mothering polecats that go cheep-cheep and we find people complying for no just reason.

The First Step

Automatic responding to a single, highly representative piece of information constitutes the fundamental form of heuristic behavior. But within this general category are numerous specific heuristics, many of which guide the process of compliance. An intriguing question is, "How do the major compliance heuristics work?" If we could analyze the workings of the rules of thumb that most people use to decide when they should and should not comply with a request, we would have information of both conceptual and practical interest. Then we would know not only about the rules of thumb but also about the basic principles of human social behavior from which they are derived.

When I began to investigate the major heuristics of compliance, my approach was destined to provide only an incomplete answer to my question. My work concentrated on highly controlled laboratory settings. Moreover, I was deciding which effects to study in those settings on the bases of theoretical considerations and prior experimental literature. Eventually, I realized that this controlled experimental approach—in which methodological precision is valued and all extraneous influences are removed or equated— would work only if the compliance heuristics were important in the course of naturally occurring compliance action. After all, my initial interest was in understanding the *major* heuristics of compliance, those that most people engaged in most often. Yet neither theory nor the prior experimental literature provided evidence of the strength or prevalence of compliance phenomena in everyday interaction.

From this I saw that my rigorous experimental procedure would also be of limited help in answering my primary question. If anything, the precision of expert technique and measurement may often mislead us regarding the potency and prominence of the phenomenon under investigation. By relying on laboratory results alone, we may be deluded into thinking we have found genuinely powerful effects.[2]

Despite their undeniable value, factors of theory, prior literature, and experimental precision were weighted heavily too early in the sequence of my investigation. These things would tell me, once I had something ecologically important to examine, exactly what I had. But the discovery of what is ecologically important had to take place by some other, prior process. Only after the most powerful and regular naturally occurring compliance heuristics had been identified could I begin investigating their theoretical underpinnings. Otherwise, I might spend my time experimentally analyzing effects that were ecologically meaningless epiphenomena of the research setting.

The first order of business, then, was to identify the major, naturally occurring compliance heuristics. The process by which such identification might take place seemed to involve a research strategy, systematic personal observation, which was at the time almost wholly alien to me. It was the approach of anthropologists and of certain sociologists (for example, Irving Goffman), but not that of my fellow experimental social psychologists and myself. Nonetheless, it appeared to be the appropriate course of action.

In preparation, I studied the anthropological and participant observational sociological methodologies; I found these tactics quite helpful. But perhaps the most instructive procedural insight came rather unexpectedly from ethology. Ethologists have long been interested in identifying their animal subjects' automatic behavior sequences. Instead of the mostly instinctive response sequences of other animals, human automatic behavior patterns normally derive from well-learned psychological principles. Yet the functional similarity of these two forms of automaticity inspired me to examine how the ethologists went about finding fixed action patterns.

One intriguing source of ethologists' information lay not so much in the behaviors of the kind of animals under study as in the behaviors of a particular variety of other animals. Termed *mimics,* the members of this latter group have evolved in such a way as to possess the trigger feature for the fixed action patterns of other species. When a mimic displays the trigger feature of another species, it causes the automatic behavior sequence to unroll, even in wholly inappropriate situations. For instance, one species of spider of the genus *Ero* employs mimicking to hunt its favorite victim, another species of spider that builds orb webs. The orb web females sit on their webs waiting to respond to the courtship signals of their male counterparts. One mating signal consists of a distinctive vibration on the strands of her web made by a prospective mate. The hunter has cracked the orb web spider's code and has evolved a way to pluck out the special vibratory pattern on the outer strands of the web. Thus the female's courtship behavior is activated, causing her to begin a dance that propels her into death's, not love's embrace (Bristowe 1958). A similar trick is played by the predator female of one kind of firefly (*Photurus*) on the males of another firefly species (*Photenus*). By mimicking the unique blinking courtship code of its victims, the hunter female is able to cause victims to fly headlong in an attempt to mate with a natural enemy (Lloyd 1965).

Insects are not the only class of organisms that include mimics. Mimics also can be found among birds, reptiles, fish, plants and even humans. My main point is that ethologists have gained a valuable perspective on the fixed action patterns of certain species by observing what mimics do. In this way, we can learn both about the fixed action patterns themselves and the specific trigger features that elicit them. This particular insight provided me an important direction for my research program. To identify the major compliance heuristics, I should examine closely the actions of individuals who have evolved ways to activate those heuristics so that they may benefit from them. To put this insight into the language of the marketplace: It would be wise to study the psychology of the buyer by watching the seller. Or, to put things in somewhat grander terminology: The major compliance heuristics, as well as the trigger stimuli that engage them and the psychological principles from which they derive, may well be revealed in a thoroughgoing analysis of the actions of compliance professionals.

Evolution

Who are these compliance professionals, and why do I have such confidence that their actions will prove instructive to my particular interest in compliance heuristics? Let us take the questions in order. The first function of compliance professionals is to induce others to comply with requests. Thus the category includes but is not limited to salespeople, fundraisers, advertisers, political lobbyists, labor-management negotiators, recruitment officers, and so on would fit the definition as well. These people's job success depends on their ability to get others to say yes.

Now we can begin to see why the systematic behavior of compliance professionals lends insight into the factors that stimulate compliance: A law not unlike that of natural selection assures it. That is, because the livelihoods of compliance professionals depend on the effectiveness of their procedures, those professionals who use procedures that work well to elicit compliance responses will survive and flourish. Further, they will pass these successful procedures on to succeeding generations (for example, trainees). However, those practitioners who use unsuccessful compliance procedures either will drop them or will quickly go out of business; in either case, the procedures themselves will not be passed on to newer generations.

The ineluctable upshot of this process is that, over time and over the range of naturally occurring compliance contexts, the strongest and most adaptable procedures for generating compliance will rise, persist, and accumulate. Further, these procedures will point a careful observer toward the major rules and heuristics that people use to decide when to comply. The observer must resist the temptation to find these generally effective procedures at any single time or in a particular compliance setting, profession, or practitioner. In any one of these specialized instances, the observer may find regular, idiosyncratic practices that are only effective there or then. The key for an observer wishing to identify the major principles governing the compliance process is the ubiquitousness of the compliance practices that tap into those principles for their power. That observer might well be advised, then, to begin the entire investigative process with an assessment of the cross-situational prevalence of certain compliance tactics over a range of diverse compliance professionals. Later steps in the process for the observer would involve: (1) the classification of the most common of these tactics according to the psychological principles that account for their effectiveness and (2) recourse to experimentation, theory, and prior research literature to try to understand precisely how and why the tactics work.

Implementation

Several years ago I resolved to become such a careful observer of compliance issues. This decision meant (were I to be true to the lessons learned from my colleagues in ethology, anthropology, and participant observational sociology) that I should orient myself initially to the study of compliance professionals, that I should conduct this study in the natural environment, and that I should do so from the inside. Accordingly, I embarked on an extended program of observation in which I took training or employment in a host of compliance professions wherein my true identity and purposes were unknown to those around me.[3] In this fashion, it was possible to learn which compliance procedures were being used and taught across an array of merchandising, advertising, direct-sales, promotion, and fundraising concerns. These first-hand experiences were supplemented with information from more traditional research sources such as instructional materials (for example, salesmanship texts, handbooks on lobbying techniques) and personal interviews with especially successful practitioners.

In seeking to determine the prominence of a particular compliance practice, I asked several questions.

1. *How varied is it?* A truly potent and general influence on the compliance process is likely to appear in a multitude of forms and variations. Therefore those practices that I registered in numerous versions were given high marks by this criterion. For example, one such practice—gaining an initial small commitment that logically implies later, larger compliance—appears in a plethora of techniques (foot-in-the-door, low-ball, bait and switch, four walls, building agreements, and so forth).

2. *Does it appear across the range of compliance professions?* Those procedures that successfully activate the fundamental principles of human compliance will have likely risen to prominence in all long-standing compliance professions. Furthermore, such procedures are likely to be carried from one profession to another by migrating practitioners. Thus to the extent that I noted the consistent incidence of a practice over a broad range of diverse professions, I rated its so-called star quality as greater.

3. *Within the professions observed, how widespread is its use among the practitioners?* I observed that within individual professions (for example, public relations/promotion), certain procedures were employed almost universally (for example, gifting) while others were used by only a few practitioners. By my scoring system, the former were graded commensurately higher than the latter. The rationale was that practices that can be implemented effectively by most practitioners are sufficiently powerful and general to sustain their effects through the many differences in style, appearance, and experience within categories of practitioners.

4. *How long has it been used and prescribed?* Some practices are traditionally successful. Indeed, the essence of certain practices can be traced back for centuries (for example, friendship referrals; see *The Illiad*, 700 B.C., book XI, 1. 793). By my survival-of-the-fittest argument, those practices that have stood the test of time must be considered more noteworthy. These practices seem to engage persisting features of the human condition. Of course, it is not necessary to establish a centuries-old history for a procedure to gain confidence. A simple examination of old and new practitioners' manuals often sufficed for me.

After slightly more than two years of collecting compliance techniques and assessing their pervasiveness, I ended this initial stage to do some structuring. It was quite evident that many of the common tactics I had observed clustered into groups. More importantly, each group seemed to illuminate one of a very few major rules that people use to determine when to comply. Most of these rules were the rule-of-thumb variety and, because of my interest in compliance heuristics, I chose to concentrate on them. In each case, the rule could be seen as stemming from a fundamental social psychological principal through which the rule acquired its power to influence behavior. In each case as well the rule was apparently triggered by a specific grouping of compliance tactics. The most notable thing about the rules for me was that they all governed in classic heuristic form, providing behavioral direction on the basis of one (or two) highly diagnostic stimulus feature of the situation rather than on the basis of a more complete analysis of the situation's relevant information. I found it fascinating that, in the most pervasive compliance tactics I observed, each contained one of those single stimulus features.

I believe that certain compliance tactics are ubiquitous because they normally spur wholly appropriate compliance. In addition, these tactics are ubiquitous because they can spur an individual to comply even when compliance is not objectively called for. Thus, provided the individual is responding heuristically, such a trigger tactic would likely work for compliance professionals whether or not they had the merits of the case on their side. In the latter instance, the compliance professional would act as a mimic, presenting just the critical trigger feature and benefitting from the inappropriate action it elicits.

Although a more detailed account appears elsewhere (Cialdini 1984), the material below offers a summary of the results of my investigations. It is organized around the supraordinate social psychological principles that appear to be most implicated in naturally occurring compliance. The heuristic rule that derives from each principle is also discussed, as is a brief sample of common trigger tactics that activate the rule. Additionally, the treatment of each principle includes an attempt to offer data about the relevant hows and whys of the compliance process. These treatments bring to bear experimental methodology, existing theory, and the findings of the prior experimental literature. Recall that these are the factors that were seen as ill-suited to the starting-point question of which are the major compliance heuristics. When the questions shift from "which" to "how and why," however, these factors are highly suitable.

Before presenting results, a sizeable caveat is in order. My survey of compliance practices, ratings of their pervasiveness, and interpretation of the implications are all *subjective*. No matter how careful and thorough I tried to be, the practices I observed were seen only through my eyes and registered through the filter of my expectations and previous experience. Furthermore, the settings I chose to investigate were neither exhaustive nor random. Therefore the judgments of tactic prevalence, on which most of what follows is based, must be seen as those of one person, made in a moderately large but not necessarily representative set of compliance contexts. I feel decidely better about the evidence that comes from experimental procedures, as it was obtained through more standardized and easily replicable operations. Nonetheless, I very much hope that my conclusions as to the major compliance heuristics will be tested by other investigations.

Principles, Heuristics, and Some Trigger Tactics

Consistency Principle

Social psychological theorists have repeatedly noted that most people possess a strong need to be consistent about their attitudes, beliefs, words, and deeds. Several of the most prominent of these theorists have incorporated the strain for consistency into their perspectives on important areas of human behavior, assigning it the role of prime motivator (for example, Festinger 1957; Heider 1946, 1958; Newcomb 1953). Recently, recognition concerning a somewhat different type of consistency drive than the private, intrapersonal variety that concerned the early theorists has grown. The desire to *appear* consistent is currently seen as having substantial influence over much human action as well (Baumeister 1982; Tedeschi 1981). According to this view, the appearance of personal consistency is a socially desirable thing, and individuals will be consistent with their prior pronouncements and actions to project a positive public image.

It is not difficult to understand why the tendency to look and be consistent is so strong. First, good personal consistency is highly valued by other members of the society, whereas poor such consistency is negatively valued. The former is commonly associated with such positive traits as stability, honesty, and intellectual strength. The latter often indicates such undesirable traits as indecisiveness, confusion, weakness of will, deceitfulness, or even mental illness. Second, aside from its effect on public image, generally consistent conduct provides a reasonable and gainful orientation to the world. Usually, we will be better off if our approach to the world is consistent. Otherwise our lives would be difficult, erratic, and disjointed. Finally, good personal consistency provides a valuable shortcut through the density of modern life. Once we have made up our minds about an issue or have decided how to act in a given situation, we no longer have to process all of the relevant information when subsequently confronted with the same (or similar) issue or situation. We only need to recall the earlier decision and respond consistently with it. The advantage of such a shortcut should not be minimized; it allows us a convenient, relatively effortless method of dealing with our complex environments, which make severe demands on our mental energies and capacities. Furthermore, provided that the first decision was thoughtful and that circumstances have not changed drastically, we will probably be correct in our subsequent decisions by simply relying on consistency.

In keeping with these reasons, people frequently respond to compliance requests in a rather unthinking fashion characterized by automatic consistency with a previous commitment. A heuristic that governs such situations follows: *After committing oneself to a position, one should be more willing to comply with requests for behaviors that are consistent with that position.*

Thus the pressure for consistency is engaged though the act of commitment. A variety of strategies may be used to produce the instigating commitment. Certain of these do so by asking for initial agreements that are quite small but nonetheless effective in stimulating later agreement with related, larger requests. One such start-small-and-build strategy is called the four walls technique. As far as I know, this technique has never been experimentally investigated. Yet it is a frequent practice of door-to-door salespeople, who use it primarily to gain permission to enter a customer's home. I first encountered it while training as an encyclopedia salesman. The technique consists of asking four questions to which the customer will be very likely to answer yes. To be consistent with the previous answers, the customer must then say yes to the crucial final question. In the encyclopedia sales situation, the technique proceeded as follows. *First wall:* Do you feel that a good education is important to your children? *Second wall:* Do you think that a child who does his or her homework well will get a better education? *Third wall:* Don't you agree that a good set of reference books will help a child do well on homework assignments? *Fourth wall:* Well, then, it sounds like you will want to hear about this fine set of encyclopedias I have to offer at an excellent price. May I come in?

A similar start-small procedure is embodied in the much more researched foot-in-the-door technique. A solicitor using this technique will first ask for a small favor that is virtually certain to be granted. The initial compliance is then followed by a request for a larger, *related* favor. It has been found repeatedly that people who have agreed to the initial, small favor are more willing to do the larger one (*cf.* Beaman et al. 1983; DeJong 1979 for reviews), seemingly to be consistent with the implication of the initial action.

Other, less savory techniques induce a commitment to an item and then remove the inducements that generated the commitment. Remarkably, the commitment frequently remains. For example, the bait-and-switch procedure is used by some retailers who may advertise certain merchandise (e.g., a room full of furniture) at a special low price. When the customer arrives to take advantage of the special, s/he finds the merchandise to be of low quality or sold out. However, because customers have by now made an active commitment to getting new furniture at that particular store, they are more willing to agree to examine and, consequently to buy, higher priced merchandise. A similar strategy is employed by car dealers in the low-ball technique, which proceeds by obtaining a commitment to an action and *then* increasing the costs of performing the action. The automobile salesperson who throws the low-ball induces the customer to decide to buy a particular model car by offering a low price on the car or an inflated one on the customer's trade-in. After the decision has been made (and, at times, after the commitment is enhanced by allowing the customer to arrange financing, take the car home overnight, etc.), something happens to remove the reason the customer decided to buy. Perhaps a price calculation error is found, or the used car assessor disallows the inflated trade-in figure. By this time, though, many customers have experienced an internal commitment to that specific automobile and proceed with the purchase. Experimental research (Cialdini et al. 1978; Burger & Petty 1981) has documented the effectiveness of this tactic in settings beyond automobile sales. On the conceptual level, this research indicates that the tactic is effective primarily when used by a single requester and when the initial commitment is freely made.

A uniting feature of these procedures (and others like them) is the induction of a commitment that is consistent with a later action desired by the compliance professional. The need for consistency then takes over to compel performance of the desired behavior. In distinctive heuristic fashion, all that is necessary for enhanced compliance is the single stimulus feature of a proper commitment, even when the reasons for that commitment are rendered irrelevant or are eliminated. Of course, not all behaviors constitute proper commitments. However, research evidence suggests the types of commitments that lead to consistent future responding. This context does not allow sufficient space for a thorough discussion of that evidence. Nonetheless, I would argue that a fair summary of the research literature is that a commitment is likely to be maximally effective in producing consistent future behavior to the extent that it is active (Bem 1967), effortful (Aronson & Mills 1959), public (Deutsch & Gerard 1955) and viewed as internally motivated (that is, noncoerced, Freedman 1965).

Reciprocity Principle

According to the sociologist Alvin Gouldner (1960), who made an extensive review of the subject, every human society abides by a norm for reciprocation that directs us to provide to others the sort of behaviors they have provided us. By virtue of the norm for reciprocation, we are *obligated* to the future repayment of favors, gifts, invitations, and the like. A widely shared feeling of future obligation made an enormous difference in human social evolution because it meant that one person could give something (for example, food, energy, care) to another with confidence that it was not being lost. For the first time, one individual could give away any of a variety of resources without *actually* giving them away. The result was the lowering of the natural inhibitions against transactions that must be begun by one person providing personal resources to another. Thus a person could provide help, gifts, defense, or trade goods to others of the group knowing that, when the time came, s/he could count on repayment. Sophisticated and coordinated systems of gift-giving, defense, and trade became possible, bringing immense benefit to the societies that possessed them. With such clearly adaptive consequences for the culture, it is not surprising that the norm for reciprocation is so deeply implanted in us by the process of socialization we all undergo.

By working to help ensure fairness in exchanges between people, the norm strengthens the society. But because it is so thoroughly ingrained, it acquires a heuristic status, at times directing us to behave in a mindless manner that results in unfair exchanges—with ourselves on the short end. The reciprocity heuristic for compliance can be worded as follows: *One should be more willing to comply with a request to the extent that the compliance constitutes a reciprocation of behavior.*

Under this general rule, then, people will sometimes be willing to return a favor with a larger favor (for example, Regan 1971). A number of sales and fundraising tactics use this factor to advantage. The compliance professional initially gives something to the target person, thereby causing the target to be more likely to give something in return. Often, this something in return is worth much more than the initiating favor.

The unsolicited gift, accompanied by a request for a donation, is a commonly used technique that utilizes the norm for reciprocation. One example experienced by many people is the Hare Krishna solicitor who gives the unwary passerby a book or a flower and then asks for a donation. Other organizations send free gifts through the mail; legitimate as well as unscrupulous missionary and disabled veterans organizations often employ this highly effective device. These organizations count on the fact that most people will not go to the trouble of returning the gift and will feel uncomfortable about keeping it without reciprocating in some way. The organizations also count on the willingness of people to send a contribution that is larger than the cost of the gift they received.

Retail stores and services also make use of the powerful social pressure for reciprocation in their sales techniques. It is not uncommon to find exterminating companies that offer free home inspections. These companies bargain on the fact that, once confronted with the knowledge that a home is infested with termites, the consumer will not delay action until he or she has done some comparison shopping. A customer who feels indebted to a particular company will buy its services to repay the favor of a free examination. Certain companies, knowing that the customer is unlikely to comparison shop, have been known to raise the quoted price of extermination above normal for those who have requested a so-called free inspection.

One extremely successful technique that incorporates the reciprocation norm is used by the Amway Corporation. A housewife will be given a tray of products to try at her leisure for a particular period of time. The products often are provided in half-full bottles, but enough is provided to allow the customer to test it. After using a portion of one or two of these products, the consumer often feels obligated to buy at least something—often the majority of the products on the tray. When the Amway representative returns to collect the products the customer puts in her order. The same tray, replenished as necessary, is then passed on to the next customer, who in turn feels obligated to reciprocate the favor.

A variation of the norm for reciprocation of favors is that for reciprocation of concessions. A reciprocal concessions procedure (or door-in-the-face technique) for inducing compliance has been documented by Cialdini et al. (1975). When one bargaining party retreats from an initial demand to a second, smaller one, social conventions require the other party to reciprocate that concession. However, if the first party intentionally begins with a request much greater than that which is actually desired, when it is rejected, s/he may make a compliance-enhancing retreat to the level of request that was really wanted in the first place. This tactic often is used in appliance sales: The salesperson starts with a large request of the consumer by offering the top of the line. When this request is refused, the salesperson appears to retreat by making a concession and offering a lower-priced product. The customer feels a pressure to meet the salesperson halfway by agreeing to buy the lower-priced product, which may still be more expensive than the one s/he meant to buy in the first place.

This reciprocal concessions strategy also can be successfully used in door-to-door solicitations. Cialdini and Ascani (1976) used this technique in soliciting blood donors. They first requested a person's involvement in a long-term donor program. When that request was refused, the solicitor made a smaller request for a one-time donation. This pattern of a large request, which is refused, followed by a smaller request significantly increased compliance with the smaller request, as compared to a control condition of people who were asked only to perform the smaller, one-time favor (50 percent versus 32 percent compliance rate).

Social Validation Principle

People frequently use the beliefs, attitudes and actions of others, particularly similar others, as a standard of comparison against which to evaluate the correctness of their own beliefs, attitudes, and actions (cf. Festinger 1954). Thus it is common for individuals to decide on appropriate behaviors for themselves in a given situation by searching for information as to how similar others have behaved or are behaving (for example, Latane & Darley 1970; Schachter & Singer 1962). Powerful modeling effects of similar others have been found in both adults and children and in such diverse activities as altruism (for example, Hornstein, Fisch & Holmes 1968), phobia remission (for example, Bandura & Menlove 1968) and suicide (Phillips 1974).

Normally, the tendency to see an action as more appropriate when similar others are doing it works quite well. As a rule, we will make fewer mistakes by acting in accord with social evidence than contrary to it. As such, social validation allows us another convenient shortcut. By processing what similar people do, we can usually decide what we should do, with a minimum of additional effort. When this reliance on social evidence alone becomes automatic, however, we can find ourselves behaving in objectively inappropriate ways. For example, research indicates (for example, Cupchik & Leventhal 1974) that people rate comedy funnier and laugh more and longer at it when the sound of others' laughter is present—even when they know that the others' laughter is on a manufactured laugh track! As regards compliance, the social validation heuristic can be worded as follows: *One should be more willing to comply with a request for behavior to the degree that similar others are or have been performing it.*

Charity and other nonprofit organizations frequently make use of social validation information to encourage people to donate. It is typical for the master of ceremonies at a telethon to read incessantly from a handful of pledge cards. The pledges are structured to represent a cross-section of the viewing public so that all may have evidence of the similarity of contributors. The message being communicated to the holdouts is clear, "Look at all the people like you who have decided to give; it must be the correct thing to do." Church collection plates (as well as bartender's tip jars) are often "salted" beforehand with folding money to provide social validation for the donation of sizeable amounts. Evangelical preachers are known to seed their audiences with ringers, people who are rehearsed to come forward at a specified time to give witness and offerings. Research by Reingen (1982) has demonstrated that individuals shown lists of prior contributors are more likely to donate to charity; further, the longer the list, the greater the effect.

Social validation techniques are also used extensively by profit-making organizations. Advertisers love to inform us that a product is the largest-selling or fastest-growing because they do not have to convince us directly that the product is good; they need only imply that many others think so. Salespeople are trained to spice their presentations with numerous accounts of other individuals who have purchased the product. When such individuals will testify in writing to the product's effectiveness, these testimonials are collected and prominently displayed.

Authority Principle

Legitimately constituted authorities are extremely influential persons (for example, Aronson, Turner & Carlsmith 1963; Milgram 1974). Whether they have acquired their positions through knowledge, talent, or fortune, their positions bespeak superior information and power. From childhood, these people (for example, parents, teachers) knew more than we did, and we found that taking their advice proved beneficial—partly because of their greater wisdom and partly because they controlled our rewards and punishments. As adults, our authority figures have changed to employers, judges, police officers, and the like, but the benefits associated with doing as they say have not. For most people, then, conforming to the dictates of authority figures produces genuine practical advantages. Consequently, it makes great sense to comply with the wishes of properly constituted authorities. It makes so much sense, in fact, that people often do so when it makes no sense at all.

This paradox is, of course, the same one that attends all of the major compliance principles. When a principle normally counsels correctly, there is a tendency to respond according to it in an unthinking fashion that leads to errors. In the instance of the authority principle, the compliance heuristic can be worded as follows: *One should be more willing to follow the suggestions of an individual who is a legitimate authority.*

Authorities may be seen as falling into two categories: (1) authorities with regard to the specific situation and (2) more general authorities. Compliance practitioners employ techniques that seek to benefit from the power invested in authority figures of both types. In the case of authority relevant to a specific situation, we can note how often advertisers inform their audiences of the level of expertise of product manufacturers (for example, "Fashionable Men's Clothiers since 1841." "Babies are our business, our only business.") At times, the expertise associated with a product has been more symbolic than substantive, for instance, when actors in television commercials wore physician's white coats to recommend a product. It is instructive that the mere symbols of a physician's expertise and authority are enough to trip the heuristic mechanism that governs authority influence. One of the most prominent of these symbols, the title "Dr.," has been shown to be devastatingly effective as a compliance device among trained hospital personnel. In what may be the most frightening study I know, a group of physicians and nurses conducted an experiment that documented the dangerous degree of blind obedience that 95 percent of hospital nurses accorded to an individual whom they had never met but who had claimed over the telephone to be a doctor (Hofling, Brotzman, Dalrymple, Graves, & Pierce 1966).

In the case of influence that generalizes outside of a specific situation, the impact of authority (real and symbolic) appears equally impressive. For instance, Bickman (1974) found that, when wearing a security guard's uniform, a requester could produce more compliance with requests (for example, to pick up a paper bag on the street, to stand on the other side of a bus stop sign) that were irrelevant to a security guard's domain of authority. Less blatant in its connotation than a uniform, but nonetheless effective, is another kind of attire that has traditionally indicated authority in our culture, the well-tailored business suit. Lefkowitz, Blake, and Mouton (1955) found that three and one-half times as many people were willing to follow a jaywalker into traffic when he wore a suit and tie versus a work shirt and trousers.

Scarcity Principle

As opportunities and the items they contain become more scarce, they are perceived as more valuable. There seem to be two major reasons for this. First, it is normally the case that what is less available *is* more valuable. Precious metals and stone, for instance, are precious (in both major meanings of the word) precisely because of their limited supply. The fundamental relationship between supply and assigned worth appears so commonly that an item's availability can be taken as an indication of its quality. Worchel, Lee, and Adewole (1975) have provided data concerning how and when an item's scarcity affects its perceived value. They found that cookies were rated as more desirable, more attractive to consumers, and more costly when they were scarce rather than abundant. Further more, the effect was greater when the scarcity replaced previous abundance and when it was caused by a social demand. Other research and theorizing by Brock and Fromkin has suggested that in addition to commodities, limited access to information makes the information more desirable and more influential (Brock 1968). A recent test of Brock and Fromkin's thinking by one of my students found good support in a business setting. Wholesale beef buyers who were told of an impending imported beef shortage purchased significantly more beef when they were informed that the shortage information came from certain exclusive contacts that the importer had (Knishinsky 1982). Apparently, the fact that the news was itself scarce made it more valued and persuasive.

A second reason that increasing scarcity leads to increasing attraction is that, as things become less available, the freedom to have them decreases. According to Brehm's reactance theory (Brehm & Brehm 1981), the loss of free access to an item increases the drive to have it. Thus when increasing scarcity limits prior access to something, reactance will be generated, causing individuals to want and try to possess the thing more than before. Much laboratory evidence exists to support reactance theory predictions (*cf.* Brehm & Brehm 1981). In addition, some support has been found in naturally occurring settings. For example, Mazis (1975) showed that newly limited access to a certain type of detergent enhanced its attractiveness for customers.

One should want to try to secure those opportunities that are scarce. With the scarcity principle operating powerfully on the worth assigned to things, it should not be surprising that compliance professionals have a variety of techniques to convert this power to compliance. Probably the most frequently used technique I witnessed was the limited number (or SRO) tactic in which the customer is informed that membership opportunities, products, or services exist in a limited supply that cannot be guaranteed to last for long. In some instances, the limited number information was true; in others, it was not. In each case, however, the intent was to convince prospects of an item's scarcity and thereby increase its immediate worth in their eyes. At one appliance store, it was not uncommon for sales-people to raise the value of a particular sale item for a customer by announcing that "the last one has just been sold, and I'm sure we have no more in the back; however, I can check with our other store and, if I can get it for you at the sale price, would you like to buy it?" In this way, customers were induced to make a commitment at a time when the scarcity principle would render the merchandise most attractive. Many of the customers agreed eagerly and were uniformly pleased (even relieved) when the salesperson invariably reported that, yes, the other store location still had one in stock.

Related to the limited number tactic is the deadline technique, in which an official time limit is placed on the customer's opportunity to get what is being offered. Newspaper ads abound with admonitions to the customer regarding the folly of delay. One rather single-minded movie advertiser managed to load three separate appeals to the scarcity heuristic into just five words: "Exclusive, limited engagement, ends soon." The purest form of a decision deadline occurs in a variant of the deadline technique in which customers are told that, unless they make an immediate purchase decision, they will have to buy the item at a higher price or they will not be able to purchase it at all. This tactic is used in numerous compliance settings. A large child-photography company urges parents to buy as many poses and copies as they can afford because "stocking limitations force us to burn the unsold pictures of your children within 24 hours." A prospective health club member or automobile buyer might learn that the deal offered by the salesperson is good for that one time; should the customer leave the premises, the deal is off. One home-vacuum-cleaner sales company instructed me as a trainee to claim to prospects that "I have so many other people to see that I have the time to visit a family only once. It's company policy that even if you decide later that you want this machine, I can't come back and sell it to you." For anyone who thought about it carefully, this was nonsense; the company and its representatives are in the business of making sales, and any customer who called for another visit would be accommodated gladly. The real purpose of the can't-come-back-again claim was to evoke the scarcity heuristic.

Recall that in the Worchel el at. (1975) study, scarcity was the most effective when it was produced by social demand. This finding highlights the importance of competition in the pursuit of limited resources. We want a scarce item even more when in competition for it. Advertisers often try to commission this tendency in their behalf. In their ads, we see crowds pressing against the doors of a store prior to the start of a sale; we watch a flock of hands quickly deplete a supermarket shelf of a product. There is much more to such images than the idea of ordinary social validation. The message is not just that the product is good because other people think so, but also that we are in direct competition with those people for it. Real estate agents are taught to convey a similar idea to hesitant customers. A realtor trying to sell a house to a fence-sitting prospect sometimes will call with news of another potential buyer (real or fabricated) who has seen the house, liked it, and is scheduled to return the following day to talk about terms. The tactic, called in some circles "goosing them off the fence," works by turning a hesitant prospect into a competitor for a scarce resource.

Friendship/Liking Principal

A fact of social interaction that hardly needs belaboring is that people are favorably inclined toward those they know and like. A compliance heuristic consequence of this tendency could be worded as follows: *One should be more willing to comply with the requests of friends or other liked individuals.*

Compliance professionals may make use of the tendency to comply more readily to the requests of friends by enlisting the friends of prospects in the request presentation. The clearest illustration of this strategy that I know is the home-party concept, made prominent by the Tupperware Company but now used to sell everything from cookware to lingerie. In the case of Tupperware, the real compliance-inducing power of the party comes from a particular arrangement that trades on friendship. The true request to purchase the product does not come from the stranger who is the company sales representative; it comes from a friend to every person in the room. Usually, it is a woman who has called her friends together for the product demonstration in her home and who, everyone knows, makes a profit from each piece sold at the party. In this fashion, the company arranges for customers to buy from and for a friend rather than an unknown salesperson. Of course, other compliance practitioners also recognize the increased pressure to say yes to a friend. Charity organizations prefer to have volunteers canvass for donations close to their homes. They understand how much more difficult it is to turn down a charity request when it comes from a friend or neighbor. Other compliance professionals have found that the friend need not be present to be effective; often the mention of the friend's name is sufficient and, consequently, friendship referral systems are common in direct sales.

But what do compliance professionals do when the already-formed friendship is not present for them to employ? Here the professionals' strategy is quite direct: They first get their customers to like them. Tactics designed to generate liking occur in a variety of forms that cluster around certain factors that have been shown by research to increase liking: similarity, praise, cooperation, and physical attraction.

Similarity of attitude (for example, Byrne 1971) or background (for example, Stotland & Patchen 1961) can increase liking. Consequently, compliance professionals often point to (or manufacture) similarities between themselves and target persons before making a request. Car salespeople, for example, are trained to look for evidence of a prospect's background and hobbies while examining the trade-in car. Later, the salesperson can mention an interest that is similar to the customer's. Similarity of dress is another way to induce liking, probably because it provides a basis for assumptions about other more important areas of similarity, such as opinions and values. For instance, in a study done on peace marchers in the early 1970s (Suedfeld, Bochner, & Matas 1971), subjects were significantly more likely to sign the petition (without reading it) of a similarly dressed requester. This latter finding once again suggests the automatic and mindless quality of much compliance that is triggered by a single cue, in this case, similarity of dress.

Praise and other forms of positive estimation also stimulate liking (for example, Byrne & Rhamey 1965). The actor Maclain Stevenson once described how his wife tricked him into marriage: "She said she liked me." Although designed for a laugh, the remark is as much instructive as humorous. The simple information that someone fancies us can be a bewitchingly effective device for producing return liking and willing compliance. Although there are limits to our gullibility—especially when we can be sure that the flatterer's intent is manipulative (Jones & Wortman 1973)—we tend as a rule to believe praise and to like those who provide it. Evidence for the power of praise on liking comes from a study (Drachman, deCarufel, & Insko 1978) in which men received personal comments from someone who needed a favor from them. Some of the men got only positive comments, some only negative comments, and some got a mixture of good and bad. Three interesting findings resulted: (1) the evaluator who offered only praise was liked best; (2) this was so even though the men fully realized that the flatterer stood to gain from their liking of him; (3) unlike the other types of comments, pure praise did not have to be accurate to work. Compliments produced just as much liking for the flatterer when they were untrue as when they were true.

It is for such reasons that direct salespeople are educated in the art of praise. A potential customer's home, clothes, car, taste, and so forth are all frequent targets for compliments. One famous compliance practitioner, Joe Girard (named the "World's Greatest Salesman" by the *Guinness Book of World Records* for his phenomenal car sales record), makes an extensive and expensive habit of statements of positive evaluation. Each month he sends every one of his over 13,000 former customers a holiday greeting card containing a personal message. The holiday greeting changes from month to month ("Happy New Year" or "Happy Thanksgiving," etc.), but the message printed on the face of the card never varies; it reads, "I like you." As Joe explained in an interview, "There's nothing else on the card. Nothing but my name. I'm just telling 'em that I like 'em.'' Could this cost be worth the expense? Joe Girard thinks so; and someone who sells five cars and trucks every working day deserves our attention on the topic of compliance.

Cooperation is another factor that has been shown to enhance positive feelings and behavior (*cf.* Aronson, Bridgeman, & Geffner 1978; Cook 1978). Those who cooperate toward the achievement of a common goal are more favorable and helpful to each other as a consequence. That is why compliance professionals frequently strive to be perceived as cooperating partners with a target person. Automobile sales managers frequently set themselves as villains so that the salesperson can do battle in the customer's behalf. The cooperative, pulling-together kind of relationship consequently produced between the salesperson and customer naturally leads to a desirable form of liking that promotes sales. A related technique is employed by police interrogation officers to induce a suspect to confess to a crime. Called good cop/bad cop, the tactic begins when two interrogators use vastly different styles to confront a suspect. One officer takes a harsh, hard approach and pretends to try to bully the suspect into confessing. S/he then leaves the suspect alone with the second officer who takes a soft, conciliatory approach. The good cop tries to convince the suspect that s/he does not approve of the bad cop's style nor methods and that s/he is allied with the suspect against the bad cop. If s/he will only confess, good cop will work with the suspect to see that s/he gets fair treatment from the judicial system and that the bad cop's threats of severe punishment will go unrealized. This cooperative orientation is often effective in winning trust and confessions from the suspect.

Finally, physical attraction and its effect on liking have long been acknowledged as producing an advantage in social interaction. Recent research findings indicate, however, that the advantage may have been sorely underestimated. There appears to be a halo effect for physical appearances that generalizes to such favorable trait perceptions as talent, kindness, honesty, and intelligence (for example, Dion, Berscheid, & Walster 1972; Rich 1975). Consequently, attractive individuals are more persuasive both in terms of changing attitudes (Chaiken 1979) and getting what they request (Benson, Karabenic, & Lerner 1976). For instance, a study of the 1974 Canadian Federal elections found that attractive candidates received more than two and one-half times the votes of unattractive ones (Efran & Patterson 1976). Equally impressive results seem to be obtained in the judicial system. In a Pennsylvania study, researchers rated the physical attractiveness of seventy-four separate male defendants at the start of their criminal trials. When, much later, the researchers checked the results of these cases through court records, they found that the better-looking men received significantly lighter sentences. In fact, the attractive defendants were twice as likely to avoid incarceration as were the unattractive defendants

(Stewart 1980). When viewed in the light of such powerful effects, it is not surprising that extremely attractive models are employed to promote products and services, that sales trainers frequently include appearance and grooming tips in their presentations, or that con men and women are good-looking.

Ethics of Heuristic Compliance

At the outset, I described how automatic behavior patterns in lower animals are sometimes triggered by a single stimulus feature that is highly correlated with a complex and influential array of stimuli. Automatic responding to such highly representative single stimuli was said to be economical because it normally allows an animal to behave correctly by attending to and processing just one signal in its environment, thereby conserving its limited mental resources for other situations and decisions. I argued further that parallel forms of automatic responding and trigger features exist within *human* action, also for reasons of cognitive economy. Whether for human or infrahuman, such responding is seen to be vulnerable to error because it is stimulated by only a piece (albeit a usually reliable piece) of the entire array of relevant information. This vulnerability is especially telling when the trigger feature is purposefully removed from the larger stimulus array it traditionally occupies and is presented by itself. Under these circumstances, always generated by animal mimics and sometimes generated by human compliance professionals, we are likely to see inappropriate and exceedingly exploitable behavior.

Later, I described what I believe to be the trigger stimuli that typically engage the major human compliance heuristics. Briefly, they are: commitments, opportunities for reciprocation, the compliant behavior of similar others, cues of legitimate authority, cues of scarcity, and cues of friendship or liking. Compliance professionals who infuse their requests with major human compliance stimuli are more likely to be successful both when compliance is objectively called for (by the other cues of the situation) and when it is not. In the negative case, an important ethical issue is raised concerning the use of these triggers of mechanical, heuristic responding. When is it morally objectionable to press the triggers to gain compliance?

To answer this question, we might first decide when pressing those triggers is not objectionable. There is no necessary ethical problem of using the trigger stimuli for compliance. Indeed, the triggers naturally function to provide a valuable and efficient shortcut to those who respond to them. When seen in this light, the compliance practitioner who presents trigger features as they naturally occur may be seen as acting in a way that facilitates the usefulness of these increasingly important shortcuts. With the

pace and demands of our society accelerating as they are, shortcut processing will become an even more valuable device, provided that the shortcuts
are, indeed, good ones that take us where we want to go faster than the
safe but slow routes.

Here is where the potential for misuse lies. The practitioner who seeks
not to point out, reveal, or merely discuss the naturally present trigger
stimuli of a situation but who seeks to manufacture, counterfeit, or
fabricate the presence of such stimuli in the situation is acting in an exploitative manner. An insurance agent can, for instance, point out a
couple's existing monetary commitment to their home and suggest that a
commensurately larger policy would be consistent with that commitment; it
is quite another thing for the agent to produce a commitment to home insurance by the bait and switch technique. Similarly, it is far different for a
real estate agent to honestly convey scarcity information involving a particular type of house in the market than it is to create a false sense of scarcity
by announcing the interest of nonexistent other bidders. In each case, the
ethical key is whether the trigger feature is a representative and natural part
of the compliance situation or has been imported artificially to the situation
by the compliance agent.

Aside from the ethical implications, there are certain pragmatic reasons
that would counsel practitioners against the falsification of trusted compliance signals. First, respect for compliance practitioners will be reduced
when such an approach is used. A recurring theme in the profession is the
importance of a strong positive regard for one's work (i.e., a sense of pride
and professionalism) in generating high levels of job satisfaction *and* performance. It seems best to adopt the socially beneficial style of trigger
feature influence and to avoid the exploitative style. In the long run, practitioners are more likely to feel happy and respected in their work and to be
productive as a consequence. The second practical reason to take into account is the likelihood of further laws and constraints designed to regulate
the compliance professionals. That is, if we grant that the incidence of
shortcut responding is destined to increase throughout the society because
of the accelerating nature of modern life, then we can anticipate an enhanced
interest on the part of social and legal institutions to protect the integrity of
the shortcuts. Formal (i.e., regulatory) and informal (i.e., normative) sanc-
tions are likely to develop in an attempt to provide such protection. The
prospects of increased governmental and popular disapproval of compliance activities is hardly the sort of thing practitioners would want to
foster.

Thus it seems advantageous for compliance professions to undertake
training programs designed to clarify the vital distinction between trigger
feature influence that fairly presents to prospects the opportunity for socially
and mutually beneficial heuristic responding and that which exploits the heur-

istic rule in the interests of short-term benefit for only one party. In the latter instance, the long-term welfare of both parties is destined to suffer, whereas in the former instance, it is likely to grow in a context of cooperation.

Notes

1. Although there are functional similarities, several important differences exist between the automatic responding of humans and infrahumans. Our mechanical responses tend to be learned while infrahumans' tend to be innate. Ours are also more flexible and responsive to a larger number of triggers than are those of infrahumans.

2. For a more complete treatment of these issues, the interested reader may wish to consult Cialdini (1980).

3. In certain cases, a highly placed individual within an organization was informed of my research aims and cooperated both to conceal my identity and to arrange for a proper placement. In most instances, however, I remained incognito to all in an organization throughout my association with it. On leaving an organization, I gave a full revelation of my intent and identity, along with a promise that I would protect the organization's anonymity.

References

Aronson, E.; Bridgeman, D.L.; and Geffner, R. (1978). "The Effects of a Cooperative Classroom Structure on Student's Behavior and Attitudes," in D. Bar-Tal and L. Saxe (eds.), *Social Psychology of Education: Theory and Research.* Washington, D.C.: Hemisphere.

Aronson, E., and Mills, J. (1959). "The Effect of Severity of Initiation on Liking for a Group." *Journal of Abnormal and Social Psychology* 59, 177–181.

Aronson, E.; Turner, J.A.; and Carlsmith, J.M. (1963). "Communicator Credibility and Communication Discrepancy as a Determinant of Opinion Change." *Journal of Abnormal and Social Psychology* 67, 31–36.

Bandura, A., and Menlove, F.L. (1968). "Factors Determining Vicarious Extinction of Avoidance Behavior Through Symbolic Modeling." *Journal of Personality and Social Psychology* 8, 99–108.

Baumeister, R.F. (1982). "A Self-Presentational View of Social Phenomena." *Psychological Bulletin* 91, 3–26.

Beaman, A.L.; Cole, C.M.; Preston, M.; Klentz, B.; and Steblay, N.H. (1983). "A Meta-analysis of Fifteen Years of Foot-in-the-Door Research." *Personality and Social Psychology Bulletin* 9, 181–196.

Bem, D.J. (1967). "Self-Perception: An Alternative Interpretation of Cognitive Dissonance Phenomena." *Psychological Review* 74, 183-200.

Benson, P.L.; Karabenic, S.A.; and Lerner, R.M. (1976). "Pretty Pleases: The Effects of Physical Attractivenss on Race, Sex, and Receiving Help." *Journal of Experimental Social Psychology* 12, 409-415.

Bickman, L. (1974). "The Social Power of a Uniform." *Journal of Applied Social Psychology* 4, 47-61.

Brehm, S.S., and Brehm, J. (1981). *Psychological Reactance*. New York: Academic Press.

Bristowe, W.S. (1958). *The World of Spiders*. London: William Collins.

Brock, T.C. (1968). "Implications of Commodity Theory for Value Change," in A.G. Greenwald, T.C. Brock, and T.M. Ostrom (eds.), *Psychological Foundations of Attitudes*. New York: Academic Press.

Burger, J.M., and Petty, R.E. (1981). "The Low-Ball Technique: Task or Person Commitment." *Journal of Personality and Social Psychology* 40, 492-500.

Byrne, D. (1971). *The Attraction Paradigm*. New York: Academic Press.

Byrne, D., and Rhamey, R. (1965). "Magnitude of Positive and Negative Reinforcements as a Determinant of Attraction." *Journal of Personality and Social Psychology* 2, 884-889.

Chaiken, S. (1979). "Communicator Physical Attractiveness and Persuasion." *Journal of Personality and Social Psychology* 37, 1387-1397.

Cialdini, R.B. (1984). *Influence*. New York: Morrow.

————. (1980). "Full-Cycle Social Psychology," in L. Bickman (ed.), *Applied Social Psychology Annual,* (vol. 1). Beverly Hills, Calif.: Sage.

Cialdini, R.B., and Ascani, K. (1976). "Test of a Concession Procedure for Inducing Verbal, Behavioral, and Further Compliance with a Request to Give Blood." *Journal of Applied Psychology* 61, 295-300.

Cialdini, R.B.; Cacioppo, J.T.; Bassett, R.; and Miller, J.A. (1978). "Low-Ball Procedure for Producing Compliance: Commitment, Then Cost." *Journal of Personality and Social Psychology* 36, 463-476.

Cialdini, R.B.; Vincent, J.E.; Lewis, S.K.; Catalan, J.; Wheeler, D.; and Darby, B.L. (1975). "Reciprocal Concessions Procedure for Inducing Compliance: The Door-in-the-Face Technique." *Journal of Personality and Social Psychology* 31, 206-215.

Cook, S.W. (1978). "Interpersonal and Attitudinal Outcomes in Cooperating Interracial Groups." *Journal of Research and Development in Education* 12, 28-38.

Cupchik, G.C., and Leventhal, H. (1974). "Consistency Between Expressive Behavior and the Evaluation of Humerous Stimuli: The Role of Sex and Self-Observation." *Journal of Personality and Social Psychology* 30, 429-442.

DeJong, W. (1979). "An examination of Self-Perception Mediation of the Foot-in-the-Door Effect." *Journal of Personality and Social Psychology* 37, 2221-2239.

Dion, K.; Berscheid, E.; and Walster, E. (1972). "What Is Beautiful Is Good." *Journal of Personality and Social Psychology* 24, 285-290.

Drachman, D.; deCarufel, A.; and Insko, C.A. (1978). "The Extra-Credit Effect in Interpersonal Attraction." *Journal of Experimental Social Psychology* 14, 458-467.

Deutsch, M., and Gerard, H.B. (1955). "A Study of Normative and Individual Judgments." *Journal of Abnormal and Social Psychology* 51, 629-636.

Efran, M.G., and Patterson, E.W.J. (1976). "The Politics of Appearance." Unpublished manuscript, University of Toronto.

Festinger, L. (1954). "A Theory of Social Comparison Processes." *Human Relations* 2, 117-140.

_____ . (1957). *A Theory of Cognitive Dissonance.* Stanford, Calif.: Stanford University Press.

Fox, M.W. (1974). *Concepts in Ethology: Animal and Human Behavior.* Minneapolis: University of Minnesota Press.

Freedman, J.L. (1965). "Long-Term Behavioral Effects of Cognitive Dissonance." *Journal of Experimental Social Psychology* 1, 145-155.

Gouldner, A.W. (1960). "The Norm of Reciprocity." *American Sociological Review* 25, 161-178.

Heider, F. (1958). *The Psychology of Interpersonal Relations.* New York: Wiley.

Hofling, C.K.; Brotzman, E.; Dalrymple, S.; Graves, N.; and Pierce, C.M. (1966). "An Experimental Study in Nurse-Physician Relationships." *Journal of Nervous and Mental Disease* 143, 171-180.

Hornstein, H.A.; Fisch, E.; and Holmes, M. (1968). "Influence of Model's Feeling About His Behavior and His Relevance as a Comparison Other on Observer's Helping Behavior." *Journal of Personality and Social Psychology* 10, 222-226.

Jones, E.E., and Wortman, C. (1973). *Ingratiation: An Attributional Approach.* Morristown, N.J.: General Learning Corp.

Knishinsky, A. (1982). "The Effects of Scarcity of Material and Exclusivity of Information on Industrial Buyer Perceived Risk in Provoking Purchase Decision." Doctoral dissertation, Arizona State University.

Lack, D. (1943). *The Life of Robin.* London: Cambridge University Press.

Langer, E. (1978). "Rethinking the Role of Thought in Social Interaction," in *New Directions in Attribution Research,* vol. 2, Harvey, Ickes, and Kidd (eds.). Potomac, Md.: Lawrence Erlbaum Associates.

Langer, E.; Blank, A.; and Chanowitz, B. (1977). "The Mindlessness of Ostensibly Thoughtful Action: The Role of Placibic Information in Interpersonal Interaction." *Journal of Personality and Social Psychology* 36, 635–642.

Latane, B., and Darley, J.M. (1968). *The Unresponsive Bystander: Why Doesn't He Help?* New York: Appleton-Century-Crofts.

Lefkowitz, M.; Blake, R.R.; and Mouton, J.S. (1955). "Status Factors in Pedestrian Violation of Traffic Signals." *Journal of Abnormal and Social Psychology* 51, 704–706.

Lloyd, J.E. (1965). "Aggressive Mimicry in Photuris: Firefly *Femme Fatates.*" *Science* 149, 653–654.

Mazis, M.B. (1975). "Antipollution Measures and Psychological Reactance Theory: A Field Experiment." *Journal of Personality and Social Psychology* 31, 654–666.

Milgram, S. (1974). *Obedience to Authority.* New York: Harper.

Newcomb, T.M. (1953). "An Approach to the Study of Communicative Acts." *Psychological Review* 60, 393–404.

Phillips, D.P. (1974). "The Influence of Suggestion on Suicide: Substantive and Theoretical Implications of the Werther Effect." *American Sociological Review* 39, 340–354.

Regan, D.T. (1971). "Effects of a Favor and Liking on Compliance." *Journal of Experimental Social Psychology* 7, 627–639.

Reingen, D.H. (1982). "Test of a List Procedure for Inducing Compliance with a Request to Donate Money." *Journal of Applied Psychology* 67, 110–118.

Rich, J. (1975). "Effects of Children's Physical Attractiveness on Teacher's Evaluations." *Journal of Educational Psychology* 67, 599–607.

Schachter, S., and Singer, J.E. (1962). "Cognitive, Social, and Physiological Determinants of Emotional States." *Psychological Review* 69, 379–399.

Stewart, J.E. (1980). "Defendant's Attractiveness as a Factor in the Outcome of Trials." *Journal of Applied Social Psychology* 10, 348–361.

Stotland, E., and Patchen, M. (1961). "Identification and Change in Prejudice and Authoritarianism." *Journal of Abnormal and Social Psychology* 62, 250–256.

Suedfeld, P.; Bochner, S.; and Matas, C. (1971). "Petitioner's Attire and Petition Signing by Peace Demonstrators: A Field Experiment." *Journal of Applied Social Psychology* 1, 278–283.

Tedeschi, J.T. (1981). *Impression Management Theory and Social Psychological Research.* New York: Academic Press.

Worchel, S.; Lee, J.; and Adewole, A. (1975). "Effects of Supply and Demand on Ratings of Object Value." *Journal of Personality and Social Psychology* 32, 906–914.

2

Attitude Change and Personal Selling: Central and Peripheral Routes to Persuasion

Richard E. Petty,
John T. Cacioppo, and
David Schumann

The typical personal selling situation involves a salesperson and a customer. The salesperson's goal is get the customer to agree to purchase some product. The customer's goal is to obtain the best possible product at a reasonable price. Yet salespeople are sometimes unable to close a transaction, and customers sometimes end up with products that they do not really need or want. What are some of the factors that determine whether or not the salesperson and/or customer will be satisfied? Three literatures within social psychology appear most relevant to this question: compliance, bargaining, and attitude change.

Over the last twenty years, social psychologists have documented a wide variety of *compliance* techniques. In one technique, the door-in-face procedure, a salesperson asks a customer to make a very expensive purchase, and when the customer refuses, the salesperson comes back with a more modest request. Thus a student selling door-to-door might ask a customer to help him or her through school by purchasing a $500 set of encyclopedias. The customer would like to help, but the request is too large, so the customer says no. The student, however, immediately comes back with a more modest request. Would the customer be willing to subscribe to just one magazine? Research shows that more people are likely to agree to the second more modest request after they have refused the initial large request than if no initial large request were made. Research supports the view that this effect occurs because the customer, feeling that the salesperson has made a reasonable compromise, feels subtle pressure to compromise also (see Cialdini et al. 1975). Importantly, in compliance techniques, one person gets another to agree to some request *without changing the person's attitude about the product in question.* So in the example, our hypothetical customer has agreed to subscribe to a magazine, but the customer's attitude about the magazine has not changed as a result of the customer's interaction with the salesperson. Several other compliance techniques have been shown to be effective in getting people to agree to requests without changing their attitudes about the issue or product under consideration (for example, the foot-in-the-door technique, see Freedman & Fraser 1966; DeJong 1979; the low-ball technique, see Cialdini, Cacioppo, Bassett, & Miller 1978; Burger & Petty 1981, and so forth).

A second relevant area of research in social psychology is that on *bargaining* and *negotiation*. Consider the same magazine salesperson who wants the customer to purchase a magazine subscription. After hearing the price of a one-year subscription, the customer may indicate that the price is too high but that s/he might subscribe for half the price. The salesperson says that the half-price deal is impossible, but that s/he might be able to offer 25 percent off. The customer and salesperson finally close the sale at one-third off the listed price. A large number of social psychological studies have investigated a variety of factors that may determine whether the final selling price is more advantageous to the customer or the salesperson (see review by Miller & Crandall 1980). For example, in one study Cialdini, Bickman, & Cacioppo (1980) found that new-car customers who were able to demonstrate that they were tough bargainers in an initial discussion with a salesperson subsequently obtained a better price in bargaining over a second car than customers who did not bargain over the initial car. It is important to note that in the typical bargaining situation, just as with the compliance techniques noted above, the interaction between salesperson and customer does *not* involve an attempt to change the customer's attitude about the product. All that is at stake is how much the customer will pay for the product or what conditions will be attached to the sale.

A third approach to obtaining agreement, highlighted in this chapter, relies on changing a person's attitude about the product under consideration. In this approach, our hypothetical magazine salesperson might have attempted to get the customer to *like* the magazine more than s/he did initially prior to asking him/her to subscribe to it. This approach assumes that the more favorable the customer's attitude toward the magazine, the more likely s/he is to subscribe to it. Our primary goal in this chapter is to present a general framework for thinking about attitude change: We call it the Elaboration Likelihood Model (ELM). The ELM specifies two distinct routes to attitude change—central and peripheral—that have different antecedents and consequents. We will review some empirical evidence for the model and address the relevance of the model for personal selling situations. We believe that the ELM may provide some insight into how salespeople influence the attitudes of customers. We hope that this understanding will help produce better consumer decisions.

Central and Peripheral Routes to Persuasion

It is not uncommon for textbooks on the psychology of attitude change to describe ten to twenty unique theories of persuasion. These various theories, all with periods of ascendency and decline, have competed over the years for the attention of researchers and practitioners. In a recent review, we suggested that—even though the different theories of persuasion have unique terminology, postulates, underlying motives, and particular effects, that they specialize in explaining—the different theories can be thought of as emphasizing one of two relatively distinct routes to attitude change (Petty & Cacioppo 1981). First, the *central route* views attitude change as resulting from a person's diligent consideration of information that is central to what that person feels are the true merits of the product. The theoretical approaches that fall under this route have emphasized factors such as (1) a person's attempt to cognitively justify dissonant behavior (for example, Cummings & Venkatesan 1976; Festinger 1957); (2) a person's attempt to comprehend, learn, and retain product-relevant information (for example, Hovland, Janis, & Kelley 1953; McGuire 1976); (3) a person's attempt to scrutinize a message and evaluate whether the arguments are cogent or specious (for example, Cacioppo & Petty 1981; McGuire 1974; Petty, Ostrom, & Brock 1981); and (4) a person's attempt to combine and integrate product-relevant information and beliefs into an overall evaluative reaction (for example, Anderson 1981; Azjen & Fishbein 1980). Attitude changes induced by the central route are postulated to be relatively enduring and predictive of subsequent behavior (Cialdini, Petty, & Cacioppo 1981; Petty & Cacioppo 1980).

In contrast to this focus on the extensive cognitive activity that is central to an evaluation of the personal worth of a product, a second group of theoretical approaches to persuasion has developed that emphasizes a more *peripheral route* to attitude change. Attitude changes that occur through the peripheral route do not occur because an individual has personally and carefully considered the pros and cons of the product. Rather, they result because the product is associated with positive or negative cues or because the person makes a simple inference about the merits of the product based on various simple cues in the persuasion context. For example, rather than diligently considering the product-relevant arguments presented, a person may favor a product simply because s/he heard about it during a pleasant lunch, because the person telling him/her about it is believed to be an expert, or because there appear to be many arguments in favor of it. Similarly, a person may decide against a product simply because the salesperson is unattractive or too dissimilar. These cues (for example, good food, many arguments, attractive sources) may shape attitudes or allow a person to decide what attitudinal position to adopt without the need for engaging in any extensive thought about the actual product-relevant arguments presented. The approaches that fall under the peripheral route to persuasion have emphasized factors such as (1) whether or not a simple attitudinal inference can be made based on observing one's own behavior (for example,

Bem 1972; Scott 1978); (2) whether or not the position advocated in a message falls within one's predetermined latitude of acceptance or rejection (for example, Sherif, Sherif, & Nebergall 1965; Newman & Dolich 1979); (3) whether or not some immediate personal benefit is associated with expressing a particular attitude (for example, Schlenker 1978, 1980); and (4) whether or not a product is associated with basic but product-irrelevant cues such as food and pain (for example, Janis, Kaye, & Kirschner 1965; Sternthal & Craig 1974) or is associated with secondary cues such as pleasant pictures and attractive endorsers (for example, Kelman 1961; Mowen 1980). Attitude changes induced through the peripheral route are postulated to be relatively temporary and unpredictive of subsequent behavior.[1]

Unfortunately, none of the unique theories of persuasion has yet provided a comprehensive view of attitude change. A general framework for understanding persuasion must consider that attitudes toward issues and products sometimes are formed and changed in a thoughtful manner after a careful consideration of issue or product-relevant arguments (central route) but attitudes sometimes are formed and changed as a result of relatively simple cues in the persuasion situation (peripheral route). Also, variables that enhance and reduce the likelihood that extensive cognitive activity will accompany attitude change should be specified as well as the consequences of thoughtful and nonthoughtful persuasion. Since a salesperson can presumably induce attitude change toward a product by either the central or the peripheral route, it is important to understand the influential variables and the differential consequences of the two routes to persuasion. Before proceeding to a discussion of the implications of our ELM for personal selling situations, we need to outline the model in some detail.

The Elaboration Likelihood Model of Persuasion

Figure 2-1 presents an abbreviated diagram of the ELM specifying the two routes to persuasion (see Petty & Cacioppo, in press, for further details). The basic tenet of the ELM is that different methods of inducing attitude change should work best depending on whether the elaboration likelihood of the communication situation (i.e., the probability of message or issue-relevant thought occurring) is high or low. When the elaboration likelihood is high, the central route to persuasion should be particularly effective, but when the elaboration likelihood is low, the peripheral route will likely be better. Two classes of variables affect whether or not the elaboration likelihood will be high or low. First, people will not be *motivated* to think about every message that they receive. Since it is estimated that people may receive over 1500 persuasive messages a day from national advertisers alone (Will 1982), far too much effort would be required to carefully scrutinize

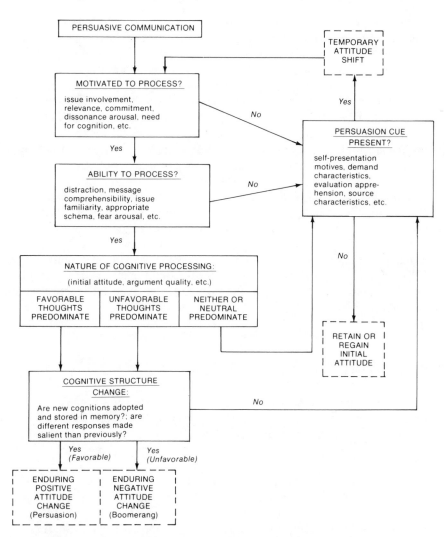

Figure 2-1. The Elaboration Likelihood Model of Attitude Change

every argument. Furthermore, even if people were willing to think about every message they received, it is unlikely that they would have the *ability* to do so.

One assumption of the ELM is that when people have both the motivation and ability to think about the arguments in a message or the arguments that a salesperson might present, they attempt to determine the personal implications of the arguments. This may involve relating the persuasive arguments to prior personal experiences or information previously stored in memory. For example, if a salesperson encourages a customer to buy a television with automatic fine tuning for the best reception, this argument might elicit a favorable thought from one customer (for example, I sure can use better reception than I get now) but an unfavorable thought from another (for example, my present television doesn't have automatic fine tuning and my reception is fine). A second assumption is that the more favorable the thoughts a message elicits, the greater the likelihood of positive attitude change, but the more unfavorable the thoughts a message elicits, the greater the likelihood of resistance or boomerang (see Cacioppo & Petty 1981; Wright 1980, for documentation). In short, the ELM holds that one way a variable can affect attitude change is by affecting the number and nature of issue or product-relevant thoughts that a message elicits. As noted earlier, however, attitudes may also be changed without thinking about the issue or product-relevant arguments if a salient positive or negative cue is present in the persuasion situation. In sum, according to the ELM, a variable can affect attitudes by affecting the motivation or ability to think about and evaluate the available issue or product-relevant arguments (central route) or by serving as a positive or negative cue (peripheral route).

Consequences of the Route to Persuasion

It is important to know *how* a variable affects persuasion because current research supports the view that attitudes changed by the central route tend to be more enduring and more predictive of behavior than those changed by the peripheral route (Chaiken 1980; Cialdini et al. 1976; Petty, Cacioppo, & Schumann 1983). When an attitude change is based on an extensive foundation of self-generated favorable thoughts and beliefs about an issue or product, the attitude change is likely to persist because the issue or product-relevant beliefs are likely to remain salient (see Slamecka & Graf 1978). Furthermore, even if a few of the favorable cognitions elicited at the time of message exposure are forgotten, others are likely to remain. On the other hand, attitude changes that result from one prominent cue (for example, an attractive source) would appear to be much more vulnerable to forgetting. These changes are likely to endure only if the person has been exposed to the persuasive message in the same persuasion context many times, thereby rendering the cue relatively permanent. Even then, however, such attitude changes would appear to be highly susceptible to counterpropaganda because the person has so little on which to base a positive or negative opinion. Thus the new attitude would be difficult to defend if challenged severely. The fact that attitudes induced via the central route have a more extensive informational basis than those induced via the peripheral route may render people more confident in acting on these attitudes, and the fact that central attitudes are more salient in memory than peripheral attitudes may make people more able to act on them (*cf.* Fazio & Zanna 1981).

Testing Central versus Peripheral Routes

Because of the different consequences of the two routes to persuasion, it is important to know how a variable affects persuasion. When an attitude change is produced, it is unclear how long it will last or how predictive it will be of subsequent behavior. So how can it be determined whether a variable works by the central or the peripheral route? In the typical basic or applied study on attitude change, one cannot tell. For example, trial attorneys have long suspected that the use of a dramatic rhetorical question in a closing argument could enhance persuasion over the use of simple declarative statements. Research has supported the view that when argument summary statements are presented in declarative sentences (for example, the car gets good gas mileage), they are typically less persuasive than when the argument summary statements are phrased as rhetorical questions (for example, the car gets good gas mileage, doesn't it?; see Zillmann 1972). But *why*?

Zillmann (1972) suggested that for most naturally occurring messages, rhetorical questions are used only with especially strong arguments. Because of this, he proposed that over time the use of rhetorical questions eventually comes to signal the presence of good arguments. Therefore people might agree more with rhetorical messages because they make the inference that the arguments are good. Note that Zillmann's theory does not require people to actually think about the merits of the arguments. It only requires them to notice the presence of the rhetorical questions, which serve as a peripheral cue as to the validity of the advocacy. Others have argued that the use of rhetorical questions makes the speaker appear more polite, and people prefer to agree with polite others (see Bates 1976). Again, rhetoricals serve as a peripheral cue.

In contrast to these theories, we have proposed that when people are unmotivated to think about a message, the use of rhetorical questions motivates increased thinking about the arguments provided. Thus when the salesperson says, "This car gets good gas mileage, doesn't it," the customer is more likely to think about whether or not the car really does get good gas mileage than when the salesperson just asserts that the gas mileage is good. Thus if the person knows that the car really does get good gas mileage, the message using rhetorical questions should be more likely to elicit a favorable thought than the message using declarative sentences, thereby enhancing the persuasive impact of the message. However, if the person knows that the car really doesn't get good gas mileage, the message using rhetorical questions should be more likely to elicit a counterargument than the message using declarative sentences, thereby reducing the persuasiveness of the message. Our reasoning suggests how to conduct a crucial test of the central versus peripheral explanations of the effectiveness of rhetorical questions: Compare the effectiveness of both strong and weak arguments summarized in both declarative form and as rhetorical questions. If they serve as a positive peripheral cue, rhetorical questions should enhance the persuasive impact of both strong and weak messages. If the central theory is correct, however, then rhetorical questions should improve agreement only for messages with strong arguments. If the arguments are weak and rhetorical questions strengthen thinking about them, agreement should be reduced.[2]

To compare the two approaches to rhetorical questions, we exposed college undergraduates to a message very low in personal relevance. The message contained relatively strong arguments (that is, they elicited primarily favorable thoughts when undergraduates were asked to think about them in a pilot test) or relatively weak ones (that is, they elicited primarily unfavorable thoughts when undergraduates were asked to think about them). Each of the major arguments in the regular version of the message ended with a summary sentence. In the rhetorical version, six of the eight argument summarizing statements were transformed to rhetorical questions. Afterward, students indicated their extent of agreement with the comprehensive exam idea (see Petty, Cacioppo, & Heesacker 1981).

Figure 2–2 presents the results. Our pattern of data clearly suggests that rhetorical questions do not serve simply as acceptance cues. When strong arguments were presented, the use of rhetoricals enhanced persuasion, but when the arguments were weak, rhetoricals reduced persuasion. If we had only included strong arguments in our messages, both peripheral and central explanations could have accounted for the results. Thus one indication that a variable affects attitudes by affecting the motivation and/or ability to think about the message arguments is that the variable affects the acceptance of strong and weak arguments *differently*. The more a variable improves the motivation and/or ability to scrutinize message arguments, the more people should realize the positive implications of cogent arguments and the negative implications of weak ones and the more their attitudes should be affected by these argument differences. If a variable affects attitudes simply by serving as an acceptance or rejection cue, then the quality of the arguments should be relatively unimportant.

Variables Affecting Motivation and Ability to Think

Perhaps the most important motivational variable affecting a person's willingness to think about a persuasive message is the personal relevance of the

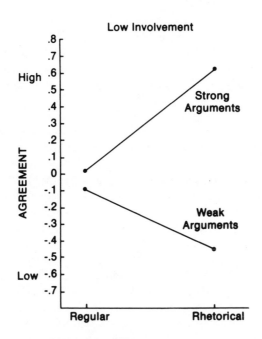

Source: Petty, Cacioppo, and Heesacker, 1981.

Figure 2–2. Rhetorical Questions and Message Processing

message. As a message becomes more personally involving or there are more personal implications of the advocated position, it becomes more important and adaptive to form a reasoned and veridical opinion. Thus as a message increases in personal relevance, the quality of the arguments in the message becomes a more important determinant of attitude change, and the number and nature of a person's message-relevant thoughts become a more important predictor of the amount of message agreement (Petty & Cacioppo 1979a, 1979b). In addition, we have found that in general people are more motivated to think about messages or anticipated messages that take disagreeable rather than agreeable positions (Cacioppo & Petty 1979a, 1979b). Counterattitudinal messages indicate that one's attitude may be incorrect; therefore these messages may warrant more careful consideration than proattitudinal messages that do not challenge one's viewpoint.

Just as some messages may typically evoke more thought than others, we have also found that some people are typically more motivated to think about messages and are more likely to extract meaning from them (for example, Cacioppo & Petty in press, b; Heesacker, Petty, & Cacioppo in press). In particular, in a series of studies on the *need for cognition*, we have found that some people tend to find tasks requiring extensive cognitive activity to be fun, whereas others prefer to avoid them (Cacioppo & Petty 1982). As might be expected based on our ELM, the quality of the arguments contained in a message is a more important determinant of attitudes for people high than low in their need for cognition (Cacioppo, Petty, & Morris 1983).

Of course, many variables can affect a person's motivation to think about a message. Finally, we note that the more people responsible for evaluating a message, the less motivated any individual is to exert effort in order to evaluate the message (Petty, Cacioppo, & Harkins 1983). Thus the impact of some messages delivered to groups may be diffused. For example, if a husband and wife are listening to a salesperson explain the benefits of home insulation, it is likely that their attitudes would be less affected by the quality of the arguments the salesperson provides than if either were listening alone and felt solely responsible for evaluating the message (see Petty, Harkins, & Williams 1980).

As figure 2-1 indicates, having the motivation to think about a persuasive message is not sufficient to ensure that the central route will be followed. A person must also have the ability to think about the issue-relevant information presented. Some people will naturally have a greater ability to think about certain kinds of information because of their superior intelligence (Eagly & Warren 1976) or because of their greater experience with or knowledge about an issue (Cacioppo & Petty 1980b; Wood 1982). In addition, a large number of situational variables have been shown to affect a person's ability to think about a message. For example, to the extent that a message is accompanied by distracting stimuli, the ability to think about it is decreased, and people thus are less able to differentiate strong from weak arguments (Petty, Wells, & Brock 1976). On the other hand, as a message is repeated a moderate number of times, people have a greater opportunity to think about the arguments and show greater differentiation of cogent from specious arguments (Cacioppo & Petty 1980a; in press, -a). How a message is presented may also affect a person's ability to engage in issue-relevant thought. When a person reads a message about a product (as opposed to hearing it on a radio, television, or face-to-face) it is possible to stop the message presentation to think about it. An oral message, however, may be presented too quickly to permit careful scrutiny (Chaiken & Eagly 1976). As a persuasive message becomes more complex and difficult to understand, the more advantageous it becomes to screen out distractions, to repeat the major message arguments, and to perhaps provide the customer with a written summary of the major points made.[3]

Inducing persuasion by presenting a customer with cogent product-relevant arguments is an effective sales strategy when the elaboration likelihood of the persuasion situation is relatively high. A salesperson can estimate the elaboration likelihood by carefully considering the variables discussed above. Does the product have important personal implications for the customer? If not, prior to presenting the arguments for a product, can the salesperson point out some personal implications that the customer might not have considered? Can the salesperson ask the customer questions during the presentation to induce more thinking about the arguments presented? How much knowledge does the customer have about the product? Will the customer be able to evaluate the facts and figures that are part of the sales presentation? According to the ELM, when the elaboration likelihood is high, attitudes will be determined mostly by the quality of the product-relevant arguments available; but when the elaboration likelihood is low, peripheral cues in the persuasion situation will be more important determinants of attitudes. What variables serve as peripheral cues, and what is the evidence for their operation?

Peripheral Cues

As noted earlier, a customer might decide in favor of a product simply because of the salesperson's likeability or because some other simple positive cue was present. According to the ELM, peripheral cues should be especially important determinants of attitudes when people are either relatively unmotivated or relatively unable to think about the issue or product-relevant information presented. In order to provide an appropriate test of the two routes to persuasion, it is necessary to construct two kinds of persuasion contexts: one in which the elaboration likelihood is high and one in which the elaboration likelihood is low. In the experiments described next, we specifically attempted to validate the prediction that there were two relatively distinct routes to persuasion. We held the ability of our subjects to think about the message at a relatively high and constant level across experimental conditions (for example, the messages and issues employed were easy to understand, no extraneous distractions were present, etc.), but we experimentally varied their motivation to think about the message by varying the extent to which the message had personal consequences for the message recipient. Following the procedure of Apsler & Sears (1968), subjects in the high and low relevance conditions were exposed to the same experimental stimuli. But subjects in the high relevance conditions were led to believe that the issue or product under consideration would likely have direct personal consequences for them, whereas subjects in the low relevance conditions were led to believe that the issue or product had few personal implications. Given that all subjects have the same ability to think about the arguments presented, subjects in the high relevance conditions should be more likely to follow the central route to persuasion whereas subjects in the low relevance conditions should be more likely to follow the peripheral route.

In addition to varying the personal relevance of the message in each of our experiments, we manipulated the quality of the arguments contained in the message, and a peripheral cue that would permit assessment of the message without the need for issue- or product-relevant thinking. As explained above, a manipulation of message quality allows us to assess the extent to which subjects are carefully scrutinizing the message arguments. The greater the scrutiny, the more they should realize the strengths of cogent arguments and the flaws in specious ones. Furthermore, if subjects are basing their attitudes on a careful assessment of the validity of the arguments presented, the peripheral cue manipulations should have little effect on their attitudes. On the other hand, if subjects are not thinking carefully, then their post-message attitudes should not differ greatly as a function of the strength of the arguments in the message but should vary because of the peripheral cue presented.

Source Cues. In our initial test of the two routes to persuasion (Petty, Cacioppo, & Goldman 1981) we had university undergraduates listen to a message advocating that seniors be required to pass a comprehensive exam in their declared major as a requirement for graduation. In the high-involvement conditions, the speaker advocated that the policy be instituted at the students' own university next year, thereby affecting all of the students personally. In the low-involvement conditions, the speaker advocated that the policy begin in ten years, thereby affecting no current students. Half of the students heard eight cogent arguments in favor of the recommendation and half heard eight weak arguments. Finally, for half of the students, the source of the message was described as a Professor of Education at Princeton University (expert source), and for the other half the source was described as a junior at a local high school (non-expert source). The expertise of the message source provides a peripheral cue that permits an assessment of the advocacy without any need to think about the issue-relevant arguments.

The results of this study are graphed in the left panel of figure 2–3. When the students thought that the exam proposal had little personal relevance, their post-communication attitudes were influenced only by the expertise of the message source (peripheral cue); the actual quality of the arguments had no effect. On the other hand, when the students thought that the exam proposal had direct personal consequences, their attitudes were affected only by the quality of the issue-relevant arguments presented; the source expertise manipulation had no effect.

To test the utility of the ELM in a situation wherein product rather than issue attitudes were involved, we conducted a study in which university undergraduates were asked to examine a booklet containing twelve magazine advertisements (Petty, Cacioppo, & Schumann 1983). One of the ads in the booklet was for a fictitious new product, "Edge disposable razors." Before beginning to look through the ad booklet, the students were

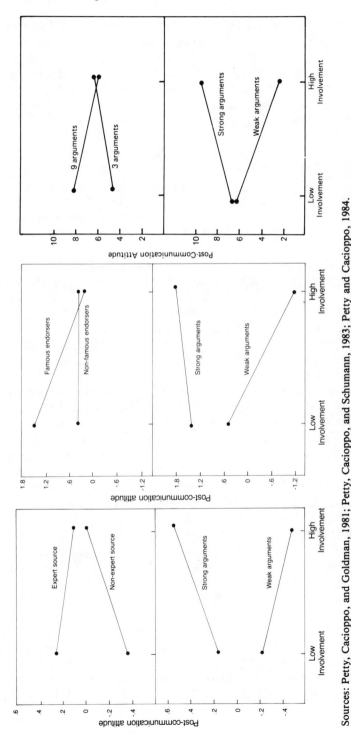

Figure 2-3. Results of Source-Cue Study

Sources: Petty, Cacioppo, and Goldman, 1981; Petty, Cacioppo, and Schumann, 1983; Petty and Cacioppo, 1984.

Note: The top half of each panel shows that peripheral cues are effective under low involvement; bottom halves show that arguments are processed under high involvement.

informed that at the end of the study they would be asked to select a modest gift. Students in the high-involvement group were told that they would be able to select from a variety of disposable razor products, rendering our bogus razor ad highly relevant. Subjects in the low-involvement group were told that they would be able to select from a variety of toothpaste products (one ad for toothpaste was included in the ad booklet). For these subjects, the razor ad was relatively irrelevant.

Four different versions of the ad were constructed. Two featured photographs of two well known and liked sports celebrities, and two featured middle-aged citizens described as Californians. The product endorser served as the manipulation of a peripheral cue. In addition, two of the ads featured very persuasive arguments for the product (for example, "handle is tapered and ribbed to prevent slipping"), and two featured weak arguments (for example, "designed with the bathroom in mind"; see example ads in figure 2-4).

After exposure to the ad booklet containing one of the four Edge ads, subjects rated their attitudes toward the products. The attitudes toward Edge razors are presented in the middle panel of figure 2-3. When subjects anticipated making an imminent decision about the product class (high involvement), the quality of the product-relevant information provided in the ad had a stronger impact on attitudes than when no decision was imminent (low involvement). On the other hand, under low involvement, the nature of the product endorsers (famous or not) had a significant effect on attitudes toward the product, but the endorsers had no effect on product attitudes under high involvement. In addition to the attitude measures, students were asked to rate the likelihood of purchasing Edge razors the next time they needed a product of this nature. Attitudes toward Edge razors proved to be a better predictor of behavioral (purchase) intentions under high ($r = .59$) than under low-involvement conditions ($r = .36$). Thus as expected by the ELM, attitudes changed by the central route were more predictive of behavior than those changed through the peripheral route.

The accumulated persuasion literature in social psychology is generally consistent with the ELM view that attributes of the source of a persuasive message are particularly likely to serve as simple acceptance or rejection cues when people are relatively unmotivated or unable to think about the message arguments presented. When motivation and thinking ability are high, source factors become relatively unimportant in their role as cues. Thus source factors are more likely to serve as cues when the personal consequences of a message are low rather than high (see also Chaiken 1980; Rhine & Severance 1970). In addition, source factors have been shown to gain importance as the ability to process a message decreases. Thus, source factors have been shown to have a greater impact on persuasion when distraction is high rather than low (Kiesler & Mathog, 1968) and when a

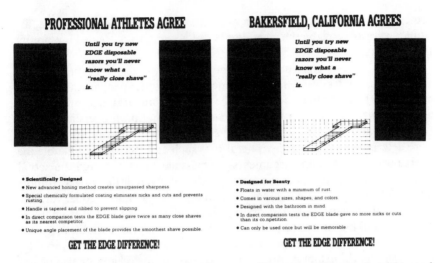

PROFESSIONAL ATHLETES AGREE

Until you try new EDGE disposable razors you'll never know what a "really close shave" is.

● Scientifically Designed
● New advanced honing method creates unsurpassed sharpness
● Special chemically formulated coating eliminates nicks and cuts and prevents rusting.
● Handle is tapered and ribbed to prevent slipping
● In direct comparison tests the EDGE blade gave twice as many close shaves as its nearest competitor.
● Unique angle placement of the blade provides the smoothest shave possible

GET THE EDGE DIFFERENCE!

BAKERSFIELD, CALIFORNIA AGREES

Until you try new EDGE disposable razors you'll never know what a "really close shave" is.

● Designed for Beauty
● Floats in water with a minimum of rust
● Comes in various sizes, shapes, and colors
● Designed with the bathroom in mind
● In direct comparison tests the EDGE blade gave no more nicks or cuts than its competition
● Can only be used once but will be memorable

GET THE EDGE DIFFERENCE!

Note: The left panel features celebrity endorsers with strong arguments; the right panel features average citizen endorsers with weak arguments. Photographs have been blacked out to preserve anonymity.

Figure 2–4. Mock Magazine Ads for Razors

message is externally paced (such as when presented orally) than when self-paced (such as when presented in print; Chaiken & Eagly 1983; Worchel et al. 1975).

Message and Other Cues. Although in the experiments just described, the peripheral cues resided in the message source, cues may also reside in the persuasive message or the persuasion context. To document this, we briefly describe a study designed to show that the mere number of arguments contained in a message can serve as a peripheral cue and affect attitudes when people are unmotivated to think about the issue. In this study, we once again exposed college students to a message advocating that seniors be required to pass a comprehensive exam in their major. We once again manipulated the personal relevance of the proposal and the quality of the arguments in support of the exam, but this time we included a peripheral cue within the message. Specifically, half of the students received a message containing only three arguments and half received a message containing nine (see Petty & Cacioppo 1984). If a person is not thinking about the arguments in a message, then it may be reasonable to infer that the more arguments in favor of the proposal, the better it must be. The results of our study are graphed in the right panel of figure 2–3. As expected by the ELM, when the issue had high relevance, subjects' attitudes were affected only by the quality of the arguments in the message; the mere number of arguments presented had no effect. However, when the issue was of low relevance, attitudes were affected by the mere number of arguments presented but not by their quality.

In sum, in our experiments on the different routes to persuasion, we found that under very high-relevance conditions, people exerted the cognitive effort required to evaluate the issue-relevant arguments presented, and their attitudes were a function of this information processing activity (central route). Under very low-relevance conditions, however, attitudes were determined by salient peripheral cues such as how expert or likable the source was or how many arguments the message contained, and the actual quality of the arguments in the message had relatively little impact. Importantly, although our research has focused on how the motivational variable of personal relevance affected whether attitude changes resulted from issue-relevant thinking or peripheral cues, other motivational variables (for example, the number of people evaluating the message) and ability variables (for example, the extent of prior knowledge about the issue) can also be important in determining the route to persuasion.

Implications of the ELM for Personal Selling

Since a great deal of personal-selling research has focused on particular characteristics of salespersons and how these attributes affect product attitudes and sales, this is where we will begin our discussion.

First, it is clear that a wide variety of attributes of salespeople have been studied, including the salesperson's expertise, physical attractiveness, similarity to the customer, and others (see Reingen & Woodside, 1981, for further discussion). It is noteworthy that some studies have found attributes of salespeople to exert a significant impact on attitudes and sales, but others have failed to detect any impact. In addition, many different theories have been proposed to account for the diversity of findings obtained. The diversity of findings and the multitude of theories available to account for significant and non-significant results has led to considerable disagreement in the literature as to how important salesperson attributes such as perceived expertise, similarity, and attractiveness really are. Some investigators have concluded that these variables do exert an important influence on sales (for example, Reingen, Ronkainen, & Gresham 1981) whereas others have concluded that salesperson attributes more often are not important (for example, Wilson & Ghingold 1981).

Consider the impact of a salesperson's perceived expertise on his/her ability to close a sale. In one study, Obermiller & Sawyer (1981) varied the perceived expertise of a salesperson who attempted to convince college students to sign up for a new tennis course in which personalized instruction would be offered for $30. The expert salesperson was described as a former tennis instructor whereas the non-expert was described as a novice. In addition, the expert salesperson used more tennis jargon than did the non-expert. Each was trained to deliver the same 1500-word sales message. After the talk, the students were asked whether or not they wanted to sign up for the course. Overall, 30 percent of the students signed up for the course; this figure did not differ for the expert and the non-expert salesperson.

On the other hand, Woodside & Davenport (1974) conducted a study in which the manipulated expertise of the salesperson did affect sales. In their study, a salesclerk attempted to induce the purchase of a cassette-tape-head cleaner kit. In addition to manipulating the amount of knowledge the clerk displayed about the cleaner kit (expertise), they also manipulated how similar the clerk's stated taste in music was to the customer's (similarity). In this study, both increased expertise and increased similarity induced greater sales.

Why did these two studies achieve different results? One possibly important difference between the two studies concerns the customer's motivation and/or ability to evaluate and scrutinize the product-relevant information provided. Most college students are interested in sports and are quite familiar with tennis and the benefits of exercise. Thus it is likely that in the Obermiller & Sawyer study, most of the potential customers had the requisite motivation and ability to evaluate the arguments presented by the salesperson. It was not necessary for them to rely on the salesperson's presumed level of expertise in order to evaluate the tennis course offer. On the other hand, most owners of tape recorders probably know very little about their maintenance and the real utility of a tape-head cleaner kit. If so, then most potential customers for this product would be relatively unable to evaluate the true merits of the arguments presented and would therefore be more likely to base a decision on the salesclerk's apparent expertise or on how much they liked the salesclerk. We suggest that in the first study, customers followed the central route to persuasion because the elaboration likelihood was relatively high, but in the second study, customers followed the peripheral route to persuasion because the elaboration likelihood was relatively low. Similar analysis of the likely extent of message elaboration in previous research on source factors in personal selling might be useful in accounting for the conflicting pattern of data obtained in these studies.

Source Factors as Motivators of Thought

We suspect that in many of the personal selling situations typical of actual buyer-seller exchanges, the elaboration likelihood is neither as high nor as low as we deliberately created in our laboratory tests of central and peripheral routes to persuasion. For example, in our initial study (Petty, Cacioppo, & Goldman 1981) we varied the personal relevance of a message to create different elaboration likelihood conditions. In the high-relevance conditions, our subjects were told that the proposal they were to evaluate had important and relatively immediate personal consequences for them (for example, If they didn't pass the comprehensive exam that was to be instituted next year, they would be unable to graduate). Low-involvement subjects were led to believe that the proposal would have absolutely *no* personal consequences for them. These manipulations were designed to induce relatively pure forms of the central and peripheral routes to persuasion. As already noted, under conditions of very high involvement, attitudes were affected only by the relevant arguments, and not by source expertise; conversely, with low involvement, attitudes were affected only by source expertise, not by the quality of the arguments.

What would happen if the level of personal relevance was less clear? For example, what if we told students that the university was considering the institution of senior comprehensive exams, but it was not clear when or if they would be instituted. This situation more closely parallels typical day-to-day persuasion situations. Before the President of the United States begins a nationwide television address on arms control or before a salesperson begins a presentation on tax sheltered annuities, most potential voters or customers are not sure how personally relevant or important the information will be. So how much effort should they put into processing what the speaker has to say? We have proposed that when people are only moderately interested in the topic of the message or are uncertain as to its relevance, source factors may influence the extent of thought about the message (Petty & Cacioppo 1981). Consistent with this expectation, in our own research we have found that when a message is counterattitudinal and involvement is moderately high, people scrutinize the arguments of expert sources more than sources who are inexpert (Heesacker, Petty, & Cacioppo, in press). Also, people scrutinize arguments presented by attractive sources more than those of unattractive sources (Puckett, Petty, Cacioppo, & Fisher 1983). Counterattitudinal messages are potentially threatening because they indicate that one's attitude may be incorrect and one's behavior may be maladaptive. This threat should be especially strong when the counterattitudinal message is presented by an expert or by an attractive source who is believed to be more intelligent, witty, and interesting than an unattractive source (Berscheid & Walster 1974). When the counterattitudinal information is presented by an inexpert or unattractive source, it can be dismissed more easily as untrue without thought. Thus when the message is counterattitudinal it may make more sense for people to devote more effort in order to process what an expert or attractive source rather than an inexpert or unattractive source has to say. On the other hand, when the message is proattitudinal, it may be more threatening to find that a favored position is supported by an inexpert or an unattractive source. Under these circumstances, people may choose to think more about what the normally less desirable source s⁻   hal, Dholakia, & Leavitt 1978).

In sum, whe⟨   ⟩ʋnal relevance of a message is very apparent, it doesn't matter w⁻·ʋ says it, but it is very important for the person to attempt to evaluate the true merits of the proposal. When the personal relevance is clearly low, however, it doesn't matter *what* is said and it may be sufficient to express an opinion simply based on the characteristics of the message source. When the relevance of the message is less clear but the topic is potentially important, people appear to use the source of the message as an indication of whether or not the message is worth thinking about. When the message contains cogent arguments, enhanced thought leads to increased agreement, but when the message contains weak arguments, increased thought leads to decreased agreement. Thus in some situations, characteristics of the source (salesperson) may determine how much effort people put into processing a message (see figure 2–5).

Some Final Implications and Conclusions

We can conclude that when the elaboration likelihood of a persuasion situation is very low, source factors will tend to serve as positive or negative peripheral cues. When the elaboration likelihood is at some intermediate level, source factors may be used to determine whether an issue is worth thinking about. When the elaboration likelihood is very high, source factors will tend to be relatively unimportant as simple acceptance or rejection cues or as motivators of thought; under high involvement, argument processing is prepotent. It is important to note that sometimes source factors may serve as persuasive arguments. For example, if a salesperson is selling cosmetics and claims to use the product that is being sold, the attractiveness of the salesperson can serve as a cogent product-relevant indication of the effectiveness of the product. In this case, the attractiveness of the salesperson is not peripheral, but central to the true merits of the product, and the attractiveness of the salesperson would be expected to have an impact on attitudes even when the elaboration likelihood was high (Petty & Cacioppo 1980). In most instances, however, salesperson characteristics are likely to be peripheral to the true merits of the product and therefore are likely to affect product attitudes primarily when the elaboration likelihood is low.

We noted earlier that attitudes changed through the central route tended to be more enduring and more predictive of behavior than those changed by the peripheral route. What are the implications of this for personal selling? When people are exposed to an advertisement in the mass media, the goal of

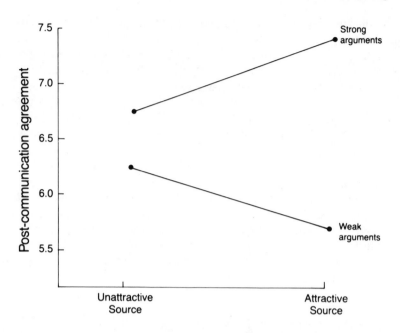

Source: Puckett, Petty, Cacioppo, and Fisher, 1983.

Figure 2-5. The Impact of an Attractive Source on a Moderately Involving
    Counterattitudinal Message

the ad is to entice the person to purchase the product at some time in the
future. Thus the central route to persuasion has important advantages over
the peripheral route because if an attitude is to influence subsequent
behavior, it must be relatively enduring. In personal selling situations,
however, the purchase behavior is requested immediately, not at some
vague point in the future. In this situation, even attitudes formed via the
peripheral route may be salient enough to influence behavior. In fact, the
peripheral cue that created the positive attitude is often physically present at
the time of the purchase decision. Thus the personal selling situation may be
one persuasion context in which the peripheral route to attitude change has
considerable utility. Importantly, however, if a person has a favorable attitude about a product due to the operation of a peripheral cue rather than
because the person has carefully considered the true merits of the product,
the attitude is relatively unlikely to persist and influence *subsequent* product
purchases. One important implication of this is that if a person comes to
dislike a product because the salesperson is rude and unattractive, and not

because the person has carefully considered and rejected the arguments presented, the dislike for the product will be temporary and irrelevant to future product purchases. It is interesting to note that although a salesperson's courteousness may be peripheral to evaluating the true merits of a product, it is central to evaluating the merits of a retail establishment. Therefore, although the negative attitude toward a particular product induced by a rude salesperson may decay quite rapidly—since this information about the salesclerk is unlikely to be integrated with other information about the product—the information about the rude salesclerk is likely to be integrated with other information that the person has about a particular store and create a more permanent negative change in attitude toward that establishment. The lesson is that a feature that produces a peripheral change in one attitude may induce a more central change in another.

Notes

1. It is important to note that the various theoretical approaches to attitude change and the variables whose effects they try to explain may not fall clearly under one or the other route in all circumstances. For example, the theoretical process of self-perception (Bem 1972) might lead to attitude change via a simple inference under most circumstances but to extended issue-relevant thinking in others (Liebhart 1979). Additionally, we note that the distinction that we have made between the central and the peripheral routes to persuasion has much in common with the recent psychological distinctions between deep versus shallow processing (Craik & Lockhart 1972), mindful versus scripted or mindless processing (Langer 1978), systematic versus heuristic processing (Chaiken 1980), and earlier formulations on different kinds of persuasion (e.g., Kelman 1961; Kelman & Eagly 1965). For more details on similarities and differences among the approaches, see Petty & Cacioppo (in press).

2. Our expectation that the use of rhetorical questions should enhance thinking for relatively unmotivated people applies only if the message recipients are also *able* to elaborate the arguments. If not, rhetorical questions might serve as peripheral cues.

3. Our discussion has so far assumed that variables affecting motivation and/or ability to process a message do so relatively objectively. This is not necessarily so; for example, some variables appear to *bias* the nature of information-processing activity, thereby motivating or enabling people to be more favorable or more unfavorable than they otherwise would be (Cacioppo, Petty, & Sidera 1982; Petty & Cacioppo 1979a; Wells & Petty

1980). A discussion of these processes is beyond the scope of this chapter; interested readers should consult Petty and Cacioppo (1983; in press) for reviews.

References

Ajzen, I., and Fishbein, M. (1980). *Understanding Attitudes and Predicting Social Behavior*. Englewood Cliffs, N.J.: Prentice-Hall.

Anderson, N.H. (1981). "Integration theory applied to cognitive responses and attitudes." In R.E. Petty, T.M. Ostrom, and T.C. Brock (eds.), *Cognitive Responses in Persuasion*. Hillsdale, N.J.: Erlbaum.

Apsler, R., and Sears, D. (1968). "Warning, personal involvement, and attitude change." *Journal of Personality and Social Psychology* 9, 162–166.

Bem, D.J. (1972). "Self-perception theory." *Advances in Experimental Social Psychology* 6, 2–57.

Berscheid, E., and Walster, E. (1974). "Physical attractiveness." In L. Berkowitz (ed.), *Advances in Experimental Social Psychology* (vol. 8). New York: Academic.

Burger, J., and Petty, R.E. (1981), "The low-ball compliance technique: Task or person commitment?" *Journal of Personality and Social Psychology* 40, 492–500.

Cacioppo, J.T., and Petty, R.E. (1979*a*). "Attitudes and cognitive response: An electrophysiological approach." *Journal of Personality and Social Psychology* 37, 2181–2199.

Cacioppo, J.T., and Petty, R.E. (1979*b*), "Effects of message repetition and position on cognitive responses, recall and persuasion." *Journal of Personality and Social Psychology* 37, 97–109.

Cacioppo, J.T., and Petty, R.E. (1980*a*). "Persuasiveness of communications is affected by exposure frequency and message quality: A theoretical and empirical analysis of persisting attitude change." In J. Leigh & C. Martin (eds.), *Current Issues and Research in Advertising*. Ann Arbor: University of Michigan.

Cacioppo, J.T., and Petty, R.E. (1980*b*). "Sex differences in influenceability: Toward specifying the underlying processes." *Personality and Social Psychology Bulletin* 6, 651–656.

Cacioppo, J.T., and Petty, R.E. (1981). "Social psychological procedures for cognitive response assessment: The thought-listing technique." In T. Merluzzi, C. Glass, and M. Genest (eds.), *Cognitive Assessment*. New York: Guilford.

Cacioppo, J.T., and Petty, R.E. (1982). "The need for cognition." *Journal of Personality and Social Psychology* 42, 116–131.

Cacioppo, J.T., and Petty, R.E. (in press,*a*), "Central and peripheral routes to persuasion: The role of message repetition." In L. Alwitt and A. Mitchell (eds.), *Psychological Processes and Advertising Effects: Theory Research and Application.* Hillsdale, N.J.: Erlbaum.

Cacioppo, J.T., and Petty, R.E. (in press,*b*), "The need for cognition: Relationships to social influence and self influence." In R. McGlynn, J. Maddux, C. Stoltenberg, and J. Harvey (eds.), *Social Perception in Clinical and Counseling Psychology.* Lubbock, Tx.: Texas Tech University Press.

Cacioppo, J.T., Petty, R.E., and Morris, K. (1983). "Effects of 'need for cognition' on message evaluation, argument recall, and persuasion." *Journal of Personality and Social Psychology* 45, 805–818.

Cacioppo, J.T., Petty, R.E., and Sidera, J. (1982). "The effects of a salient self-schema on the evaluation of proattitudinal editorials: Top-down versus bottom-up message processing." *Journal of Experimental Social Psychology* 18, 324–338.

Chaiken, S. (1980). "Heuristic versus systematic information processing and the use of source versus message cues in persuasion." *Journal of Personality and Social Psychology* 39, 752–766.

Chaiken, S., and Eagly, A.H. (1976). "Communication modality as a determinant of message persuasiveness and message comprehensibility." *Journal of Personality and Social Psychology* 34, 605–614.

Chaiken, S., and Eagly, A.H. (1983). "Communication modality as a determinant of persuasion: The role of communicator salience." *Journal of Personality and Social Psychology* 45, 241–256.

Cialdini, R.B.; Bickman, L.; and Cacioppo, J.T. (1980). "An example of consumeristic social psychology: Bargaining tough in the new car showroom." *Journal of Applied Social Psychology* 9, 115–126.

Cialdini, R.B.; Cacioppo, J.T.; Bassett, R.; and Miller, J.A. (1978). "The low-ball procedure for producing compliance: Commitment then cost." *Journal of Personality and Social Psychology* 36, 463–476.

Cialdini, R.B.; Levy, A.; Herman, P.; Kozlowski, L.; and Petty, R. (1976). "Elastic shifts of opinion: Determinants of direction and durability." *Journal of Personality and Social Psychology* 34, 663–672.

Cialdini, R.B.; Petty, R.E.; and Cacioppo, J.T. (1981). "Attitude and attitude change." *Annual Review of Psychology* 32, 357–404.

Cialdini, R.B.; Vincent, J.; Lewis, S.; Catalan, J.; Wheeler, D.; and Darby, B. (1975). "Reciprocal concessions procedure for inducing compliance: The door-in-the-face technique." *Journal of Personality and Social Psychology* 31, 206–215.

Craik, F., and Lockhart, R. (1972). "Levels of processing: A framework for memory research." *Journal of Verbal Learning and Verbal Behavior* 11, 671–684.

Cummings, W.H. and Venkatesan, M. (1976). "Cognitive dissonance and consumer behavior: A review of the evidence." *Journal of Marketing Research* 13, 303–308.

DeJong, W. (1979). "An examination of self-perception mediation of the foot-in-the-door effect." *Journal of Personality and Social Psychology* 37, 2221–2239.

Eagly, A.H., and Warren, R. (1976). "Intelligence, comprehension, and opinion change." *Journal of Personality* 44, 226–242.

Fazio, R.H., and Zanna, M. (1981). "Direct experience and attitude-behavior consistence." In L. Berkowitz (ed.), *Advances in Experimental Social Psychology* (vol. 14). New York: Academic.

Festinger, L. (1957). *A Theory of Cognitive Dissonance.* Stanford: Stanford University Press.

Freedman, J., and Fraser, S. (1966). "Compliance without pressure: The foot-in-the-door technique." *Journal of Personality and Social Psychology* 4, 195–202.

Heesacker, M.; Petty, R.E.; and Cacioppo, J.T. (in press). "Source credibility can alter persuasion by affecting message-relevant thinking." *Journal of Personality.*

Hovland, C.I.; Janis, I.; and Kelley, H.H. (1953). *Communication and Persuasion.* New Haven: Yale University Press.

Janis, I.; Kaye, D.; and Kirschner, P. (1965). "Facilitating effects of 'eating while reading' on responsiveness to persuasive communications." *Journal of Personality and Social Psychology* 1, 181–186.

Kelman, H. (1961). "Processes of opinion change." *Public Opinion Quarterly* 25, 57–78.

Kelman, H., and Eagly, A.H. (1965). "Attitude toward the communicator, perception of communication content, and attitude change." *Journal of Personality and Social Psychology* 1, 63–78.

Kiesler, S., and Mathog, R. (1968). "The distraction hypothesis and attitude change: The effects of interference and credibility." *Psychological Reports* 23, 1123–1133.

Langer, E. (1978). "Rethinking the role of thought in social interaction." In J. Harvey, W. Ickes, and R. Kidd (eds.), *New Directions in Attribution Research* (vol. 2). Hillsdale, N.J.: Erlbaum.

Liebhart, E.H. (1979). "Information search and attribution: Cognitive processes mediating the effect of false autonomic feedback." *European Journal of Social Psychology* 9, 19–37.

McGuire, W.J. (1964). "Inducing resistance to persuasion: Some contemporary approaches." In L. Berkowitz (ed.), *Advances in Experimental Social Psychology* (vol. 1). New York: Academic.

McGuire, W.J. (1976). "Some internal factors influencing consumer choice." *Journal of Consumer Research* 2, 302–319.

Miller, C., and Crandall, R. (1980). "Bargaining and negotiation." In P. Paulus (ed), *Psychology of Group Influence*. Hillsdale, N.J.: Erlbaum.

Mowen, J.C. (1980). "On product endorser effectiveness: A balance model approach." In J. Leigh and C. Martin (eds.), *Current Issues and Research in Advertising*. Ann Arbor: University of Michigan Press.

Newman, L.M., and Dolich, I.J. (1979). "An examination of ego-involvement as a modifier of attitude change caused from product testing." *Advances in Consumer Research* 6, 180–183.

Obermiller, C., and Sawyer, A. (1981). "Cognitive responses in buyer/seller interaction." In P. Reingen and A. Woodside (eds.), *Buyer-Seller Interactions: Empirical Research and Normative Issues*. Chicago: American Marketing Association.

Petty, R.E., and Cacioppo, J.T. (1979*a*). "Effects of forewarning of persuasive intent and involvement on cognitive responses and persuasion." *Personality and Social Psychology Bulletin* 5, 173–176.

Petty, R.E., and Cacioppo, J.T. (1979*b*). "Issue involvement can increase or decrease persuasion by enhancing message-relevant cognitive responses." *Journal of Personality and Social Psychology* 37, 1915–1926.

Petty, R.E., and Cacioppo, J.T. (1980). "Effects of issue involvement on attitudes in an advertising context." In G. Gorn and M. Goldberg (eds.), *Proceedings of the Division 23 Program*. Montreal, American Psychological Association.

Petty, R.E., and Cacioppo, J.T. (1981), *Attitudes and Persuasion: Classic and Contemporary Approaches*. Dubuque, Iowa: Wm. C. Brown.

Petty, R.E., and Cacioppo, J.T. (1983). "Central and peripheral routes to persuasion: Application to advertising." In L. Percy and A. Woodside (eds.), *Advertising and Consumer Psychology*. Lexington, Mass.: D.C. Heath, Lexington Books.

Petty, R.E., and Cacioppo, J.T. (1984). "The effects of involvement on responses to argument quantity and quality: Central and peripheral routes to persuasion." *Journal of Personality and Social Psychology* 46, 69–81.

Petty, R.E., and Cacioppo, J.T. (in press). *Attitude Change: Central and Peripheral Routes to Persuasion*. New York: Springer/Verlag.

Petty, R.E.; Cacioppo, J.T.; and Goldman, R. (1981). "Personal involvement as a determinant of argument-based persuasion." *Journal of Personality and Social Psychology* 41, 847–855.

Petty, R.E.; Cacioppo, J.T.; and Harkins, S.G. (1983). "Group size effects on cognitive effort and attitude change." In H.H. Blumberg, A.P. Hare, V. Kent, and M. Davies (eds.), *Small Groups and Social Interaction* (vol. 1). London: John Wiley.

Petty, R.E.; Cacioppo, J.T.; and Heesacker, M. (1981). "The use of rhetorical questions in persuasion: A cognitive response analysis." *Journal of Personality and Social Psychology* 40, 432–440.

Petty, R.E.; Cacioppo, J.T.; and Schumann (1983). "Central and peripheral routes to advertising effectiveness: The moderating role of involvement." *Journal of Consumer Research* 10, 135–146.

Petty, R.E.; Harkins, S.G.; and Williams, K.D. (1980). "The effects of group diffusion of cognitive effort on attitudes: An information processing view." *Journal of Personality and Social Psychology* 38, 81–92.

Petty, R.E.; Ostrom, T.M.; and Brock, T.C. (1981). "Historical foundations of the cognitive response approach to attitudes and persuasion." In R. Petty, T. Ostrom, and T. Brock (eds.), *Cognitive Responses in Persuasion*. Hillsdale, N.J.: Erlbaum.

Petty, R.E.; Wells, G.L.; and Brock, T.C. (1976). "Distraction can enhance or reduce yielding to propaganda: Thought disruption versus effort justification." *Journal of Personality and Social Psychology* 34, 663–672.

Puckett, J.; Petty, R.E.; Cacioppo, J.T.; and Fisher, D. (1983). "The relative impact of age and attractiveness stereotypes on persuasion." *Journal of Gerontology* 38, 340–343.

Reingen, P.; Ronkainen, I.; and Gresham, L. (1981). "Consequences of the physical attractiveness stereotype in buyer-seller interactions: Affect, intention and behavior." In P. Reingen and A. Woodside (eds.), *Buyer-Seller Interactions: Empirical Research and Normative Issues*. Chicago: American Marketing Association.

Reingen, P., and Woodside, A. (1981). *Buyer-Seller Interactions: Empirical Research and Normative Issues*. Chicago: American Marketing Association.

Rhine, R., and Severance, L. (1970). "Ego-involvement, discrepancy, source credibility, and attitude change." *Journal of Personality and Social Psychology* 16, 175–190.

Schlenker, B. (1978). "Attitudes as actions: Social identity theory and consumer research." *Advances in Consumer Research* 5, 352–359.

Schlenker, B. (1980). *Impression Management: The Self-Concept, Social Identity, and Interpersonal Relations*. Monterey, Calif.: Brooks/Cole.

Scott, C. (1978). "Self-perception processes in consumer behavior: Interpreting one's own experience." *Journal of Consumer Research* 5, 714–720.

Sherif, C.W.; Sherif, M.; and Nebergall, R. (1965), *Attitude and Attitude Change*. Philadelphia: Saunders.

Sternthal, B., and Craig, S. (1974). "Fear appeals: Revisited and revised." *Journal of Consumer Research* 1, 22–34.

Sternthal, B.; Dholakia, R.; and Leavitt, C. (1978). "The persuasive effect of source credibility: Tests of cognitive response." *Journal of Consumer Research* 4, 252–260.

Wells, G.L., and Petty, R.E. (1980). "The effects of overt head movements on persuasion: Compatibility and incompatibility of responses." *Basic and Applied Social Psychology* 1, 219–230.

Will, G.F. (1982). "But first a message from . . ." *Newsweek*, May 10, 98.

Wilson, D.T., and Ghingold, M. (1981). Similarity-dissimilarity: A reexamination. In P. Reingen and A. Woodside (eds.), *Buyer-Seller Interactions: Empirical Research and Normative Issues.* Chicago: American Marketing Association.

Wood, W. (1982). "The retrieval of attitude-relevant information from memory: Effects on susceptibility to persuasion and on intrinsic motivation." *Journal of Personality and Social Psychology* 42, 798–810.

Woodside, A., and Davenport, W. (1974). "The effect of salesman similarity and expertise on consumer purchasing behavior." *Journal of Marketing Research* 11, 198–202.

Worchel, S.; Arnold, S.; and Baker, M. (1975). "The effects of censorship on attitude change: The influence of censor and communication characteristics." *Journal of Applied Social Psychology* 5, 227–239.

Wright, P. (1980). "Message-evoked thoughts: Persuasion research using thought verbalizations." *Journal of Consumer Research* 7, 151–175.

Zillmann, D. (1972). "Rhetorical elicitation of agreement in persuasion." *Journal of Personality and Social Psychology* 21, 159–165.

3

Behavioral Influence Applied to Retail Selling Situations: When Actions Speak Louder Than Words

Jerome B. Kernan and
Peter H. Reingen

Traditional discussions of personal selling in retailing distinguish between situations in which customers know what they want and those in which even the decision to buy (much less what) has not yet been made. Since in the former case consumers are pre-sold, the retail task is reduced to one of service selling, order taking, or some similar designation. The latter case, however, is said to require ingenuity of the highest order; it necessitates creative selling if browsers are to be converted into buyers.

This chapter focuses on creative selling: situations in which persuasion is necessary to bring a retail sale to fruition. We present a comprehensive notion of creative selling: We do not argue that traditional notions about how to sell are incorrect but hope to convince the reader that they are more restricted than is commonly accepted and that certain alternatives can complement traditional forms of persuasion.

The chapter comprises four parts. First we review some traditional notions about persuasion and suggest how, in view of recent scientific findings from consumer and social psychology, these notions should be regarded as limited. Next, we introduce a set of procedures (variously called compliance induction tactics or behavioral influence strategies) whose efficacy is based on a set of assumptions about retail consumers very different from that associated with traditional persuasion. We suggest this set of procedures as a new look in persuasion, which can produce sales without the pressure commonly associated with traditional persuasion and which promises to complement it to form a more comprehensive notion of creative selling. Third, we enumerate several of these behavioral influence strategies—in each case explaining what it is, how and why it works, and where it might apply in retail selling situations. Finally, we summarize our comments and suggest a general guide to applying various influence procedures in creative retail selling.

Traditional Persuasion

We begin by recognizing that all influence attempts, whatever their particular characteristics—represent social interaction phenomena. One person attempts to shape, reinforce, or change the responses of another person through noncoercive means. Negotiations conducted in an atmosphere of power, threats, fear, guilt, or embarrassment are beyond our scope. This is noteworthy because we must continuously recognize that the persons whose responses we hope to influence frequently are neither willing nor passive targets. They do not want to do what we suggest, and they do not have to. Yet retail salespeople are taught that, in order to sell, they must somehow convince customers that buying is an appropriate idea. The effective salesperson maneuvers the client's mind through a hierarchy of stages that culminate in a conviction that the proffered sale is a prudent choice.

If we reflect on this conception of selling, however, it becomes apparent that its efficacy depends on a particular set of assumptions. Specifically, this traditional notion of persuasion assumes that influence attempts: (1) are obtrusive; (2) flow from the seller to a passive buyer; and (3) emphasize attitude change as a precursor to behavior.

Consider each of these assumptions as it applies to retail selling. First, are influences attempts commonly obtrusive? That is, when a person's responses are shaped, reinforced, or changed, is this commonly traceable to the efforts of some other person? Or can a strong case be made for people convincing themselves—that is, doing something in the absence of any apparent external influence? Recent psychological research suggests that both phenomena occur regularly. People behave on the basis of information and the source of it can be external (X tells Y what to do) or internal (Y tells himself or herself). Thus to the question "Are influence attempts obtrusive?" the answer is yes. To the question "Must they be obtrusive?" the answer is no, however.

Does influence flow from sellers (who act) to buyers (who simply react)? Or is influence a bi-directional phenomenon, with both parties acting and reacting? Again, extant research suggests that the convention of regarding influence attempts as a form of rhetoric is seriously flawed. More than the seller's most ingenious efforts to combine source, message, and channel characteristics determine persuasive effectiveness. Buyers are now recognized as being far more than passive receptacles. Indeed, the seller's message is now recognized as only the beginning of the process of influence. The buyer's own information processing activities appear to be far more significant in determining his/her subsequent behavior.

Finally, is attitude a precursor to behavior? Is it necessary to convince people to like something before they will buy it? Or is it also common for people to buy things in order to ascertain whether they like them? The fact is that both situations occur with great frequency.

So our current understanding of consumer psychology suggests that the traditional notion of persuasion—obtrusive attempts by a seller to convince a passive buyer to like a proposed product/service—portrays only part of reality. Influence is a much more comprehensive phenomenon; paradigms in addition to the traditional model are needed to deal with those scenarios in which the original assumptions break down. In the next section we describe a set of procedures that promises to complement the traditional model of persuasion such that a more comprehensive view of the influence process, creative selling, comes into relief.

A New Look in Persuasion

It is no secret that many people do not like to be sold things. They would prefer to believe that they chose to buy in the absence (or in spite) of external pressure to do so. This is understandable, inasmuch as persuasion carries an inherently negative connotation. Moreover, some view a transaction and its attendant negotiations as a battle of wits, which one must win in order to save face. Thus sellers have long been interested in devising procedures that produce sales but that do not concomitantly seem unsavory.

Researchers have likewise demonstrated an interest in understanding influence attempts that might be regarded as more palatable than traditional persuasion. Although it is common knowledge that people sometimes persuade themselves, only recently have we come to understand how and why this phenomenon occurs. Thus we are now in a position to formalize some of the things that we have understood only intuitively. Our understanding is far from complete and supporting evidence is still somewhat fragmentary. Yet behavioral influence or compliance induction procedures are well enough understood for us to position them within the broader context of persuasion. We allude to them as a new look because they are largely unfettered by the assumptions of the traditional model; because of that, they constitute a powerful complement to it.

Consider these assumptions. Where the traditional model assumes obtrusiveness, the newer procedures assume just the opposite. Indeed, they are frequently introduced under the rubric of compliance without pressure. A common characteristic of these compliance induction tactics is that the target person regards the impetus for behavior as internal; s/he, not some salesperson, causes the behavior to occur.

Where the traditional model assumes that influence flows from seller to buyer, the new look does not. This does not mean that the seller has no part in the process, but it recognizes that there is a bilateral flow of influence and, most importantly, that the buyer is not a passive entity. Indeed, the buyer's information processing activities are central to the outcome of the influence attempt.

Finally, regarding the assumption of attitude as a precursor to behavior, the new look procedures focus directly on behavioral change. In some cases, this is because attitude change occurs after, and as a result of, behavioral change. In other cases, it is because attitude change is not treated as an elaborate precondition to behavioral change. (Frankly, there is some dispute as to whether attitude change always occurs before behavioral change; but it is widely agreed that, even if it does, this is not a condition of subsequent behavioral change.)

A Brief Digression

To highlight the underlying differences between traditional and new look persuasion, we digress briefly into two areas of research. One concerns the structural responses people make to communications while the other deals with how people process the information contained in communications in order to arrive at those structural responses.

As already suggested, the traditional notion of selling assumes that target persons respond to persuasive communications by modifying their attitudes toward the product/service in question and that this modification in turn leads to their purchase behavior. Such a conception has been characterized by Michael Ray (1982) as a *feel→do* response hierarchy, inasmuch as it reflects the case where people do things because of how they feel about them.

Some behavior is not conditioned by prior mental commitment, however. Such cases are characterized as a *do→feel* response hierarchy because people so inclined buy products in order to gain experiential information which they use as the basis for forming their attitudes. In simple terms, they behave in order to determine how they feel. It follows that the appropriate selling strategy in a *do→feel* situation is to focus directly on the target person's behavior and *not* on elaborate justifications for it. The person doesn't need to be convinced to buy; only encouragement is needed. S/he will do whatever convincing is to occur after the purchase, based on personal sensory experience with the product.

Obviously, retailers must know which response hierarchy is likely to prevail in the selling situations they encounter. The very efficacy (to say nothing of the efficiency) of their efforts depends on their being directed at the appropriate *kind* of consumer response. Communications directed at developing prospects' attitudes will accomplish little when a *do→feel* hierarchy obtains and direct encouragements to buy will prove ineffectual when the consumer assumes a *feel→do* posture. Thus the retailer must know what to look for in a selling situation in order that the appropriate selling communication can be brought to bear.

Although many factors appear to contribute to the prevalence of one or another of the consumer's response hierarchies, the overarching condition (therefore the one to which the retailer must be most alert) seems to be the consumer's involvement with the advocated behavior. If the consumer has well formed, strong feelings about the matter, it is likely that a *feel → do* situation exists. On the other hand, if the consumer has weak or uncertain feelings about the advocated behavior, a *do → feel* hierarchy likely exists. In general, the former situation would call for the retailer to employ a strategy of traditional persuasion whereas the latter situation is better suited to a compliance induction procedure. Unfortunately, consumers do not usually announce their involvement, so the retailer must be alert to subtleties in the consumer's negotiating behavior that evince involvement. For example, an argumentative shopper almost certainly is highly involved; people rarely are contentious about matters they know little about or which are of slight concern to them.

Thus a principal distinction between traditional and new look persuasion lies in the assumptions they make about how people respond to persuasive communications. Traditional persuasion is grounded in the notion that consumers must be talked into buying, so it emphasizes the deft manipulation of the buyer's cognitive structure prior to the purchase. New look persuasion, on the other hand, recognizes that actions sometimes speak louder than words, so it focuses directly on behavior and relies on the buyer to develop attitudes after, and as a consequence of, the purchase.

This distinction is further highlighted by interpreting it in the vernacular of information processing theory (Sternthal and Craig 1982). This perspective emphasizes two facts important to our discussion. First, consumers acquire information from two sources: the environment and themselves. Information acquired from the environment is exemplified by advertising, salesperson's efforts, and the like; that acquired from self is exemplified by a consumer's sensory experiences with products and services. Second, despite its source, information is organized and used very actively. It is accepted, magnified, attenuated, distorted, refuted, and so on as a consequence of active comparison processes within the consumer's mind. In a simplified way, every piece of information we ask a consumer to accept undergoes a kind of tug-of-war with the consumer's existing beliefs and feelings. Only information more powerful than the thoughts it replaces changes a consumer's mind.

In traditional persuasion, the consumer has well formed feelings about the advocated behavior. Thus s/he has a strong set of what are called own thoughts (either positive or negative). A typical sales presentation constitutes a set of message thoughts. The consumer's cognitive response to the presentation involves the processing of message thoughts and own thoughts. If the consumer already agrees with the message (own thoughts are positive), a favorable attitude is enhanced and the persuasive effort likely will be effective. If the consumer is negatively disposed, however, message thoughts will be played off against own thoughts and the persuasive attempt will fail unless the message is very powerful or otherwise disarming (for example, using highly credible spokespeople, clever humor, two-sided arguments, and so on). Thus, when a consumer is negatively disposed toward the advocated behavior, persuasion attempts to inhibit his/her own thoughts in the hope that s/he will focus on message thoughts. As anyone who has ever attempted to sell realizes, however, this is no mean task.

Behavioral influence strategies—since they are recommended only where the consumer has a weak set of own thoughts about the advocated behaviors—take a rather different tack. The message presented to the consumer is quite minimal. Assuming that the behavior occurs, the consumer now has a source of information (his/her experience with the product/service), hence the basis for a better formed set of own thoughts. Since people tend to trust their own sensory experiences far more than others' words, persuasion by a behavioral influence route tends to be reasonably effective. These procedures nevertheless have weaknesses; unless the consumer can be induced to behave initially, the subsequent processing will not occur.

Some Behavioral Influence Strategies

Our treatment of these techniques is quite spartan; the interested reader can consult other sources (Kernan and Reingen 1983) for more detailed discussion of them. Second, some of our comments are speculative because the scientific evidence supporting these procedures is still fragmentary. For example, much of the research that has demonstrated the efficacy of compliance induction used prosocial, relatively altruistic requests. The reader should consider whether more blatantly commercial requests would militate against these procedures' effectiveness. Further, since this area of research is still in an evolutionary stage, some of its findings are mixed. That is, although the *general* rule appears to be that the strong-feelings case yields better to traditional persuasion and that the weak-feelings one better to new look procedures, we cannot evince an invincible bloc of evidence to support that rule. We believe the exceptions to it are just that, however.

Legitimization of Paltry Favors

The first procedure resembles traditional persuasion in that it commonly is used in cases in which consumers exhibit moderate to strong feelings about the advocated behavior. Unlike traditional persuasion, however, this technique is used as a fall-back strategy.

Suppose a life insurance agent senses a client's reluctance to purchase a large amount of coverage. The traditional way of dealing with such reluctance is to sell harder, to offer additional reasons why the coverage is needed or isn't as expensive as initially assumed. The problem with such an approach, of course, is that it is an all-or-nothing gamble. An alternative approach is to disarm the client, to preclude a variety of excuses s/he might have for refusing to buy, and to invoke his/her image-maintenance mechanisms. To illustrate, it is difficult to claim that one does not have the resources to provide for a *minimum* amount of life insurance and, in addition, failure to do so conveys the impression of being an especially uncaring person. It is important to emphasize that this strategy calls for the legitimizing (not actual requesting) of small amounts. If we ask for but a little, we'll get but a little. If we use the paltry amount to emphasize the importance of *having* life insurance, however, the client is very likely to agree with us (so that some level of compliance is assured) and to talk him- or herself up the the coverage ladder.

The evidence for this technique's efficacy is traced to studies by Cialdini and Schroeder (1976), who asked homeowners for contributions to the American Cancer Society. In one condition, a standard request was made; in the other, the same request was followed by the sentence, "Even a penny will help." The latter appeal produced nearly twice the compliance rate as the former (50 percent versus 29 percent) and, most interestingly, the conditions had essentially equal average contributions. This suggests that the paltry amount is perceived by target persons as a legitimation of the issue being advocated (the American Cancer Society really needs money; I really need life insurance) and not as a presribed level of compliance. Accordingly, the technique likely has application wherever a target consumer can be induced to believe that s/he is the sort of person who cares about worthwhile causes.

Social Labeling

Social labeling is grounded in people's tendencies to be consistent. Most of us do what is expected and labeling is a procedure that draws consumers' attention to that social convention, especially when they are not clear as regards exactly what is expected of them.

The classic evidence for the efficacy of the procedure is due to Kraut (1973) who, during a door-to-door charity drive, had half of the people who contributed labeled as charitable ("You're the kind of person who supports charitable causes"), while the other half of contributors received no label. A week later, a second solicitor called on the same donors with the result that, among the previously labeled people, both the incidence and level of giving to the second charity was higher than among the previously unlabeled (but otherwise equivalent) donors.

Continuing with our life insurance illustration, labeling might be used to denote a prospect as the sort of person who, because of his/her stature in the community, obviously requires periodic assessment of his/her personal estate. The insurance agent is in an ideal position to do exactly this, and an appointment with the client will show how. Thus the prospect should comply with the agent's request for an appointment.

Labeling is more palatable to prospects than a let-me-sell-you-something appeal because the latter is likely to produce reactance in the prospect. But a person whose feelings about estate planning are not well formed might well yield to the notion that the right people do this sort of thing and willingly comply with the agent's request for an appointment. Similar applications for labeling exist in the prospecting for banking and financial services, automobiles (especially higher-price ones), correct clothing, educational services, and so on.

But all this assumes that the person doing the labeling is credible. If s/he is not credible, his/her attempts to label the prospect will be ineffective: Who is this person to say who (what) I am? In such a case, a different tack is necessary.

Informational Social Influence

Social influence also attempts to provide a consumer with reasons to behave as advocated. One difference, though, is labeling encourages the prospect to think "*I* am the sort of person who does this" whereas social influence provides him/her with a list of *others* who already have done it. Thus since the prospect is uncertain regarding the appropriateness of the advocated behavior, s/he can substitute the judgment of respected others for his/her own.

Note that the person providing the list of other compliers need not be especially crdible; s/he merely provides the list. So long as the list is a truthful one, its members' credibility influences the consumer.

Experiments by Reingen (1982) have demonstrated the efficacy of this influence procedure. He determined that a number of attributes of the list affect results. For example, although lists in general produce both higher levels and incidences of compliance, the length of the list and the social prominence of its members can influence target consumers, especially those who are not well informed about the advocated behavior. If one is uncertain that a behavior is appropriate, a longer list of compliers is more influential, especially if it contains the names of persons who might exert a normative influence on the target person. Similarly, if one is uncertain regarding the appropriate level of compliance, a list that indicates who has given how much is quite influential.

Practical examples of this technique abound. College textbooks are marketed by featuring lists of schools already using them; numerous consumer services are sold through referral techniques; satisfied-customer lists and testimonial letters commonly are exhibited in retail establishments; television commercials feature clips of consumers already enjoying the product; and so on.

Door-in-the-Face

We now turn to three procedures useful when consumers are to be approached with more than one request. Such multiple-request procedures are used when it is determined that a single request or contact with the consumer is too restrictive. But our critical request will always be made during the second contact. The initial contact serves merely to set up the prospect.

The reader will recall from our discussion of social labeling that it can be used in the context of multiple requests. There is nothing about the technique's efficacy that depends on prior contact, however. The three behavioral influence strategies that are inherently multiple-request procedures are called the foot-in-the-door, low-balling, and the door-in-the-face. The former two (foot-in-the-door and low-balling) are used when there is a delay between the initial and (second) critical request while the latter is used when the two requests are made in hard juxtaposition.

The door-in-the-face technique works as follows. Returning to our life insurance example, suppose we know of a prospect whom we suspect is a hard sell, the sort who would refuse most any request. Let us give in by intentionally requesting something we know will be refused. Perhaps we suggest that s/he buy a $1 million whole-life policy. When refused, we engage in a bit of conciliation, some comments to the prospect that form a transition from our initial request to the one we're about to make, such that s/he perceives the second request as a concession on our part. The second request might be something like: "Well, I see you're not interested in a whole-life policy; perhaps a term-life arrangement, requiring considerably less cash, but sacrificing no protection, would suit your needs better."

The door-in-the-face works because each of us understands the notion of social reciprocation. That is why it is important that our transition from first to second request be interpreted unambiguously as a concession. The transition comments must accept the prospect's rejection of the initial request (not explain why the refusal is ill-considered) and the second (critical) request must be significantly smaller (as perceived by the prospect) than the first. Otherwise, the mechanism will not work.

Scientific evidence to support the face technique is attributable to the work of Cialdini and his associates (Cialdini et al. 1975). In a series of experiments they determined that target persons who perceive that a requester has made concessions to them are more likely to comply with a second, moderated request than are those persons who are asked to yield only to the second request. For example, one group was asked to serve as counselors to juvenile delinquents for a period of two years and, having refused, were then asked to chaperone these delinquents on a two-hour trip to the zoo. An equivalent group of people received only the chaperoning request. Whereas only 17 percent of the latter group complied, 50 percent of the former (door-in-the-face) group yielded to the chaperoning request.

The face procedure has been studied widely and, as a consequence, certain conditions have been established that govern its efficacy. These concern invoking the consumer's perception of concessions having been made by the requester and may be summarized as follows:

1. The initial request must be rejected by the target consumer.
2. The perception of a concession must be clearly established (that is, the second request must be unambiguously smaller than the initial one, must be made by the same requester, and must be made in the same contact as the initial request).
3. The second request must not be too small, and the initial request must not be unreasonably large such that resentment or hostility in the target consumer occurs, overwhelming any possibility that a concession might be perceived.

When these conditions are present, the consumer's mind focuses on message thoughts which, because the larger-then-smaller request is made immediately, are perceived as a concession. Because there is no delay between the requests, the consumer has little time to reflect on the advocated behavior. S/he realizes only that s/he has just rejected the seller's initial request and hence interprets the second (smaller) one as equitable.

Salespeople understand the notion of social reciprocity very well, and forms of it in retail selling abound. Salespersons on commission, for example, typically work from the high side of their product lines down, since it is easier to move a prospect from a higher-cost item to a lower-cost one than vice versa. Similarly, when offering price concessions, it is common to quote the reduction in small, odd numbers, to create the illusion that the last drop of profit has been squeezed out of the proposal. Most anything a salesperson can do that creates within a prospect a sense of obligation, a psychic debt, invokes the principles of the face technique. Thus the Fuller Brush tactic of giving a gift to homemakers regardless of whether they buy anything, the Electrolux offer to clean your carpeting free, personal computer retailers' offer to assess your computing needs, and so on all fall under the genre. Indeed, the very notion of entertainment expenses in

American commerce is based on the hope that their beneficiaries will feel beholden to their providers. We should note that some prospective buyers are uneasy about all this, to the point that they dislike the feeling of obligation. In such cases, it is probably better simply to provide the favor, avoiding any prior negotiation or posterior recognition.

Foot-in-the-Door

Turning now to situations in which there is to be a delay between the initial and the second, critical request, two compliance induction tactics are available to us. In contrast to the door-in-the-face procedure, each of these tactics involves a small-then-larger request sequence. Yet these are different strategically, in that one (the foot-in-the-door) is used when the second favor represents an increase (over the initial request) in the amount or size of compliance while the other (low-balling) is used when the first-to-second increase has to do with the cost or price of compliance to the target consumer.

The foot-in-the-door technique is named because of its reference to the archtypical salesperson working house-to-house who inserted one foot in the door to forestall abrupt dismissals. In a more contemporary context, it works as follows. In the case of our life insurance example, perhaps our judgment or experience suggests that in order to sell the amount of insurance coverage a particular client really needs we must proceed in steps.

We make an initial contact with the prospect in which we solicit compliance with a small (but not trivial) request. Perhaps we ask him/her, as a responsible household head, to provide us with personal and family financial goals. Whatever the request's particulars, it is crucial that it be granted and that such compliance triggers the prospect's self-perceptions ("I am a responsible person; I care enough to plan for my family's future"). We then allow some time to pass because (1) we want these self-perceptions to germinate and (2) an immediate sales pitch would overwhelm them in the prospect's mind.

After a brief period (one to two weeks, perhaps) we make our critical request. It is larger, considerably larger, but does not seem outrageous to the prospect because by now his/her mind contains the self-perception of a caring person who plans for his/her family's financial future. The requested insurance program strikes the client as altogether reasonable, given his/her financial goals.

Freedman and Fraser (1966) were the first to investigate the scientific basis for the foot procedure. Among their studies was one in which California residents were asked to display in their front lawns a large sign which read "Drive Carefully." Some residents had been asked a smaller favor two weeks previously: to place a small sign promoting either safe driving (in their cars) or keeping California beautiful (in their house windows) or to sign a petition advocating legislation in behalf of safe driving or keeping California beautiful. Thus two-request residents received either similar requests (safe-driving/safe-driving) or dissimilar ones (California-beautiful/safe-driving). Moreover, the second request was made by a different person (earlier work used the same person for both requests). Nevertheless, prior compliance increased the degree of compliance with the second, critical request. Whereas fewer than 17 percent of the residents who had been asked only to place the large sign in their yards complied, some 55 percent of those who had previously complied with the initial request agreed to place the large sign—whether their initial compliance had to do with safe driving or keeping California beautiful—and in spite of the fact that the initial and second requests were made by different people.

The apparent explanation for the foot effect lies in what is sometimes called attribution theory (Mizerski et al. 1979). As suggested above, the target consumer initially is uncertain regarding his/her feelings about the advocated (critical-request) behavior. Thus s/he turns to whatever informaion *is* available that might reduce the uncertainty. One source of information is the target's past behavior (that is, his/her response to the initial request). If s/he has complied with that request, that behavior is stored in memory as own thoughts and, given a delay between the initial and critical requests, s/he has time to reflect on the likely reasons for initial compliance. Assuming there are no circumstantial moderators ("My friends were watching me; I had to do it"), the inevitable conclusion is that s/he did it because s/he is the kind of person who does this sort of thing. A self-perception of being a complier thus motivates the target consumer to respond favorably to the critical request.

The foot procedure is the most widely documented technique we have discussed. Based on many studies, it appears to work best under the following conditions:

1. The initial request must be unambiguously smaller than the critical request and the initial request must enjoy compliance.
2. The initial request must induce self-perceptions that commit the target person to compliance with the critical request. This can be accomplished by (a) allowing enough time between initial and critical requests so that targets reflect on their initial compliance rather than merely on the requester's critical petition, (b) inducing the target to comply behaviorally, rather than just verbally, with the initial request, or (c) making the initial request non-trivial.
3. The critical request can be made by the same or a different person, so long as the target relates the initial-request compliance attitudinally to the critical request.

Not surprisingly, day-to-day applications of the foot-in-the-door technique are pervasive. Everyone who believes in a step-by-step process of building accounts, whether in office supplies, financial services, cosmetics, household products, or whatever, implicitly subscribes to the foot rationale. In direct counterpoint to the door-in-the-face philosophy, the foot procedure implies that it is easier to sell larger items or amounts if consumers are first sold smaller items or amounts. In addition to the self-perception explanation for this, one can think of several other reasons why getting one's foot in the door make sense. Clients feel more comfortable dealing with sellers who have previously treated them well, who know them and their particular needs, and whose products have proved satisfactory in prior use.

Another widespread application of the foot technique can be found in closing sales. If one subscribes to the notion that most sales comprise a number of small sales (that is, each sale effectively consists of a series of mini decisions, each one of which must be concluded before the purchase can occur), then orchestrating a prospective buyer through this series of steps can be interpreted as a series of foot exercises. The common ploy of bringing about a close by getting a prospect to agree to a series of relatively minor issues ("Will this be cash or charge?," "Where would you like it delivered?," and so forth) is an example. With each incidence of agreement, the likelihood of next-stage agreement increases, until the buyer signs on the dotted line.

Low-Balling

Finally, we consider the multiple-request case in which the second, critical request represents an increase in cost to the target consumer: Here the low-balling technique is recommended. Although this technique's applicability is relatively limited, and it contains some significant ethical questions, it applies to some situations.

The term low-balling means to get a prospect committed to compliance on the strength of an attractive price and then to raise the price in the hope that the prospect will persevere in spite of the increased cost. The procedure is attributed (correctly or otherwise) to certain unscrupulous car dealers.

We might imagine an ethical application of low-balling as follows. Suppose we know of a person who really needs life insurance coverage but, for reasons of a poor medical history, cannot buy an individual policy except at premium rates. Suppose further that this rated individual has inadequate coverage through his/her employer and has always assumed that s/he couldn't afford life insurance because of his/her medical history.

It is reasonably likely that the rates this person assumes s/he must pay are far higher than those s/he actually would have to pay, given the increased sophistication reflected in contemporary actuarial tables. In such a case, it would seem altogether reasonable for an insurance agent to quote such a person a ball-park rate (in fact, the lowest rate at which s/he possibly could be covered), in order to get him/her committed to the idea of an individual policy. When the contracted rate turns out to be higher than the original quote, his/her commitment to having adequate insurance coverage likely will be sufficient to swallow the additional cost. Such a mild, effectively innocent deception would seem well within the bounds of propriety.

The basic experimental work on low-balling was done by Cialdini and his associates (Cialdini et al 1978). In a series of studies, they determined that target subjects who agreed to perform a behavior before understanding its full cost were significantly more likely actually to perform that behavior than were subjects who were informed of the full cost of the behavior initially. The explanation for this seems to be that, once persons have freely committed themselves to a behavior (or to the person requesting it), they are reluctant to abrogate that commitment, even though the cost of honoring it increases substantially. These same people are more reluctant to agree to behaviors whose full cost they understand initially, however.

As commonly observed in commerce, low-balling operates by inducing consumers to buy something, largely on the strength of an especially attractive price. Once the decision to buy is confirmed by the salesperson, s/he removes the price advantage, thus rendering the purchase decision more costly to the consumer. The widespread practice of advertising price specials of the bait-and-switch variety is a common example of the technique. Automobile sales (as well as other transactions in which negotiated prices are customary) also use the procedure. Whether the item is a car, a house, tires, an appliance, or whatever, the quoted price commonly used to stimulate the buyer's interest frequently turns out to be significantly less than the amount necessary to consummate the transaction. The difference in prices may represent add-ons, accessories, handling charges, taxes, or any number of legitimate sources of cost to the seller, but these so-called minor adjustments are rarely revealed until the consumer has somehow demonstrated that s/he is already committed to the purchase.

Summary: Some Comments on Applying
Influence Procedures

The thought processes that apply to everyday life naturally apply to consumer choices as well. Retail selling is effective to the extent that it conforms to the human condition. There are many ways to persuade people, and anyone who believes otherwise is not realistic.

The reader should regard our comments as general guidelines. Similarly, creative salespeople will recognize that the procedures we have described singly can be used in combination with one another. The refusal of a critical request in a foot strategy being interpreted as the initial request in a face strategy comes immediately to mind.

Finally, retailers will recognize some ethical limits in the application of influence procedures. Knowing how consumers' minds work does not give license to prey on the least endowed of these minds with manipulative techniques. We do not forsee the dawn of a Machiavellian society (shrewd consumers understand how to use behavioral influence procedures too), but we will gain little by furthering the sometimes-negative reputation of selling.

References

Cialdini, R.B.; J.T. Cacioppo; R. Bassett; and J.A. Miller. (1978). "The Low-Ball Procedure for Producing Compliance: Commitment then Cost." *Journal of Personality and Social Psychology* 36, 463–476.

Cialdini, R.B., and D.A. Schroeder. (1976). "Increasing Compliance by Legitimizing Paltry Contributions: When Even a Penny Helps." *Journal of Personality and Social Psychology* 34, 599–604.

Cialdini, R.B.; J.E. Vincent; S.K. Lewis; J. Catalan; D. Wheeler; and B.L. Darby. (1975). "Reciprocal Concessions Procedure for Inducing Compliance: The Door-in-the-Face Technique." *Journal of Personality and Social Psychology* 33, 206–215.

Freedman, J.L., and S.C. Fraser. (1966). "Compliance without Pressure: The Foot-in-the-Door Technique." *Journal of Personality and Social Psychology* 4, 195–202.

Kernan, J.B., and P.H. Reingen. (1983). "Behavioral Influence: A New Look in Persuasion Research." In J.N. Sheth (ed.), *Research in Consumer Behavior* (vol. I.). Greenwich, Conn.: JAI Press.

Kraut, R.E. (1973). "Effects of Social Labeling on Giving to Charity." *Journal of Experimental Social Psychology* 9, 551–562.

Mizerski, R.W.; L.L. Golden; and J.B. Kernan. (1979). "The Attribution Process in Consumer Decision Making." *Journal of Consumer Research* 6, 123–140.

Ray, M.L. (1982). *Advertising and Communication Management.* Englewood Cliffs, N.J.: Prentice Hall.

Reingen, P.H. (1982). "Test of a List Procedure for Inducing Compliance with a Request to Donate Money." *Journal of Applied Psychology* 67, 110–118.

Sternthal, B. and C.S. Craig. (1982). *Consumer Behavior: An Information Processing Perspective.* Englewood Cliffs, N.J.: Prentice-Hall.

4 Some Social Psychological Perspectives On Closing

Jacob Jacoby

Selling takes various forms. In some cases, such as when a customer orders merchandise from a retailer's mail order catalogue, there is no direct interaction between the seller and the purchaser. The sales transaction is basically impersonal. In contrast, other forms of selling do involve some direct, person-to-person interaction and communication. Despite this personal component, however, not all such selling warrants being termed *personal selling*. For the interaction to be considered personal selling, the salesperson must also attempt to exert some influence over the customer. Without any such influence attempt, personal selling is reduced to order-taking or clerking. Thus though it may involve much more (from prospecting through post-sale follow-up), the distinguishing feature of *all* personal selling is that there is an attempt by the seller to exert some influence over the buyer's behavior.

In practitioners' language, attempting to exert influence over the customer is referred to as *closing*. Broadly defined, this means getting the customer to go along with the seller's recommendations. There can be many different closes during a single sales interaction. For example, during a single interview, the life insurance salesperson may try to influence the prospect to provide or authorize access to certain information, to take a physical exam, to buy insurance, to permit his/her name to be used by the salesperson in contacting another prospect, and so forth.

This chapter's central thesis is that the behavioral sciences, particularly social psychology, have much to offer those interested in understanding and improving the practice of closing. Among other things, behavioral science theory can provide an understanding of the conditions under which various closing techniques will and will not work and explain why and how they work. Beyond explaining current closing techniques, behavioral science theory can be used to suggest new closing techniques. This chapter attempts to illustrate both types of contributions. First, a few observations regarding the ethics of personal influence and persuasion are in order.

While individuals are often influenced by others to do things (such as make a purchase) that may not be in their own interests, influence is also often exerted in a manner consistent with their needs. So exerting personal influence is not, by itself, necessarily evil and may be positive.

When used effectively, closing techniques can be very powerful influence techniques. As such, they place an obligation on those who use them to act ethically and responsibly. Clearly, their use should be limited to those circumstances in which a genuine need exists and in which the prospect or buyer has the ability to pay. In all other instances, their application appears inappropriate. This means that the salesperson accepts and operates on the belief that the prospect's needs come first, and that the prospect should not be sold something unnecessary. Aside from the not-being-fair-to-the-prospect issue, there are practical reasons for following this precept. First, it is generally much easier to sell something when the prospect can see and understand its relevance. Second, products that satisfy the customer's genuine needs are less likely to be returned. Finally, ethical selling makes the vendor less vulnerable to competition and increases the likelihood that the prospect will continue to patronize that establishment and that salesperson. It is important to have the customer become a repeat customer, since even retail giants could not stay in business long if every individual in the country purchased a product from them only once.

This chapter is divided into three sections, each of which provides a different focus on closing. The first describes an actual case study in which behavioral science theory was used to help a salesperson better understand the underlying causes of problems being experienced during closing and then to take appropriate corrective action. Section two describes an approach toward closing derived from social psychological theory, which seems to have not yet surfaced in the sales training literature. This also includes the results of an exploratory test of this technique. Finally, the third section outlines a number of closing techniques culled from the sales training literature.

A Case Study: Closing to Stay Closed

The case, which might be subtitled "When high credibility and expertise can backfire," is very familiar to me, since it involves my wife, Fran, a life insurance sales agent. Though now a member of the Million Dollar Round Table's elite "Top of the Table," she experienced a variety of problems during her early years as a salesperson. One such problem took the following form.

She would go out on an initial get-acquainted interview, with no expectation of selling any life insurance during this first interview. At this point, the objective was primarily fact-finding to identify the specifics of the prospect's problem. Yet as the parameters of the problem and its solution were being outlined, a good number of prospects became sufficiently motivated that Fran frequently returned home with a signed application for insurance.

Unfortunately, by the time the policy was issued by the company several weeks later, a number of these prospects had changed their minds and declined to take the insurance. What was the problem? Why were these sales, which seemed so perfectly fine earlier, now coming unglued?

According to widely accepted behavioral science theory, persasive communication involves a process whereby a source (in this case, the salesperson) transmits a message (in this case, the proposed solution to the prospect's problem, life insurance) over a particular medium to a receiver (that is, the prospect) for the purpose of achieving some desired effect (in this case, the purchase of life insurance). This sequence is depicted in figure 4-1. Generally (*cf.* Petty, Cacioppo and Schumann, this volume), to be effective, the source must convey reasonably high credibility, that is, sell him- or herself before there is hope of selling the message. It also helps if the source is liked (*cf.* Chestnut & Jacoby, this volume). However, being liked and credible may be insufficient, especially when the persuasive effect must persist over a period of time. This is generally the case with life insurance, in which there is usually a several-week interval between when a prospect signs an application and the point at which the policy is available for delivery.

Analysis of Fran's experiences suggested that she was being very effective in selling herself, the source, but was being somewhat less than effective in selling her message (that is, the solution to the prospect's problem). In fact, it seemed that being so effective in selling herself was partly responsible

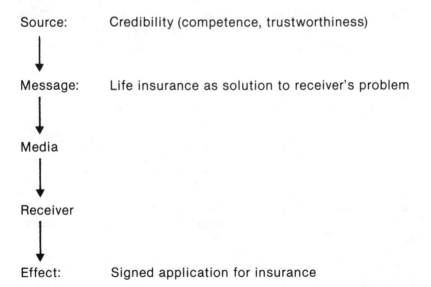

Source: Credibility (competence, trustworthiness)

Message: Life insurance as solution to receiver's problem

Media

Receiver

Effect: Signed application for insurance

Figure 4-1. Applying the General Communication Model to the Sales Process

for her difficulty in selling her message. Because the prospects bought Fran as a likable and credible (that is, knowledgeable and trustworthy) source, and given that many people experience difficulty comprehending complicated financial matters, they really didn't listen as closely as they should have to her analysis of their problem and the reasons for her proposal. After all, since they had accepted her as being likable, trustworthy, and competent, to them there seemed no real reason to pay close attention to her recommendations. They correctly perceived that she was looking out for their best interests and therefore felt no need to be critically attentive to her message.

Several days after this initial interview, however, when Fran was no longer immediately available to answer questions, many prospects could no longer remember the logical, important reasons that they had for buying life insurance. So, despite their positive feelings about Fran, they cancelled.

From a behavioral science perspective, the solution seemed relatively simple. Fran could not be content with obtaining the signature on the application. Rather, once she had successfully sold herself, Fran needed to do a more thorough job of selling her message. Particularly when a time interval is involved between making the sale and delivering the product, the general principle is: "After selling yourself, don't neglect to sell your message." Armed with this insight, Fran was able to virtually eliminate the cancellations she had experienced just a short while earlier.

This case study illustrates the potential that the social sciences offer for diagnosing and clarifying just what it is that is going on during the sales process and for indicating why certain practices might or might not be effective and the circumstances under which they are more likely to be effective (see also, Jacoby and Jacoby 1979).

Suggestions for Closing Derived from Psychological Theory

One of the simplest yet most appealing models of social influence to have surfaced in psychology is Heider's (1944, 1946, 1958) Balance Model. It concerns a target person (P), some other person (O), and an object (X) which, for present purposes, may be considered a product. The focus of the model is on the target person's thoughts regarding three things: his/her own feelings toward the other, his/her feelings toward X, and how he/she thinks O feels about X. These relationships are depicted by the arrows in figure 4–2 and may be either positive (denoting liking) or negative (denoting disliking).

The basic proposition is that if all three signs are positive, or if any two are negative and one positive (for example, the example depicted in figure 4–2, namely, P dislikes O, P dislikes X, and P perceives that O dislikes X),

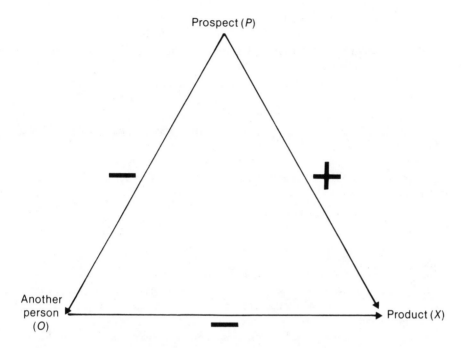

Figure 4-2. Generating a Positive Reaction to the Product, According to the Balance Model, − − + Condition

the system is in a state of *balance.* All other combinations are *unbalanced.* The important point to note, at least in terms of attempting to exert influence, is that unbalanced states are supposed to generate uncomfortable psychological tensions within the individual such that he becomes motivated to restore balance. Accordingly, using this knowledge a salesperson can create certain types of unbalanced states, the resolution of which will cause the prospect to be more positively inclined toward the salesperson's proposal.

The typical selling strategy essentially represents Heiders triple positive (+ + +) condition. It involves the salesperson telling the prospect something to the effect that someone whom the prospect *likes likes* the product, so it makes sense that s/he should also *like* it. However, the model also suggests a second, non-obvious strategy for generating increased consumer preference for product X, namely pointing out that someone whom the prospect *dislikes dislikes* the product. Much like the old adage "The enemy of my enemy is my friend," this should elicit a *like* reaction from the prospect. The post-Watergate 1976 Indiana election for U.S. Senator offers a more up-to-date example. The author recalls a large billboard in Indianpolis paid for by the Democrats, which proclaimed "Lugar, Nixon's favorite mayor," a nickname which Lugar had enjoyed as the Republican mayor of Indianapolis during Nixon's term in office.

The present study provided a test of the hypothesis that, given two negatives, the Heider model can correctly predict the sign (+) given to the third relationship. Note that this hypothesis incorporates two of the six principles outlined by Cialdini (this volume), namely, consistency and liking.

Note also Heider's contention that the Balance Model applied to both sentiment and unit (or belonging) relationships. That is, not only can liking be affected, but knowing that a liked Other owns a product should theoretically make us want to own it as well. Hence, the present investigation tested the ability of the model to correctly predict both sentiment and unit relationships.

Procedure

Two-hundred sixty-five subjects (122 males and 143 females from ten introductory psychology classes) were placed into hypothetical purchasing situations involving knowledge that people whom they disliked had said that they disliked specific new products. They were then asked to indicate their probable feelings and purchasing tendencies toward these products. Four versions of each of two questionnaires, one for males and the other for females, were randomly interspersed so that each subject's assignment to one of four hypothetical situations was randomly determined through distribution of the questionnaires. Situations involved products that were either highly visible when used (shoes, suits, dresses) and therefore likely to be the subject of reference group comments and/or ones on which individuals might solicit the opinions of others (movies, make-up, cologne). Consider the following example:

"You are thinking about buying a new pair of shoes from among several new shoe styles that have just come on the market. You know that someone you *dislike* said that he *disliked* one particular style. Based simply on this information, how do you think you would tend to feel about this particular shoe style?" Subject's responded on a five-point Likert scale ranging from "like it very much" to "dislike it very much." The questionnaire continued: "Given the situation above, would you be more or less likely to buy that particular style of shoe?" A forced-choice (more likely–less likely) response format was provided.

Attention is directed to the fact that, while Heider's model permits only + and − responses, in order to more accurately reflect reality and to accommodate criticisms of the model (Kiesler, Collins & Miller 1969; Zajonc 1960), the liking scale used here allowed for a neutral response and two different intensities of + and − responses. In contrast, given that one can only end up buying or not buying when behavioral intentions are translated into actual behavior, the belonging scale contained only two alternatives. Inasmuch as no appreciable decrement in reliability or validity results when Likert scales with as many as nineteen response categories are collapsed to two- or three-point scales (Matell & Jacoby 1971), data from the first question were reduced to a two-point format, and Chi-square tests for one sample with two classes (Edwards 1960) were conducted.

Results

Table 4–1 presents the pattern of responses by sex and product. Inspection reveals the predicted tendencies in six of the eight groups, with eleven of the sixteen Chi-square tests being significant in the predicted direction and two being significant in the opposite direction.

Discussion

In general, learning that a negatively balanced source had expressed a dislike for a product seems sufficient to generate increases in preference for and intention to purchase that item. The few failures of the model occur primarily with two products: cosmetics and cologne. Insasmuch as the

Table 4–1
Patterns of Like-(Neutral)-Dislike and More Likely-Less Likely to Buy Responses by Sex and Product
(Given two minuses; predicting +)

	Liking Relationship				Purchasing Relationship		
	Like	(Neutral)	Dislike	p^a	More Likely	Less Likely	p^a
Females (N = 143)							
Shoes ($n=38$)	15	(19)	4	< .02	24	14	.10
Movies ($n=36$)	12	(20)	4	< .05	24	12	.05
Dress ($n=36$)	13	(19)	4	< .05	24	12	.05
Make-up ($n=33$)	1	(23)	9	< .02[b]	7	26	.01[b]
Males (N = 122)							
Shoes ($n=29$)	11	(16)	2	< .01	20	9	< .05
Movies ($n=31$)	8	(22)	1	< .01	22	9	< .02
Suit ($n=32$)	6	(26)	0	< .01	19	13	n.s.
Cologne ($n=30$)	3	(22)	5	n.s.	14	16	n.s.

[a]Based on two-tailed Chi-square tests for one sample with two classes (Edwards 1960, pp. 64–65), with the (neutral) responses omitted.
[b]Significant in the direction opposite to that predicted.

respondents were from ten different classes and were tested at different times with respondents in all eight groups being tested concurrently in each class, the most plausible explanation for the two counter-tendencies revolves around a consideration of the type of products involved. Perhaps personal hygiene products are not highly visible and/or vulnerable to the opinions of others. Attempts to introduce such influence might therefore generate psychological reactance (Brehm 1966), resulting in the individual's moving in a direction opposite to that intended.

In any event, these preliminary results suggest that making reference to a disliked source who had expressed a dislike for a product may be an effective strategy for exerting influence. Further research, especially with more sophisticated variants of the Balance model (*cf.* Feather 1964, 1967), seems warranted.

Seventeen Basic Closing Techniques

A review of the applied sales literature reveals a variety of recommended closing techniques. Seventeen of the more commonly described approaches have been extracted and are described below. Some appear quite manipulative; others do not. Some appear ethical and legitimate; others appear somewhat less so. By describing these here, I should emphasize that no endorsement of any of these techniques is implied or intended.

However, I contend that playing ostrich will not make these techniques go away. Rather, these techniques currently enjoy widespread use in a variety of personal selling spheres, and failure to give them due attention would mean, among other things, that behavioral scientists would be forfeiting a valuable opportunity to improve their understanding of the personal influence and persuasion process. Such improved understanding could be used to serve a variety of purposes, including some that have individual and social benefit. Accordingly, my purpose is to note these techniques and to suggest that a more formal conceptual and empirical approach with respect to these techniques would benefit three broad sectors: practitioners, scholars, and consumers.

For practitioners, especially those in retailing, the implementation of the more ethical of these techniques can assist in converting what is a clerking operation into one involving personal selling. Such a conversion would not only lend a measure of job enrichment but is seen as one way of increasing both productivity and sales and also effectively coping with an ever-increasing competitive environment, one that will soon also include shopping by in-home computers. There will always be products that will need to be seen, touched, or tried on, or that are too complex or abstract (for example, life insurance) to be easily explained over a computer and telephone hook-up, so that there will always be a need for skilled salespeople. Indeed, personal selling directed toward the genuine needs of the customer may be one of the most appropriate ways for differentiating, in the customer's mind, between different types of store environments, as well as between in-store versus non-store retailing.

For the scholar, these closes are seen to represent three opportunities. First, virtually all are in need of explanatory theory. Only then will we be able to achieve the necessary understanding of how and especially why they work, of important interaction effects, and the boundary conditions that circumscribe their effectiveness. Second, beyond the application of existing theory is the potential that one or more of these techniques will lead to the extension of theory. Accounting for the operation of these techniques may require theory development. Third, beyond the excitement of theory application and theory development remains the challenge provided by attempts at empirical confirmation. All of these are necessary if behavioral scientists are to maintain that their theories of personal influence generally apply across the broad spectrum of human interaction.

Finally, for the consumer, simply knowing what these techniques are and understanding how they are used may be sufficient to moderate their effect. Such knowledge may even confer a degree of resistance to persuasion. Whether such effects will occur, however, remains an empirical question—one which those interested in creating a more equal balance of power between the salesperson and the customer (*cf.* Kulich, Curran, Jacoby and Mariotto, submitted) are encouraged to address.

Finally, all of what is described below assumes ethical selling.

The seventeen closing techniques are:

assumed consent

closing on a specific objection

closing on a general objection

closing on a question (contingent decision close)

tallying the pros and cons (Ben Franklin validation)

closing on a minor point (secondary question)

fatal alternative (alternative choice)

the take-away close

impending event

story telling

special incentive close

puppy-dog close

no-risk close

delayed cost close

medical close

asking outright

the lost-sales close

Some professional sales trainers are fond of saying that most salespeople know two different closes and typically use only one. Interestingly, studies of top-notch salespeople show that their repertoire of closing techniques tends to be larger than average. Moreover, such salespeople often credit a large part of their success to being able to employ several different closing techniques during the same sales interaction. At least in regard to the selling of life insurance, research shows that more sales are closed on the fourth or fifth closing attempt than on the first or second. So the folk wisdom that successful salespeople are persistent holds. The one important catch is that this persistence is based on being able to effectively use and integrate a *different* closing approach each time. Clearly, it must be very difficult to make a second and a third closing attempt if all the salesperson has at his/her disposal was one basic closing approach. In other words, the skilled salesperson operates adaptively and has somehow internalized a set of "if A, then B" contingency propositions, much like the notion of scripts discussed by Leigh and Rethans (this volume).

Moreover, not all of the closing approaches can be used with equal ease and effectiveness at all points in the sales interview. Some can only be used early in the interview, others can only be used as a last resort, while yet others can be used at most any point in time. Skillful salespeople have learned how to properly weave closes into sequences that move the prospect nearer and nearer to making a favorable purchase decision.

Assumed Consent

The most basic, natural close in any salesperson's tool bag is assumed consent. To ease descriptions of this and subsequent closes, the reader is asked to assume that he/she is the salesperson. Assume further that you and the prospect have thoroughly discussed his/her situation and found a genuine need for your product. This approach requires that you simply assume that the prospect recognizes the importance of his/her problem and the need for acting on it right away. Thus you begin asking for the information you need in order to complete the sales form (for example, "What is your correct address, John?''). In other words, you simply *assume* that s/he goes along with you.

The prospect can then do one of two things: either accept the reasonableness of your proposal and go along with you or object. In either case, you have benefited. If the prospect goes along with you, then you have made the sale, because as long as s/he doesn't stop you, s/he has bought. If s/he brings up an objection, then you've moved a major step toward closing the sale because you have identified the objection without having to waste time or play games. As a result, you now know what it is that you have to attend to in order to make this sale.

In other words, few, if any, negative consequences result from using an assumed consent close, but there are two positive consequences: Either you close the sale, or you quickly identify the prospect's objection(s). Further, the assumed consent close can be used in conjunction with just about any other closing approach and is appropriate at just about any point in the sales interview after the need has been identified and a program to solve that need has been described.

Closing on a Specific Objection

Suppose, while you are attempting to close a prospect using assumed consent, s/he brings up a specific objection. If you can effectively answer this objection, it is possible to turn it into a final objection and use it as the basis for closing the sale. Attempting to close on a specific objection involves the following seven-step approach.

1. Listen to every word. Let the prospect describe his/her objection fully. Don't finish any sentence for him/her or jump to conclusions; let him/her speak without interruption. Make certain that you understand the objections.
2. Sell him/her the objection. This involves expanding on it, perhaps looking a bit defeated in the process. For example, say something like, "As I understand it, you feel that these benefits just aren't adequate." If you have sold the prospect the objection, s/he will usually reply affirmatively.
3. Confirm the objection. This involves saying something like, "That's the only thing standing between us, isn't it?" or "If it wasn't for this, you would go along with the plan, wouldn't you?" Chances are, the prospect will agree with you.
4. Begin to question the objection. Start by saying something like: "Just to clarify my thinking, why do you feel . . . ?" Three things can happen when the prospect tries to answer this question. First, the prospect

may confirm the fact that this is his/her real objection. S/he may even explain the basis for it, and this can be important information for you to know. Second, in the process of trying to answer your question, another more basic objection may pop up. This then becomes the objection you must close on. Third, in the process of trying to explain it to you, the prospect may begin to feel that the objection was pretty foolish and that s/he really does not have an objection.

5.   Answer the real objection. This involves a genuine attempt on your part to realistically and fairly handle the problem that the prospect has raised. In doing so, you need to maintain both empathy and the understanding that short-term gains from making that particular sale are often negligible compared to the long-term gains that come from treating the customer fairly.

6.   Confirm the answer. This can be done by saying, "Now that completely settles that problem, doesn't it?"

7.   Close the sale by moving directly into an assumed consent close. For example, ask the prospect: "Now what did you say your address was?"

Closing on a General Objection

Suppose you have tried to close using assumed consent and the prospect comes up with a general objection. For example, s/he might say, "Well, I don't think I really want it." Such general objections are usually impossible to handle. In such cases, your first job is to identify the *specific* objection that underlies the prospect's reluctance. Chances are that unless you can identify this specific objection, you won't be able to close the sale.

The way to proceed is to ask the prospect a series of questions that begins as follows: "Just to clarify my thinking, John, what is it about my proposal that you don't like? Is it the integrity of (name of your firm)? Is it my personal integriry? . . . Is it this? Is it that? Is it the money?"

Note several things about this series of questions. First, to identify the specific objection involved, it is important not to pause after asking the opening general question "What is it about the program that you don't like?" As a rule, general questions yield general responses and specific questions yield specific responses—and what you want is a very specific response. If you pause here and the person says something like "the whole thing," you might as well pack up. Second, if both spouses are present, don't be hesitant about including a question such as: "Is it that you think your wife doesn't really need a dishwasher to help her unload some of the drudgery of her household chores?" If the need is genuine, particularly if the spouse is present, the prospect will be very reluctant to say "yes." Third, note that every time the prospect says "no," s/he is actually indirectly saying "yes" to your proposal. Finally, save questions about money for last. Even if money is the prospect's real objection, it will seem less important after s/he has said "yes" to your proposal a number of times.

Usually, one of two things will happen as a result of your asking such a series of questions. Either both the prospect and you begin to realize that there really is no objection, in which case you can then move into an assumed consent close. Or you identify a specific objection, in which case you can move directly into closing on that specific objection.

Closing on a Question (Contingent Decision Close)

It may be that the prospect's objection to your proposal might come in the form of a question. For example, the prospect might ask, "Does this product have Feature X?" Most salespeople would instinctively respond with either a "yes" or a "no." However, this kind of reply doesn't really help them very much. Generally, the best way to handle most questions is with a question of your own. For example, you might reply, "Would you like to have Feature X?" This puts the issue back in the prospect's lap and no matter how s/he answers your question, you will obtain some useful information.

Moreover, it is always possible to use the prospect's question as a basis for a closing attempt. For example, you could reply to the prospect's question regarding by asking, "If we could get Feature X put into this product, would you take it?" In other words, "Do you want it if it does?" Again, this puts the issue squarely back into the prospect's lap and s/he will respond with either a "yes," "no," or an "I-don't-know" type of answer. If the answer is "yes," you move into an assumed consent. If it's "no" or "I don't know," then you move into identifying the objection and closing on that objection.

Tallying the Pros and Cons

If your fact-finding shows that there is a genuine need for insurance, but the prospect is indecisive and can't seem to give any specific objection, you might try what is sometimes called Tallying the Pros and Cons, or the Ben Franklin Validation. The latter version begins with a story about Benjamin Franklin, which goes like this:

> As you know, John, Ben Franklin has always been considered one of the wisest men America has ever had. Whenever he found himself in a situation where he couldn't quite make up his mind, he felt pretty much as you do now. If it was the right thing, he wanted to be sure that he did it. If it was the wrong thing, he wanted to be just as sure that he avoided it. Isn't that

about the way you feel? So here's what he would do to arrive at a decision. He would take out a clean sheet of paper and draw a line down the middle, like this. On one side of the line he would list all the reasons why he should make a "yes" decision and on the other side of the line he would list all the reasons against making this decision. When he was through, he would count the number of reasons that he was able to tally on each side, and his decision was made for him. Why don't we try it here and see what happens.

At this point, put the paper in front of the prospect, hand him/her your pen and say: "Let's see how many reasons we can think of for taking this plan." Help him/her think of the reasons for favoring this decision. Offer help.

After you've listed as many different reasons as both of you can think of for making an affirmative decision, ask the prospect to start listing all the possible reasons against making the decision. When doing this, leave the prospect entirely alone. Don't provide any assistance. In a good number of instances, the prospect will find it difficult to generate more negative than positive reasons. When he/she is done, tally up the number of "yes" and "no" reasons. Count out loud; then say, "Well the answer is pretty obvious, isn't it John?"

More often than not, the number of reasons "for" making the decision far outnumber the number of reasons "against." So as soon as the score is tallied, the salesperson will move right into an Assumed Consent close. Often, if the prospect doesn't go along at this point, the prospect's specific objection will have surfaced during the process of listing the pros and cons, in which case the salesperson would then move into closing on a Specific Objection.

Minor Point (or Secondary Question)

Another approach, similar to Assumed Consent and which can be used before, with, or after trying an Assumed Consent close, is called Closing on a Minor Point. In this approach, the salesperson asks the major question (that is, does the prospect want to buy your plan?) and immediately follows this with a question about a minor point, the answer to which carries over to a decision on the major point. For example, s/he might say, "It would seem that you really want to buy this model refrigerator, now would you like to order it in white, yellow, or green?" The prospect can respond to this secondary question in one of two ways. S/he can say s/he wants to have the refrigerator in a certain color or can raise an objection. If s/he replies that s/he would prefer one of the colors, this implies that s/he has bought the program. Answers to the secondary question carry along with them agreement on the major point.

Note that the secondary question used in the example provided the prospect with a choice between two alternatives. Another variation is to ask a question that provides only a single alternative. For example, "Now when would be the most convenient time for you to take delivery?" In this case, we have a combination of the Assumed Consent with a Closing on a Minor Point.

Fatal Alternative (or Alternative Choice)

The minor point approach is similar to an approach sometimes called either Fatal Alternative or Alternative Choice. The principal difference is that the Minor Point close avoids asking a question regarding the basic issue of purchase, while the Fatal Alternative approach tackles this issue head on. The Fatal Alternative close involves providing the prospect with a choice between two or more alternatives so that the selection of either of these alternatives actually results in a purchase decision. For example, consider the following questions: "Which do you prefer: the ElDorado or the Seville?" Regardless of which alternative the prospect selects, the answer implies a purchase. Of course, the prospect could select none of the alternatives and bring up an objection instead; but then the good salesperson would simply cycle back to Closing on an Objection.

The Take-Away Close

Another useful close is the Take-Away close. (Note: This is essentially the same as the notion of ostensible demarketing described by Barclay, this volume.) This strategy involves stressing the actual or potential unavailability of your product. That is, the salesperson holds out the needed program or product and then makes it seem unavailable. For example, you might say something like, "I'm not sure you even qualify for this insurance, John. It all depends on how the results of a medical examination come out." Note that this statement tells the prospect that the purchase is less than automatic.

Generally, the more scarce or difficult an item is to obtain, the more desirable it tends to become. Fear of loss can be a powerful motivating force. Once the prospect experiences and appreciates the potential unavailability, one can lead quite naturally into an Assumed Consent close.

Impending Event

A related technique is termed the Impending Event close. The basic ingredient underlying this approach is the fact that it calls attention to changes that might, or will, occur either in the product or in the situation. An example statement is, "Our rates are scheduled to go up in two months. Why not take advantage of the lower rates now?"

The Impending Event close tends to be more effective when an element of uncertainty or risk is built in. An example of an impending event that includes an element of uncertainty is as follows: "We only have one more dress available in your size in that style. The way it's been selling, I don't think it will be here if you wait until Saturday." Another example would be, "In a few weeks you'll be going on a long trip. Le'ts get your family protected before you leave." Again, the natural follow-up to an impending event would be an Assumed Consent close.

Story Telling

The Story Telling closing technique has a long history in the life insurance selling. This tends to be used when the salesperson runs across a prospect who will agree with his/her analysis of financial need, but who doesn't really recognize the significance of the problem in human terms. The Story Telling approach seems to work well under these circumstnces. This involves telling a story about what happened to some other family (or business) when someone who was adequately covered by insurance died unexpectedly (the happy-ending approach), or when the person was inadequately covered and died unexpectedly (the unhappy-ending approach). It usually is best if the story is about someone the prospect can identify with, and even better if it is about someone whom he knew.

It is not a good idea to make up stories; they sound phony, and that is the last thing you want. There is actually no need to contrive stories since there are so many appropriate, true ones. For example, my wife remembers placing a $300,000 policy on a young man with three children who had a heart attack and died only two months after paying the first premium; his family was protected. In contrast, another prospect did not want to write out a check at the time he took out the application; hence he remained uninsured. He was killed in a hunting accident the day before the policy came down from the home office to be placed; his family received no monthly insurance check to help them out.

Regardless of what kind of story has been told, the objective is to have the prospect become emotionally involved. In selling life insurance, once the prospect becomes emotionally involved in experiencing his/her need and understanding the impact his/her death could have on those near and dear, the salesperson generally finds it easier to move directly into an Assumed Consent close.

Special Incentive

In many instances, the salesperson can discount the merchandise on the spot, thereby providing a special inducement to purchase, for example, "I'll give you 30 percent off if you take this order today." Another variant, useful when the merchandise cannot be discounted, involves throwing in something else for free or at a special price, for example, "I can't lower the price anymore on that item, but if you take it for that price, I can lower the price on this other item that you're interested in."

Puppy-Dog Closing

It is the rare person who, after enjoying the company of a healthy puppy dog for a while, would be able to return it to the store. It is equally difficult to do so with products that are socially visible and whose possession bring its owner positive social recognition. Accordingly, consider how this Puppy Dog close has been used in selling such products as cars. "I know that you're not certain you want a Cadillac, Mr. Jones, so why don't you take this one home for the weekend, then come back on Monday and we'll see how you feel about it." Note that the salesperson doesn't require the prospect to actually buy the car. He/she simply permits the prospect to use it for a few days for a free trial. After the neighbors have seen Mr. Prospect drive up in this car all weekend, he's not very likely to relinquish it on Monday.

No-Risk Close (Money-Back)

One of the most commonly used techniques is the money-back if you're not completely satisfied close. Unlike the Puppy-Dog close, the money-back close does require that the prospect purchase the product before taking it from the premises. However, much like the Puppy-Dog close, the elements of a free trial and "How can I return this product now that I find it gives me great pleasure?" are both present.

Delayed/Minimized Cost Close

Another effective closing technique is to provide payment terms that either delay or effectively minimize the cost. Examples include such things as "Buy now, pay later" or "No payment required for 90 days" and "Your payments can be as low as X dollars a month."

Medical Close

This particular closing technique may be unique to selling life insurance. In using the Medical Close, the salesperson begins by telling the prospect, "Actually, two decisions have to be made—yours and the company's. The company's decision is based upon both your financial status and especially your physical health. Since they're going to be taking a $150,000 risk on your life, they want to be pretty sure to begin with that you are in at least average physical condition for your age. So until they approve this program that we've been talking about, we can't really talk about your taking it. What we need now is for you to take a medical exam. When would be the most convenient time for you to see the doctor—Tuesday or Thursday?"

The Medical Close is used most often in cases in which the prospect is firm about not making a final decision that day, or in which the salesperson needs to check on a few things before quoting a specific premium. There are several advantages to using the medical close, including the fact that it obtains commitment from the prospect and effectively blocks competition in the process. In fact, some salespeople have even been known to use it in certain cases in which physical exams are not necessary, even if this means they have to pay for the physical exam themselves.

Asking Outright

Unlike the Fatal Alternative approach (which subtly asks the prospect to choose between two alternatives) Asking Outright involves the not-so-subtle request to purchase a single alternative. There are contrasting opinions as to whether or not a salesperson ought to ask the prospect for the sale outright. Some authorities argue that this is one of the poorest forms of salesmanship, while others contend that it is one of the best. Some advocate that this direct approach only be used with self-confident prospects; others believe that it should only be used on prospects who are assumed to have an inferiority complex. Regardless, because many salespeople are afraid of direct confrontation on the major question, the Ask Outright Close is probably not used often enough. There is really very little reason to fear such direct confrontation, especially when you're doing both yourself and the prospect a service. In fact, many people don't say "yes" until they are asked directly.

Some salespeople who do Ask Outright use this as their first closing attempt. This can be very effective, particularly when the sales interview has proceeded in a logical and straightforward manner, and the prospect's objections have been handled satisfactorily. Such a close might proceed as follows: "Well, John, the program I've outlined fills your unique needs to a T. It's just what you need, and you know that, so let's take care of this thing right now. Why don't you write out a check for $287.80 and we'll get this purchase order processed."

Most times, however, sales people who Ask Outright save it to use as one of their last closing attempts. The philosophy seems to be: If you've tried all the indirect closes that you feel are appropriate and you have nothing else to lose, why not try it? Even if only one out of twenty prospects then decides to buy, that is a 5 percent higher sales ratio than would be the case had the salesperson accepted defeat and left.

The Lost Sales Approach

As a last resort, if nothing you have tried seems to be working and you are just about ready to give up with no possibility of seeing this prospect again, another recommended close is the Lost Sales approach. This involves behaving as if you have given up on the possibility of making a sale. Say something like, "Let me apologize for being such a poor salesman, John. You see, according to the information you gave me and the figures we came up with, you definitely have a need for this program/product. Now perhaps had I had been a better salesman, I could have made you see the importance of having this program/product. I want you to know it's all my fault and I'm truly sorry. Just so I don't make the same mistake again with someone else, would you please tell me what it was that I did wong?" Prospects are often disarmed by this approach and quite willing to indicate to the salesperson what they feel was wrong. In the process, they often reveal their real objections. Once this happens, the salesperson can move quite easily into Closing on a Specific Objection.

Conclusion

These techniques are of value to social scientists interested in social influence as well as to salespeople. By trying to explain, in broader theoretical terms, and then empirically exploring how, why, and when these techniques work, social scientists will necessarily extend the range of his/her basic theoretical propositions regarding social influence. If these propositions do not have demonstrable applications in the context of personal selling, then they clearly are not as generalizable nor as tenable as might have been claimed or thought. Therein lies the challenge for social scientists.

References

Barclay, D.W. (1984). "Toward understanding ostensible demarketing as a personal selling strategy." [This volume.]

Brehm, J.W. (1966). *A Theory of Psychological Reactance.* New York: Academic Press.

Chestnut, R.W., and Jacoby, J. (1984). "The Impact of Attractiveness on Salesperson Effectiveness: Consumer Behavior in the Marketing of Complex Financial Services. [This volume.]

Cialdini, R. (1984). "Principles of Automatic Influence." [This volume.]

Edwards, A.L. (1960). *Experimental Design in Psychological Research.* New York: Holt, Rinehart, and Winston.

Feather, N.T. (1964). A Structural Balance Model of Communication Effects." *Psychological Review* 71, 291–293.

Feather, N.T. (1967) "A Structural Balance Approach to the Analysis of Communication Effects." In L. Berkowitz (ed.), *Advances in Experimental Social Psychology.* Vol. 3. New York: Academic Press, pp. 100–166.

Heider, F. (1944). "Social Perception and Phenomenal Causality." *Psychological Review* 51, 358–374.

Heider, F. (1946). "Attitudes and Cognitive Organizations." *Journal of Psychology* 21, 107–112.

Heider, F. (1958). *The Psychology of Interpersonal Relations.* New York: Wiley.

Jacoby, J. (1975). "Consumer Psychology as a Social Psychological Sphere of Action. *American Psychologist* 30, 977–987.

Jacoby, F., and Jacoby, J. (1979). "The Psychology of Persuasion." *Proceedings of the Million Dollar Round Table* 2, 899–906. Des Plaines, Ill.: Million Dollar Round Table.

Kiesler, C.A.; Collins, B.E.; and Miller, N. (1969). *Attitude Change: A Critical Analysis of Theoretical Approaches.* New York: Wiley.

Kulich, R.J.; Curran, J.P.; Jacoby, J.; and Mariotto, M. The Application of Assertiveness Training to Consumer–Salesperson Interactions. Unpublished manuscript.

Leigh, T.W., and Rethans, A.J. (1984). "Consumer Scripts for Insurance Salesperson Behaviors in Sales Encounters." [This volume.]

Matell, M.S. and Jacoby, J. (1971). "Is There an Optimal Number of Alternatives for Likert Scale Items? Study I: Reliability and validity." *Educational and Psychological Measurement* 31, 1657–674.

Petty, R.E.; Cacioppo, J.T.; and Schumann, D. (1984). "Attitude Change and Personal Selling: Central and Peripheral Routes to Persuasion." [This volume.]

Zajonc, R.B. (1960). "The Concepts of Balance, Congruity, and Dissonance." *Public Opinion Quarterly* 24, 280–296.

5

An Attribution Theory Perspective on Using Two-Sided Messages to Increase Seller Credibility

James M. Hunt,
Michael F. Smith, and
Jerome B. Kernan

Marketing communicators have long been interested in understanding how individuals assess the truthfulness of persuasive appeals. The reason for this is relatively straightforward. Success of promotional activities such as advertising and personal selling is thought to be directly related to peoples' acceptance of information contained in seller-related messages. It is essential, therefore, that marketers understand the process by which people come to accept (or reject) the contents of persuasive appeals.

One theory—from social psychology—helpful in dealing with this issue is that of attribution theory (Heider 1958). Attribution theory suggests that the causal inferences (attributions) people make regarding the nature of a persuasive message influence their judgments about the accuracy of that message. As such, attribution theory is a useful perspective for analyzing persuasion.

This chapter attempts to bring attribution theory to bear on persuasion as that process pertains to personal selling. More specifically, we present a model that incorporates the related processes of attribution and persuasion into the context of personal selling. This gives rise to several hypotheses concerning concepts critical to sellers, that is, message acceptance, recall of information, and seller credibility. These hypotheses are offered not only as a set of directions for future research but also as a guide for tactical considerations on the part of those enaged in personal selling.

Background

The presence of attribution theory in marketing and consumer studies is not novel. Various investigations have been conducted using attribution theory to model processes relevant to buying behavior (for example, Golden 1977; Hansen and Scott 1976; Hunt, Domzal, and Kernan 1982; Mizerski 1982; Settle 1972; Settle and Golden 1974; Smith and Hunt 1978; Sparkman 1982;

Sparkman and Locander 1980). Most of these researchers have related attribution to promotion.

Generally speaking, the term *attribution* refers to the process by which individuals interpret events "as being caused by particular parts of the relatively stable environment" (Heider 1958, p. 297). That is, attribution is said to be the process of assigning cause to events. In a personal selling situation, for instance, a prospective buyer can be thought of as making judgments regarding the underlying cause(s) of a particular seller's appeal or persuasive attempt (an event). Attribution theory attempts to explain this kind of inference process.

How attribution relates to persuasion and other promotion-related phenomena has been the focus of a great deal of research in social psychology (see Eagly and Chaiken 1975; Eagly, Wood and Chaiken 1978; Festinger and MacCoby 1964; Hovland and Mandel 1952; Jones et al. 1971; Koeske and Crano 1968; McPeek and Edwards 1975; Mills and Jellison 1967; Steiner and Field 1960; Thibaut and Rieken 1955; Walster, Aronson and Abrahams 1966; Walster and Festinger 1962). The central notion of this research is that message acceptance is dependent, to a large degree, on the attributions people make regarding various persuasive appeals. This proposition appears to be quite broad in domain and capable of explicating the persuasive effects of much marketing communication. As such, this proposition serves as a perspective for the analysis presented here.

A Model of Seller Credibility and Persuasion

The model proposed here is based on the work of Eagly, Wood, and Chaiken (1978) and Hunt, Domzal, and Kernan (1982). The grist of the model is the notion that when message recipients anticipate receiving a persuasive communication, they develop pre-message expectancies regarding the content of that communication. Simply put, people expecting to deal with persuasive communication are thought to engage in pre-message cognitive processes; and these processes result in expectations (lay hypotheses) about what will be communicated. In terms of personal selling, therefore, prospective buyers are viewed as anticipating the likely position of a would-be seller.

As modeled here, pre-message expectancies guide peoples' judgments concerning the accuracy or truthfulness of a persuasive communication. When people anticipate receiving a persuasive communication, it is likely they develop expectancies that are one-sided. That is, they tend to expect a message that is skewed, or slanted, toward the communicator's position. Such pre-message expectancies can be said to exhibit *bias* (situational bias) since the communicator obviously has something to gain from message acceptance.

Whether, and to what degree, message recipients actually do accept the communicator's message depends on whether the message confirms their biased pre-message expectancies. If the message actually *confirms* these bias-related expectancies (if, for example, a seller actually takes a one-sided stand favoring his/her position or product), message recipients tend to attribute the message to situational bias and thus discount the validity of the message. In essence, the cause of the message is seen to reside in factors such as the desire to sell or profit from the interaction, *not* the communicator's own true issue-related opinions. Accordingly, little persuasion occurs and communicator credibility pales.

Contrasting effects are posited for situations in which expectancy disconfirmation occurs. When a communicator *disconfirms* bias-related expectancies (a seller takes a stand that is *not* one-sided, rather one that reveals information unfavorable to his/her position), message recipients tend to discount the biasing factors. Instead, they attribute the cause of the message to other factors such as the communicator's own true (unbiased) disposition. Such attributions are more likely to result in message acceptance than are those involving situational bias. Simply stated, the communicator's appeal is judged to be bias-free and under control of his/her own true feelings. Further, since the communicator appears willing to reveal information opposed to his/her own best interest (unfavorable information disconfirming one-sided expectations), s/he is more likely to be judged as a credible message source. In sum, when bias-related expectancies are disconfirmed, communicator credibility is enhanced and persuasion more likely. Figure 5–1 represents the pattern of these effects.[1]

Preliminary Predictions Concerning Personal Selling

The model presented here posits that those engaged in personal selling can enhance their credibility by employing selling appeals that disconfirm prospective buyers' pre-message expectancies when those expectancies reflect bias. This involves the use of negative information—that is, information that is not all one-sided, but unfavorable in some way to the seller's product—in communicating promotional appeals. It is argued here that such appeals will be more likely to lead to message acceptance and enhanced seller credibility. In other words, sellers who are willing to discuss weaknesses of their products (disconfirm buyer expectancies) should be judged as more credible than those sellers who are disposed to one-sided selling appeals. Further, persuasive appeals that disconfirm expectancies should produce greater message acceptance than traditional one-sided messages. Given that sellers who admit product weaknesses are judged to be relatively credible, it follows that they should be more persuasive in terms of their selling efforts.

The following hypotheses formally summarize the preceding analysis. The first of these is descriptive in nature, whereas the latter predictions are causal.

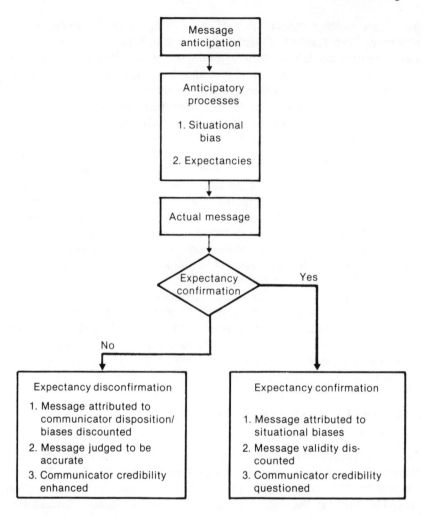

Figure 5-1. The Effects of Expectancy Confirmation/Disconfirmation

1. Prospective buyers who anticipate receiving a promotional message from a seller will develop bias-related expectancies concerning that appeal, that is, will anticipate the appeal to consist only of one-sided (positive) information.
2. Prospective buyers who receive a promotional message that disconfirms their bias-related expectancies—that is, one containing some negative information about the seller's product—will be more likely to attribute that message to the seller's own disposition than will those who receive an appeal that confirms bias-related expectancies.

3. Prospective buyers who receive a promotional message that disconfirms their bias-related expectancies will be more likely to accept that message (as an accurate account of the seller's product) than will those who receive an appeal that confirms bias-related expectancies.
4. Prospective buyers who receive a promotional message that disconfirms their bias-related expectancies will be more likely to judge the seller as credible than will those who receive an appeal that confirms bias-related expectancies.

Theoretical Considerations

The preceding analysis does not make predictions that differ radically from more traditional models of attribution. In this sense, the model is reminiscent of Kelley's (1972a, 1973) discounting and augmentation principle and Jones and Davis's (1965) model of correspondent inference. The value of the present model is how it hypothesizes persuasive effects. First, it gives explicit recognition to cognitive processes that precurse actual message reception. Thus message recipients are viewed as engaging in cognitive processes as a result of simply *anticipating* a persuasive communication (*cf.* Cialdini, Petty, and Cacioppo 1981). This is to assert that in personal selling situations, prospective buyers do not just attend a seller's presentation. They approach that stage of promotion with some preconception regarding what the seller is about to communicate.

In addition to recognizing the presence of anticipatory processes, the model details the relationship between those processes and subsequent attribution. Specifically, expectancies, which are products of anticipatory pre-message processing, are modeled as inputs to post-dictive attributions made by message recipients; and these attributions are directly linked to persuasion. Thus we can say that the present analysis elaborates the cognitive processes that the more traditional models of attribution propose.

Recent Research

Two recently conducted studies bear on the model proposed here. The first (Hunt, Domzal, and Kernan 1982) assessed the expectancy-attribution-persuasion sequence in the context of advertising. The second (Mizerski 1982) explored recipient response to information from a personal source— that is, fictitious product evaluations made by fictitious other subjects.

Study 1. In the Hunt *et al.* study, subjects were exposed to one of two different experimental advertisements involving a new clock-radio, characterized as a test product. Subjects received either an ad that made superior claims (expectancy confirmed) on all product features—sound of the radio, accuracy of the clock-radio, clock and alarm reliability, and styling—or a commercial message that made such claims on only three of these attributes. On the fourth attribute, sound, the information given to subjects in the expectancy disconfirmation group was that the radio did not perform in a superior manner.

To ensure that subjects actually held bias-related expectations regarding the experimental advertising (that is, they expected claims about the radio to be relatively superior ones), some subjects were randomly assigned to an expectancy group. The rationale for including this group was to measure premessage expectancies without contaminating subsequent responses to the experimental ads. Thus subjects assigned to the expectancy group did not actually view the experimental advertising. Instead, they responded to a set of items pertaining to their expectancies about what would be said in the advertising. To ensure these responses were a product of actual ad anticipation, expectancy subjects were given the same pre-message instructions as subjects who actually viewed the experimental advertising. Thus they were led to believe that they would view a test commercial.

Results from the study demonstrated that subjects anticipating the reception of an advertisement tend to hold bias-related expectancies regarding that ad—that is, expectancy subjects exhibited positive, or superior, message expectancies regarding all product attributes. More importantly, however, the study demonstrated relatively clear support for the proposed effects of expectancy disconfirmation. Subjects who viewed ads that *disconfirmed* bias-related expectancies were more likely to accept the content of that advertising (as an accurate account of the test product) than were those who received ads confirming such expectancies. This can be seen from table 5-1, which summarizes subjects' post-message belief scores regarding the experimental product. On three of the four product attributes, subjects accepted the advertising appeal more when they received a message that disconfirmed expectations.

Table 5-1
Mean Attribute Belief Scores by Expectancy Disconfirmation

Product Attribute	Expectancy Disconfirmation	
	Confirmed	Disconfirmed
Sound quality	9.28	4.31[a]
Accuracy	9.98	10.90[b]
Reliability	10.44	11.42[c]
Styling	10.52	10.38

Source: Adapted from Hunt, Domzal, and Kernan 1982.
Note: Scales ranged from "strongly disagree" ($+1$) to "strongly agree" ($+15$) regarding product performance on each attribute.
[a] $F(1,110) = 117.39$, $p < 0.001$
[b] $F(1,110) = 4.63$, $p < 0.03$.
[c] $F(1,110) = 5.17$, $p < 0.02$.

The difference in message acceptance appears to have been due to differences in causal ascriptions. That is, subjects who received ads that disconfirmed biased expectancies tended to attribute the experimental advertising to actual true *facts* about the product. Subjects exposed to expectancy confirmation, on the other hand, were more likely to attribute the cause of the advertising to the firm's desire to sell products. Results concerning advertiser (source) credibility, however, were not as congenial to the expectancy-disconfirmation hypothesis. Judgments of advertiser credibility were not found to differ over the expectancy disconfirmation manipulation.

Study 2. The Mizerski (1982) study involved attributional processes related to the receipt of information from a personal source (another student) who supposedly had just tested and evaluated one of two new products. Subjects received evaluative information about either a car or a movie, depending on their experimental assignment. The information consisted of product performance ratings made on three attributes for each of the two products. One attribute for each product was used as the basis of manipulating information presented to subjects and ascertaining attributional responses. Half of the subjects received an evaluation that described the test product as performing favorably on this attribute, whereas the other half received an unfavorable report concerning how the product performed on that attribute. Product perfomance on the remaining two attributes was described to both groups as average.

Of the findings reported in this study, two are congenial to the model proposed here. First, subjects who received unfavorable information were more likely to attribute the experimental (fictitious) product evaluations to the product itself than were those who received favorable information. That is, subjects exposed to negative information tended to attribute the cause of the performance report to the product itself, indicating greater message acceptance. The second finding relevant to the present analysis concerns the impact of unfavorable information on the strength of subjects' beliefs. Analysis of post-message beliefs indicated that exposure to unfavorable product evaluations produced relatively stronger beliefs. This result was obtained for both products. Finally, the study revealed that the majority of subjects approached the experimental task with favorable expectations regarding how other students would evaluate the test products. This was ascertained through questions designed to assess the general expectancies of pretest subjects.

Other Studies. Other studies (Settle and Golden 1974; Smith and Hunt 1978) have produced results similar to those discussed above. However, these studies did not assess pre-message expectancies. Rather, their focus was confined solely to the actual presentation of information. They lend only partial support to the expectancy-disconfirmation hypothesis proposed here.

Issue of Effectiveness

From the preceding discussion, it appears that sellers can increase their persuasive effectiveness by presenting information that disconfirms prospective buyers' bias-related message expectancies. This section addresses two
issues thought to involve the degree to which such presentations and appeals
are effective. The first pertains to the informational content of those appeals—that is, the type of product attribute used in formulating the
message. The second concerns the placement, or timing, of disconfirming-
type information. Is it more or less effective to place this kind of information at the beginning or at the end of a persuasive appeal?

Message Content

The overall effectiveness of expectancy disconfirmation appears to depend,
in part, on the nature of the attributes used in constructing a persuasive appeal. This can be seen from table 4-1 pertaining to the Hunt et al. study. As
noted previously, subjects in that study were found to be more receptive to
persuasive communication when that communication disconfirmed their
pre-message expectancies. This finding was exhibited for three of the four
experimental product attributes. Both the accuracy and reliability of the
clock-radio were rated significantly higher (indicating greater message acceptance) in the expectancy-disconfirmed group. Sound quality, the first
product attribute, received a significantly lower rating from the disconfirmed group. Presumably, this was due to its role in imparting unfavorable, or disconfirming, type information to that group. Thus its significantly lower score indicates greater message acceptance.

Results such as these were *not* obtained in conjunction with the styling
attribute, however. No significant difference was found to exist between the
confirmed and disconfirmed group with respect to the radio's style. Thus an
expectancy disconfirmation explanation cannot be said to order the results
for all product attributes.

One possible reason for this difference concerns the less objective nature of the styling attribute. In contrast to the other experimental attributes,
styling is a product feature with fewer verifiable qualities. On the other
hand, product features such as accuracy, reliability, and sound quality can
be more directly evaluated.

Hirschman (1980, 1981) references this dichotomy in terms of a "tangible" versus "intangible" classification scheme. According to her, tangible
product characteristics can be judged or detected through touch, sight,
taste, and so forth. Thus they can be considered objective attributes in that
their assessment tends to be independent of the individual. Hirschman

terms attributes such as the styling feature *intangible*. These are said to be less palpable (verifiable) and thus more subjective in nature. That is, judgment regarding intangible attributes tends to be more dependent on the scrutinizer rather than the object being scrutinized.

We suggest here that this difference in judgment accounts for the differential efficacy of expectancy disconfirmation. Simply put, the effect of expectancy disconfirmation is greater when used in conjunction with tangible attributes; this difference is thought to arise from the variation in judgment occurring across the tangible-intangible continuum. This can be seen by considering the judgment of intangible attributes. Opinion shifts along these intangible dimensions should be more difficult to effect, even though bias-related expectancies on other attributes may have been disconfirmed. It is as if message recipients elicit (rehearse) their own thoughts regarding intangible features.

In contrast, tangible product features involve judgment processes that depend less on the person (message recipient) making the judgment. Rather, judgments concerning tangible attributes are related more closely to the object, or product, under scrutiny. Therefore message recipients will tend to be more receptive to information about such attributes.

This reasoning gives rise to a second set of hypotheses intended to elaborate those stated previously.

5. Given that a seller's promotional message disconfirms bias-related expectancies, prospective buyers will be less likely to accept that message in its entirety when it contains positive (superior) product information on intangible attributes than when it contains similar information on tangible attributes.
6. Given that a seller's promotional message disconfirms bias-related expectancies, prospective buyers will be less likely to judge the seller as credible when the message contains positive information on intangible attributes than when it contains similar information on tangible attributes.

Comments. Hypotheses 5 and 6 imply that in formulating persuasive appeals, sellers should consider the type attributes they employ. We suggest here that messages containing positive product information on intangible attributes may offset the beneficial effects of expectancy-disconfirmation. Thus even though sellers, using unfavorable information, disconfirm bias-related expectancies on one dimension, their simultaneous use of positive information on intangible attributes may have a detrimental effect on persuasion.

Message Format

A second factor that possibly affects the operation of expectancy disconfirmation is information placement. Placing negative, or disconfirming, information at the beginning of a persuasive appeal may be less problematic and more effective than placing such information at the end of the message. This assertion stems from a great deal of evidence involving memory and cognitive response to persuasive communication.

Memory Updating. We noted previously that when prospective buyers receive persuasive messages that disconfirm bias-related expectancies, they tend to discount the bias-related factors (that is, the situation, selling motive, and so forth) as being message causes. We also discussed the notion that such discounting led to more favorable judgments concerning the seller's credibility. Mental shifts such as these can be thought of as instances of memory updating. That is, message recipients, or buyers, revise their memories for the communication event based on outcome (actual message) feedback. The result is a causal explanation much different from what was expected—that is, the set of causal relationships leading to the original bias-related expectancies. This updating phenomenon is reminiscent of Fischhloff's (1975) "knew it all along" effect in which old information (the bias-related expectancy) is erased and replaced by the more current outcome data. In other words, "memory is malleable" (Loftus 1979, 1980).

That perspective buyers (as message recipients) make such revisions greatly affects how they interpret and ultimately accept a seller's message designed to disconfirm biased expectancies. It is well known, for instance, that both interpretation and recall of information from an event depend somewhat on the status of the observer's existing knowledge. That is, information intake is largely dependent on whatever memory structure is activated at the time the event occurs (Bartlett 1932; Bransford and Johnson 1972; Loftus 1980). In terms of personal selling, this means that a buyer's interpretation and later recall of a seller's message is a function of the buyer's existing knowledge. As noted above, however, this knowledge structure becomes updated when disconfirming (unfavorable) information is encountered in the message. In essence, the buyer's knowledge structure should somehow reflect a less biased and more credible representation of seller and message. We can reason, therefore, that subsequent message processing will be influenced largely by a new, unbiased knowledge structure. So expectancy disconfirmation leads to memory updating; and this revision directs the remainder of message processing.

Primary versus Recency. Given these observations, we can make certain predictions regarding the placement of negative, or disconfirming, product information. Usually, these predictions lead to the conclusion that unfavorable information is more effectively placed at the beginning of a persuasive apeal.

When buyers receive disconfirming type information and engage in a memory updating process, biased expectancies are replaced with an unbiased representation. From the standpoint of persuasion, it is likely that the timing of such updating moderates the efficacy of expectancy disconfirmation. When instigation of updating occurs early in the message reception sequence, expectancy disconfirmation is seen as relatively effective. On the other hand, updating occurring toward the end of message reception should produce little, if any, disconfirmation effect.

This reaffirms what is known about information interpretation. When memory updates of the kind just discussed occur relatively early in the message reception sequence, message interpretation depend largely on an unbiased knowledge structure. Expectancy disconfirmation occurring during the later stages of the message, however, should produce message interpretations that depend to a large extent on bias-related expectancies.

This analysis meshes with current knowledge about cognitive response to persuasive communication. The cognitive response approach (see Cialdini, Petty, and Cacioppo 1981; Greenwald 1968; Petty, Wells, and Brock 1980; and Wright 1980) proposes that persuasive communication is mediated by thoughts that message recipients generate in response to (or anticipation of) the reception of a persuasive communication. Such thoughts can be opposed to the message viewpoint (counter-arguments) or in favor of it (pro-arguments). Two propositions are central to the cognitive response approach. The first maintains that there is an inverse relationship between counterargumentation and message acceptance. When people elicit counter-arguments in response to persuasive appeals, they are thought to become more resistant to persuasion. The second proposition states that message acceptance is directly related to proargumentation. The more support arguments people generate in conjunction with message reception, the more likely they will shfit toward the position advocated in the appeal.

Counterargumentation would be expected to be greater in situations in which expectancy disconfirmation does not occur until the end of a persuasive appeal. When unfavorable information is placed at the beginning of a message and expectancy disconfirmation occurs relatively early, the message source will be judged as operating free of bias throughout the entire message or appeal. This should result in less counterargumentation throughout the remainder of message reception. As Sternthal *et al.* (1978) note, a highly credible source is normally thought to inhibit counterargumentation. In the case of delayed expectancy disconfirmation, counterargumentation should be significant throughout the early portions of message reception. Since memory updating does not occur until the end of the message, there will be a greater propensity to counterargue throughout.

In that counter-argumentation is thought to be greater when unfavorable/disconfirming information is placed at the end of a message than when such information is placed at the beginning, message acceptance should be greater. When bias-related expectancies are disconfirmed at the beginning of a message, the source is viewed as relatively credible and the impetus to counterargue diminished. Thus message acceptance is greater.

The following hypotheses summarize the discussion of message format and expectancy disconfirmation.

7. Given that a seller's promotional message disconfirms bias-related expectancies, message interpretation will be more heavily weighted with situational biases when unfavorable information is placed at the end of the message rather than at the beginning.
8. Given that a seller's promotional message disconfirms bias-related expectancies, message recall will be more heavily weighted with situational biases when unfavorable information is placed at the end of the message rather than at the beginning.
9. Given that a seller's promotional message disconfirms bias-related expectancies, counterargumentation will be greater when unfavorable information is placed at the end rather than at the beginning of the message.
10. Given that a seller's promotional message disconfirms bias-related expectancies, message acceptance will be greater when unfavorable information is placed at the beginning rather than end of the message.

Comments

In terms of personal selling, the preceding hypotheses suggest that using unexpected information to enhance believability should be accomplished early in the selling appeal. It should be noted, however, that these hypotheses may not constitute an adequate description of the persuasion process for those cases in which buyers already possess a favorable attitude toward the seller's offering. Sternthal *et al.* (1978) have shown that when such circumstances exist, source credibility and persuasion take on an inverse relationship. Underpinning this finding is the notion that support arguments are elicited when source credibility is relatively low, thus facilitating greater persuasion.

Conclusion

A few comments on the limitations of the model are in order. First, it appears that the model is limited to situations in which sellers are making initial contact with prospects. In such cases, the credibility of the seller is yet untested in the mind of the buyer. Expectancy disconfirmation, therefore, becomes one avenue to gaining initial trustworthiness and acceptance.

Along these same lines, the analysis is not meant to cover situations in which buyers have an already-developed favorable attitude toward the seller's offering. Rather, it is intended for situations in which buyers are neutral, unfamiliar, or perhaps somewhat skeptical and negative.

Finally, the model presumes sellers can identify a priori those features of their offering that influence buyers' decision processes. Although these need not be perfomance-type attributes (see Lutz 1979), they should nevertheless be relevant to the buyer decision process.

The model presented here may assist sellers in formulating persuasive appeals designed to gain initial acceptance and believability. It also serves as a basis for future research in the area of causal inference and persuasion.

Note

1. The model depicted in figure 5-1 assumes that, since the message sources involved are marketing communicators, they are not regarded as especially credible sources by message recipients. Further, the variable element in source credibility is assumed to be the seller's trustworthiness, or his/her reporting bias. Were this assumption *not* to hold, of course, message recipients' own thoughts likely would not enter prominently into the cognitive processing picture, as they would be overwhelmed by the highly credible source's message thoughts.

References

Bartlett, F.C. (1932). *Remembering: A Study in Experimental and Social Psychology*. Cambridge: Cambridge University Press.

Bransford, J.D, and M.K. Johnson (1972). "Contextual Prerequisites for Understanding: Some Investigations of Comprehension." *Journal of Learning* 11, 717-721.

Cialdini, Robert B., Richard E. Petty, and John T. Cacioppo (1981). "Attitude Change." *Annual Review of Psychology* 32, 357-404.

Eagly, Alice H., and Shelly Chaiken (1975). "An Attribution Analysis of the Effect of Communicator Characteristics on Opinion Change: The Case of Communicator Attractiveness." *Journal of Personality and Social Psychology* 32, 136-144.

Eagly, Alice H., Wendy Wood, and Shelly Chaiken (1978). "Causal Inferences about Communicators and Their Effect on Opinion Change." *Journal of Personality and Social Psychology* 36, 424-435.

Festinger, Leon, and Nathan Maccoby (1964). "On Resistance to Persuasive Communications." *Journal of Abnormal and Social Psychology* 79, 350-366.

Fischhoff, Baruch (1975). "Hindsight and Foresight: The Effect of Outcome Knowledge on Judgement under Uncertainty." *Journal of Experimental Psychology: Human Perception and Performance* 1, 288-299.

Golden, Linda L. (1977). "Attribution Theory Implications for Advertising Claim Credibility." *Journal of Marketing Research* 14, 115–117.

Greenwald, Anthony (1968). "Cognitive Learning, Cognitive Response to Persuasion, and Attitude Change." In *Psychological Foundations of Attitudes*, ed. A. Greenwald *et al.* New York: Academic Press, pp. 147–170.

Hansen, Robert A., and Carol A. Scott (1976). "Comments on Attribution Theory and Advertiser Credibility." Journal of Marketing Research 13, 193–197.

Heider, Fritz (1958). *The Psychology of Interpersonal Relations*. New York: Wiley.

Hirschman, Elizabeth C. (1980). "Attributes of Attributes and Layers of Meaning." In *Advances in Consumer Research*, ed. J.C. Olson. Ann Arbor, Mich.: Association for Consumer Research.

———— (1981). "Cognitive Complexity and the Perception of Intangible Attributes." In *Educator's Conference Proceedings*, ed. K.C. Bernhardt et al. Chicago: American Marketing Association.

Hovland, Carl I., and Wallace Mandell (1952). "An Experimental Comparison of Conclusion Drawing by the Communicator and by the Audience." *Journal of Abnormal and Social Psychology* 47, 581–588.

Hunt, James M., Teresa J. Domzal, and Jerome B. Kernan (1982). "Causal Attributions and Persuasion: The Case of Disconfirmed Expectancies." In *Advances in Consumer Research*, ed. A. Mitchell. Ann Arbor, Mich.: Association for Consumer Research.

Jones, Edward E., and Keith E. Davis (1965). "From Acts of Dispositions." In *Advances in Experimental Social Psychology*, ed. L. Berkowitz. New York: Academic Press, 219–266.

Jones, Edward E., Steven Worchel, George R. Goethals, and Judy Grumet (1971). "Prior Expectancy and Behavioral Extremity as Determinants of Attitude Attribution." *Journal of Experimental Social Psychology* 7, 59–80.

Kelley, Harold H. (1972). "Attribution in Social Interaction." In *Attribution: Perceiving the Causes of Behavior*, ed. E.E. Jones et al. Morristown, N.J.: General Learning Press, pp. 1–26.

———— (1973). "The Process of Causal Attribution." *American Psychologist* 28, 107–128.

Koeske, Gary F., and William D. Crano (1968). "The Effect of Congruous and Incongruous Source Statement Combinations upon the Judged Credibility of a Communication." *Journal of Experimental Social Psychology* 4, 384–399.

Loftus, Elizabeth F. (1979). "The Malleability of Human Memory." *American Scientist* 67, 312–320.

———— (1980). *Memory*. Reading, Mass.: Addison-Wesley.

Lutz, Richard J. (1979). "A Functional Theory Framework for Designing and Pretesting Advertising Themes." In *Attitude Research Plays for High Stakes*, ed. J.C. Maloney and B. Silverman. Chicago: American Marketing Association.

McPeek, Robert W., and John D. Edwards (1975). "Expectancy Disconfirmation and Attitude Change." *Journal of Social Psychology* 96, 193–208.

Mills, Judson, and Jerald M. Jellison (1967). "Effect on Opinion Change of How Desirable the Communication Is to the Audience the Communicator Addressed." *Journal of Personality and Social Psychology* 6, 98–101.

Mizerski, Richard W. (1982). "An Attribution Explanation of the Disproportionate Influence of Unfavorable Information." *Journal of Consumer Research* 9, 301–310.

Petty, Richard E., Thomas M. Ostrom, and Timothy C. Brock (1980). "Historical Foundations of the Cognitive Response Approach to Attitudes and Persuasion." In *Cognitive Responses in Persuasion*, ed. R.E. Petty et al., Hillsdale, N.J.: Erlbaum.

Settle, Robert B. (1972). "Attribution Theory and Acceptance of Information." *Journal of Marketing Research* 9, 85–88.

Settle, Robert B., and Linda L. Golden (1974). "Attribution Theory and Advertiser Credibility." *Journal of Marketing Research* 11, 181–185.

Sparkman, Richard M. (1982). "The Discounting Principle in the Perception of Advertising." In *Advances in Consumer Research*, ed. A. Mitchell. Ann Arbor, Mich.: Association for Consumer Research.

Sparkman, Richard M., and William B. Locander (1980). "Attribution Theory and Advertising Effectiveness." *Journal of Consumer Research* 7, 219–224.

Smith, Robert E., and Shelby D. Hunt (1978). "Attributional Processes and Effects in Promotional Situation." *Journal of Consumer Research* 5, 149–158.

Steiner, Ivan D., and William L. Feild (1960). "Role Assignment and Interpersonal Influence." *Journal of Abnormal and Social Psychology* 61, 239–246.

Sternthal, Brian, Ruby Dholakia, and Clark Leavitt (1978). "The Persuasive Effect of Source Credibility: Tests of Cognitive Response." *Journal of Consumer Research* 4, 252–260.

Thibaut, John W., and Henry W. Reicken (1955). "Some Determinants and Consequences of the Perception of Social Causality." *Journal of Personality* 24, 113–133.

Walster, Elaine E., Elliot Aronson, and Darcy Abrahams (1966). "On Increasing the Persuasiveness of a Low Prestige Communicator." *Journal of Experimental Social Psychology* 2, 325–342.

Walster, Elaine E., and Leon Festinger (1962). "The Effectiveness of 'Over-
    heard' Persuasive Communication." *Journal of Abnormal and Social
    Psychology* 65, 395–402.
Wright, Peter (1980). "Message-Evoked Thoughts: Persuasion Research
    Using Thought Verbalizations." *Journal of Consumer Research* 7,
    151–175.

6 Ostensible Demarketing as a Personal Selling Strategy

Donald W. Barclay

Ostensible demarketing as a personal selling strategy has been used successfully in the industrial marketplace. Kotler and Levy (1971) describe ostensible demarketing as discouraging a customer from accepting your product or offering in hopes of making the product even more desirable to that customer.

As with many other strategies, tactics, and techniques associated with personal selling, this behavioral influence strategy seems to be "what some salespersons have stumbled upon in their effort to become more successful" (Yalch 1979). If we understand how and why ostensible demarketing may be effective, and under what conditions, we can make more appropriate use of the strategy. Toward this end, a multi-theoretic conceptualization based on the psychology of reactance and theories of inducing resistance to persuasion is proposed to enhance our understanding of ostensible demarketing. The basic conceptual model is shown in figure 6–1.

This chapter first outlines ostensible demarketing as a selling strategy and indicates the role of determinant attributes in such a strategy. The conceptual model is then developed by discussing the psychology of reactance and reviewing the attention given to this concept in the marketing literature. Next, the conditions that enhance reactance are discussed along with the differences between reactance and commodity theory. Finally, the incremental benefits of an ostensible demarketing strategy in terms of inducing resistance to persuasion are examined.

Ostensible Demarketing

Demarketing is "that aspect of marketing that deals with discouraging customers in general or a certain class of customers in particular on either a temporary or permanent basis" (Kotler and Levy 1971). The dimension of ostensibility is added when the marketer creates "the appearance of trying to discourage demand as a device for actually increasing it" (Kotler and Levy 1971). Thus the apparent objective is to dissuade a customer whereas the real objective is to persuade the customer. Given the focus of this

Comments by Michael J. Ryan on an earlier draft of this chapter were most helpful and appreciated.

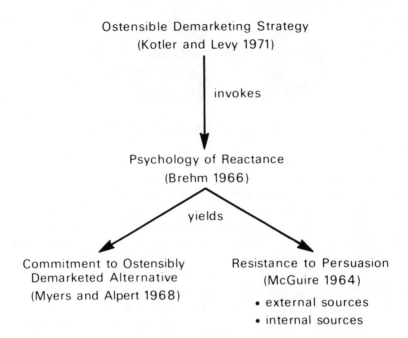

Ostensible Demarketing Strategy
(Kotler and Levy 1971)

invokes

Psychology of Reactance
(Brehm 1966)

yields

Commitment to Ostensibly
Demarketed Alternative
(Myers and Alpert 1968)

Resistance to Persuasion
(McGuire 1964)
- external sources
- internal sources

Figure 6-1. Conceptual Model of Ostensible Demarketing

chapter, ostensible demarketing is more narrowly defined as a personal selling strategy that appears to discourage a customer from choosing a specific solution within his/her evoked set, that solution being one offered by the salesperson's organization. The real objective is to increase the customer's desire for the determinant attributes of the demarketed alternative so that a commitment to this alternative will result.

Before expanding on the actual ostensible demarketing strategy, I will outline the concept of determinant attributes. For the salesperson to completely withdraw a specific solution from the customer's evoked set would appear foolish. What should be withdrawn or held back temporarily is the ability to deliver certain determinant attributes of the demarketed solution. A determinant attribute is a "feature which predisposes consumers to action" (Myers and Alpert 1968). A determinant attribute must be both important to the customer *and* be perceived by the customer as being provided by different suppliers in quite different ways. If all suppliers offer an important feature or function in a similar fashion, no one has a competitive advantage and this important feature will not be determinant. For example, if all steel companies provide equal-quality sheet metal, quality is not a determinant attribute. If the technical support provided by steel companies is perceived as being varied and is important to the customer, then this becomes a determinant attribute.

The personal selling strategy proceeds as follows. Through a series of interactions prior to the demarketing phase of the strategy, the salesperson presents a solution to a customer's problem, or a bundle of benefits, so that this solution is accepted as a member of the customer's evoked set. The interactions also establish and elaborate on the determinant attributes relevant to the customer's decision. The salesperson helps the customer to focus clearly on those determinant attributes where his/her solution has a competitive advantage. This phase thus involves the creation of interest in, and a somewhat positive attitude toward, the proposed solution: a set-up for the demarketing phase. The subsequent demarketing of the determinant attributes of this product-solution threatens to reduce the customer's freedom of choice since s/he is told that the solution may not be readily available to him/her. For example, the salesperson may claim delivery difficulties with respect to certain desired attributes, a long lead time to develop a desired feature, manpower constraints on providing desired support services; or the salesperson may argue that a determinant aspect of the proposed solution is not really appropriate for the customer. The salesperson has in effect told the customer that s/he cannot or should not have what s/he wants.

The psychology of reactance predicts that as a reaction to this threat to freedom of choice, the customer's desire for the demarketed alternative will increase and s/he may insist on committing to this alternative as a way of restoring the perceived loss of freedom (Brehm 1966). If the salesperson's objective was to gain a commitment to the demarketed alternative in the first place, s/he has had success. For a more complete understanding, we now turn to the psychology of reactance.

Psychology of Reactance

Brehm outlines the concept of psychological reactance as follows:

> when a person believes himself free to engage in a given behavior, he will experience psychological reactance if that freedom is eliminated or threatened with elimination. Psychological reactance is defined as a motivational state directed toward the reestablishment of the threatened or eliminated freedom and should manifest itself in increased desire to engage in the relevant behavior (Brehm 1966, pp. 15–16).

Arousal and Manifestation

There are three key antecedents to the arousal and manifestation of reactance. First, a person must believe that s/he actually has a particular freedom. This expectation could result from past experience exercising similar freedoms, from observing others exercise freedoms, or from formal and informal agreements with others (Brehm 1972). If a person does not expect a free choice, then the elimination or threatened elimination of a choice alternative should not matter. In the marketplace, consumers and industrial buyers in most cases feel that choice is their prerogative; thus this element is in place as an antecedent. Second, reactance will only be aroused if the assumed freedom of choice is eliminated, or threatened with elimination, and the threat is accompanied by implicit or explicit power that makes the threat meaningful (Clee and Wicklund 1980). Threat in this case is "the perception by an individual that there is pressure on him to behave in a specific way" (Brehm 1968, p. 283). Third, reactance will only be in evidence if the reactance aroused is greater than the offsetting persuasion inherent in the arguments used to restrict the individual's freedom. This latter antecedent becomes important in the ostensible demarketing strategy since the intent is to have the reactance more than counterbalance the demarketing arguments presented to the customer.

The threats to freedom of choice can be social or non-social in nature. A social threat exists when a person attempts to persuade another to adopt a certain position or threatens to eliminate a potential option. A non-social threat or barrier exists when some restriction is introduced which may block goal directed behavior. In a sales situation, both types of threats may exist. An example of a social threat would be an industrial salesperson forcefully attempting to persuade a customer to purchase his/her product. This social influence is an attempt to reduce the customer's flexibility with respect to choosing among alternatives and could be perceived as threatening. An example of a non-social threat in a sales situation would be an unexpected increase in the delivery lead time of one alternative; again, this could be viewed by the customer as a potential restriction of his/her flexibility to choose.

What are the possible consequences of a person being in the aroused state of reactance? How does s/he go about restoring the threatened or lost freedom? Reactance can only be detected by its behavioral manifestations and by changes in a person's perception of and attitudes toward choice options. The most obvious—and in the case of ostensible demarketing the hoped-for consequence of reactance—is a direct attempt to engage in the restricted behavior. If a salesperson says that the customer cannot or should not have a solution and its associated determinant attributes, the customer may well want to buy that solution to show that his/her freedom cannot be curtailed. In the case of a barrier, there would be a tendency to try to overcome the barrier and to engage in the threatened behavior.

A second behavioral manifestation of reactance could be an attack on the threatening agent, the salesperson, if it is likely that the threat would be withdrawn or if the recipient of the threat is not overly concerned about the threat agent's power to retaliate (Brehm 1972). The likelihood of this type of behavior may be less in the industrial as opposed to the retail sales environment as a valued relationship may exist between the customer and salesperson in the former situation.

Freedom to behave and choose can also be restored by the intervention of a third party, provided that the person who intervenes has some power over the behavioral freedom in question (Worchel and Brehm 1971). For example, if an industrial buyer feels that his/her freedom to choose has been restricted by a salesperson, s/he could well receive assurances from his/her own superior that any threats to freedom put forth by the salesperson could be taken care of through higher-level customer-to-supplier contacts. This freedom-restoration process returns the buyer to the state of free choice.

Finally, if the exercising of freedom is not possible due to significant barriers or due to the fact that an option has been truly eliminated, reactance should result in an increase in positive attitude toward the eliminated option and an increased desire for this option (Hammock and Brehm 1966).

What do these anticipated consequences mean in the light of ostensible demarketing? By demarketing a product-solution's determinant attributes, the salesperson hopes to create reactance in the customer that will increase his/her desire for the demarketed alternative and will result in the customer's freedom being restored through purchasing the demarketed option. The typical application of the psychology of reactance is as a warning: A strong communication strategy may well backfire due to reactance's creating a boomerang effect. In the strategy delineated here, this boomerang effect is exactly what is desired.

I should indicate that confirmation of Brehm's notion of psychological reactance has been somewhat ambivalent. The difficulty stems mainly from attempting to deal with a theory that focuses on a motivational construct such as reactance which cannot be directly tapped. Researchers resort to measuring outcomes suggested by the theory, but this does not directly confirm the motivational mechanism proposed by Brehm.

Reactance in the Marketing Literature

As reactance may well help marketers understand consumers' and industrial buyers' possible responses to personal sales influence, influence from advertisements, and product unavailability, one would expect to see this concept given attention. In fact, there are very few articles in the marketing literature. The most substantial article by Clee and Wicklund reviews reactance theory research in a variety of psychological journals and relates the findings to the field of consumer behavior. Freedom-threatening events were broadened to encompass government regulations and the concept of marketing was broadened to encompass nonprofit, social, and political marketing. Clee and Wicklund carefully point out constructs—such as the existence of group norms, which can inhibit the manifestation of reactance—that can intervene in the reactance process.

In an experimental study, Venkatesan (1966) found that in a group situation, an individual in the absence of any objective standards tended to conform to group norms. However, when there was pressure to go along with the group, the individual tended to resist group pressure. Venkatesan claimed that this latter tendency was due to reactance. There is some feeling, however, that the experimental manipulation did not really restrict freedom of choice but rather introduced group indecision. Thus the results should probably not be cast in a reactance framework.

Mazis, Settle, and Leslie (1973) examined consumers' responses to the elimination of phosphate detergent in the Miami area. Compared to Tampa consumers—whose freedom was not restricted by such government legislation—the Miami residents expressed more favorable attitudes toward the eliminated phosphate laundry detergent. This would be consistent with reactance theory. Furthermore, those consumers who not only had to switch from a phosphate to a non-phosphate detergent but also had to switch brand names in the process showed even more reactance due to more restrictions.

The research that has addressed reactance in the marketing literature seems to support the theory; however, none of this research was involved with personal selling or the industrial marketplace.

Determinants of Reactance

If we can appreciate the conditions under which reactance will most likely occur, we can better judge this strategy's appropriateness in a given situation. A review of psychology literature reveals that we can expect reactance and the manifestations thereof to be enhanced or reduced under the following conditions:

1. When a freedom is important to a person, restriction of that freedom will generate more reactance than when the freedom is not important (Hammock and Brehm 1966). In the case of an industrial buyer, the freedom to choose among suppliers of a given product is generally important since it is the essence of his/her position. An industrial buyer expects to be free to choose; this sets the stage for reactance if choices are restricted. For less important purchases, the buyer may not be too upset if an alternative is eliminated.

2. When a person feels competent to make a choice or form an opinion, the threatened elimination of an alternative will generate more reactance than when this competence is not felt (Greibitz-Gniech 1971). If a person does not feel capable of judging alternatives, s/he may be willing to accept the advice of others, even though doing so restricts freedom. Again, in the case of the industrial buyer, s/he is expected to be competent and thus would generally experience reactance in the face of pressure to accept another's view.

3. More reactance will be generated if one among a few options is eliminated versus the elimination of one among many (Hammock and Brehm 1966). By threatening to eliminate one of two members of the buyer's choice set, choice has essentially been eliminated; by threatening to eliminate one of five, the restriction of freedom is not as great as 80 percent of the original options remain open.

4. More reactance will result where the choice alternatives being considered contain a low degree of cognitive overlap. If a person is considering equally attractive alternatives with quite different features, more reactance will emerge than in the case in which s/he is considering equally attractive options with very similar features (Weiner and Brehm 1966). This concept becomes important in the demarketing of determinant and distinguishing attributes. The attributes demarketed must be such that the buyer feels that not being able to choose them is truly a restriction. For example, if plastic and steel could both be used in a certain car component (low overlap), significant reactance would be aroused on the part of a buyer of materials if one of these were unavailable. In an application in which only steel suppliers were being considered for a component, the elimination of one of several steel alternatives (high overlap) would not be viewed as restrictive as was the elimination of plastic in the first case.

5. If a person views a specific threatened freedom as holding implications for other related or future freedoms, reactance will be greater (Sensenig and Brehm 1968). Threatening one freedom may threaten a network of associated freedoms. In the case of the industrial buyer, for example, a situation in which buying a piece of equipment commits the buyer to purchase future supplies and accessory equipment from the same manufacturer will be a situation in which greater reactance could be expected. The initial decision is linked to subsequent purchases, and thus this decision restricts future freedom.

6. The possibility of future interaction between the person whose freedom is threatened and the threatening agent may dampen reactance. The threatened person may be willing to give up some freedom in order to maintain future harmonious relations (Pallak and Heller 1971). In the salesperson-customer dyad, this effect could reduce the amount of reac-

tance generated by demarketing. But reactance in no way would be eliminated. If the customer-salesperson relationship is fairly secure, the customer would probably feel that any impact on the relationship due to his/her manifesting reactance could be smoothed over and thus s/he should not feel too restrained by the thought of subsequent interactions.

7. In a similar vein, if the influencer has the opportunity to retaliate, reactance may be reduced (Heilman 1976). In the case of the industrial buying situation, the opportunity for salesperson retaliation is probably not great. It would not be strategic for the salesperson to threaten not to sell to the customer in the future if the customer did not go along with the salesperson's ideas this time. The salesperson cannot easily retaliate and hence the customer should feel free to display reactance to the salesperson's suggestions in most selling situations.

8. Worchel and Brehm (1971) have studied the likelihood of reactance developing in a group situation in which it is possible for the group member whose choice has been restricted to have this freedom restored by another group member. The member may have his/her freedom restored by another group member who states that s/he has not yet made up his/her own mind. A related idea studied by Greibitz-Gniech (1971) suggests that reactance may be suppressed in the face of a group norm. If a group norm exists with respect to the choice of a specific alternative, a person may be willing to give up some of his/her individual freedom to comply with the norm. Reactance may not emerge because restoring freedom is far less important than compliance with the group. Both of these related ideas have implications for the use of demarketing when dealing with a multi-person buying center. Demarketing to a buying-center member may not prove effective if his/her freedom can be restored by another center member or if a group norm precludes reactance.

    As an example of Worchel and Brehm's idea, consider a group decision about the acquisition of a computer. Suppose the data processing manager feels pressured to go with a given supplier, that is, s/he feels that his/her freedom has been restricted. If other members of the buying center appear to hold open several options still, the manager may feel likewise; his/her freedom has been restored, not by a commitment to a threatened option but by elimination of the threat to freedom of choice. Demarketing to *key* buying-center members might still prove effective—even given this freedom-restoring alternative.

9. The nature of the demarketing communication and the communicator can affect the amount of reactance generated. Brehm (1968) suggests that a communication will appear as more of a threat, and thus generate more reactance, if it appears one-sided and unfair or if conclusions do not follow from the facts or arguments. Also, if the com-

municator tries too hard or has a vested interest in the recipient's adopt-
ing the advocated position, more reactance will be generated (Wicklund,
Slattum, and Solomon 1970).

10. Linder, Wortman, and Brehm (1971) established that the less time a
person has to make a decision, the more his/her freedoms are threatened and the more reactance is aroused. As a person moves towards the
point at which one alternative must be chosen, reactance emerges. The
salesperson may be able to capitalize on this naturally occurring reactance by using ostensible demarketing as a sales closing technique. By
demarketing specific features of a proposed solution when the customer
feels very threatened by having to make a choice, the reactance generated may well push the customer to insist on the demarketed alternative.

Reactance Theory versus Commodity Theory

We could suggest that commodity theory and the concept of scarcity (*cf.*
Brock 1968; Worchel, Lee, and Adewole 1975) be proposed as the basis for
ostensible demarketing. Brock views scarcity as the starting point for his
analysis and examines the direct and indirect behavioral consequences stemming from scarcity. A commodity will be valued to the extent that it is
perceived as unavailable or scarce.

Most commodity-theory research focuses on how the selective dissem-
ination of information or the restricted access to information enhances its
value and increases people's efforts to obtain it. The concept of scarcity of
information was extended to the idea of the scarcity of any commodity;
hence its applicability to purchasing behavior. The scarcity of a good influences the consumer's taste and preference for the good and increases
his/her attempts to obtain it. Fromkin et al. (1971) found such a response to
scarcity in their study of a new hosiery product.

Brock developed a series of eight hypotheses that explicate how the perceived unavailability of a commodity can be enhanced. Many of these com-
modification propositions have been empirically tested, mostly with respect
to information as a commodity.

Should this apparently simple notion of unavailability leading to increased desire for a product be accepted as the explanation of how ostensible demarketing functions? I suggest not. The main reason is that commodity theory lacks an underlying psychological mechanism that explains how
and why scarcity leads to increased desire. It is essentially a stimulus-
response theory with the eight hypotheses showing how the stimulus can be
enhanced to generate more response. Reactance theory, on the other hand,
proposes that the perceived restriction of freedom and the arousal of a

motivation labeled reactance intervenes between the stimulus and response. It is this mechanism that gives us the understanding of how reactance, and hence ostensible demarketing, may work. Clee and Wicklund (1980) go so far as to propose that reactance theory can explain commodity theory; hence the latter is subsumed under the former. Brock recognized the lack of a mechanism as a problem as he saw that "at present the theory lacks a dynamic explanatory principle" (1968). He suggests that a person's desire for uniqueness may be the motivation underlying the desire for scarce commodites. This does not seem to be a reasonable supposition in industrial buying, however, as one would expect the buyer to be more concerned with acquiring the best solution.

Overall, reactance theory appears more robust and useful and can be viewed as incorporating commodity theory. The use of the psychology of reactance seems to provide a definite approach to understanding ostensible demarketing.

Inducing Resistance to Persuasion

An incremental benefit of ostensible demarketing as a personal selling strategy is the customer's development of resistance to attacks leveled against the demarketed and subsequently chosen solution. Inducing resistance to persuasion focuses on the "uncovering of pretreatments which when applied to the person, make him less susceptible to persuasive messages than he is found to be without the pretreatments" (McGuire 1964). The ostensible demarketing strategy faces the customer with arguments against accepting the salesperson's proposal. This small dose of counterarguments inoculates the customer and prepares him/her for stronger arguments that could be put forth by others within his/her company or by suppliers offering different solutions.

While restoring freedom of choice by selecting the demarketed alternative, the customer justifies to the threatening agent (salesperson) why this alternative is appropriate, hence reinforcing the alternative's benefits. In addition, the customer addresses the salesperson's stated objections to the alternative. This interesting reversal of roles during the counterarguing process firmly fixes in the customer's mind the benefits of the solution to which s/he has become mentally committed and has also allowed for extensive rehearsal of the alternative's determinant benefits. Brehm suggests that "when a person is motivated by reactance to change his position on an issue, he may also seek information supportive of that change, be receptive to such information and be resistant to information that is disconfirmatory" (Brehm 1968).

McGuire (1964) conceived the concept of how different inoculation techniques build up resistance to attack. An effective defense provided to a buyer results in the buyer's recognizing the vulnerability of his/her beliefs to attack and also provides or develops information that gives the buyer the ability to defend him-/herself against attack (Ray 1968). Based on this, researchers have found (*cf.* McGuire and Papageorgis 1961) that refutational defenses in which the salesperson refutes the customer's beliefs confer greater resistance to subsequent persuasion than do arguments supporting his/her beliefs.

As in the case of reactance, there are circumstances under which inducing resistance will be more or less effective. Bither (1977) outlines the "situational domain of the construct," which suggests that the dimensions of the beliefs involved, the individual holding the beliefs, and the immunization treatment should be assessed to understand how effective the resulting inoculation might be. For example, the individual must be sufficiently committed to a belief and must have sufficient intellectual capacity to comprehend attacks on beliefs or attitudinal positions. These clues can be used by the salesperson to determine whether resistance can be developed through demarketing.

Two studies in the marketing literature focus on immunization. Bither, Dolich, and Nell (1971) studied the resistance to persuasion for a controversial belief: censorship of movies. Three factors were examined: level of immunization; level of attack; and prestige of the immunization source. Immunization provided some protection against subsequent attacks, even though the attacks induced some negative change in the attacked person's attitude. Bither, Dolich, and Nell's contribution to marketing was that their belief was not a cultural truism but a disputable belief (similar to a belief that a consumer could hold with respect to a product).

Szybillo and Heslin (1973) went even further in trying to test inoculation theory in a marketing context. The attacked belief concerned the use of air bags in cars; the inoculation and attack instruments consisted of advertisements. Predictions from inoculation theory were generally confirmed.

In summary, it is hypothesized that the resistance to persuasion induced by the demarketing strategy and associated counterarguing will allow the customer to fend off competitors offering alternatives to the demarketed solution. The customer also will be better prepared for any members of his/her organization who are in positions to question, challenge, or attempt to dissuade him/her from following through with the commitment to the ostensibly demarketed alternative. Heightened customer involvement in the sales interaction process resulting from the ostensible demarketing/reactance strategy develops into heightened resistance to persuasion.

Conclusion

Two areas require further comment. First, it may be valuable to gain some perspective on ostensible demarketing as a personal selling strategy by examining it in the context of a broader framework. The behavioral influence discussed in this chapter is just that; it is not an answer to successful selling. In Sheth's (1976) conceptual framework of buyer-seller interaction, ostensible demarketing would fit mainly into the "style of seller communication" dimension; if considered in this framework, it can be seen that many other factors, including the content of the communication, must be considered to be successful. Even though it is important to understand how and under what conditions behavioral influence strategies work, this should be kept in perspective.

Second, from a theoretical perspective, explanation of why this behavioral influence strategy may be successful enriches our understanding of the personal selling process. This crucial area—the final meeting of minds between the customer and salesperson—is underdeveloped in the research. I have tried to demonstrate that the starting point for further research in this area lies in attempting to establish the underlying process behind influence strategies. Based on this, further research can develop that would most likely involve experimental settings in which predictions from the conceptualization would actually be tested in the personal selling context. For example, with respect to demarketing, one would want to see if an experimental demarketing manipulation could generate a net positive change in attitude and purchase intention as predicted by the psychology of reactance. The determinants of reactance, such as felt competence, could also be tested in an experimental/personal selling context.

From a managerial perspective, then, increased understanding of how and under what conditions ostensible demarketing functions should lead to judicious use of the strategy. At a more general level, this chapter demonstrates how discovering the theoretical bases for often-used sales approaches enhances their use in the field.

References

Bither, Stewart W. (1977). "Resistance to Persuasion: Inoculation and Distraction." In *Consumer and Industrial Buying Behavior,* pp. 243–250. Edited by Arch G. Woodside, Jagdish N. Sheth, and Peter D. Bennett. New York: Elsevier North-Holland.

Bither, Stewart W.; Dolich, Ira J.; and Nell, Elaine B. (1971). "The Application of Attitude Immunization Techniques in Marketing." *Journal of Marketing Research* 8 (February):56–61.

Brehm, Jack W. (1966). *A Theory of Psychological Reactance.* New York: Academic Press.

Brehm, Jack W. (1968). "Attitude Change from Threat to Attitudinal Freedom." In *Psychological Foundations of Attitudes,* pp. 277–296. Edited by Anthony G. Greenwald, Timothy C. Brock, and Thomas M. Ostrom. New York: Academic Press.

Brehm, Jack W. (1972). *Responses to Loss of Freedom: A Theory of Psychological Reactance.* Morristown, N.J.: General Learning Press.

Brock, Timothy C. (1968). "Implications of Commodity Theory for Value Change." In *Psychological Foundations of Attitudes,* pp. 243–275. Edited by Anthony G. Greenwald, Timothy C. Brock, and Thomas M. Ostrom. New York: Academic Press.

Clee, Mona A., and Wicklund, Robert A. (1980). "Consumer Behavior and Psychological Reactance." *Journal of Consumer Research* 6 (March): 389–405.

Fromkin, Howard L.; Olson, Jerry C.; Dipboye, Robert L.; and Barnaby, David A. (1971). "A Commodity Theory Analysis of Consumer Preferences for Scarce Products." *Proceedings of the 79th Annual Convention of the APA* 6, 653–654.

Greibitz-Gniech, Gisla. (1971). "Some Restrictive Conditions for the Occurrence of Psychological Reactance." *Journal of Personality and Social Psychology* 19 (August):188–196.

Hammock, Thomas, and Brehm, Jack W. (1966). "The Attractiveness of Choice Alternatives when Freedom to Choose Is Eliminated by a Social Agent." *Journal of Personality* 34 (December):546–554.

Heilman, Madeline E. (1976). "Oppositional Behavior as a Function of Influence Attempt Intensity and Retaliation Threat." *Journal of Personality and Social Psychology* 33 (May):574–578.

Kotler, Philip, and Levy, Sidney J. (1971). "Demarketing, Yes, Demarketing." *Harvard Business Review* 49 (November–December):74–80.

Linder, Darwyn E.; Wortman, Camille B.; and Brehm, Jack W. (1971). "Temporal Changes in Predecision Preferences among Choice Alternatives." *Journal of Personality and Social Psychology* 19 (September): 282–284.

Mazis, Michael B.; Settle, Robert B.; and Leslie, Dennis C. (1973). "Elimination of Phosphate Detergents and Psychological Reactance." *Journal of Marketing Research* 10 (November):390–395.

McGuire, William J. (1964). "Inducing Resistance to Persuasion." In *Advances in Experimental Social Psychology,* Vol. 1, pp. 191–229. Edited by Leonard Berkowitz. New York: Academic Press.

McGuire, William J., and Papageorgis, Demetrios (1961). "The Relative Efficacy of Various Types of Prior Belief-Defense in Producing Immunity against Persuasion." *Journal of Abnormal and Social Psychology* 62 (March):327–337.

Myers, James H., and Alpert, Mark I. (1968). "Determinant Buying Attitudes: Meaning and Measurement." *Journal of Marketing* 32 (October):13–20.

Pallak, Michael S., and Heller, Jack F. (1971). "Interactive Effects of Commitment to Future Interaction and Threat to Attitudinal Freedom." *Journal of Personality and Social Psychology* 17 (March): 325–331.

Ray, Michael L. (1968). "Biases in Selection of Messages Designed to Induce Resistance to Persuasion." *Journal of Personality and Social Psychology* 9 August, 335–339.

Sensenig, John, and Brehm, Jack W. (1968). "Attitude Change from Threat to Attitudinal Freedom." *Journal of Personality and Social Psychology* 8 (April):324–330.

Sheth, Jagdish N. (1976). "Buyer-Seller Interaction: A Conceptual Framework." In *Advances in Consumer Research*, Vol. 3, pp. 382–386. Edited by Beverlee B. Anderson. Atlanta: Association for Consumer Research.

Szybillo, George J., and Heslin, Richard. (1973). "Resistance to Persuasion: Inoculation Theory in a Marketing Context." *Journal of Marketing Research* 10 (November):396–403.

Venkatesan, M. (1966). "Experimental Study of Consumer Behavior, Conformity and Independence." *Journal of Marketing Research* 3 (November):384–387.

Weiner, Judith, and Brehm, Jack W. (1966). "Buying Behavior as a Function of Verbal and Monetary Inducements." In Jack W. Brehm, *A Theory of Psychological Reactance,* pp. 82–90. New York: Academic Press.

Wicklund, Robert A.; Slattum, Valerie; and Solomon, Ellen. (1970). "Effects of Implied Pressure Toward Commitment on Ratings of Choice Alternatives." *Journal of Experimental Social Psychology* 6 (October):449–457.

Worchel, Stephen, and Brehm, Jack W. (1971). "Direct and Implied Social Restoration of Freedom." *Journal of Personality and Social Psychology* 18 (June):294–304.

Worchel, Stephen; Lee, Jerry; and Adewole, Akanbi. (1975). "Effects of Supply and Demand on Ratings of Object Value." *Journal of Personality and Social Psychology* 32 (November):906–914.

Yalch, Richard F. (1979). "Closing Sales: Compliance Gaining Strategies for Personal Selling." In *Sales Management: New Developments from Behavioral and Decision Model Research,* pp. 187–198. Edited by Richard P. Bagozzi. Cambridge, Mass.: Marketing Science Institute.

7

Sales Effectiveness through Adaptation to Situational Demands

Barton A. Weitz

In 1981, the average cost of an industrial sales call was \$178.00 (McGraw-Hill Research, 1982*a*). Since 5.1 calls typically were required to close an industrial sale, the average selling cost associated with each sale was \$907.80. This average selling cost per sales call increased at the rate of 25 percent per year between 1979 and 1981 (McGraw-Hill Research, 1982*b*). These rapidly increasing sales costs illustrate the need to improve sales force productivity.

One approach is to replace traditional face-to-face personal selling with less costly communication vehicles such as telemarketing, direct response marketing, industrial stores, and demonstration centers (Shapiro and Wyman 1981). This chapter focuses on another approach for improving productivity: increasing the effectiveness of the salesperson.

Sales management techniques for improving salesperson productivity can be classified in terms of the two components of job performance: *effort* and *ability*. Effort is related to the quantity of work performed by the salesperson, whereas ability is related to the quality of the work performed. Motivation programs; time mangement training; efficient allocation of salespeople across products, customers, and territories; and the selection of highly motivated individuals are directed toward increasing the level of effort expended by salespeople. Improvements in ability are achieved through the careful selection of people with sales abilities and training programs directed toward improving sales skills and product knowledge.

This chapter concentrates on a specific sales skill, adapting sales behaviors to meet the needs of the sales situation, and suggests how academic research and sales training programs can be directed toward improving sales effectiveness through increasing our understanding of how to select, train, and motivate adaptive salespeople.

Importance of Adaptive Selling

The importance of adaptive sales skills to salesperson effectiveness can be illustrated by a review of the results of empirical research on effective sales behaviors and by an examination of the unique properties of personal selling as a marketing communication vehicle.

123

Research on Effective Sales Behaviors

Over the last twenty years, a substantial amount of research has been directed toward identifying sales behaviors or behavioral predispositions (personality traits) related to sales effectiveness (see Weitz 1979 for a detailed review). The results have been equivocal. In some studies, a behavioral predisposition such as forcefulness was related to sales effectiveness, whereas in other studies forcefulness was not related to effectiveness. Social orientation was related to performance in some studies and unrelated in others. Furthermore, some results are contradictory. Greenberg and Mayer (1964) report consistent positive relationships between empathy and sales performance, whereas Lamont and Lundstrom (1977) found that empathy was marginally significant and negatively related to sales performance.

Finally, a number of studies have examined the impact of specific sales behaviors. These tightly controlled experimental studies also have failed to uncover consistently effective sales behaviors. There were no significant differences in effectiveness for product-oriented versus personal-oriented messages (Farley and Swinth 1967); hard sell, emotional appeals versus soft sell rational appeals (Reizenstein 1971); or six different appeals based on Bales Interaction Process Analysis categories (Capon 1975). In fact, the use of a customer-oriented selling approach is more effective in some selling situations than others (Saxe and Weitz 1982).

The lack of consistent results from this research on selling effectivenes may be due to the underlying premise. These research efforts have attempted to uncover behaviors or behavioral predispositions that enable salespeople to perform effectively across a wide range of sales situations. Thus these studies have attempted to answer the following types of questions: Are aggressive salespeople more effective than passive salespeople? Are salespeople who use rational appeals more effective than those who use emotional appeals? The results suggest that sometimes aggressive behavior is more effective than passive behavior and sometimes rational appeals are more effective than emotional appeals.

The conclusion therefore is that there are no universally effective sales behaviors. The effectiveness of a sales behavior is contingent upon characteristics of the sales situation (Weitz 1981). "Every contact a salesman has . . . involves different human problems or situations. In brief there is no one sales situation and no one way sell" (Thompson 1973, p. 8). Thus effective salespeople need to adapt their sales approach to the specific situation in which they are engaging.

*Personal Selling as a Marketing
Communication Vehicle*

In fact, the personal selling research directed toward uncovering universally effective sales behaviors has ignored the unique advantage of personal selling as a marketing communication vehicle. Personal selling is the only marketing communication vehicle that has an opportunity to match the marketing message to the specific customer's needs and beliefs. Salespeople can do market research on each customer and develop a unique marketing message that is maximally effective for that customer. In addition, they can observe the customer's reaction to the marketing communications (the sales presentation) and make real time alterations.

In contrast, marketing managers must aggregate customers into segments in order to communicate effectively with them through advertising, sales promotion, and packaging vehicles. Although marketing managers collect market research information in a more systematic manner, their information is indirect, filtered by the marketing research process. Marketing managers are left with an abstract description of typical customers in a market segment rather than a description of a specific individual. Since they must develop communication strategies based on a typical customer, advertising strategies will be most effective with a small group of customers similar to the typical customer. In addition, due to the substantial delay and error involved in monitoring customer reactions to advertising, marketing managers have limited ability to make adjustments based on customer feedback (Weitz and Wright 1978).

Even though most empirical research has ignored this unique advantage of personal selling, academics and practitioners have recognized the importance of this adaptive capability to selling effectiveness. Adaptive behavior is incorporated in many models of the sales process (Green and Tonning 1979; Grikscheits and Crissy 1973; Hakansson, Johanson, and Wootz 1977; Robertson and Chase 1968; Spiro, Perreault, and Reynolds 1976; and Weitz 1978) and sales training programs developed by Wilson Learning and Xerox Learning Systems.

Managerial Implications

Since the effectiveness of a sales approach varies with the nature of the sales situation, there are two approaches for increasing personal selling productivity by improving sales ability and skills: (1) Management can recruit and train salespeople who are specialists in one type of sales behavior and have them sell only to customers for which that sales approach is effective; (2) management can recruit and train salespeople who are effective at adapting their behavior to the sales situation.

The use of specialized sales forces implements the first approach (Kahn and Shuchman 1971). Through this, the variety of sales situations encountered by a salesperson is reduced. For example, if the sales forces are specialized by customer type, one computer salesperson will only call on retail establishments whereas another salesperson will only call on financial institutions. Thus the retail-institutions salesperson can develop specialized sales skills and product knowledge that are effective with retail customers. Since the salesperson only calls on retail customers, the salesperson can use the same sales approach on all of his/her customers. The second approach presumes that the salesperson encounters a wide variety of sales situations. Thus, to be effective, s/he needs to develop adaptive rather than specialized skills.

The effectiveness of each approach depends upon the variance between sales situations within a customer group versus the variance between the typical sales situation across customer groups. The specialized sales force will be most effective when the variance across groups is much greater than the variance within groups. However, the second approach based on adaptive skills is needed when there is high within-group variance.

In general, there will always be substantial within-group variance. Not all retail institutions are the same, and there are substantial individual differences within each institution. The appropriate sales approach will vary depending on the nature of buying task and the specific individuals in the buying center. It is unlikely that the variance between sales situations can be reduced through segmentation and specialization to the point where adaptive selling skills are no longer needed. In fact, if such segmentation could be done, the need for personal selling would be eliminated. Under these circumstances, marketing communications could be delivered through less adaptive, more cost-effective vehicles such as advertising, direct response marketing, and telemarketing.

Adaptive Selling and Sales Effectiveness

In this section, adaptive selling is defined and some research concerning the use of adaptive selling is reviewed. Then a model refuting adaptive selling to sales effectiveness is presented. The section concludes with a discussion of the skills needed to be an effective adaptor.

Definition of Adaptive Selling

Salespeople practice adaptive selling when they alter their sales behavior during a customer interaction or across customer interactions based on information about the nature of the sales situation. Delivering the same canned sales presentation (Jolson 1975) to all customers would be an extreme example of non-adaptive behavior. In contrast to this non-adaptive behavior, salespeople are extremely adaptive when they employ unique sales behaviors for each customer and even alter their behavior during the interaction. Thus the variance in sales behavior across and within interactions is a measure of the degree to which a salesperson practices adaptive selling.

Adaptive selling can be effective or ineffective; simply altering sales behaviors is not enough. Effectiveness depends on selecting the appropriate level of adaptation and selecting the appropriate sales behaviors. There is an optimal level of adaptation in sales behavior. Both too little and too much adaptation can result in using inappropriate sales behaviors. This optimal level of adaptation occurs when the variance in sales situations matches the variance in sales behaviors. Even if salespeople employ the appropriate level of adaptation, their effectiveness depends on the degree to which they use the appropriate sales behavior for the sitaution in which they are engaging.

Some dimensions on which sales behaviors can be adapted include:

1. base of influence established—expert, referent, coercive, legitimate, or reward power bases.
2. influence technique used—open versus closed, rational versus emotional.
3. cognitive element toward which messages are directed—specific beliefs and values or importance weights.
4. communication style—aggressive versus passive, high pressure versus low pressure.
5. message format employed—one-sided versus two-sided.
6. services, delivery dates, price, terms offered.

It seems reasonable to assume the effectiveness of influence bases, influence techniques, specific messages and formats and communication style varies across situations encountered by a salesperson. Thus salespeople could increase their effectiveness by making appropriate adjustments in their behavior along the above-mentioned dimensions.

Research on Adaptive Selling

While little empirical research has examined adaptive behavior directly, there is some evidence that salespeople do adapt their behavior based on perceptions of their customers and that such adaptation does result in improved sales performance. In a field experiment, Wise (1974) found that the price quoted and treatment offered to customers by automobile salespeople varied as a function of customer's race and dress style. While the objective of this study was to determine the extent to which race and socioeconomic status affects treatment in the marketplace, the results indicate that salespeople use visual cues to alter their sales behaviors.

Spiro and Perrault (1979) found relationships between influence tactics used by wholesale salespeople during a customer interaction and characteristics of the interaction. The consistency of the findings suggest that salespeople adapt their influence tactics to specific characteristics of the interaction; however, the adaptation of a salesperson across customers was not examined explicitly.

Although studies indicate that salespeople adapt their behaviors in terms of influence tactics, price quoted, and treatment offered, descriptive studies of retail appliance salespeople indicated the level of adaptation is limited. More variation in attributes discussed (Olshavsky 1973) and types of comments made (Willett and Pennington 1966) were found across salespeople than across customers for a salesperson. This suggests that the salespeople used a similar sales approach for each of their customers.

Model of Adaptive Selling

A model relating adaptive selling to sales effectiveness is shown in figure 7–1. This model indicates that dispositional and organizational characteristics motivate salespeople to engage in adaptive selling. However, adaptive selling is not directly related to sales effectiveness. The relationship between adaptive selling and sales effectiveness is moderated by (1) the variance in the selling situations encountered by the salesperson, (2) the resources available to the salesperson, and (3) the salesperson's skills for engaging in adaptive selling. These three factors result in a strong relationship between adaptive selling and sales effectiveness. In other words, they determine the effectiveness of adaptive selling.

The impact of situational variance on the effectiveness of adaptive selling has been discussed previously. Clearly, if salespeople face little situational variance, varying their sales behaviors has a negative impact on their selling effectiveness. Thus situational variance provides the opportunity for effective adaptive selling.

However, to be effective at adaptive selling, salespeople must possess the resources to appropriately alter their behavior. When salespeople are selling a broad product line or products with many features and options, they have a greater opportunity to tailor their presentation to meet the needs of their customers. Thus companies give their salespeople more opportunities to practice adaptive selling when they offer products and product lines for which a wide range of sales presentation can be developed.

In addition, salespeople need internal resources to practice effective adaptive selling. They need the knowledge and skills to select the appropriate sales behavior for the situation. To be effective adaptors, salespeople need to have (1) a wide range of customer stereotypes, (2) an ability to correctly classify customers, and (3) a set of contingency selling theories that enable the salesperson to select an appropriate sales behavior for the customer.

The three salesperson characteristics needed for effective adaptive selling are closely related to the first, second, and fifth step in the ISTEA (im-

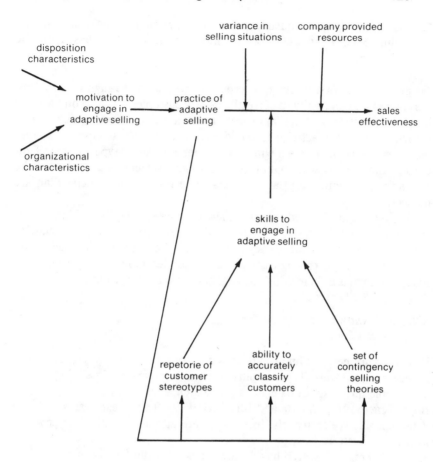

Figure 7-1. Adaptive Selling and Sales Effectiveness

pression formation, strategy selection, transmission of messages, evaluation of impact, and adaptation) sales process model (Weitz 1978). The ISTEA model suggests that salespeople engage in the following activities during a sales interaction:

1. develop an accurate impression of the customer by collecting information through observation and direct questions
2. use information contained in this impression to formulate an effective influence strategy
3. implement the influence strategy by developing and transmitting messages
4. evaluate the effects of the transmitted messages by assessing the customer's reactions through additional observation and questions

5. make appropriate adjustments in the impression of the customer, the influence strategy used, or the messages transmitted based on the evaluation.

To perform the first activity, salespeople need a wide range of customer stereotypes and an ability to correctly classify customers. The second activity involves selecting a sales approach from a set of contingency selling theories. The fifth activity is based on an ability to uncover customer behavior that is inconsistent with the salesperson's stereotypes. Research indicates that experts with elaborated knowledge structures use more of the available information and are better at detecting inconsistencies than are novices.

Finally, figure 7–1 indicates the mere practice of adaptive selling will increase the salesperson's repertoire of stereotypes, ability to classify customer, and set of contingency theories. By altering their sales behaviors, salespeople will go through a trial and error learning process that, over time, will increase their skills for engaging in adaptive selling.

Skills and Knowledge Needed for Adaptive Selling

People do not perceive an infinite variety of objects, social events, or people in their environments. They simplify their environment by classifying objects and people into a set of categories (*cf.* Rosch, Mervis, Gray, Johnson, and Boyes-Braen 1976; Cantor and Mischael 1979). The categorization scheme determines how effective the individuals are at dealing with their environment.

For example, research has demonstrated that the quality of chess playing exhibited by expert and novice players is in part determined by differences in their categorization schemes for patterns of pieces on a chess board (Chase and Simon 1973). Expert chess players have a very elaborate scheme for categorizing configurations of chess pieces. They recognize a wide variety of patterns and have a well-developed set of rules describing how to proceed when a particular pattern arises. In addition, experts are able to quickly distinguish patterns that occur infrequently or are inconsistent with some basic principles of chess play. On the other hand, novice chess players have difficulty recognizing patterns of chess pieces and thus do not have a variety of contingency rules for playing based on the configuration of pieces. When chess pieces are placed randomly on a chess board, experts immediately recognize the pattern as atypical, while novices do not. However, the quality of subsequent play by experts relative to novices is degraded because the experts are not able to draw upon their existing categorization scheme and contingency rules to determine the appropriate course of action.

Based on this research, one would hypothesize that expert salespeople have a more elaborate scheme for classifying customers and sales situations than do novices. Novices see all sales situations as the same and therefore they use the same sales approach in all situations. Experts are able to recognize a wide variety (although not an infinite variety) of sales situations.

In addition, experts have a theory for how to successfully sell in each situation. These contingency theories are a set of "if . . . then" propositions such as:

> if the sales situation involves a hostile customer making an involving purchase about which he has little prior experience or knowledge, I should first attempt to develop rapport with the customer to reduce the hostility level. Then I should spend considerable time educating the customer about the factors that should be considered in making a purchase decision.

These contingency selling theories are analogous to the productions discussed in problem solving contexts by Newell and Simon (1972).

In addition to an elaborated knowledge structure concerning sales situations, effective adaptation requires skills in using this knowledge structure. Effective adaptation will only occur if salespeople are able to collect information about a sales situation and use this information to correctly classify the sales situation.

Measures of Knowledge Structures and
Adaptive Skills

There are no well accepted methods for measuring the degree of elaboration of an individual's knowledge structure. Suggested approaches are based on presenting salespeople with different sales situations and asking them to describe the situations and/or their behavior in the situation. For example, salespeople could be presented with brief descriptions of eight sales situations generated from combinations of the following three factors: (1) customer has purchased the product before versus not purchased before; (2) customer has a good relationship versus a poor relationship with the salesperson; and (3) purchase decision is important versus unimportant to the customer. Then the salespeople would be asked to list all of their thoughts concerning each of these eight situations. A measure of the degree of similarity for thoughts across situations would be developed. High similarity would indicate low elaboration of knowledge structure (few stereotypes) while low similarity would indicate high elaboration (many stereotypes).

Kelly's (1955) Role Construct Repertory (Rep) Test is typically used as a measure of cognitive complexity and could be used as a measure of the complexity of a salesperson's knowledge structure for sales situations. The salesperson would be asked to list ten customers. Then s/he would be asked to indicate which customers are the most similar, which are the least similar, and why the customers are the most similar and the least similar. Using this information, a measure of knowledge-structure complexity can be developed.

There has been some research directed toward examining adaptive behavior in salespeople that explored simultaneously both the knowledge structure and adaptive skills. Grikscheidt (1971) used a unique methodology to study adaptive behavior. In his study, salespeople viewed a film of a customer-salesperson interaction. Ten times during the interactions, the salespeople were asked to list the verbal and non-verbal cues they observed about the customer in the film. In addition, they were asked to indicate what sales strategy they would use if they were the salesperson in the film. Thus this study explored the degree to which salespeople collect information about customers and how this information is used to develop sales strategies.

Similarly, Weitz (1978) studied the ability of salespeople to understand the needs and beliefs of their customers and to use this information about customers to develop sales strategies. He found that sales performance was significantly related to the accuracy of information about customers and the quality of sales strategies selected.

Developing Adaptive Selling Capabilities

In this section, training and motivation approaches for developing adaptive selling capabilities are examined.

Training Adaptive Salespeople

There are two training approaches for developing the skills and knowledge required for adaptive selling: (1) sales training can be used to teach salespeople a set of customer stereotypes, rules for classifying customers, and contingency sales approaches to be used when interacting with the different types of customers. The training program developed by the Wilson Learning Corporation of Edina, Minnesota is an example of this approach for developing adaptive salespeople (Ingrasci 1981).

Communication Style Matrix. The Wilson Learning Corporation Program provides a set of stereotypes, identification rules, and contingency selling approaches. In this program, salespeople are taught that there are four basic types of customers (and salespeople). This categorization scheme, shown in figure 7–2, is based on the social style of the customer as defined by customer's behavior on two dimensions: assertiveness and responsiveness. Assertiveness is the amount of effort people use to influence the thoughts and actions of others, whereas responsiveness is the amount of effort that people use to control their emotions when relating to others.

Using the dimensions of assertiveness and responsiveness, the following four customer stereotypes are developed: (1) analytical style (system specialist), (2) driver style (control specialist), (3) amiable style (support specialist), and (4) expressive style (relations specialists).

After developing the set of stereotypes, the Wilson Learning Program provides a set of rules for classifying customers. Some of these cues for recognizing the social style of the customer are shown in table 7–1. Knowing these cues, salespeople can classify customers by simply observing them

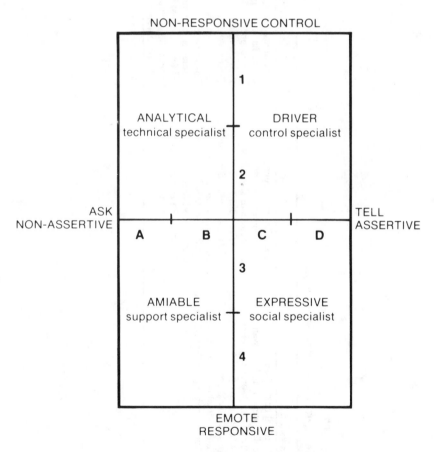

Figure 7–2. Types of Sales Behaviors

Table 7-1
Cues for Recognizing Social Styles

Analyticals	Drivers	Amiables	Expressives
Technical background	Technical background	Liberal arts background	Liberal arts background
Achievement awards on wall	Achievement awards on wall	Office has friendly, open atmosphere	Motivational slogan on wall
Office is work-oriented, showing a lot of activity	No posters or slogans on office walls	Pictures of family displayed	Office has friendly, open atmosphere
Conservative dress	Calendar prominently displayed	Personal mementos on wall	Cluttered, unorganized desk
Prefer individual leisure activities such as reading, individual sports	Desk placed so that contact with people is across desk	Desk placed for open contact with people	Desk placed for open contact with people
	Conservative dress	Casual or flamboyant dress	Casual or flamboyant dress
	Prefer group activities such as politics, team sports	Prefer individual leisure activities such as reading, individual sports	Prefer group activities such as politics, team sports

and the place in which they work and asking a few simple questions. In addition, the training program provides information that enables the salespeople to classify themselves into one of the four basic stereotypes.

Then the training program offers a set of contingency selling approaches. These "if . . . then" rules are based on the classification of the salesperson and the customer. The basic principle is for the salespeople to alter their communications style so that it is in congruence with the customer's communication style. For example, if a driver salesperson is interacting with an analytical customer, then the salesperson should reduce assertiveness by asking for the customer's opinions, listening without interruption, and letting the customer direct the flow of the conversation. However, if the driver salesperson is interacting with an expressive customer, then the salesperson should increase responsiveness by verbalizing feelings, expressing enthusiasm, and spending more time on relationships than business.

This extended discussion of the Wilson Learning Program should not be taken as an endorsement of the program. It simply illustrates how one popular sales training program provides salespeople with the three key ingredients for effective adaptive selling: (1) a set of customer stereotypes, (2) rules for classifying customers, and (3) contingency selling approaches. Little academic research has been done to demonstrate the effectiveness of the specific knowledge structure instilled by the Wilson Learning Corporation's approach. Thus a number of unanswered questions remain: Do the two dimensions capture the critical aspects of communication style? Are the four stereotypes appropriate for all sales situations? Are stereotypes based simply on communication style (as opposed to customer needs) adequate for developing effective sales approaches? Are four stereotypes sufficient or do salespeople need a richer repertoire? Can customers be accurately classified using the cues shown in table 7-1? Does the communication style congruence principle on which the contingency sales approaches are based increase the effectiveness of influence attempts?

Providing Idiosyncratic Knowledge Structures and Skills. Rather than using a general purpose set of stereotypes, companies can develop a set of stereotypes, classification rules, and contingency selling approaches that are idiosyncratic to their selling environments. One possible approach would be to tap knowledge structures and skills for the best salespeople working for the company. Presumably these expert salespeople have developed the knowledge and rules required to be effective in the selling environment facing the company.

There are no well-developed methodologies for collecting information about a salesperson's knowledge structure, although such structures for simple tasks such as ordering a meal in a restaurant have been examined (Bower, Black, and Turner 1979). However, the procedures used to collect this information might not be appropriate when examining the more complex selling tasks that includes a number of contingencies.

Perhaps a cognitive response methodology could be used to develop idiosyncratic knowledge structures. High- and low-performing salespeople would be videotaped as they interact in a series of role playing exercises. Then the salespeople would be asked to verbalize their thoughts during the role play as they watched a videotape replay. These recalled thoughts or retrospective cognitive responses would reveal the knowledge structure and decision rules used by the salespeople. During the videotape replay, the salespeople would identify specific cues and the subsequent sales behaviors triggered by the cues. A comparison of cognitive responses collected from high- and low-performance salespeople would suggest aspects of knowledge structures potentially related to sales performance. This information could then be used to develop a training program that would educate salespeople so that they would possess the knowledge structure and decision rules of the best salespeople.

Learning Knowledge Structures and Skills. To develop adaptive sales skills through the Wilson Learning Program or the development of idiosyncratic programs, an appropriate knowledge structure is determined and then this knowledge structure is transferred to trainees through an educational process. Another approach for developing adaptive selling capabilities is to facilitate the process by which salespeople develop their own knowledge structure for adaptive selling. Rather than teaching a specific set of stereotypes and contingency selling rules to salespeople, in this approach the salespeople would be placed in a training environment in which they would be encouraged to develop their own stereotypes and rules.

Such learning could be achieved by exposing salespeople to a wide variety of selling situations using role playing exercises. After participating in the role playing exercise, the sales trainees would be asked to indicate why they engaged in specific behaviors during the role play. Such retrospective analysis would encourage salespeople to think about how their sales behaviors are related to specific cues in the sales environment. This thinking process should emphasize the need to engage in adaptive selling and lead to the development of stereotypes and decision rules for simply the process of selecting an appropriate sales behavior.

Motivating Salespeople to Engage in
Adaptive Selling

As the model in figure 7–1 suggests, salespeople can develop their adaptive capabilities by simply practicing adaptive selling. By altering their sales behaviors and observing the effects of sales behaviors in different situations, salespeople will improve their adaptive capabilities through a trial-

and-error learning process. Given that the mere practice of adaptive selling, over time, improves the effectiveness of adaptive selling, it becomes important to motivate salespeople to engage in adaptive selling. A model describing the factors affecting motivation of salespeople is shown in figure 7-3.

There are three facets of motivated behavior: intensity, persistence, and choice (Atkinson 1964). When salespeople are motivated to increase the intensity of their work, they will be more energetic. Salespeople can also be motivated to increase their persistence and thus encouraged to spend longer hours attempting to realize a goal.

Both the intensity and persistence aspects of motivation are non-directional. They are related to the quantity of effort expended, not to the goals or behaviors toward which the effort is directed. However, the third facet of motivation, choice, has a directional aspect. When salespeople are motivated to choose between alternative behaviors, they will analyze and evaluate alternatives to select an appropriate behavior. The choice aspect of motivation is directed toward getting salespeople to work smarter. Working *smarter* involves analyzing sales situations and selecting among alternative sales approaches. On the other hand, the intensity and persistence aspect of motivation is associated with getting salespeople to work *harder*.

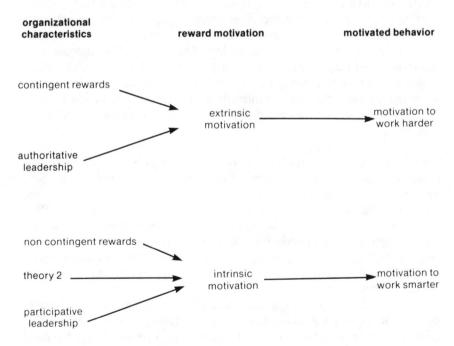

Figure 7-3. Motivation to Engage in Adaptive Selling

Research on salesperson motivation has focused on the working-harder aspects of motivation and largely ignored the working-smarter aspect of motivation (see Walker, Churchill, and Ford 1977). However, the working-smarter aspect of motivation is directly related to motivating salespeople to practice adaptive selling and eventually learning to improve their adaptive selling capabilities through practice.

Reward Orientation and Motivated Behavior. Figure 7–3 indicates that the degree to which salespeople are motivated to work harder or smarter is a result of their reward orientation.

There are two reward orientations: extrinsic and intrinsic. When salespeople have an extrinsic reward orientation, they engage in selling activities because they wish to get externally mediated rewards such as pay, promotions, or achievement awards. Salespeople with an intrinsic reward orientation engage in selling activities because they get a reward from simply performing the activities. They enjoy selling, the challenge of influencing customers, and the opportunity to exercise their selling skills.

When salespeople have an intrinsic reward orientation, they are motivated to learn how to improve their selling skills. They want to try new approaches, to think about why certain approaches have been effective while others have been ineffective, and to analyze the nature of the selling situations confronting them. On the other hand, salespeople with an extrinsic reward orientation are motivated to increase the amount of effort expended on selling rather than improve the quality of their effort. Salespeople with an extrinsic reward orientation are motivated to work harder, while salespeople with an intrinsic reward orientation are motivated to work smarter. When management develops an intrinsic reward orientation in salespeople, the salespeople will be motivated to alter their sales behaviors in different sales situations.

Organizational Factors and Reward Motivation. Figure 7–3 indicates some organizational factors than influence the reward motivation of salespeople. Research indicates that contingent rewards—based on performance—increase extrinsic motivation and reduces intrinsic motivation (Deci 1975, Pittman, Emery, and Boggiano 1982). Individuals engaging in an activity with contingent rewards tend to focus on the reward rather than the task. Thus salespeople compensated by straight commission will be more extrinsically motivated while salespeople compensated by straight salary will be more intrinsically motivated.

Organizational culture can influence the reward motivation of salespeople. Ouchi and his colleagues (Ouchi 1981; Ouchi and Jaeger 1978; Ouchi and Price 1978) have examined a number of American firms that have an organizational culture similar to Japanese firms. These firms, referred to as Type Z, are characterized by stable, long-term employment; an identifiable management philosophy; and the use of informal, non-hierarchical versus formal, hierarchical control mechanisms. Due to the nature of Type Z organizations, employees tend to develop a close identification with their company and their work, and thus they develop a strong intrinsic reward orientation.

Finally, the leadership style of first-level sales management can affect the reward orientation of salespeople. Participative leaders provide feedback to salespeople and encourage salespeople to participate in decision making. The feedback and participation should foster an intrinsic reward orientation. On the other hand, authoritarian leaders probably focus the attention of salespeople away from the intrinsic rewards in the job and toward extrinsic rewards the job offers.

Conclusion

Effective personal selling requires salespeople to adapt their sales approach to meet the demands of sales situation. No single sales approach is effective in all sales situations. Even though adaptive selling is a critical aspect of effective selling, little research has been directed toward identifying the capabilities needed to practice effective adaptive selling and measuring the extent to which these capabilities are possessed by salespeople. This chapter proposes that effective adaptive selling requires a rich knowledge structure composed of a variety of customer stereotypes, rules for classifying customers, and a set of contingency selling approaches. Some measures of the knowledge structure are suggested. In addition, research needs to be directed toward developing methods for improving the adaptive capabilities of salespeople and motivating salespeople to practice adaptive selling. One method for improving adaptive capabilities is providing salespeople with a knowledge structure. Another promising approach is facilitating the process by which salespeople can develop their own knowledge structure. By providing an organizational climate and reward structure conducive to the development of an intrinsic reward orientation, salespeople will be motivated to work smarter: to try new sales approaches, learn from their mistakes, and improve their adaptive selling capabilities.

References

Atkinson, J.W. (1964). *An Introduction to Motivation.* Princeton, N.J.: Van Nostrand.

Bower, Gordan H.; John B. Black; and Terrence J. Turner (1979). "Scripts in Memory for Text." *Cognitive Psychology* II (April):177–220.

Cantor, N., and W. Mischel (1979). "Prototypes in Person Perception." In L. Berkowitz (ed.), *Advances in Experimental Social Psychology*, Vol. 12. New York: Academic Press.

Capon, Noel (1975). "Persuasive Effects of Sales Messages Developed from Interaction Process Analysis." *Journal of Applied Psychology* 60 (April):238–244.

Chase, William G., and Herbert A. Simon (1973). "Perceptions in Chess." *Cognitive Psychology* 4 (January):55–81.

Deci, E.L. (1975). *Intrinsic Motivation.* New York: Plenum Press.

Farley, John, and R. Swinth (1967). "Effects of Choice and Sales Message on Customer-Salesman Interaction." *Journal of Applied Psychology* 51 (April):107–110.

Green, Paul C., and Wayland A. Tonning (1979). "The Behavior Process Model of the Sales Interview." In R. Bagozzi (ed.), *Sales Management: New Developments from Behavioral and Decision Model Research.* Cambridge, Mass.: Marketing Science Institute.

Greenberg, Herbert, and David Mayer (1964). "A New Approach to the Scientific Selection of Successful Salesmen." *Journal of Psychology* 57 (January):113–123.

Grikscheit, Gary M. (1971). "An Investigation of the Ability of Salesmen to Monitor Feedback." Ph.D. dissertation, Michigan State University.

Grikscheit, Gary M., and William J.E. Crissy (1973). "Improving Interpersonal Communication Skills." *MSU Business Topics* 21 (Autumn): 63–68.

Hakansson, Hakan; Jan Johanson; and Bjorn Wootz (1977). "Influence Tactics in Buyer-Seller Processes." *Industrial Marketing Management* 5 (Fall):319–332.

Ingrasci, Hugh J. (1981). "How to Reach Buyers in their Psychological 'Comfort Zone.' " *Industrial Marketing* (July):60–64.

Jolson, Marvin A. (1975). "The Underestimated Potential of the Canned Sales Presentation." *Journal of Marketing* 39 (January):75–78.

Kahn, George N., and Abraham Shuchman (1961). "Specialize Your Salesmen!," *Harvard Business Review* 39 (January/February):90–98.

Kelly, George A. (1955). *The Psychology of Personal Constructs*, Vols. 1 and 2. New York: Norton.

Lamont, Lawrence M., and William J. Lundstrom (1977). "Identifying Successful Industrial Salesmen by Personality and Personal Characteristics." *Journal of Marketing Research* 14 (November):517–529.

McGraw-Hill Research (1982*a*). "An Industrial Sales Call Now Costs $178.00." LAP Report #8013-6. Laboratory for Advertising Performance/McGraw-Hill Research.

McGraw-Hill Research (1982*b*). "Average Cost to Close an Industrial Sale Increases to $907.80." LAP Report #8051-1. Laboratory for Advertising Performance/McGraw-Hill Research.

Newell, Alan, and Herbert A. Simon (1972). *Human Problem Solving.* Englewood Cliffs, N.J.: Prentice-Hall.

Olshavsky, Richard W. (1973). "Customer-Salesmen Interaction in Appliance Retailing." *Journal of Marketing Research* 10 (May):208-212.

Ouchi, William (1982). *Theory Z: How American Business Can Meet the Japanese Challenge.* Reading, Mass.: Addison-Wesley.

Ouchi, William, and A.M. Jaeger (1978). "Type 2 Corporation: Stability in the Midst of Mobility." *Academy of Management Review*, April, 293-317.

Ouchi, William, and Raymond L. Price (1978). "Hierarchies, Clans, and Theory 2: A New Perspective on Organization Development." *Organizational Dynamics*, Autumn, 25-44.

Pittman, Thane S.; Jolee Emery; and Ann U. Boggiano (1982). "Intrinsic and Extrinsic Motivation Orientation: Reward Induced Changes in Preference for Complexity." *Journal of Personality and Social Psychology* 42 (May):787-797.

Reizenstein, Richard C. (1971). "A Dissonance Approach to Measuring the Effectiveness of Two Personal Selling Techniques through Decision Reversal." *Proceedings*, Fall Conference. Chicago: American Marketing Association, pp. 176-180.

Robertson, Thomas S., and Richard B. Chase (1968). "The Sales Process: An Open System Approach." *MSU Business Topics* 16 (Autumn): 45-52.

Rosch, Eleanore; Carol B. Mervis; Wayne D. Gray; David M. Johnson; and Perry Boyes-Braen (1976). "Basic Objects in Natural Categories." *Cognitive Psychology* 8, 382-439.

Saxe, Robert, and Barton A. Weitz (1982). "The Customer Orientation of Salespeople: Measurement and Relationship to Performance." *Journal of Marketing Research* 19 (August):343-351.

Shapiro, Benson P., and John Wyman (1981). "New Ways to Reach Your Consumers." *Harvard Business Review* 59 (July-August):103-110.

Spiro, Rosann L., and William D. Perreault, Jr. (1979). "Influence Used by Industrial Salesmen: Influence Strategy Mixes and Situational Determinants." *Journal of Business* 52 (July):435-455.

Spiro, Rosann L.; William D. Perreault, Jr.; and Fred D. Reynolds (1976). "The Selling Process: A Critical Review and Model." *Industrial Marketing Management* 5 (December):351-363.

Thompson, Joseph W. (1973). *Selling: A Managerial and Behavioral Science Analysis.* New York: McGraw-Hill.

Walker, O.C., Jr.; G.A. Churchill; and W.M. Ford (1977). "Motivation and Performance in Industrial Selling: Existing Knowledge and Needed Research." *Journal of Marketing Research* 14 (May):156-168.

Weitz, Barton A. (1978). "The Relationship Between Salesperson Performance and Understanding of Customer Decision Making." *Journal of Marketing Research* 15 (November):501-516.

Weitz, Barton A. (1979). "A Critical Review of Personal Selling Research: The Need for a Contingency Approach." In G. Albaum and G. Churchill (eds.), *Critical Issues in Sales Management: State-of-the-Art and Future Research Needs*. Eugene, Oreg.: University of Oregon, College of Business Administration.

Weitz, Barton A. (1981). "Effectiveness in Sales Interactions: A Contingency Framework." *Journal of Marketing* 45 (Winter):85–103.

Weitz, Barton A., and Peter Wright (1978). "The Salesperson as a Marketing Strategist: The Relationship Between Field Sales Performance and Insights About One's Customers." MSI Working Paper No. 78–120. Cambridge, Mass.: Marketing Science Institute.

Willett, Ronald P., and Alan L. Pennington (1966). "Customer and Salesman: The Anatomy of Choice and Influence in a Retail Setting." In Raymond M. Hass (ed.), *Science, Technology, and Marketing*. Chicago: American Marketing Association, pp. 598–616.

Wise, Gordon L. (1974). "Differential Pricing and Treatment by New Car Salesmen: The Effects of Prospect's Race, Sex, and Dress." *Journal of Business* 47 (April):218–230.

8 Bargaining Behavior in Personal Selling and Buying Exchanges

Arch G. Woodside

Browne (1976) provides a useful definition of bargaining behavior: a compromise between what one has and what one is willing to lose in exchange for what one wants. The term *exchange* implies that two or more persons are always involved in bargaining. Browne's definition is enriched by Morley's (1978) five defining characteristics of negotiations: (1) Negotiation is a process of joint decision-making; (2) negotiators have different preferences concerning the set of actions which may be taken; (3) negotiations are mixed-motive situations, that is, each party has a motive for cooperation in order to reach a mutually agreeable solution, and simultaneously, a motive for competition in order to gain at the other's expense; (4) negotiation allows the possibility of strategic decision-making of one sort or another where each party's actions may be guided by expectations of what the other will accept; and (5) negotiation involves talking about a relationship before doing anything about it.

While several other definitions of negotiation and bargaining have been developed (*cf.* Rubin and Brown 1975 for a review), Morley and Stephenson (1977) provide definitions for both that are useful particularly for personal selling and buying exchanges:

> Negotiation is any form of verbal communication, direct, or indirect, whereby parties to a conflict of interest discuss, without resort to arbitration or other judicial processes, the form of the joint action they might take to manage a dispute between them. Bargaining is one form of negotiation, namely negotiation for agreement.

Given these characteristics and definitions, there are extremely few laboratory or field studies available in social psychology or marketing that may be classified as negotiation or bargaining research. On this basis, Nemeth (1970) has criticized the substantial body of empirical research and propositions generated from the Prisoner's Dilemma analogue. These games lack an adequate social context; communication is restricted to an extent that the partner may be forgotten; negotiation lacks multidimensionality; there is a lack of clarity as to which are the exchangeable resources. "These may be the reasons why behavior in experimental games has proven to be extremely instruction dependent and has included less reciprocity in interaction than behavior in naturalistic settings" (Schuler 1978, p. 170).

Stern, Sternthal, and Craig (1973) provide several brief criticisms of their own "parasimulation" of distribution channel bargaining, including: "relaxation on the ban on oral communication within each firm would increase mundane realism" (p. 177).

Stern and colleagues (1973) define a parasimulation as more complete than a game but less complete than a full-blown simulation: "On the other hand, a parasimulation affords less participant interaction than a game but greater control than is usually found in simulation exercises. Finally, in all three types of paradigms, specification of relationships is generally quite high" (p. 170). Using 282 students as subjects, two firms of three subjects each bargained for a limited time period over the price and quantity at which the one firm, Surgical Manufacturing, would sell microscalpels to the other, Wholesale Hospital Supply. The researchers found that an exchange-of-persons condition brought about more effective long-term problem-solving behavior among the conflicting parties than an outside threat condition.

The terms *parasimulation, laboratory paradigm,* and *game* are used interchangeably in this chapter. The focus is directed toward briefly describing the problems in developing parasimulations of real-life economic bargaining tasks. A simple laboratory analogue (the Car Dealers' Game) of an actual marketing exchange is presented. Empirical results are described of a test of several propositions on the strategies developed by subjects participating in the game.

Problems with Laboratory Games

Parasimulations are designed to include some features of real-life situations and exclude others. Games are experimenters' attempts to build simple laboratory situations that preserve the essential aspects of some real-life cases. Thus "the fact that an experimental situation differs in obvious ways from the real world does not *ipso facto* make it irrelevant as a possible source of valid generalizations" (Kelman 1965, p. 598). The purpose of the game is to provide the experimenter with easy access to critical features of a real-life situation for developing and testing hypotheses through observing and manipulating some of the features.

The external validity of research hypotheses supported by games can be established only by direct tests in real-life situations. The specifics to this argument have been presented in detail by Cialdini (1980) and Morley (1978). Two related points should be noted here: (1) Given that problems of generalizing the results of laboratory research are specific and cannot be settled once and for all, it is surprising that very few experimental studies of negotiations have derived inspiration from field data. By and large, most laboratory studies have been suggested by other laboratory research. (2) One way of increasing the relevance of laboratory research is to integrate it into a program of study that also involves the analysis of real cases (Morley and Stephenson 1977).

Marketing games share some weaknesses with the games of exchange developed by social psychologists. The marketing games developed by Busch and Wilson (1976), Stern, Sternthal, and Craig (1973), and Levitt (1965) lack an adequate social context. The use of videotaped sales messages (*cf.* Busch and Wilson 1976; Leavitt 1965) as a surrogate of selling behavior is too far removed from an essential feature of the natural situation. Communication is restricted in the Stern and associates (1973) game to an extent that the other firm may be forgotten. The need and failure to include critical features of real-life marketing exchanges in marketing simulations has been expressed before (*cf.* Capon, Holbrook, and Hulbert 1972; Weitz 1981).

A related but less severe criticism is that there are apparently no marketing or social psychology games that allow subjects to change the nature of the agenda items on the table; such integrative bargaining behavior has not been reported in laboratory research.

Morley (1978) and Schuler (1978) have stressed the need to incorporate the essential features of natural situations in mixed-motive games of exchange. The experimenter must deal with three sorts of problems: (1) define the behavior s/he is trying to simulate; (2) identify certain key components of that behavior; and (3) translate those components into components of a laboratory task.

The marketing game reported in the following section aimed to provide easy access to a simple, everyday marketing exchange wherein both seller and buyer have near-equal power in the negotiation process. The term *simple* here means that a natural setting was selected where (1) neither previous nor future interactions would likely occur between the parties, (2) one person is the seller and one person is the buyer, and (3) the exchange would be expected to be completed by both parties in one face-to-face meeting. *Equal power* means that both the buyer and seller would expect each other to attempt to influence the terms of the agreement to be negotiated because both have substantial control over such terms. Such an exchange has been called a functional equivalence system.

> Function equivalence means that in an issue-specific sense neither party is so weak that one can overtly influence by force, for example, or use manipulational punishments without the other retaliating, thus promoting a very costly interchange that does not accomplish exchange and hurts both parties. The asking price is viewed as an initial starting point, not as any fixed entity that a buyer may take or leave (*cf.* Bonoma 1977).

The game was designed to incorporate all the major defining characteristics of negotiations mentioned in the introduction and summarized in table 8–1.

The Car Dealers' Game

The Car Dealers' Game is a mixed-motive parasimulation requiring some degree of cooperation and conflict between two car dealers negotiating an agreement to sell and to buy a specific car. The subject assigned the role of seller is given the information shown in figure 8–1 and asked to make several strategic decisions shown in the exhibit. The seller is asked to explain each decision. The subject assigned the role of buyer is given the information shown in figure 8–2 and similar instructions to those given to the seller. Each person is informed that s/he will meet with the other party after completing the worksheet provided.

Each is given a bill of sale after completing their respective worksheets. The buyer and seller are introduced to each other and requested to meet together to reach an agreement, complete and sign one of the bill of sales provided, and return when the meeting is concluded. The bill of sale is shown as figure 8–3.

This game was developed and revised with the cooperation and suggestions of four car dealers in Columbia, South Carolina in September and October 1979. An extreme price range of likely expectations was included by confidentially informing the subject in the selling role that s/he intended to sell the car for $300; the subject in the buying role was informed that s/he had a customer willing to pay $20,000 for such a car. This extreme range was included to permit substantial flexibility in outcomes to the negotiation.

Table 8–1
Defining Characteristics of Bargaining and Personal Selling and Buying

Bargaining Characteristic	Stern, Sternthal, and Craig (1973)	Busch and Wilson (1976)	Levitt (1965)	Woodside and Davenport (1974)	Car Game (1983)
Process of joint decision making	Yes	No	No	No	Yes
Different preferences on actions to be taken	Yes	N/A	N/A	N/A	Yes
Mixed-motive situation	Yes	N/A	N/A	N/A	Yes
Strategic decision making allowed	No	No	No	No	Yes
Talking before doing	No	No	No	Yes	Yes

Confidential Information to the Seller

The following information is confidential. However, you may give some or all of the information to other persons during the game.

You are a new and used car dealer in Columbia, South Carolina. Presently you have an inventory of 250 cars. Half of the cars are late models or new. Your oldest model is a 1952 Packard four-door sedan.

You are known locally for offering used cars with a one-week guarantee: "If you can't start it, return it for a full refund in the first week after purchase."

You have decided to junk your older inventory of used cars. All pre-1960 cars will be sold next week to the local iron works at $300 per car.

Today you have received a phone call from another dealer in Washington, D.C. This dealer is looking for a 1952 four-door Packard sedan in working order for a customer. The dealer heard that you had such a car: The dealer asked if s/he could meet with you tomorrow to purchase the car. S/he said the s/he will stop on his/her way to Florida where s/he will be vacationing for two weeks. You agree to meet him/her tomorrow for lunch.

You decide to get the 1952 sedan washed and cleaned. You are now thinking about the meeting tomorrow with the dealer from Washington, D.C.

Worksheet for the Seller

1. What price do you *expect to sell* the 1952 four-door Packard sedan to the dealer from Washington, D.C.? $ _____
   Why? _____
   _____

2. What price would you *like to sell* the 1952 four-door Packard sedan to the dealer from Washington, D.C.? $ _____
   Why? _____
   _____

3. What is the *lowest price* that you would accept for selling the car to the Washington dealer? $ _____
   Why? _____
   _____

4. Briefly explain how you plan to handle the meeting at lunch tomorrow with the car dealer from Washington, D.C.
   _____
   _____
   _____

5. Will you insist on buying lunch tomorrow or will you let him/her pay for it? Please check the most appropriate answer.

   (   ) I will insist on buying lunch.
   (   ) It doesn't matter who buys lunch.
   (   ) I will let him/her buy lunch.

Figure 8–1. The Car Dealers Game: Seller's Role

Confidential Instructions to the Buyer

The following information is confidential. However, you may give some or all of the information to other persons during the game.

You are a new and used car dealer in Washington, D.C. One day last week a diplomat from the Libyan Embassy requested that you locate a 1952 four-door Packard sedan. The diplomat wants the car for a present to his/her father back home. If this car is found in working order, s/he will pay $20,000 or $10,000 if it is in good, but not running, condition.

After three hours on the phone this morning, you have located a dealer in Columbia, South Carolina, who has a 1952 four-door Packard in working order. You talked with the dealer personally. You asked the dealer in Columbia if you could meet him/her tomorrow. You told him/her that you would stop in Columbia on your way to Florida for a two week vacation. The dealer in Columbia agreed to meet you tomorrow for lunch.

You have arranged to have a truck ready to bring the 1952 sedan back to Washington. Your travel plans are complete.

You are now thinking about the meeting tomorrow with the car dealer in Columbia.

Worksheet for the Buyer

1. What price do you *expect to pay* for the 1952 four-door Packard sedan from the dealer in Columbia? $ _____
    Why? _____

2. What price would you *like to buy* the 1952 four-door Packard sedan from the dealer in Columbia? $ _____
    Why? _____

3. What is the *highest price* that you would pay for buying the car from the Columbia dealer? $ _____
    Why? _____

4. Briefly explain how you plan to handle the meeting at lunch tomorrow with the car dealer in Columbia. _____

5. If you do buy the car tomorrow, at what price will you sell the car to the diplomat from Libya? $ _____
    Why? _____

Figure 8–2. The Car Dealers Game: Buyer's Role

Several of the game's features could be altered to make the game into a simulation of a commonly occurring marketing situation. However, the game was designed purposely to represent an uncommon, yet realistic, negotiation situation in which both parties had a lot to gain or lose.

I, Columbia car dealer, hereby sell 0247653 Packard 4-door sedan to Washington, D.C., car dealer for the following price: $ _____.

This bill of sale is subject to the following conditions and terms (state conditions and terms, if any):

1. _____

2. _____

3. _____

_____   _____
Date   Signature, Columbia Car Dealer

_____   _____
Date   Signature, Washington, D.C. Car Dealer

Figure 8–3. The Car Dealers Game: Bill of Sale

To include an opportunity for integrative bargaining, the participants were told that they could add any agreed-upon conditions and terms onto the bill of sale. No time limit was mentioned to the subjects to complete their meeting.

The game developed is less complex than the games of economic exchange developed by Siegel and Fouraker (1960), Kelley and Schenitzki (1972), and Stern et al. (1973) in that the subjects are given profit tables and asked to agree upon a price/quantity combination at which goods are to be exchanged. Only one unit, a single car, is the quantity included in the negotiation, unless the subjects add additional cars or other items to the negotiation (which did occur in a few instances!).

Subjects

The study subjects were fifty-four managers participating in an executive-development course on marketing decision-making in the College of Business Administration, University of South Carolina, in the fall of 1979 and spring of 1980. The average length of service with their respective firms was eight years with a range of two to twenty-four years. The average age of the subjects was forty-two. None of the subjects was a car dealer.

A Framework of Buyer-Seller Exchanges

A simple framework of buyer and seller exchanges should include four sets of global variables and several relationships as shown in figure 8-4. The

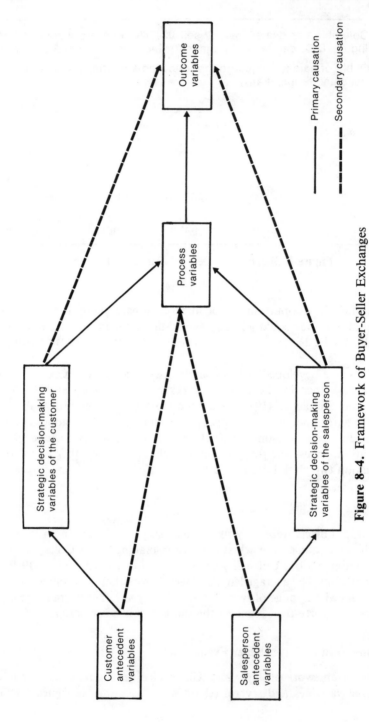

Figure 8-4. Framework of Buyer-Seller Exchanges

one-directional arrows in the figure are intended to imply causation. More complex frameworks of such exchanges are available based on theory (Sheth 1975) and direct observation (Taylor and Woodside 1980).

The antecedent variables shown in figure 8-1 include personal, organizational, and product-specific factors. Such variables as buying or selling experience, need for achievement, and profit orientation of one's firm are examples of antecedent variables. These are hypothesized to have the primary influence on strategic decision-making of buyers and sellers and a secondary influence on the process of verbal and written exchanges.

Strategic decision-making variables include planning for meetings with the buyer (seller); developing a fall-back price, expected price, and asking price; and developing strategies for quantity and trade discounts and other terms and conditions in the purchase contract. Such variables are hypothesized to have the primary influence on the actual negotiation process and a secondary effect on the outcome of the negotiation.

Process variables include verbal and nonverbal communications between buyers and sellers, physical arrangements and environments of meetings, and the number and length of the meetings between the parties. Such variables are hypothesized to have the primary influence on the outcomes of the negotiation.

Outcome variables include the agreement, contract price, terms and conditions, feelings of satisfaction, attitude toward the other party, and willingness to meet again.

Only a limited number of strategic decision variables and how they may affect outcome variables are reported here for the Car Dealers' Game. Additional data are needed on the relationships of primary influence shown in figure 8-1. Both audio-video and audio-only recordings of negotiations are planned in a study of the primary influences of strategic decision-making and process variables.

A Few Propositions

Buyers and sellers are likely to develop strategies regarding the respective highest and lowest price that they would be willing to pay or accept in negotiation when they have some knowledge of the value of the product to be exchanged.

1. Based on Homans' (1974) exchange theory and economic reasoning, for the buyer in the game, a price somewhat less than $20,000 is hypothesized to be the highest price s/he would be willing to pay.
2. For the seller in the game, a price somewhat above $300 is hypothesized to be the lowest price s/he would be willing to accept.

3. The highest willing-to-pay price is hypothesized to be greater than the lowest willing-to-accept price based on the design of the game.
4. The price the buyer expects to pay is hypothesized to be greater than the price the seller expects to sell.
5. However, the difference in buyer-seller expectations is hypothesized to be less than the difference in their fall-back positions.

The rationale for the fifth hypothesis is that the buyer and seller are each likely to consider the power of the other party when mentally calculating a fair price or a price somewhat but not extremely favorable to their own position when planning on an expected price.

6. The like-to-buy price is hypothesized to be the lowest price of the three buying prices formulated by the buyer.
7. The like-to-sell price is hypothesized to be the highest price of the three prices formulated by the seller. (These prices are wish prices by the buyer and seller, that is, prices they each believe unlikely and extremely favorable to their own circumstances.)
8. The contract price is hypothesized to be less than the buyer's expect-to-pay price.
9. The contract price is hypothesized to be greater than the seller's expect-to-sell price. (Given the range in the written price offers to buy the car reported initially to both parties, most subjects should contract for prices better than their expectations.)

Will the negotiated price be closer to the seller's or buyer's wish price?

10. Given the custom of the seller's first stating an asking price and thus enabling the buyer to learn some information about the seller's preference, the contract price is hypothesized to be closer to the buyer's wish price than the seller's wish price.
11. The lower the buyer's expect-to-pay price, the lower the contract price.
12. The higher the seller's expect-to-sell price, the higher the contract price.

These hypotheses are based on the strategic rules-of-thumb that it pays to start low if you are the buyer or start high if you are the seller and then compromise. These hypotheses are supported by prior laboratory research in which subjects bargained against simulated opponents programmed to follow given schedules of bids (Chertkoff and Conley 1967; Komorita and Brenner 1968; Liebert, Smith, Hill, and Keiffer 1968; Pruitt and Johnson 1970).

Results and Discussion

Two dyads were eliminated from the data analysis for misunderstanding the information and instructions.

The means and standard deviations for the price strategies and contract price are listed in table 8-2. The first nine hypotheses are supported. The strategic decision-making of the subjects meet a set of reasonable hypotheses.

The average difference between the buyer and seller strategies ($11,291) for their highest (lowest) price willing to pay (sell) is more than twice the difference between their expected prices ($5,106). This confirms the fifth hypothesis. The average difference in the expected prices between the buyers and sellers was substantially greater than the difference in their like-to or wish prices ($308). Given the relatively small difference the buyers' and sellers' like-to prices, it is not surprising that the average length of time to complete the negotiation was only eighteen minutes and all twenty-five groups reached an agreement.

Hypothesis 10 is unsupported. The average contract price is closer to the seller's wish price than the buyer's wish price. Assuming that the seller was the first to ask for a specific price, this information was likely used by the buyer to influence an agreement even better than the buyer's own wish price. This strategy was apparent in two observed negotiations and reported in the debriefings by several buyers.

Hypothesis 11 is unsupported. The contract prices were unrelated to the levels of the buyers' expect-to-pay ($r = .03$), like-to-pay ($r = .25$), or highest pay prices ($r = .08$). Hypothesis 12 is supported. The contract prices were related to the sellers expect-to-sell ($r = .69$, $p < .01$), like-to-sell ($r = .68$, $p < .01$), and lowest price willing to accept ($r = .50$, $p < .01$). Thus the buyer was willing to acquiesce to the seller's preferences—not a bad strategy given the likely substantial profit margin involved.

From the average seller's perspective, a price of $5,180.60 is over seventeen times greater than s/he expected to receive before the telephone call from the buyer. Thus the average seller likely believed that s/he realized an extremely favorable outcome from the negotiation. The average buyer would have had to pay $1,158.75 to receive the same profit rate as actually received by the average buyer. The contract price would be $2,450 for both to receive the same rate of profit, assuming a $20,000 future selling price.

The most important conclusion is that strategic decision-making of buyers and sellers is likely to be most influenced by their perceptions of their own bargaining positions, not their perceptions of the other party's bargaining positions. For the seller, to plan negotiation strategies in terms of customer value—that is, develop demand oriented pricing instead of cost-oriented pricing—may require special training. For the buyer, to plan negotiation strategies in terms of value analysis—that is, establish vendor's costs of materials, labor, overhead and profit instead of accepting list price—may require special training.

Table 8-2
Average Buyer and Seller Price Strategies and Contract Price
(standard deviations)

Decision	Buyer Strategy n=25	Seller Strategy n=25	A–B	p[a]
Highest (lowest) price that you would pay (accept)	(1) $12,960 (4,659)	(2) $ 1,669 (2,184)	$11,291	<.01
Price you expect to pay (sell)	(3) 8,120 (5,280)	(4) 3,014 (3,935)	5,106	<.05
Price you would like to buy (sell), the parties' wish price	(5) 6,032 (4,217)	(6) 5,724 (11,066)	308	n.s.
Price on the bill of sale (contract price)		(7) 5,180.60 (5,381) n=50		

Additional comparisons:

$$(1) - (7) = \$ 7,779.40, \ t = 5.69$$
$$(2) - (7) = - 3,511.60, \ t = 3.74$$
$$(3) - (7) = 2,939.40, \ t = 1.96$$
$$(4) - (7) = - 2,166.60, \ t = 2.79$$
$$(5) - (7) = 851.40, \ t = 0.71$$
$$(6) - (7) = 543.40, \ t = 0.32$$

$t = 1.71, p$ .05,
$d.f. = 24$
(one-tailed test).

[a]t-test results for unrelated samples, $d.f. = 48$ for each test.

Examples of Strategies and Outcomes

Examples of willing, expected, and like-to prices and negotiation strategies for subjects in two dyads are presented in tables 8-3 and 8-4. The contract price is $675 for the dyad presented in table 8-3. The contract price if $13,500 for the dyad is presented in table 8-4. These examples were selected as typical strategy price decisions and reasons among cases of extreme contract prices.

The predominant differences between tables 8-3 and 8-4 are the seller's price strategies. The seller in table 8-3 agreeing to a low contract price, developed a strategy of low minimum willing-to-sell, expected, and like-to-sell prices compared to the seller in table 8-4. Note in table 8-3 that the difference in the seller's willing and like-to-sell prices was $200 versus a difference of $29,000 between these two prices in table 8-4.

The seller agreeing to the low contract price reported that s/he planned to handle the meeting by telling the buyer the "asking price offer. . . ." The seller agreeing to the high contract price referred to the car as antique, "no other like it in the South," as part of his/her strategy to handle the meeting.

These findings offer additional insight into the findings of the study. The seller's expected and like-to prices may be particularly important in influencing the contract price agreed to in the negotiation. Learning the other party's expected and willing prices before s/he learns your own pricing strategies is hypothesized to improve the price agreed to your own benefit.

Debriefing

All the subjects reported satisfaction with the contract outcome of the game. None correctly predicted the other party's likely profit margin resulting from the concluded agreement. "I don't know, I hadn't thought about it" was the most often reported response.

One subject in the seller's role objected strongly that the game was unfair to the seller since the seller was about to sell the car for $300. Most seller's reported that the benefit of the game was to learn the benefits of the product to the buyer before pricing the product.

Most subjects participating as buyers expressed the need to consider the seller's costs in planning price strategies. Buyers compared to sellers more often reported feeling foolish at the outcomes of the negotiations.

Implications for Sales Management

Several recommendations can be suggested for improving personal selling and sales management programs based on the results of the Car Dealer's

Table 8–3
Example of Buyer and Seller Strategies of a Negotiation Resulting in a Price Favorable to the Buyer

Party	Highest (Lowest) Price Willing to Pay (Sell) and Reason	Expect to Pay (Sell) Price and Reason	Like to Buy (Sell) Price and Reason	Plan to Handle the Meeting
Buyer	$18,000 Need: There is a demand for the car and an opportunity to make a profit.	$10,000 Realizing that the car is a collector's item and would be almost impossible to find elsewhere, I expect to pay at least $10,000.	$ 8,000 I feel that would give him/her what the car is worth and allow me to make some money in return.	The lunch will be friendly and casual. I will *not give* all the details for wanting the car. I will approach the negotiations with the amount of money the seller would like to get.
Seller	$ 600 Would recover $300 if sold to iron works; write off remainder as loss.	$ 700 Paid $600 two years ago; stored and kept in operating condition which cost $100.	$ 800 Ten percent over my cost; R.O.I.	Tell him/her about car; tell asking price offer to show car.
Contract Price and Conditions:	$ 675	Guaranteed to be in running condition. Car is guaranteed to make the trip to D.C. If it fails, seller will be responsible for getting the car back to Columbia.		

Table 8-4
Example of Buyer and Seller Strategies of a Negotiation Resulting in a Price Favorable to the Seller

Party	Highest (Lowest) Price Willing to Pay (Sell) and Reason	Expect to Pay (Sell) Price and Reason	Like to Buy (Sell) Price and Reason	Plan to Handle the Meeting
Buyer	$17,500 Any higher cost would be a no-profit deal.	$15,000 In line with normal profit margin.	$ 7,500 Would like to buy at price willing to pay for a non-running vehicle.	Would not discuss fact that I have a buyer.
Seller	$ 1,000 S/he is en route to Florida; bus the money and the customer.	$15,000 Customer needs this antique; then I would make clear profit.	$30,000 Then I could sell other cars at clear profit; probably less than $300.	Explain the beauty of the almost-antique car; no other like it in the South.
Contract Price and Condition:	$13,500		"Deliver car to Washington. Allow our maintenance people to inspect car to see that it is in good working order when it arrives in Washington. Paid cash in Columbia."	

Game. The following recommendations need to be supported by additional studies in other settings before assuming wide applicability.

1. Sellers need to be trained to set prices based on customer value and not based solely on costs. Sellers need to learn how to acquire customer's reasons for buying. Lower gross margins will likely result otherwise.
2. Sellers need to acquire customer value information before presenting price information. Otherwise, lower seller performance levels will result.
3. Sellers need to ask more questions about customers' plans and search behaviors. The tendency of asking too few questions has been observed in real-life seller-buyer exchanges (Taylor and Woodside 1980).
4. Role-playing and critiques of role-playing exercises will likely increase the ability of sellers to bargain more effectively with buyers when the results of the bargain are based on the participants' own behavior. The outcome of the Car Dealers' Game is controlled by the players and not the experimenter. The resulting variability in outcomes between buyer-seller groups increases both insight and interest among the participants.

Conclusion

The Car Dealers' Game was developed to provide an easy access to a marketing exchange. The game aimed to include all the essential characteristics of a real-life negotiation. Thus it involves a process of joint decision-making by a buyer and a seller who have different preferences concerning the set of actions to be taken. Each is likely to perceive equivalent powers, but this has yet to be established. The negotiation is a mixed-motive situation allowing the possibility for strategic decision-making. Verbal communications between the buyer and seller are an integral process in the game.

The Car Dealers' Game is intended to represent a simple parasimulation of one marketing exchange. Other parasimulations are needed to study relationships and develop propositions with respect to antecedent, strategic decision-making, process, and outcome variables.

The influence of manipulations for affecting strategic decisions, process variables, and outcomes for the buyer's or seller's benefit can be tested with such games.

Propositions developed form the Car Dealers' Game can be tested in natural field settings. The hypotheses supported in Cialdini, Bickman and Cacioppio's (1979) field experiment on "bargaining tough in new car showrooms," that specific verbal reactions made by customers to sellers' offers to sell price in negotiations on one car reduce the sellers' offers to sell price in subsequent negotiations about a second car, can be verified and extended using the Car Dealers' Game. The extensions can be then verified with further field experiments. This type of full cycle behavioral research is needed urgently in research on buyer-seller interactions.

The findings and implications from the Car Dealers' Game are limited by the laboratory setting of the experiment and the fact that the experiment is designed for only one meeting between a buyer and seller. Before generalizations can be offered on bargaining behavior, different laboratory and field experiments need to be developed for real-life selling-buying interactions.

References

Bonoma, Thomas V. (1977). "Toward a Social Analysis of Consumption: Buyer-Seller Negotiations in Context." In A.G. Woodside, J.N. Sheth, and P.D. Bennett (eds.), *Consumer and Industrial Buying Behavior.* New York: North-Holland, pp. 345-354.

Browne, Joy (1976). "The Used-Car Game." In M. Patricia Golden (ed.), *The Research Experience.* Itasca, Ill.: F.E. Peacock Publishers, pp. 60-70.

Busch, Paul, and David T. Wilson (1976). "An Experimental Analysis of a Salesman's Expert and Referent Bases of Social Power in the Buyer-Seller Dyad." *Journal of Marketing Research* 13 (February):3-11.

Capon, Noel; Moris B. Holbrook; and James Hulbert (1972). "Industrial Purchasing Behavior: A Reappraisal." *Journal of Business Administration* 4 (Fall):69-77.

Chertkoff, J.M., and M. Conley (1967). "Opening Offer and Frequency of Concession as Bargaining Strategies." *Journal of Personality and Social Psychology* 7 (March):181-185.

Cialdini, Robert (1980). "Full Cycle Social Psychology." in L. Bickman (ed.), *Applied Social Psychology Annual.* Beverly Hills, Calif.: Sage, pp. 92-11.

Cialdini, Robert B.; Leonard Bickman; and John T. Cacioppo (1979). "An Example of Consummeristic Social Psychology: Bargaining Tough in the New Car Showroom." *Journal of Applied Social Psychology* 9 (May):115-126.

Homans, George C. (1974). *Social Behavior: Its Elementary Forms.* New York: Harcourt-Brace-Jovanovich.

Kelley, H.H., and D.P. Schenitzki (1972). "Bargaining." in C.G. McClintock (ed.), *Experimental Social Psychology.* New York: Holt, Rinehart and Winston.

Kelman, H.C. (1965). "Social Psychological Approaches to the Study of International Relations: The Question of Relevance." In H.C. Kelman (ed.), *International Behavior: A Social Psychological Analysis.* New York: Holt, Rinehart and Winston.

Komorita, S.C., and R. Brenner (1968). "Bargaining and Concession Making Under Bilateral Monopoly." *Journal of Personality and Social Psychology* 9, 15–20.

Levitt, Theodore (1965). *Industrial Purchasing Behavior.* Boston: Division of Research, Graduate School of Business Administration, Harvard University.

Liebert, R.M.; W.P. Smith; J.H. Hill; and M. Keiffer (1968). "The Effects of Information and Magnitude of Initial Offer on Interpersonal Negotiation." *Journal of Experimental Social Psychology* 4, 431–441.

Morley, Ian E. (1978). "Bargaining and Negotiation: The Character of Experimental Studies." In H. Brandstatter, J.H. Davis, and H. Schuler (eds.), *Dynamics of Group Decisions.* Beverly Hills, Calif.: Sage, pp. 175–206.

Morley, Ian E., and Geoffrey M. Stephenson (1977). *The Social Psychology of Bargaining.* London: George Allen and Unwin.

Nemeth, C. (1972). "A Critical Analysis of Research Utilizing the Prisoner's Dilemma Paradigm for the Study of Bargaining." In L. Berkowitz (ed.), *Advances in Experimental Social Psychology,* Vol. 6. New York: Academic Press.

Pruitt, D.G., and D.F. Johnson (1970). "Mediation as an Aid to Face-Saving in Negotiation." *Journal of Personality and Social Psychology* 14, 239–246.

Rubin, Jeffrey, and Bert R. Brown (1975). *The Social Psychology of Bargaining and Negotiation.* New York: Academic Press.

Schuler, Heinz (1978). "Part III, Mixed-Motive Interaction." In H. Brandstatter, J.H. Davis, and H. Schuler, (eds.), *Dynamics of Group Decisions.* Beverly Hills, Calif.: Sage, pp. 169–174.

Sheth, Jagdish N. (1975). "Buyer-Seller Interaction: A Conceptual Framework." In G. Zaltman and B. Sternthal (eds.), *Broadening the Concept of Consumer Behavior.* Chicago: Association for Consumer Research, pp. 131–140.

Siegel, Sidney, and L.E. Fouraker (1960). *Bargaining and Group Decision Making.* New York: McGraw-Hill.

Stern, Louis; Brian Sternthal; and C. Samuel Craig (1973). "Managing Conflict in Distribution Channels: A Laboratory Study." *Journal of Marketing Research* 8 (May):169–179.

Taylor, James L., and Arch G. Woodside (1980). "An Examination of the Structure of Buying-Selling Interactions Among Insurance Agents and

Prospective Customers." In the *1979 Proceedings of the Association for Consumer Research.* Chicago: Association for Consumer Research, pp. 281–285.

Weitz, Barton A. (1981). Effectiveness in Sales Interactions: A Contingency Framework." *Journal of Marketing* 45 (Winter):85–103.

Woodside, Arch G., and W.J. Davenport (1974). "The Effects of Salesman Similarity and Expertise on Consumer Purchasing Behavior." *Journal of Marketing Research* 11 (May):198–202.

9

Improving the Effectiveness of Salespersons' Time Allocation: A Research Program

Terry Deutscher and
Adrian B. Ryans

A major decision facing traveling salespersons, which can have a significant impact on sales performance, is the allocation of time. In several surveys salespersons report that time allocation is their most important problem (Churchill, Ford, and Walker 1981, p. 344). The importance of time allocation by salespersons seems to be recognized by sales managers. In both company and commercial sales training activities, there is a heavy emphasis on territory management training, a part of which deals with time allocation (Davis and Webster 1968, p. 485, and Bergman 1967). Companies use various sales call quota systems to influence salespersons' time allocation in what is hoped to be a productive direction. Sometimes these quotas may simply require a minimum number of calls per day. However, in some companies, particularly consumer-packaged-goods companies, call frequencies by size and/or type of account are suggested (Shapiro 1977, p. 431). Recognizing that in many situations the salesperson may have the most relevant information for making these time allocation decisions, some companies have chosen to provide models, such as CALLPLAN (Lodish 1971), to help the salespersons process judgments about their accounts' sales response so as to allocate time more effectively.

This emphasis on encouraging the effective use of available selling time does not appear to be misplaced. Lodish (1971) reported that anticipated sales increases in CALLPLAN applications generally range between 5 percent and 25 percent. In an actual experiment involving matched pairs of salespersons at United Airlines, the experimental group with access to CALLPLAN achieved 8.1 percent higher sales than a control group ($p < .025$) (Fudge and Lodish 1977). The widespread use of CALLPLAN by a number of companies (Lodish 1974) suggests that at least some managers do believe that CALLPLAN provides improved time allocations and better sales performance.

The authors gratefully acknowledge the assistance of Professor Shelby H. McIntyre of the University of Santa Clara in some of the original conceptualization that led to this chapter. Professor David B. Burgoyne of The University of Western Ontario and Steven Finlay of Lever Brothers Limited are heavily involved in the empirical research related to this research study and have contributed to our understanding of the issues.

163

In many selling situations, the salesperson has accounts concentrated in several geographical areas (for example, cities). Here, the salesperson can misallocate his/her available time in two conceptually distinct ways: first, there may be an inappropriate division of time between (a) traveling among areas and (b) calling on accounts within areas; and second, the time available for calling on accounts within areas may not be used in the most effective manner.

Given the apparent impact of time allocation on sales performance, a number of important questions need investigation.

1. Is the misallocation of available selling time a widespread and operationally significant phenomenon?

If the answer to this research question is positive, then a second question needs to be addressed.

2. Can salespersons and/or managers identify when they have a problem with time allocation?

If the answer to this second question is negative, then a third research question is suggested.

3. Is the degree of time misallocation related to identifiable characteristics of the task or the task environment, for example, the variability in travel time to the different areas and the level of competition? If so, this would indicate when attention should be paid to the problem and when such aids as decision support systems might be most useful.

Regardless of the answer to the second and third research questions a positive answer to the first question suggests:

4. Can a significant part of the misallocation of time be attributed to an inappropriate allocation of the available time between traveling and calling? Specifically do salespersons allocate too much time to calling on customers as compared to traveling between areas (a customer contact bias)?

Finally two research questions related to ways of overcoming any time allocation problems are suggested.

5. If the reasons for the misallocation of time can be identified, can salespersons be trained to allocate their time more effectively, and/or
6. Can control or quota systems be designed to encourage more optimal time allocations?

Obviously, before any of these research questions can be addressed, there is a need to develop a measure of the adequacy of the time allocation among accounts. The above research questions are presented schematically in figure 9-1.

Empirical Evidence about How Salespersons Allocate Time

There is little research on how salespersons allocate their time and which parameters of the situation have the greatest effect on the optimality of

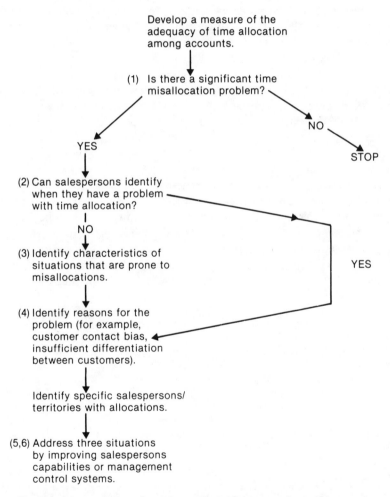

Note: Numbers in parentheses refer to the numbers of the research questions.

Figure 9-1.   Schematic Diagram of Research Questions

their allocations. In sales management case studies, where time and activity analyses for individual salespersons are occasionally presented, it is evident that they sometimes spend a disproportionately large amount of time on small accounts relative to their apparent sales potential. For example, in the Paper Distributors (B) case (Shapiro 1977), one salesperson spent almost a hundred times as many hours per unit of potential for the smallest class of accounts as for the largest class of accounts. This time allocation pattern may be partly due to the fact that salespersons want and are often encouraged to spend a high proportion of their available selling time in face-to-face contact with customers rather than spending it traveling between customers. In a way, it represents rational behavior to the salesperson, since calling on an account, (*any* account,) has the potential to generate sales, whereas travel appears to be totally unproductive. Thus once they are in particular geographic area, salespersons tend to call on most or all of the accounts in that area, whether or not it is optimal to do so. If the accounts in an area are heterogeneous, then salespersons will be spending a disproportionate amount of their time with small accounts. Calls per day quotas probably encourage this behavior, particularly if the quotas are ambitious ones.

More impressive evidence of a possible customer contact bias is apparent in two papers about the CALLPLAN model that compare present time allocations and optimal time allocations for two salespersons. Some descriptive statistics for these two salespersons are presented in table 9–1. The striking thing about this data is that the model-based optimal solution suggests a more radical allocation of calls than the present policy of the salesperson.[1] The salespersons have exercised too homogeneous a call policy and, as a consequence, have traveled less than is optimal, given their perception of customer responsiveness to call frequency. Perhaps these individuals are exhibiting a customer contact bias to the detriment of their total sales performance.

Table 9–1
Time Allocation in Sample Callplan Applications

	Lodish 1971	Fudge and Lodish 1977
Variance in calls/account (present policy)	5.36	3.42[a]
Variance in calls/account (optimal policy)	12.06	34.57[a]
Percentage increase in travel time (optimal/present)	5.4%	14.5%

[a]The authors present only 29 of the 50 accounts in the territory and these are described as "the ones where CALLPLAN recommended significant changes in call frequency." Thus the increase in variance is probably overstated.

Factors Influencing Salesperson Time Allocation

In studying performance on the time allocation task, three aspects of the situation need to be considered: the decision maker, the decision task, and the environment in which the task is performed (Newell and Simon 1972).

Factors Related to the Decision Maker

The performance of human decision makers is often viewed as being a function of ability and motivation (Mitchell 1978). In the salesperson time allocation situation, the former factor might be affected by the salesperson's previous training on time allocation and his/her previous experience with the task. The salesperson's motivation to allocate time effectively might be influenced by his/her perceptions of the importance of time allocation to effective job performance and the extent to which s/he believes s/he is evaluated on actual time allocation.

Factors Related to the Task

The characteristics of the time allocation task would include not only the various descriptors of the salesperson's territory and accounts, but also how the time allocation task is presented to the salesperson. Among the wide variety of task characteristics that could be related to performance are the following:

1. type of account response function present (concave, S-shaped, or mixed)
2. heterogeneity in response functions across accounts, in terms of affectable range and shape
3. number of areas
4. mean number of accounts per area
5. variability in number of accounts per area
6. variability in travel times to areas
7. degree of uncertainty as to how accounts will respond to call levels

The degree to which, and the manner in which, account and territory data are presented to salespersons might influence their performance on the time allocation task. By simply processing data on sales performance by size of account, type of account, and historical calling level, and presenting the salesperson with processed account data rather than raw data or no data, a company may be able to improve the performance of its salespersons.

Task Environment Factors

A variety of characteristics of the task environment, both controllable and non-controllable, might also be related to task performance. Of particular interest and importance to sales management is the impact of controllable sales force policies such as sales quotas, calls per day quotas, suggested call frequencies by size and type of account, required account planning, and the compensation system. The above discussion is summarized in table 9–2.

In designing this research program, a decision was made to focus first on the task and task environment area rather than on the decision maker. Two major considerations motivated this choice.[2] First, there is some evidence from the research literature that certain of the task characteristics may have a significant impact on a salesperson's ability to allocate time in an effective manner. If we are able to identify the types of task situations

Table 9–2
Factors Expected to Affect Task Performance

Decision Maker Factors
    Motivation
    Experience with the task
    Training on how to perform the task

Task Factors
    Task Presentation
        Cumulative vs. marginal response functions
    Task Characteristics
        Types of account response functions present
        Heterogeneity of response functions across accounts
        Number of areas
        Mean number of accounts per area
        Variability in number of accounts per area
        Variability in travel time to areas
        Uncertainty as to how accounts will respond

Task Environment Factors
    Controllable
        Quotas (calls per day and/or call frequencies by size and type of account)
        Required advance account planning
        Supervision of account planning activities
        Compensation and incentive system
    Non-controllable
        Level of competition in territory

that are related to poor time allocations, management would be advised in these circumstances to give salespersons access to call planning tools, such as CALLPLAN or processed sales data, or training in effective time allocation. Second, many aspects of the task environment are controllable by management and, if certain policies were found to have dysfunctional effects on time allocation and sales performance, these could be changed.

In the next two sections we will explore in some detail the previous literature relating the task and task environment characteristics to time allocation and sales performance in an effort to develop testable propositions.

Task Characteristics

Task-Related Factors

Seven task characteristics that may be related to task performance are listed in table 9-2. The first six are all, in a crude sense, factors that can influence the amount of information a subject must attend to if time is to be allocated optimally. The introduction of uncertainty may also impact the optimality of the time allocation decision, but this factor has received little attention in the sales literature to date (Zoltners 1979). Information load factors may be worthy of particular attention since (1) these factors appear to exhibit wide variation in the field and (2) there is evidence that information load may affect decision quality. Again, if information load were shown to have a strong influence on time allocation and sales performance, this knowledge would have important managerial implications, possibly suggesting circumstances in which salespersons will need aid (perhaps decision support systems) to allocate their time effectively.

The construct information load has received a good deal of attention in the consumer information processing literature, but there is little agreement as to how it should be operationally defined. Jacoby (1977) has advocated defining information load as "the variety of stimuli (in type and number) to which the receiver must attend," and has operationally defined it, in the consumer context, as the product of the number of alternatives and the number of attributes presented. Wright and Weitz (1977) have advocated a five factor model of information load, which adds some significant dimensions to the original definition. These factors are: (1) the time available for decision, (2) the number of factors to be considered for each option, (3) the number of levels or discriminations to be considered per factor, (4) the number of options to be evaluated, and (5) the amount of extraneous information. Even this five factor model does not fully capture the richness of the information processing load problem faced by a decision maker in the time allocation situation. Here we can imagine two problems with the same number of areas and accounts, which are essentially identical on these five dimensions, yet where the effective amount of information that must be processed if optimal decisions are to be made might be quite different. To take a simple example: If in one of these problems all the accounts within each area have identical response functions, then if it pays to visit one of the accounts in an area it will certainly pay to visit all the accounts within the area. Contrast this with the same basic problem in which response functions are quite hetergeneous. Clearly here, the amount of information that must be processed is much greater. Thus within certain limits, heterogeneity in the response functions across accounts increases the amount of information that must be attended to and hence the effective information load.[3]

Ideally, we would like an operational measure of information load that would provide an index of the effective information processing load for any given problem. This would be of great value from both research and managerial perspectives.

Conceptually, an index of the amount of information that must be effectively processed for a given problem might be the length of time it takes a standard untiring subject with an excellent set of heuristics to solve the problem to a desired degree of accuracy. This time would then provide an index of the number of information processing operations and, hence, the information processing load represented by a particular problem with a given time constraint. At this point, we are unable to develop an operational measure based on this conceptual approach.

Thus we are currently only at the stage of being able to say that if one changes a specific dimension of the problem in a given direction (within certain limits) that the information processing load will increase. With respect to the six dimensions of the salesperson time allocation problem believed to be related to information load we suggest the following propositions:

1. Type of response function: As we move from concave response functions to S-shaped response functions, the information processing load will increase and performance on the time allocation task will be poorer, that is, less optimal performance given the time available for calling on accounts. With S-shaped response functions the decision maker must pay much greater attention to future calls on an account since a low payoff call now can pave the way for a higher payoff call later.
2. Heterogeneity of account response functions: Initially as the variation in account response functions (in affectable range and shape) increases, the information processing load will increase and time allocation will be poorer. This will only hold within a certain range since under conditions of extreme heterogeneity the effective number of accounts may be reduced since it becomes obvious that certain accounts should never be called on.

3. Number of areas: The greater the number of areas (holding the mean number of accounts per area constant), the greater the information processing load since more information must be considered. Thus time allocation will be poorer.
4. Mean number of accounts per area: The larger the mean number of accounts per area, the greater the amount of information that must be processed. However, if one looks at this from the perspective of the salesperson another countervailing force is at work. If there are a large number of accounts in an area a salesperson may feel less of a need to visit all of the accounts on a particular visit to an area in order to justify his/her trip to the area. Therefore, a higher mean number of accounts per area may actually allow a salesperson to be more selective in his/her choice of accounts to visit and this may lead to *better* time allocation and *higher* sales performance. Given this apparent conflict, a specific directional hypothesis does not seem defensible here.
5. Variance in number of accounts per area: The greater the variance in the number of accounts per area, the greater the information processing load and the poorer the time allocation performance. Increased variation in the number of accounts per area will, in many situations, force the decision maker to think about the areas in a more differentiated manner since the fixed travel time cost to the different areas must now be allocated over differing numbers of accounts.
6. Variance in travel times to area: The greater the variance in travel time to areas, the greater the information processing load and the poorer the performance. Again the increased variation forces the decision maker to think about the areas in a more differentiated manner; there will frequently be a greater penalty if travel time is ignored.

Task Presentation

In several consumer information processing studies, it has been found that the manner in which information is presented affects how it is acquired and presumably processed (van Raaij 1976; Bettman and Kakkar 1977). Bettman and Zins (1979) argued that when information is presented in a format that is congruent with the type of processing required for the particular task, performance may be improved. However, in their study, they were unable to find support for their congruence notion with respect to their measure of performance accuracy.

In presenting salespersons with data relevant to making decisions about time allocation, data can be presented or elicited in a manner that may or may not faciliate processing. For example, in previous research, sales response functions have typically been elicited from salespersons in cumulative terms (for example, Lodish 1971), but it is not clear whether this choice of elecitation format is based on research as to how salespersons typically store such information or whether it is an arbitrary choice on the part of the model builder. Marginal information is probably the more useful form for decision making since, from a mathematical point of view, the marginal data is required to make an optimal time allocation, that is, in Bettman and Zins terminology format is congruent with task. Although the marginal information can be obtained by a transformation of the cumulative data, there is now evidence to suggest that people resist making even the simplest transformations of information prior to using it for decision making (Slovic and Lichtenstein 1968; Payne and Braunstein 1971; Slovic and McPhillamy 1974).

A second important aspect of task presentation in the time allocation situation is the issue of base-rate versus specific information. An example of base-rate or a priori information in a time allocation situation might be average quarterly sales to firms in a segment defined by firm size and type of firm. An example of specific or case information would be quarterly sales to firm A. Most salespersons in their time allocation decisions are probably reacting to a series of pieces of case information. Few salespersons or companies probably aggregate or process the data to provide the salesperson with base-rate data that could be more useful for decision making.

A common finding is that even when people are provided with both base-rate and case data they tend to ignore the former and rely almost exclusively on the latter (Hogarth 1980). Thus even when the base-rate data is available it tends to be ignored, unless case data is absent or the case data has apparent causal meaning for the individual (Hogarth 1980, p. 40). As Hogarth has pointed out, the base-rate information can often be presented in a way that the causal link between the base-rate data and the problem at hand becomes more obvious to the subjects. When this is done, the decision making can be improved.

In the time allocation context it would seem useful to explore whether the quality of a salesperson's time allocations over time can be improved by feeding back to him/her processed base-rate data on such things as performance or that of his/her fellow salespersons' in a particular customer segment.

Thus we have two major propositions with respect to task presentation:

7. Presentation of data in a format congruent with required processing: When data is present in a format that is congruent with the kind of information processing required for the particular task, time allocation decisions will be improved.
8. Base-rate data: The presentation of selected base-rate data on a salesperson's performance in particular customer segments will lead to improved time allocation decisions.

Task Environment

The characteristics of the task environment can be divided into two broad classes: (1) those controllable by management and (2) those that are not controllable by management. Variables of both types are likely to influence a salesperson's performance.

Examples of controllable variables include: sales quotas, calls per day quotas, suggested call frequencies by size and type of account, required account planning, the compensation system, and close supervision of account planning by management. Policies such as required account planning and suggested call frequencies by size and type of account, should, if intelligently designed, result in improved time allocation and sales performance. However, others could have a deleterious effect on sales performance. Calls per day quotas are a possible example of this. Many companies use calls per day quotas to encourage their salespersons to make a large number of calls and to spend a high proportion of their available selling time in front of customers. Unfortunately, if such quotas are ambitious they may lead salespersons to maximize calls and minimize travel time by visiting all accounts in a geographic area, even if many of the smaller accounts are not large enough to warrant such frequent calls. Thus calls per day quotas may lead to a too-even calling pattern, resulting in poor time allocation and less than optimal sales performance.

An improtant task characteristic that is not controllable by management is competition. The more competition, the more difficult it is likely to be for a salesperson to allocate his/her time effectively. Consideration of competition is likely to add to a salesperson's information processing load, resulting in poorer performance on the time allocation task. In summary, then, we suggest the following propositions:

9. Policies designed to encourage salespersons to carefully allocate their time and suggested call frequencies by size and type of account should result in improved time allocation.
10. Calls per day quotas encourage even calling on all the accounts in a given geographical area. This should result in less effective time allocation.

Toward an Empirical Investigation of the
Central Research Questions

The previous sections have developed a number of research questions about the accuracy of salespersons' time allocation and possible reasons for misallocation. In some cases, these research questions suggest a number of testable propositions. It now seems appropriate to consider just how these research questions and propositions might be empirically examined. Three possible paradigms emerge as potential means of testing the questions:

1. static laboratory experiments involving paper-and-pencil exercises
2. dynamic simulations of sales territories, period-by-period
3. field studies of actual sales representatives

Each design has its strengths and weaknesses, and no single design is dominant in all respects for addressing each of the research questions. Instead, the three alternatives are to a large extent complementary. Next, each paradigm will be described in reasonable detail, along with a succinct outline of its principal advantages and disadvantages.

The Static Laboratory Experiment

In this paradigm, subjects would be assigned to a hypothetical territory based on the framework employed in the CALLPLAN model (Lodish 1971). The territory is split into a number of geographic sub-areas, with several accounts in each. The assumption is made that after each trip to a territory, the hypothetical sales representative returns to the home area. Travel times to each sub-area and call times (including travel times within the given sub-area) for each account are specified. Subjects are also presented with data on the response functions for each account, that is, the sales that would result if one call, two calls, and so forth were made on the particular account. The account and territory information is manipulated in an experimental design. Subjects are asked to simulate allocating a specified amount of time to calling on accounts within their hypothetical territory. They are told their objective is to maximize sales or contribution.

McIntyre and Ryans' paper (1983) is an example of a study that fits this general static laboratory experiment paradigm. They manipulated the form of the individual account response functions (that is, sales for a given level of calls) and the number of sub-areas in the sales territory in the problem and measured the resulting impact on sales. They found that presenting the data in a marginal instead of a cumulative format facilitated its use in decision making. Also, performance declined when mixed response functions (that is, some were concave and some S-shaped) were present and when the number of sub-areas per territory increased.

Appraisal. One can conceive of the time allocation process for the sales representative as containing two separate steps: 1) estimating the relationship between calling level and volume or contribution at each account, and 2) making the decision about calling effort by account.

The static laboratory experiment, as employed by McIntyre and Ryans, has specified the first step (the response functions) as part of the experimental manipulation in order to focus attention on the allocation decision. As such, the design does not attempt to study how individuals process information in learning about accounts' response to different calling levels, but it provides a good test for certain other questions. Given a set of accounts with estimated response functions of a certain type, configured in a particular way to form a territory, how well can the time allocation decision be made? A static laboratory experiment seems very appropriate for addressing this question. The laboratory setting permits exclusion of the many variables besides calling time that would affect sales to an account (for example, quality of the calls, competitive efforts, suitability of the seller's marketing mix for the account, and so forth), so internal validity is high. The trade-off, of course, is on the external validity side. The experiment is conducted in a purified setting where paper and pencil measures are employed (the subjects simply write out which accounts they would visit in what order in a single time period) and the objective is clear (subjects want to maximize sales for the available calling time, and sales are a function only of number of calls). The task facing a sales representative is a great deal more complicated; calling time is only one of many determinants of sales, response functions of accounts to calling levels are far from certain, and dynamic carryover effects (where this period's calls affect the next period's sales) are present.

The Dynamic Simulation of a Sales Territory

In a simulated sales territory paradigm, a subject would be placed in charge of a sales territory similar to the one employed in the static laboratory experiment which was described previously. Potential accounts would be specified, perhaps with some information about their basic type and size. The subject's task is to decide which accounts will get sales calls in a given time period. Once again, the objective of the task is to maximize sales (or total contribution) for the amount of time available.

Having decided which accounts are called on in period t, the subject then gets feedback in terms of sales to each account. These sales can be a function of several parameters, such as size of account, its loyalty to the supplier, the time elapsed since the last call, its sensitivity to calling levels, and so forth. Sales data can be presented in raw form, account-by-account (case information), or processed for the subjects to be more amenable for their analysis (base-rate information, such as summaries of sales by size and type of account or growth in sales in response to calling levels over the last few periods). The subject processes this information, decides where to make calls in the next period, and iterates through the next cycle.

Appraisal. The essential difference between this paradigm and the one described previously is that this is a *dynamic* problem whereas the former is static. In a sense, the simulation complements the initial lab experiment by extending the task over several periods of time. Instead of being presented with data that indicate marginal or cumulative sales for each level of calls, subjects in the simulation learn about accounts' response functions in the process of calling on them. This research affords the opportunity of studying other questions than the static design does: for instance, the effects of pre-processed information (base versus case) on task performance, or the results of providing training about time allocation heuristics. It also affords the researcher an opportunity to explore how the characteristics of a territory and the accounts comprising the territory help shape the behavior of the salesperson.

This simulated sales experience would probably best be run interactively on a computer. Presumably, the experience for the subject would have more experimental realism (Aronson and Carlsmith, 1968) than the previously described static laboratory design with its paper-and-pencil measures. However, although the simulation paradigm can probably provide a more involving environment for the task than its static cousin can, it is still far short of the complexity of a field setting. Removing these real-life complexities produce many of the external/internal validity trade-offs that were discussed previously in appraising the static experiment.

A point was raised earlier about how the simulation paradigm complements the lab experiment by adding the dynamic dimension. In a sense, a similar complementary relationship could exist between a field setting and the simulation. This issue will be discussed in the next section, following a brief description of how the time allocation problem might be addressed in a field setting.

Analysis of Salesperson Time Allocation
in an Actual Field Setting

If one wanted to study allocation of time to accounts by sales representatives, an obvious approach to the problem would be to go into the field and make the necessary measurements on a number of salespersons.

The information needed from each sales representative would include the following:

1. A list of the geographic sub-areas comprising the territory (if more than one sub-area exists).
2. Travel times and costs to these sub-areas.
3. A list of accounts and prospects, organized into sub-areas.

4. Information from which a response function could be estimated for each account. CALLPLAN uses sales at zero calls, at the current calling level, at the current level plus or minus 50%, and at the saturation level of calling.
5. Time per call for each account.
6. Planned calling level on each account for the next effort period.

This information is required to perform a CALLPLAN analysis of each territory. The analysis would produce an optimal or nearly optimal schedule of calls and an estimate of the sales or gross margin that should result from this schedule of calls. This output variable could then be compared to the expected sales or margin under the current plan. A ratio of planned to optimal sales could serve as the dependent variable in a subsequent analysis of performance versus various task and environment characteristics.

Appraisal. The approach described in the previous section is conceptually straightforward. Clearly, there are significant external validity advantages in dealing with real salespersons in real sales territories. If a good cross-section of sales territories could be analyzed, generalizing the results to other situations should not be a major problem.

The advantages of the field setting are, it would seem, almost obvious. The disadvantages, on the other hand, are not so apparent. The first of these is directly related to the external validity advantage of using a real situation in which sales are really a function of a host of environmental, competitive and strategic factors, only one of which is calling level. In real sales territories, the frequency of calls may be only a minor determinant of sales, and it can be very difficult for sales representatives to estimate a response function. Furthermore, sales calls can often be made for service or competitive reasons that are not directly related to volume in the short or intermediate term. For all these reasons, sales representatives might find it difficult to provide the necessary information. Second, furnishing and analyzing the required data is very time-consuming; an initial CALLPLAN session can take upwards of three hours per sales representative. Because many of the inputs (like response functions) require explanation and coaching, it is important to have a knowledgeable researcher present at the data collection.

A final disadvantage with the field setting is that it is, understandably, usually not amenable to experimentation. To study the effect of a policy such as imposing call quotas is relatively simple in the simulation that was described earlier; to do so with actual sales territories would necessitate locating two separate samples (which, hopefully, are otherwise similar) with and without call quotas. This task would be difficult and time-consuming, particularly if a number of different policies were to be examined. However, it is on this type of problem that the field study complements the dynamic simulation. A field study would provide baseline data for many results which could also be tested by the simulation. Ebbeson and Konecni (1980) have recently reported a number of examples of situations in which laboratory simulations had poor external validity. They argue persuasively that researchers ought to collect sufficient evidence to test whether the simulation can mimic data from various aspects of the real world situation. If the simulations were able to replicate the field results, we could feel more confident about the external validity of conclusions reached from other manipulations that would be difficult to perform in the field.

Applicability to the Research Questions

As a means of summarizing the discussion, it would be appropriate to consider the extent to which the research paradigms are able to address the research question. Table 9-3 outlines the major questions and the suitability of each of the paradigms for addressing them.

1. The first research question deals with the overall magnitude of the misallocation problem. It is a particularly important question because

Table 9-3
Comparison of the Three Research Paradigms

Research Question	Static Laboratory Experiment	Dynamic Simulation	Field Setting
1. Is misallocation a significant problem?			X
2. Are people aware that they have a problem with misallocation?	X	X	X
3. Is misallocation related to identifiable task or environment characteristic?	X	X	X
4. How prominent are misallocations between travel time and call time?	X	X	X
5. Can people be trained to allocate time more effectively?		X	?
6. Can control or quota systems be designed to produce more optimal time allocations?		X	?

Notes: X means the question can be addressed within this paradigm; ? means it is conceptually possible but operationally difficult to address the question within this paradigm.

a conclusion that time misallocation was only an inconsequential problem would rule out the need to consider the other questions at all. Clearly, the appropriate place to address question 1 is in the field.

2. The second research question relates to the ability of sales representatives or experimental subjects to identify situations in which they are performing poorly at time allocation. External validity issues make it most appropriate to answer this question in a field setting with actual sales territories, but valuable insights can also be obtained in the laboratory. If subjects operating in a purified environment with a clearly specified task are unaware of the extent of their misallocations, it is likely that sales representatives suffer from the same problem, probably to an even greater extent.

3. The third research question involves an attempt to relate misallocation to specific characteristics of the task or the environment. Some of these issues (for example, shape of the response function) are particularly amenable to a controlled setting like the static experiment. A few of the environmental issues, like competition, could be addressed only in the field setting.

4. The fourth research question examines misallocation in travel time versus call time. Conclusions about this question would probably be most forceful if they were obtained in the field, but the issues could also be productively examined in the static or the dynamic simulations.

5. The next research question concerns the effects of training on time allocation performance. Because it would be desirable to measure effects over time, the static experiment would not be appropriate here. Also, though field results would certainly have the greatest external validity, it would require a lengthy experiment to obtain them. Therefore this question might initially be addressed most profitably in a dynamic simulation.

6. The final research question deals with the impact of control systems like call quotas on allocation performance. Again, these issues would be difficult to address in the field for reasons similar to those discussed for the previous question. Also, results from a one-time experiment would be very dependent upon the configuration of the territory that was chosen and its match with, for example, the selected call quota system. It would seem most productive to address these control questions in the simulation paradigm.

Notes

1. Interestingly, Montgomery, Silk, and Zaragoza (1971) made a similar finding in their application of the DETAILER model. There, in an allocation

of available detailing time across pharmaceutical products, the model suggested the current policy resulted in a time allocation that was too homogeneous.

2. Of course, we recognize that many of the potential solutions to specific time allocation problems will involve attempts to alter the ability or motivation of the decision maker. At a subsequent point in the research program, efforts to measure the impact of these attempts would be very useful, but it appears more useful to concentrate on the task and environment areas first (if for no other reason than to identify decision makers with problems).

3. Of course, extreme heterogeneity may reduce the effective dimensionality of the problem and hence the information processing load. For example, if one of the accounts is extremely small relative to the others it is obvious that it never needs to be considered.

References

Aronson, Elliot, and J. Merrill Carlsmith (1968). "Experimentation in Social Psychology." In Gardner Lindzey and Elliott Aronson, *Handbook of Social Psychology,* 2nd ed., Vol. 2, Reading, Mass.: Addison-Wesley, pp. 1–79.

Bergman, Vincent A. (1967). "Training Salesmen in the Effective Use of Time." In *The New Handbook of Sales Training,* ed. Robert F. Vizza. Englewood Cliffs, N.J.: Prentice-Hall.

Bettman, James R., and Pradeep Kakkar (1977). "Effects of Information Presentation Format on Consumer Information Acquisition Strategies." *Journal of Consumer Research* 3 (March):233–240.

Churchill, Gilbert A., Jr.; Neil M. Ford; and Orville C. Walker, Jr. (1981). *Sales Force Management.* Homewood, Ill.: Irwin.

Davis, Kenneth R., and Frederick E. Webster, Jr. (1968). *Sales Force Management.* New York: Ronald Press.

Ebbeson, Ebbe B., and Vladimir J. Konecni (1981). "On the External Validity of Decision-Making Research: What Do We Know about Decisions in the Real World?" In *Cognitive Processes in Choice and Decision Behavior,* ed. Thomas S. Wallston. Hillsdale, N.J.: Lawrence Erlbaum Associates, pp. 21–45.

Fudge, William K., and Leonard M. Lodish (1977). "Evaluation of the Effectiveness of a Model Based Salesman's Planning System by Field Experimentation." *Interfaces* 8 (November, Part 2):97–106.

Hogarth, Robin M. (1980). *Judgment and Choice: The Psychology of Choice.* Chichester: John Wiley and Sons.

Jacoby, Jacob (1977). "Information Load and Decision Quality: Some Contested Issues." *Journal of Marketing Research* 14 (November): 569–573.

Lodish, Leonard M. (1971), "CALLPLAN: An Interactive Salesman's Call Planning System," *Management Science* 18 (December, Part II), pp. 25–40.

Lodish, Leonard M. (1974). " 'Vaguely Right' Approach to Sales Force Allocations." *Harvard Business Review* 52 (January-February):119–124.

McIntyre, Shelby H., and Adrian B. Ryans (1983). "Task Effects on Decision Quality in Traveling Salesperson Problems." *Organizational Behavior and Human Performance* 32, forthcoming.

Mitchell, Terence R. (1978). *People in Organizations: Understanding Their Behavior.* New York: McGraw-Hill.

Montgomery, D.B.; A.J. Silk; and C.E. Zaragoza (1971). "A Multiple Product Sales Force Allocation Model." *Management Science* 18 (December):3–24.

Newell, Allen, and Herbert A. Simon (1972). *Human Problem Solving.* Englewood Cliffs, N.J.: Prentice-Hall.

Payne, John W., and Myron L. Braunstein (1971). "Preference among Gambles with Equal Underlying Distributions." *Journal of Experimental Psychology* 87, 13–18.

Shapiro, Benson P. (1977). *Sales Program Management: Formulation and Implementation.* New York: McGraw-Hill.

Slovic, Paul, and Sarah Lichtenstein (1968). "The Importance of Variance Preferences in Gambling Decisions." *Journal of Experimental Psychology* 78, 646–654.

Slovic, Paul, and Douglas McPhillamy (1974). "Dimensional Commensurability and Cue Utilization in Comparative Judgment." *Organizational Behavior and Human Performance.* 11, 172–194.

Van Raaij, W. Fred (1976). "Data Acquisition Processing for Different Information Structures and Formats." *Proceedings of the Annual Conference of the Association for Consumer Research,* pp. 176–184.

Wright, Peter L., and Barton Weitz (1977). "Time Horizon Effects on Product Evaluation Strategies." *Journal of Marketing Research* 14 (November):429–433.

Zoltners, Andris A. (1979). "Integer Programming Models for Sales Territory Alignment to Maximize Profit." *Journal of Marketing Research* 13 (November):426–430.

10 Determining Specialized Sales Assignments Using Job Execution and Personal Criteria: A Method and Application

*Lawrence M. Lamont,
William J. Lundstrom,* and
William G. Zikmund

Traditional efforts to improve the effectiveness of personal selling have led to specializing salespeople by industry, product line, trade channel, customer, and geographic region (Parasuraman 1975; Schwartz 1962). Other studies focusing on the content of the selling job and the behavior of salespeople have suggested the value of specializing salespeople in different ways. Kahn and Shuchman (1961), for example, have observed that some salespeople prefer sales development work whereas others are more effective at sales maintenance. They recommend specializing personal selling by organizing the sales force in this manner. Pasold (1975), focusing on sales behavior, advocates the specialization of selling effort by market type.

Most firms are able to determine the type of specialized selling required. However, the problem of identifying the salespeople capable of providing the expected sales effort is often overlooked. To successfully use specialized selling, the business must acquire an understanding of the salesperson's job, personal selling styles, and the characteristics of the salespeople whose styles of selling are congruent with the specialized effort needed. These aspects of the specialization problem have not been widely investigated or reported in the marketing literature. Thus the objectives of the research were to:

1. Define the content of an industrial sales job in terms of specific behavioral dimensions.
2. Present an approach to identifying personal selling styles which will serve as a basis for the specialization of salespeople in industrial marketing.
3. Relate the personal selling styles to the personality and personal characteristics of salespeople, their compensation, and sales performance.

183

**Behavioral Dimensions and Personal
Selling Styles**

Two related concepts provide the foundation for this chapter: the
behavioral dimensions that comprise the industrial sales job and the *personal selling styles* of salespeople. Defining what salespeople do (or should
do) has proved to be difficult. Only a few authors have studied industrial
selling and attempted to define the behavioral dimensions of the sales job
(Lamont and Lundstrom 1977; Robinson and Stidsen 1967). Personal selling styles, because they reflect patterns of behavior or how effort was applied on the behavioral dimensions, are unique. Researchers have recognized
that executives have different managerial styles, but the concept has not
been applied to salespeople. It is believed that a typology of selling styles
can be identified that will be useful for specialization and research in
marketing. Each concept is defined in the following sections.

Behavioral Dimensions of Industrial Selling

Research suggests that human behavior can be classified into basic dimensions (Cattell 1964; Wofford 1967). Similar conclusions appear to hold for
behavior in an occupational setting. Hemphill (1959), Stewart (1967), and
Wofford (1970), for example, studied managers in a broad cross-section of
businesses and found that managerial behavior was multidimensional, with
each dimension consisting of several related job activities. Applied to personal selling, the behavioral dimensions broadly define the content of the
sales job. Each dimension comprises a related group of selling activities that
salespeople perform. Customer service, for example, describes one behavioral dimension of the sales job and might include the activities of providing
customers product samples, following up on sales orders, and checking
customer inventory.

    Despite an expressed need for an improved understanding of personal
selling (Dunn and Johnson 1973; Kahn and Shuchman 1961), little empirical research exists. In the sales and marketing literature, the dimensions
of sales behavior must be inferred from case studies of sales jobs, published
job descriptions, and performance appraisal forms (Crissy and Cash 1957;
Dodge 1970; Gopel 1977; Gross 1959; McMurry 1959; National Industrial
Conference Board 1965; Rados 1946). The literature suggests that the industrial sales job is multidimensional, with the number of behavioral dimensions ranging between three and nine. Most of the job descriptions and performance appraisal instruments contain the dimensions of direct selling
(making sales presentations), customer service, and territory management.
One exploratory empirical study confirms these dimensions (Lamont and

Lundstrom 1977), but in general the literature is primarily descriptive and does not appear to rest on a foundation of marketing research.

Personal Selling Styles

The salesperson is often described as an individual possessing a wide range of skills that enable him/her to adapt to different interpersonal situations. This chapter does not attempt to refute this conception. Instead, the authors take the position that while sales behavior is adjusted to respond to individual customers, certain basic patterns of behavior (or selling styles) can be identified that are common to groups (or clusters) of salespeople. Accordingly, a personal selling style is defined as a salesperson's characteristic pattern of performance on the behavioral dimensions of the sales job.

The concept of a person selling style is based on the extensive literature in managerial behavior identifying leadership styles among managers and the research that suggests that individuals develop consistent ways of reacting to interpersonal situations (Blake and Mouton 1966; Fiedler and Chemers 1974; Hodgetts 1975; Presthus 1962). Much of the literature suggests that leaders develop styles that can be defined by the relative emphasis placed on the various behavioral dimensions of the job (Hershey and Blanchard 1977; Redding 1970). Similarly, it is hypothesized that salespeople develop characteristic styles of selling that can be defined by observing patterns of performance or from reports of performance. Thus a salesperson who emphasizes and successfully performs the customer service activities of his/her job might have his/her style described as service-oriented.

The concept of a personal selling style also relies on the premise that a salesperson's job performance and the way s/he does his/her job are influenced by individual characteristics and interpersonal skills available for responding to different selling situations (Hershey and Blanchard 1972; Parasuraman 1975). The theory is based on the relationship between personality and interpersonal behavior explored and developed by Kelly (1925); Harvey, Hunt, and Schroder (1961); Presthus (1962); and Witkin, Dyk, Patterson, Goodenough, and Karp (1962). Harrison and Lubin (1965) note that people will focus on tasks with which they can use their own special skills and pass over those in which their knowledge is lacking.

While the behavioral dimensions and personal selling styles are conceptually distinct, the concepts are interactive and related by definition: A personal selling style is defined in terms of the salesperson's actual performance on the behavioral job dimensions.

Research Methodology

Setting

The research was conducted with a leading manufacturer of industrial building materials. A divisional sales force of 143 salespeople located in thirteen regional sales districts throughout the United States participated in the study. Each salesperson sold the same product line and was assigned to a sales territory that included construction firms, original equipment manufacturers (OEMs), and building supply distributors.

The sales force was well established and experienced. There was little turnover, with the average person having twenty years of selling experience and about twelve years in the present sales territory. Salespeople made a mean number of 1227 sales calls in a year with 85 percent directed to current company accounts and 15 percent to the development of new accounts. The sales compensation plan consisted of a base salary with a commission on sales above a quota. Additional incentive compensation, based on sales of certain profitable products, was also earned by most.

Exploratory Research to Identify Selling Activities

To further define the industrial sales job and reflect the perceptions of both management and the sales force regarding its content, unstructured interviews were conducted with sales managers, product managers, and a number of salespeople. Following a content analysis of the interviews, 200 statements describing the job in terms of selling activities were prepared. Considerable effort was made to reflect the selling activities identified in the literature as well as to include those that salespeople were expected to perform.

The statements were then analyzed by the researchers and sales management to eliminate redundancy, insure presentation of the job domain, and preserve the behavioral format. Editing and the elimination of overlapping statements resulted in the final selection of sixty behavioral statements for inclusion in the research instrument. The data collected using these statements as variables became the basis for defining the behavioral dimensions of the sales job and the personal selling styles of salespeople.

Variables Associated with Personal Selling Styles

The third objective of the research study was to identify variables associated with the personal selling styles. Several classes of variables were viewed as either influencing or being influenced by the salesperson's personal selling style: personality, personal characteristics, sales performance, and compensation. Data on variables in each of these categories were collected to provide a profile on the salespeople using the different selling styles and to assess their relative effectiveness.

Personality and Personal Characteristics

The relationship between leadership style and personality and the connection between personal characteristics and behavior suggest that these two groups of variables might differentiate personal selling styles. Published research with the salespeople included in this study has already shown personality and personal characteristics to be related to sales performance (Lamont and Lundstrom 1977). The personality variables (also used in this study) were dominance, endurance, social recognition (Jackson 1967), empathy (Hogan 1969), and ego strength (Cattell, Eber and Tatsuoka 1970), while the personal characteristics included age, height, weight, formal education, family size, participation in outside activities, memberships in civic and professional organizations, and selling experience. An extensive discussion of the previous research with each variable and the rationale for their inclusion in studies of this type has been reported previously and is not repeated here. Career anchorage, family size, and selling experience are examined and reported here for the first time.

The Career Anchorage Scale (Tausky and Dubin 1965), a measure of an individual's career orientation, was included in this study along with family size and two measures of sales experience because it was anticipated that they would further differentiate the selling styles of salesmen. The Career Anchorage Scale is a model based on the principle ''that a career perspective be anchored to some reference point, which may be either the starting point of a career, or the level of maximum possible achievement'' (Tausky and Dubin 1965, p. 735). Higher scores on the scale identify salespeople who orient their career goals toward the highest position in the company (an upward orientation), while low scores identify those who view their career progress by the distance moved from an occupational starting point (a downward orientation). Table 10–1 presents the descriptive statistics for the personality variables and career anchorage as well as the source and scoring of the scales used in the research instrument.

Objective Measures of Sales Performance
and Compensation

To investigate the relationship between selling style and objective measures of sales performance and compensation, information on annual sales

Table 10-1
Summary of Personality Variables and Career Anchorage

Variable	Description of High Scorer	Scale Source	Scoring	Mean (n = 71)
Dominance	Attempts to control his/her environment and to influence or direct other people; expresses opinions forcefully; enjoys the role of leader and may assume it spontaneously	Personality Research Form	20 true-false statements Minimum score 0 Maximum score 20	12.97
Endurance	Willing to work long hours, doesn't give up quickly on a problem; persevering, even in the face of great difficulty; patient and unrelenting in work habits	Personality Research Form	20 true-false statements Minimum score 0 Maximum score 20	14.70
Social recognition	Desires to be held in high esteem by acquaintances; concerned about reputation and what other people think of him/her; works for approval and recognition of others	Personality Research Form	20 true-false statements Minimum score 0 Maximum score 20	11.53
Empathy	Possesses the ability to apprehend another's condition or state of mind	Hogan Empathy Scale	64 true-false statements Minimum score 0 Maximum score 64	36.44
Ego-strength	Exhibits emotional stability, resourcefulness, and a strong motivation for professional status	16 Personality Factor	13 multiple choice statements Minimum score 0 Maximum score 26	16.63
Career anchorage	Views career progress from the perspective of the highest position in the company	Career Anchorage Scale	6 forced choice statements Minimum score 0 Maximum score 6	1.94

volume, sales quota, and compensation was obtained from sales management for the salespeople included in the study. These data were used to develop the compensation measures—salary, sales commissions, incentive earnings, and total compensation—and the performance measures—sales, sales/quota, sales commisions/total compensation, and incentive earnings/total compensation.

Research Instrument

To prepare the data collection instrument, the sixty behavioral statements describing the sales activities were scaled on seven point Likert-type scales. The scales measured the salesperson's self-appraisal of performance on each behavioral activity, providing a measure of the quality and amount of effort expended. The self ratings were considered appropriate because of the salesperson's familiarity with each of the selling activities and their potential for revealing his/her approach to personal selling.

Extensive pretesting of different descriptive statements for rating categories and anchoring phrases for the scales was conducted. Pretests of the rating scales revealed that salespeople were somewhat reluctant to evaluate their performance unfavorably. The scales tested that anchored one pole of the scale with a negative descriptor (such as unsatisfactory) resulted in performance measurements with some restriction of range. The problem was minimized by arranging the scales so that higher scale value were associated with outstanding sales performance (7 = Outstanding) and smaller scale values indicated a lower level of sales performance (1 = Satisfactory). The research instrument instructed the salespeople that Outstanding meant that performance on the activity was superior and there was little opportunity for improvement, while Satisfactory meant that performance was adequate, but there was substantial opportunity for improvement.

The research instrument was also designed to allow an evaluation of the extent to which salespeople having different personal selling styles differed on selected personality and personal characteristics. Thus in addition to the scaled statements on selling activities, the research instrument included the personality scales, career anchorage, and a section to obtain the information on personal characteristics.

Data Collection

Data were collected from the salespeople by self-administered questionnaires. Because of the length of the personality scales and the large amount of data collected, the research instrument was administered in two parts over a six-month interval. A total of 143 salespeople were in the sales force; 94 successfully completed both questionnaires. Sales management provided information for 71 of the salespeople on sales volume, sales quota, and compensation covering the same business year as the self-appraisals of performance. Thus data collection resulted in complete information on 71 salesmen, representing each of the 13 sales districts.

Methods of Data Analysis

Factor analysis was used to reduce the behavioral statements to a smaller set of constructs and facilitate the identification of the underlying behavioral dimensions of the job. This method was considered appropriate because of the large number of variables, the correlations that existed among the statements (variables), and the need to summarize the statements for interpretation. An orthogonal (Varimax) simple structure solution defining the behavioral dimensions was selected using a discontinuity plot and the auxiliary criteria of interpretability and meaningfulness suggested by Rummel (1970). Standardized factor scores were then computed for each salesperson to provide a composite measure of performance on each behavior.

Personal selling styles were identified through the use of hierarchical cluster analysis of the standardized factor scores to classify salespeople into groups with similar patterns of performance on the behavioral dimensions. While this methodology is appropriate for testing a previously constructed typology or empirically deriving a typology, it was used here to derive a typology of selling styles (Pruden 1973). A squared interpoint distance matrix was constructed from the standardized factor scores using the diameter method of Johnson's hierarchical clustering procedure (Johnson 1967). A distinct clustering solution was selected based on: (1) a comparison of the average intersubject distance within and between clusters, (2) a plot of cluster diameter as the number of clusters decreased, (3) a comparison of cluster centroids as an indication of behavioral distinctiveness, and (4) the meaningfulness and interpretability of the clusters as judged by the authors.

The influence of personality, personal characteristics, compensation, and sales performance was evaluated by one-way analysis of variance (ANOVA) to compare cluster membership with the variables in each category. Significant differences were noted and post hoc comparisons using the method of Scheffé were used to explore the significant variables.

Research Results

Definition of the Behavioral Dimensions

Following the factor analysis of the self-appraisal measures, a seven-factor Varimax solution was selected as providing the most complete, interpretable, yet parsimonious solution. The interpretation on the solution along with the author's definitions of the factors (based on the factor loadings) follows.

The variable loadings on the seven factors suggest that the factor analysis provides a reasonably good definition of the behavioral dimensions of the sales job. Factor 1—making sales presentations—describes a general factor and includes items concerned with product knowledge, selling techniques, call frequency, and an ethical dimension of personal selling. Factor 2—providing information on markets and product supply—suggests that the salesperson's performance is related to ability to keep customers abreast of market and supply conditions. Factor 3—customer service—highlights the salesperson's regular service activities including providing information and samples, keeping customer records, and handling sales orders. The need to reach end users and purchase influencers is evident in factor 4—sales promotion and specification selling—where in the behavioral dimension includes making sales calls on materials specifiers and government offices and participating in industry trade associations and local business groups. Factor 5—working and cooperating with district management—suggests that a salesperson's willingness to assist and work with sales management is viewed as a behavioral dimension of the job, while factor 6—handling customer complaints and credit adjustments—indicates service-oriented activities dealing specifically with handling product and service complaints and credit adjustments in an ethical manner. Finally, factor 7—closing sales, obtaining orders, and meeting sales objectives—identifies the importance of completing the selling process by closing the sale and obtaining the order.

Personal Selling Styles of Industrial Salesmen

Judgment was necessary in defining the personal selling styles because the problem of identifying the optimal number of clusters remains. Since choice of a clustering solution had to be made by the authors, considerable care was taken in forming and analyzing the distance matrix and interpreting the clustering solutions. The interpoint distance matrix derived from the self-appraisal factor scores was independently constructed and analyzed. Application of the criteria previously mentioned and agreement on the number of behaviorally distinct and meaningful clusters led to the selection of four clusters, each defining a personal selling style.

The results of the cluster analysis are shown in table 10-2. The cluster centroids provide an average factor score on each behavioral dimension and can be compared within and across clusters. However, to identify the salespeople's perceptions of their own selling style, the following discussion focuses on how individuals within each cluster perform on the behavioral dimensions.

Table 10-2
Clusters of Industrial Salespeople Defined Using Behavioral Dimensions

		Cluster Centroids			
Factor	Behavioral Dimension	Cluster 1 Service Oriented (n = 19)	Cluster 2 Information Oriented (n = 6)	Cluster 3 Sales Oriented (n = 7)	Cluster 4 Marketing Oriented (n = 39)
1	Making sales presentations	-.87	-.80	-.03	.55
2	Providing information on markets and product supply	-.52	-.97	-.53	.50
3	Customer service	-.36	-1.45	-1.12	.60
4	Sales promotion and specification selling	-.36	-.86	-.74	.44
5	Working and cooperating with district management	-.72	-1.46	.10	.56
6	Handling customer complaints and credit adjustments	-.09	-1.63	-1.25	.52
7	Closing sales, obtaining orders, and meeting sales objectives	-.18	-2.48	.71	.34

The Service-Oriented Style. Cluster one contains nineteen salespeople and the cluster centroids describe a service-oriented style of selling. This style emphasizes sales promotion and contact with existing customers to provide service and handle complaints. Salespeople using this style are primarily order takers, but they are capable of closing sales. However, the service orientation suggests less interest in developing new customers for the firm. This style relies on established relationships and customer satisfaction as ways of developing sales volume with existing customers.

The Information-Oriented Style. Cluster two includes six salespeople whose style can be described as an information-oriented approach to industrial selling. These people devote effort to acquiring product and application information. Then the selling centers around the sales presentation and the use of additional information on markets and product supply to enable the customer to make a purchase decision. But for the salespeople using this soft sell style, the selling effort ends here. The information-oriented style of selling does not include careful attention to the customer service aspects of the job, the need to establish a working relationship with district management, or the skill to influence buyer behavior by closing the sale and obtaining the order.

The Sales-Oriented Style. The seven salespeople included in cluster three use a sales-oriented style of personal selling. This emphasizes an aggressive presentation of the firm's products with a strong close to overcome objections and obtain the order. Part of the selling style involves the development of a close relationship with sales management to obtain whatever support is necessary to meet the established sales objectives. The sales-oriented style of selling places less emphasis on the after-sale dimensions of the job involving customer service and handling complaints. Salespeople using this style view closing sales and short-term sales volume as their ultimate goals and are less concerned with the dimensions of the job not directly connected to making sales.

The Marketing-Oriented Style. The largest number of salespeople are in cluster four. The cluster defines a marketing-oriented selling style that reflects an understanding of the role of personal selling in the firm's marketing program. People in this cluster view all of the behavioral dimensions of the job as important and try to perform each effectively. The marketing-oriented selling style suggests an ability to look beyond the immediate sale to the long-term satisfaction of the customer. Management's satisfaction with the quality of the sales effort and the low turnover is probably a reflection of the large number of marketing-oriented salespeople in the sales force.

Variables Related to Selling Style

To profile the salespeople using each style of personal selling, personality, personal characteristics, compensation, and sales performance were evaluated across clusters using a one-way ANOVA. Significant differences between clusters were assessed using post hoc tests. In addition, the geographic location and customer composition of the sales territories were examined across clusters. No patterns of concentration were observed that suggested selling style was influenced by these latter two factors.

Table 10-3 presents the analysis of variance results. Ten of the twenty-three measures examined were significant at the .10 level or better, including three personality measures and career anchorage; the personal characteristics; age; two compensation measures; and three measures of sales performance. The large number of significant differences on the external measures provides some validity for the results of the cluster analysis and the typology of selling styles.

The significant Personality Research Form (PRF) variables, dominance, endurance, and social recognition as well as career anchorage suggest that differences in the ability to influence and direct other people, work habits, needs for recognition, and career orientations differentiate the various styles of personal selling. Age, a personal characteristic, is also significant across the four clusters.

Five of the eight measures of compensation and sales performance are significant at the .10 level or better. Compensation measures such as sales commissions and total compensation are significant, suggesting that selling styles have important implications for salespeople's earning capacity. Similar conclusions are appropriate for performance measured by yearly sales volume and the ratios sales/quota and sales commissions/total compensation. Certain selling styles are associated with higher levels of sales performance.

Salesperson Profiles for the Personal Selling Styles

The research was also useful in developing a salesperson profile for the four selling styles. These profiles provide insight into the salespeople using the different styles and should help to identify these individuals for specialization.

The Service-Oriented Salesperson. According to table 10-3, the personality characteristics low dominance and social recognition distinguish the service-oriented salesperson. These traits suggest an individual who is not particularly effective in directing the selling process and not motivated by the recognition that comes from success in selling. S/he tends to be older, established in the sales territory, and active in civic and professional organizations. Compared to the others included in the study, service-oriented salespeople are lowest in average sales volume and are average performers in terms of quota achievement. Their performance explains the below-average compensation and provides a contrast to the sales-oriented salespeople. As shown in table 10–3, service-oriented salespeople are significantly lower in dominance and social recognition, older, and have lower earnings from sales commissions. The profile describes a person who is probably in the declining stages of his/her sales career. Although s/he still holds modest aspirations for career advancement, s/he is most likely resigned to selling.

The Information-Oriented Salesperson. Information-oriented salespeople have the lowest average dominance and the highest average endurance scores. This personality profile describes those who are steady but ineffective, workers, because they have a poor understanding of the sales process and are not persuasive and assertive. The low average career anchorage scores identify salespeople who have little aspiration to advance beyond their present job and view selling as an acceptable termination point for a career. The information-oriented salesperson likes to work in his/her own way, resents interference from management, and may be alienated. Low interest in outside activities and few memberships in civic and professional organizations suggest a reserved, inward-looking person.

The performance of the information-oriented salespeople measured by sales commissions/total compensation is below average, and they form the only cluster that failed to exceed their sales quota. Average earnings from sales commissions and total compensation are also the lowest of the four clusters. The inability of these salespeople to perform all dimensions of the job appears to be reflected in their performance and earning capacity. Compared to those using sales-oriented styles of selling, these people are significantly lower in dominance, career anchorage, sales performance, and compensation.

The Sales-Oriented Salesperson. These salespeople are younger and have the highest average dominance, social recognition, and career anchorage scores, and the lowest average endurance scores. This profile describes a forceful, aggressive type who is motivated by a strong need for recognition and the prospect of advancement to management. S/he focuses his/her selling effort where sales goals can be achieved with less effort and dominates the interpersonal relationship with the customer.

Sales-oriented salespeople have a higher average educational achievement, less selling experience, and are not as well established in their sales territories. Unlike the information-oriented salespeople, they are more involved in outside activities and have diverse interests.

Table 10-3
Means of Personality, Personal Characteristic, Compensation, and Performance Measures by Salesperson Cluster

	Variable Means					
	Cluster 1 (n = 19)	Cluster 2 (n = 6)	Cluster 3 (n = 7)	Cluster 4 (n = 39)	F	Significance of F
Personality						
Dominance	11.47	11.16	17.14	13.23	3.90	.012
Endurance	13.58	15.83	12.29	15.51	3.24	.027
Social recognition	9.74	12.00	13.17	11.95	4.47	.007
Empathy	36.58	32.83	37.14	36.80	1.10	.358
Ego-strength	15.74	16.50	16.71	17.08	.45	.719
Career anchorage	2.21	1.17	2.86	1.77	2.99	.037
Personal Characteristic						
Age	48.26	46.50	38.29	47.97	2.38	.077
Height	69.68	70.83	71.14	71.00	1.43	.241
Weight	178.21	181.33	192.86	186.08	.78	.511
Formal education	14.74	14.83	16.14	14.92	1.16	.330
Family size	4.63	4.33	4.86	4.49	.15	.930
Participation in outside activities	1.95	1.50	2.43	2.38	1.24	.302
Memberships in civic and professional organizations	2.16	1.33	1.71	1.67	.87	.537
Professional selling experience	269.68	247.00	185.71	239.49	1.107	.353
Time in present sales territory	155.50	147.67	117.0	137.59	.250	.862
Compensation Measure						
Salary[a]	$ 9,074	$ 9,360	$ 8,731	$ 9,307	.78	.509
Sales commissions[a]	9,510	8,672	14,094	10,608	3.07	.033
Incentive earnings[a]	710	1,178	1,067	971	.91	.554
Total compensation[a]	19,294	19,210	23,892	20,886	2.20	.095

Performance Measure						
Sales[a]	$882,884	$923,300	$1,368,200	$934,537	2.30	.085
Sales/quota	1.15	.88	1.34	1.14	4.20	.009
Sales commissions						
Total compensation	.49	.44	.57	.50	3.54	.019
Incentive earnings						
Total compensation	.033	.051	.040	.045	1.01	.393

[a]Data multiplied by a constant to avoid disclosure.

Sales performance and compensation further distinguish the sales-oriented salespeople. These people are highest in average sales, quota achievement, and sales commissions/total compensation. Further, they have the highest average sales commissions and total compensation. The sales-oriented person is concerned with results and management aspirations, so selling probably will not be his/her career.

The Marketing-Oriented Salesperson. Marketing-oriented salespeople are almost a composite of the salespeople in the other clusters. They are average scorers on many of the personality variables and career anchorage but above average on dominance and endurance. Thus they appear to be hard, willing workers with the ability to influence and persuade others.

Average performance in terms of sales and quota achievement characterize the marketing-oriented salespeople, but they have higher average sales, commissions, and total compensation than those who use the service- and information-oriented styles. These people are dependable performers, possessing both flexibilty and versatility. Industrial selling is viewed as a career by these individuals.

Discussion

The study provides a more complete understanding of industrial selling and addresses some important issues in the specialization of sales effort. The implications for sales management and directions for future research are discussed in the following sections.

Behavioral Dimensions: Implications
for Specialization

An understanding of the behavioral dimensions of the industrial sales job is crucial to the specialization of selling because they define the basic areas in which a salesperson's effort can be focused. The research results suggest a complex selling task, so it is not surprising that many salespeople are simply not capable of performing every dimension of the job. This provides an argument for using specialized selling where it is appropriate.

The behavioral dimensions suggest a multidimensional selling task and support the findings of research on managerial behavior and the literature in marketing. The study importantly uncovered some dimensions not recognized in the marketing literature but which are important in industrial selling. These include the demand-creation factor of sales promotion and specification selling and the separate factor defined for closing sales and obtaining orders. Further, the behavioral dimension—handling customer complaints and credit adjustments—is usually included under a broad customer service category. In this study, it is identified as a distinct dimension, suggesting its importance in a market often faced with product allocation and delayed shipping dates.

Selling Styles: Implications for Specialization

The research represents a first step in the development of the selling style concept. Building on an established theoretical base linking personality and interpersonal behavior, the research defined four distinct styles of personal selling. Based on the selling styles and characteristics of the salespeople comprising the sales force of this compmany, some tentative conclusions can be reached about their specialization.

The service-oriented salespeople seem to be comfortable in selling situations in which they can build on existing product acceptance and the buyer's confidence in the company. They might be best utilized in established sales territories or with customers for whom buying patterns and good customer relations already exist. Because the service-oriented salesperson's style is not aggressive, s/he can be most effectively specialized defensively, to protect his/her firm's present business and create additional sales from existing customers.

Specializing information-oriented salespeople presents a challenge because they lack selling skills and probably sell those customers who would purchase from the firm anyway. Prior to specialization, these salespeople are candidates for sales training with emphasis on customer service, sales promotion, utilizing sales management in selling, and closing techniques. If sales training is successful, they could be utilized with small, low-potential accounts, in declining sales territories, or in a market-development capacity to identify potential customers and product applications.

Salespeople using the sales-oriented selling style seem to do an adequate job of developing business among existing customers, selling present products, and pioneering the sale of new products. However, because of their aggressive, persistent nature, these salespeople may lose some accounts and have difficulty selling others. Sales-oriented types do not appear to be suited for market development in which contact over a long period of time is needed to produce results. Instead, these salesmen might be specialized by using them in sales territories dominated by competition, where competitor's customers can be sold with an aggressive selling effort. Management should be cautious, though, to assign this salesperson to a territory where his/her style of selling is acceptable to customers.

The marketing-oriented salespeople offer the greatest flexibility in specialization because they are self starters, require little supervision, and perform all dimensions of the selling job. These people seem well suited to handle large existing and potential accounts where further strengthening of a long-term business relationship is desirable. Because they view selling as a professional career, they plan carefully to develop a productive sales territory for the future. In addition, marketing-oriented salespeople can be specialized where market development and missionary selling are needed.

Directions for Future Research

The research reported here represents an important step in the assessment of industrial selling jobs and the personal selling styles of salespeople. Additional effort is needed to further validate and refine the concepts and extend them to other businesses and different sales jobs. In addition, extensions of this research might include the use of different scaling methods for the selling activities and other ways of conceptualizing the sales job. Here, researchers might benefit from recent studies on the definition and measurement of job characteristics by Dunham (1976), Hackman and Oldham (1975), Tornow and Pinto (1976), and Sims, Szilagyi, and Keller (1976).

The personality and personal characteristic profiles developed for salespeople using the different selling styles are important findings of this research. The profiles demonstrate the possibility of using selling style as a criterion in selection research and the personality scales as predictors. Success in differentiating selling styles with the dominance, endurance, and social recognition scales of the PRF suggests the potential value of the remaining scales in this instrument. The PRF is based on Murray's theory of psychological needs; this personality model may be a useful point of departure for additional development of the selling-style concept (Jackson 1970; Murray 1958).

Summary and Conclusions

Research leading to the grouping of selling activities into broader behavioral dimensions is fundamental to developing a theoretical structure for personal selling. The industrial sales job studied was found to be multidimensional. Some of the dimensions are delineated here for the first time. We conclude that the industrial selling task is more complex than the impression conveyed by much of the literature on personal selling.

Using the behavioral dimensions and numerical taxonomic analysis, four distinct personal selling styles are defined for the seventy-one salespeople in the study. Knowledge of the different selling styles can be of significant value to sales management in providing specialized selling effort.

The concept of a selling style is in the exploratory stage of investigation. Additional research is worthwhile to refine the concept and develop a taxonomy of styles.

Selling styles were successfully differentiated using personality and personal characteristics, and profiles were developed for the salespeople using each style. The profiles are helpful in understanding the selling styles and identifying people for the purpose of specialization. The study also found that certain personal selling styles were associated with higher levels of sales performance (using objective measures) and compensation.

References

Blake, R.R., and J.S. Mouton (1966). "Managerial Facades." *Advanced Management Journal* 27 (July):30–37.

Cattell, R.B. (1964). *Personality and Social Psychology.* San Diego: Robert K. Knapp.

Cattell, R.B.; H.W. Eber; and M. Tatsuoka (1970). *Handbook for the Sixteen Personality Factor Questionnaire.* Champaign, Ill.: Institute for Personality and Ability Testing.

Crissy, W.J.E., and Harold C. Cash (1957). "The Why and the 'How to' of a Salesman's Job Description." *Sales Management* 18 (October): 102–105.

Dodge, H. Robert (1970). *Industrial Marketing.* New York: McGraw-Hill, p. 316.

Dunham, Randall B. (1976). "The Measurement and Dimensionality of Job Characteristics." *Journal of Applied Psychology* 61, 404–409.

Dunn, Albert H., and Eugene M. Johnson (1973). *Managing the Sales Force.* Morristown, N.J.: General Learning Press, p. 117.

Fiedler, F.E., and M.M. Chemers (1974). *Leadership Style and Effective Management.* Glenview, Ill.: Scott Foresman and Company.

Gopel, R.A. (1977). "A Basic Guide to Training Industrial Salesman." In James M. Comer (ed.), *Sales Management: Roles and Methods.* Santa Monica, Calif.: Goodyear Publishing Co., pp. 119–141.

Gross, Alfred (1959). *Salesmanship.* New York: The Ronald Press Co., p. 12.

Hackman, J. Richard, and Greg R. Oldham (1975). "Development of the Job Diagnostic Survey." *Journal of Applied Psychology* 31 (January): 159–170.

Harrison, Roger, and B. Lubin (1965). "Personal Style, Group Composition and Learning." *The Journal of Applied Behavioral Science* 1, 286–301.

Harvey, O.J.; D.E. Hunt; and H.M. Schroder (1961). *Conceptual Systems and Personality Organization.* New York: Wiley.

Hemphill, J.K. (1959). "Job Descriptions for Executives." *Harvard Business Review* 37 (September-October):55–67.

Hersey, Paul, and Kenneth H. Blanchard (1972). *Management of Organizational Behavior*, 2nd ed. Englewood Cliffs, N.J.: Prentice-Hall, p. 82.

Hersey, Paul, and Kenneth H. Blanchard (1972). *Management of Organizational Behavior*, 3rd ed. Englewood Cliffs, N.J.: Prentice-Hall, pp. 111–129.

Hodgetts, Richard M. (1975). *Management: Theory Process and Practice*. Philadelphia: Saunders, pp. 341–359.

Hogan, Robert (1969). "Development of an Empathy Scale." *Journal of Consulting and Clinical Psychology* 33, 308.

Jackson, Donald N. (1967). *Personality Research Form Manual*. Goshen, N.Y.: Research Psychologist Press, pp. 6–7.

_____ (1970). "A Sequential System for Personality Scale Development." In C.D. Spielberger (ed.), *Current Topics in Clinical and Community Psychology*, Vol. 2. New York: Academic Press.

Johnson, Stephen C. (1967). "Hierarchical Clustering Schemes." *Psychometrika* 32 (September):241–254.

Kahn, George N., and Abraham Scuchman (1961). "Specialize Your Salesmen." *Harvard Business Review* 39 (January-February):90–98.

Kelly, G.A. (1955). *The Psychology of Personal Constructs*. New York: Norton.

Lamont, Lawrence M., and William J. Lundstrom (1977). "Identifying Successful Industrial Salesmen Using Personality and Personal Characteristics." *Journal of Marketing Research* 14 (November):517–529.

McMurry, Robert N. (1959). "How to Draft a Useful Job Description." *Sales Management* 83 (October):152–156.

Measuring Salesmen's Performance (1965). *Studies in Business Policy*, No. 114. New York: The National Industrial Conference Board.

Murray, H.A. (1958). *Exploration in Personality*. New York: Oxford University Press.

Parasuraman, A. (1975). "Assigning Salesmen to Territories." *Industrial Marketing Management* 4 (December):335–341.

Pasold, Peter W. (1975). "The Effectiveness of Various Modes of Sales Behavior in Different Markets." *Journal of Marketing Research* 12 (May):171–176.

Presthus, Robert (1962). *The Organizational Society*. New York: Alfred A. Knopf.

Pruden, Henry O. (1973). "The Upward Mobile, Indifferent, and Ambivalent Typology of Managers." *Academy of Management Journal* 16: 454–463.

Rados, William (1946). *How to Select Better Salesmen*. New York: Prentice-Hall, pp. 16–28.

Reddin, W.J. (1970). *Managerial Effectiveness*. New York: McGraw-Hill.

Robinson, Patrick J., and Bent Stidsen. (1967). *Personal Selling in a Modern Perspective*. Boston: Allyn and Bacon, p. 225.

Rummel, F.J. (1970). *Applied Factor Analysis*. Evanston, Ill.: Northwestern University Press, pp. 349–367.

Schwartz, Kenneth (1962). "The Switch to Specialized Sales." *Duns Review and Modern Industry* 25 (August):43–47.

Sims, Henry P.; Andrew D. Szilagyi; and Robert T. Keller (1976). "The Measurements of Job Characteristics." *Academy of Management Journal* 19 (June):195–212.

Stewart, R. (1967). *Managers and Their Jobs*. London: MacMillan.

Tausky, Curt, and Robert Dubin (1965). "Career Anchorage: Managerial Mobility Motivations." *American Sociological Review* 38 (October): 725–735.

Tornow, Walter W., and Patrick R. Pinto (1976). "The Development of a Managerial Job Taxonomy: A System for Describing, Classifying, and Evaluating Executive Positions." *Journal of Applied Psychology* 61: 410–418.

Witkin, H.A.; B. Dyk; H.F. Paterson; D.R. Goodenough; and S.A. Karp. (1962). *Psychological Differentiation*. New York: Wiley.

Wofford, J.C. (1967). "Behavior Styles and Performance Effectiveness." *Personnel Psychology* 20:461–496.

11 The Personal Selling Process in the Life Insurance Industry

Elizabeth J. Johnston-O'Connor,
Robert J. O'Connor, and
Walter H. Zultowski

The purpose of this chapter summarizes what consumer research at LIMRA (Life Insurance Marketing and Research Association) and other organizations suggest about the role of personal selling in the life insurance industry.[1] In a sense, it is meant to serve as a case study of an industry in which personal selling plays a major role. The chapter is divided into three major sections. The first provides some background on the nature of the life insurance product and the ways in which it is distributed. The second section provides a description of the life insurance sales process, along with a discussion of the factors related to successful selling. Finally, the last section examines the relationship between sales process variables and the tendency to retain policies over time (that is, persistency). Throughout, comments are made about consistent findings. In the interest of space, however, only the most recent data are used to illustrate such points.

Background

Life Insurance

There is no doubt that the public views life insurance as a necessity. In a recent nationwide public opinion survey (ACLI 1982), 80 percent of the respondents agreed with the statement "most people should have some form of life insurance." Similarly, in the same survey, 72 percent agreed that "life insurance is the best way of protecting one's family financially against the premature death of the breadwinner."

LIMRA's life insurance ownership studies demonstrate that these attitudes are backed up by behavior. The most recent study in this area (LIMRA/ACLI 1978) showed that 83 percent of all U.S. households own some form of life insurance. Moreover, among households with the greatest need for life insurance coverage (that is, husband-wife families with children under 18 years of age), this figure increases to 93 percent.

Authors are listed alphabetically and would like to express their appreciation to Nancy D. Boynton and Marles D. Dolge of LIMRA staff for their assistance in the preparation of this manuscript.

Within recent years, it has become common to hear life insurance referred to as a savings or investment; this is in part attributable to the fact that many insurance companies are now producing interest-sensitive products. Consumer research conducted by LIMRA and others, however, has traditionally shown that life insurance is primarily purchased for security and protection purposes. The results illustrated in table 11-1—obtained from a survey of recent life insurance buyers conducted in 1980 show that this continues to be the case (LIMRA/ACLI 1982).

In addition, it should be pointed out that life insurance is relatively complex, and the public has traditionally had difficulty with various aspects of it. As shown in table 11-2, the results of a recent national public opinion survey (ACLI 1982) indicate that this is still true, although the proportion of respondents expressing difficulty with each of these aspects of life insurance has declined significantly since the mid-1970s.

Similarly, 55 percent of the respondents in the same survey indicated that they are not well informed about life insurance (39 percent said they are "not too well informed" and 16 percent said they are "not at all informed"). Nine percent considered themselves to be "very well informed" about the product, while the remaining 36 percent indicated that they are "fairly well informed."

Finally, it is also interesting to note that a majority of the public (56 percent in 1982) continue to believe that life insurance is more expensive now than in previous years, when in fact the cost of life insurance—when measured on a premium per $1000 of coverage basis—has steadily declined over recent years.

In summary, the public views life insurance as a necessity and purchases it primarily to provide financial protection and security. At the same time, however, life insurance is a relatively complex product, and although the

Table 11-1
Consumer Reasons for Buying Insurance

Buyer's Reason for Purchase	Percent of Buyers
Continuing security of family after death	56%
Burial and other final expenses	49
Savings for retirement	23
To guarantee that the mortgage will be paid off	19
Savings for children's college education	13
Estate liquidity	7
Savings for emergencies	7
Busienss purposes	2
Other	5
	*

[a]Totals more than 100 percent because of multiple responses.

Table 11-2
Percent of Respondents Indicating Difficulty with Each of Five Aspects of Life Insurance

	Degree of Difficulty			
	A Lot	Some	Very Little	None
Understanding policy wording	33%	35%	16%	16%
Determining one's money's worth	24	35	20	21
Determining how much a policy will cost	18	33	27	22
Deciding on the type of policy needed	16	36	23	25
Determining amount to buy	15	36	20	29

public has become more informed about it in recent years, a majority still have difficulty with various aspects of life insurance and believe that they are not well informed about it.

Distribution of Life Insurance

While those in the life insurance business talk about many different types of distribution systems, there are basically only two ways of distributing life insurance to the public. The more common means, of course, is through agents; the less common approach is direct-response marketing, including direct mail and purchases made through advertisements.

Within recent years, more and more companies have initiated direct-response marketing programs, and the public has become increasingly aware of purchase opportunities not involving agents. In 1980, for example, 50 percent of U.S. households had purchase opportunities that did not involve agents, compared with 40 percent in 1973 (LIMRA 1981). However, there was no change between 1973 and 1980 in percentage of all U.S. households that purchased life insurance policies through some direct means (4 percent). The majority of life insurance purchases continue to be made through agents.

Nonetheless, the public's attitude toward life insurance agents *in general* is not especially favorable. In the national public opinion survey mentioned earlier, for example, only 37 percent of the respondents agreed that "life insurance agents are very concerned with their clients' needs." The problem with agents is typically viewed as revolving around such things as pressure selling, selling coverage that is not needed, lack of total honesty about what is being sold, and playing on guilt feelings during the sales process.

Despite the concerns raised by the public regarding life insurance agents in general, research also shows that a majority of the public view the agent as a necessary and important component of the sales process. In a 1979 public opinion survey (ACLI 1979), for example, six in ten respondents agreed that it would be a mistake to eliminate the life insurance agent from the sales process. At first glance, this result may appear contradictory to the finding reported above, but *why* the agent is viewed as an important component of the sales process becomes clear when the public is questioned more specifically: The agent is viewed as important because of the knowledge, information, and advice that he/she can contribute to the sales process. When asked to indicate the general characteristics of agents, the most common characteristic cited by the public is knowledge.

This is supported by a 1981 national public opinion survey that asked whether the commissioned agent adds unnecessarily to the cost of life insurance (ACLI 1981). The 78 percent who believed that the agent is worth the additional cost were further questioned as to why they felt that way. The respondents more frequently cited the personal attention, information, and advice provided by the agent during the sales process.

Finally, although *the public* has concerns about life insurance agents in general, life insurance *buyers and policyowners* have much more positive attitudes about the agents from whom they have purchased coverage and about the agents whom they consider to be their "personal" agents.

In a 1977 survey of recent buyers from six specific companies (LIMRA 1979), for example, agents were found to receive extremely high marks when evaluated on their performance in various aspects of the sales process. These results are shown in table 11-3.

In addition, 85 percent of these buyers said that they would buy again from the same agent, and 46 percent indicated that they would like to have an agent contact them every two years or sooner in order to review and service their life insurance.

In summary, a large proportion of the public have negative attitudes and concerns regarding the practices of life insurance agents *in general*.

Table 11-3
Buyer's Evaluations of Agents from Whom They Purchased Coverage

	Rating of Agent			
	Excellent	Good	Fair	Poor
Being courteous and businesslike	80%	18%	2%	+
Having thorough knowledge of life insurance	72	25	3	+
Avoiding high pressure	70	23	6	1%
Describing policies openly and honestly	69	26	4	1
Helping select right *type* of coverage	66	29	4	1
Avoiding complex and technical language	65	31	4	+
Helping select right *amount* of coverage	62	31	6	1

+ Indicates less than one-half of 1 percent.

The nature of life insurance causes the agent to be seen as an important component of the sales process. This is primarily because of the knowledge, advice, and personal attention that he/she can bring to the sales process. Individuals who have recently purchased from agents typically give their agents very positive evaluations, indicate that they would buy from the same agent on a future occasion, and express interest in having regular contact with the agent in order to review and update their life insurance programs.

The Personal Selling Process in Life Insurance

The personal selling process usually begins with a contact between the agent and the prospect. A 1980 LIMRA survey showed that 35 percent of the public either approached or were approached by agents in 1980. Of those households that were contacted, half actually granted interviews with the agents. Of those consumers granting interviews, 45 percent actually purchased policies.

Because only one-third of the population actually come into contact with agents each year, it has proved difficult in the past to study the experiences consumers have when they enter the life insurance marketplace. However, in 1980, LIMRA and the American Council of Life Insurance (ACLI) conducted a special study of consumer experiences in the marketplace, focusing on those consumers who actually sat down and discussed life insurance with agents in the twelve months prior to the study. The part of the study discussed here examined the experiences of both buyers and nonbuyers who met with agents about purchasing insurance for their personal or family needs.

The Prepurchase Situation

The Consumer. Before looking at the personal selling process, it might prove useful to examine what each of the protagonists brings to the sales interview.

Most consumers do not shop around for life insurance in the way that they do for many kinds of retail purchases. In the 1980 survey of buyers and nonbuyers, only 18 percent of the consumers had compared life insurance costs in their recent experiences in the life insurance marketplace. Another 22 percent had compared costs at some previous time, but clearly the overall level of price comparison is low.

There are a variety of explanations for the lack of cost comparison in life insurance discussions, but the most basic reason may well be that fewer than four in ten consumers believe that there are large cost differences between similar life insurance policies. The frequency of cost comparison increases substantially among those consumers who do believe that large cost differences exist, as shown in table 11–4.

Similarly, only one-quarter of all consumers talk to more than one life insurance agent in their venture into the life insurance marketplace. Therefore consumers are not substituting a comparison of agents for a comparison of the cost of life insurance policies.

Finally, it is important to realize that for half of all consumers, the agent is the single most important source of information on the subject of life insurance. The next most common source of information for the consumer is the life insurance company, used by one-fifth of all consumers. Few consumers use sources of information such as newspapers and magazines, as shown by table 11–5.

The Agent. The buyer-nonbuyer survey collected some information about the characteristics of the agents with whom these consumers had sales interviews. The median age of the agents (as estimated by the respondents) was 39.4, only one year older than that of the household heads with whom the interviews were held. The purchase rate—the percentage of households that buy life insurance as a result of sales interviews—was highest when the agent was between the ages of 45 and 64.

Generally, the agents were male; only 7 percent of households surveyed had their sales interviews with female agents. The purchase rates from male and female agents are identical.

Finally, most consumers do not see the agent as a biased source of information about insurance. About four in ten consumers do not believe that agents' recommendations are biased by the commissions that agents receive, and three in ten are not sure. Three in ten do believe that agents' recommendations are biased.

The Precontact Relationship. In many instances, consumers in this study had had some contact with the life insurance agent before their most recent

Table 11–4
Incidence of Cost Comparison According to Belief in Cost Differences

| | Belief in Cost Differences | | | |
	Yes; They Are Large	Yes; They Are Not Large	No	Don't Know
Yes, compared costs	29%	19%	7%	3%
No, but compared costs previously	32	25	13	7
No, never compared costs	38	54	68	86
Did not recall	1	2	12	4
Total	100%	100%	100%	100%

Table 11–5
Sources of Consumer Information

Most Important Source of Information	Percent of Households
Life insurance agents	51%
Life insurance companies	19
Friends or relatives	16
Magazines/newspapers	5
Books	5
Advertising	4
Total	100%

experiences in the marketplace. Agent-consumer contact often occurs within family and social relationships. For example, in the buyer-nonbuyer survey, four in ten of the consumers had been friends or acquaintances of their agents before the contact leading to the interview. Another 3 percent were relatives or in-laws of their agents. For 9 percent, the agent was someone whom they had heard of but not met. Nearly half said that their agents were complete strangers.

The purchase rate is greatly influenced by the closeness of the prior contact with the agent, as illustrated in table 11–6. If the agent was a relative or in-law, the purchase rate was 85 percent; at the other end of the spectrum, agents who were complete strangers had a purchase rate of 48 percent. Clearly, the strength of the prior relationship has a direct and positive relationship to the purchase rate. Similarly, if consumers view their agents as their personal agents for life insurance, they are much more likely to purchase life insurance than if they do not.

The Initial Contact. Bearing in mind that in over half of all sales interviews, the agent is already known to the consumer, how does the initial contact

Table 11–6
Consumer's Precontact Relationship with Agent

Agent Relationship	All Households	Purchase Rate
Relative/in-law	3%	85%
Friend/acquaintance	40	70
Someone heard of but never met	9	62
Complete stranger	48	45
Total	100%	

typically occur? For 63 percent of all consumers, the agent contacted the consumer initially; 28 percent of the time the consumer initiated the contact with the agent. This level of initiation by the consumer has been documented in other studies of the life insurance purchase process, but the basic finding and its implications remain somewhat controversial in the life insurance business.

How do agents normally make their initial contacts? About half of the time, the agent called the consumer and made an appointment. For about one-quarter of the interviews in the buyer-nonbuyer study, the agent simply stopped in without an appointment. This is not a very good strategy for the agent: The purchase rate declines significantly for agents who drop in without appointments.

The extent to which prospects initiate contacts is higher if there has been some prior relationship with the agent than if there has not. Surprisingly, prospect-initiation does not increase significantly as the prior relationship moves from someone heard of but never met to a friend or relative. Prospect-initiation is most likely if the agent is seen by the consumer as his/her personal agent; prior business dealings are a stronger impetus to prospect-initiation than are friendship and social ties.

When prospects or consumers initiate (or perceive that they initiate) contacts, the purchase rate is 74 percent, compared with a purchase rate of 50 percent when agents initiate contacts.

The Sales Interview

The Setting. In recent years, agents have been encouraged to meet with clients in the agent's office, partly in the belief that this better positions the agent as a financial professional. Indeed, meeting at the agent's office produces a purchase rate 10 percentage points higher than average. It may be that asking prospects to attend meetings in the agent's office screens out the consumers who are the least serious about purchasing life insurance.

Nevertheless, 86 percent of the consumers in the recent study reported that the agents met with them in their homes. Twenty percent met with the agent at the consumer's place of employment, and only 13 percent met with the agent in the agent's office. (These add to more than 100 percent because of multiple meetings.)

The Number of Meetings. Life insurance is a complex product; nonetheless, a majority of consumers (57 percent) met only once with their agents. Nearly three in ten met twice and 15 percent met with the agent three or more times. If the personal selling process is seen as an exchange of information between the agent and the prospect, it is reasonable to expect those prospects who meet only once with their agents to have a lower purchase rate than do those who meet twice or more. As the following table shows, the buying rate does increase dramatically as the number of meetings increases, from a purchase rate of 48 percent for those who met once to a purchase rate of 78 percent when there were three or more meetings.

Number of Meetings	All Households	Purchase Rate
One	57%	48%
Two	28	69
Three or more	15	78
Total	100%	

These findings suggest that some agents use the first interview to screen out those who are definitely poor prospects for life insurance purchases. Alternatively, agents may be using the first interview to do initial fact-finding and then offering an analysis and proposed solutions in the second interview.

The Competitive Situation. A sophisticated consumer might attempt to gain more information or more leverage with the agent by contacting another agent, placing both agents in a competitive situation. This is not a common strategy, however. Only 23 percent of the consumers surveyed talked to other agents, and only 16 percent of them let the agent know that he/she was in a competitive situation. That is, in three-quarters of their sales situations, agents do not face competition.

One important part of the sales process itself is programming, the procedure by which agents analyze the consumer's financial situation, retirement plans, expected social security benefits, and current life insurance holdings. Taking all these into account, the agent can suggest a life insurance program that fits the consumer's individual needs. The insurance needs of nearly half of the consumers in the survey had been programmed by their agents in their recent sales interviews. Persons with annual household incomes of $35,000 or more are more likely to be programmed than are persons with lower household incomes.

Programming does make a difference in purchase rates. Respondents who were programmed have a purchase rate of 66 percent compared with 48 percent for those who were not programmed. The perception that life insurance has been tailored to the individual's needs seems to be a powerful inducement to purchase.

Discussion of Various Policies and Companies. In six in ten sales interviews, agents reviewed several different types of life insurance policies with their prospects. Three in ten agents talked about one specific kind of policy. Interestingly, the purchase rate was higher (64 percent) if the agent reviewed several different types of policies than if he/she did not (53 percent).

While it is fairly common for life insurance agents to review several different types of policies, it is much less common for them to show consumers policies from more than one company; only 4 percent of the agents in the study did so. Again, however, the purchase rate is higher if the prospect sees policies from more than one company (78 percent) than if they see just one company's offerings (63 percent).

There are two possible reasons for this pattern. First, prospects may respond most favorably to agents who provide them with objective information toward the goal of making the most suitable choice for that individual consumer. Second, and probably less likely, prospects who have already decided to purchase life insurance may push the agent to provide them with more information.

Reasons for Purchase: The Agent's Emphasis. Nearly two-thirds of the consumers surveyed reported that their agents stressed protection as the reason for purchasing life insurance, and only 17 percent reported that their agents stressed the savings aspect. Only 2 percent of the agents stressed the tax-deferment aspects of life insurance. Purchase rates do not vary significantly according to which purpose of life insurance is stressed by agents. As one might expect, agents of households with more than $50,000 in annual income are most likely (11 percent) to emphasize tax-deferment purposes. Interestingly, when respondents were asked about *their* reasons for purchase, there is more variety in the responses. As shown in the background discussion, family security and final expenses remain the dominant reasons for purchasing life insurance, but as many as 23 percent have specific savings objectives, such as saving for retirement.

The Agent's Recommendation. Given the consumer's reliance on the agent for information about life insurance, one might expect that agents' recommendations would carry considerable weight. Indeed, as table 11–7 shows, nearly nine in ten buyers reported purchasing the type of policy recommended by the agent. Of course, some of this effect may be attributable to some respondents' recalling the sales process in a way consistent with what was actually purchased. It may also be that the agent, through skillful interviewing, establishes what the consumer wants and then recommends that type of policy. However, when one considers that consumers' information levels about life insurance are rather low and that the dependence upon agents as a source of information is great, it is likely that the agents' recom-

Table 11-7
Buyers' Purchase Decisions by Agents' Recommendations

Type of Policy Bought	Agents' Recommendations			
	Whole Life	Term	Endowment	Whole Life and Term
Whole life	88%	2%	13%	12%
Term	5	89	—	12
Endowment	1	6	82	1
Whole life and term	3	1	3	62
Other	3	2	2	13
Total	100%	100%	100%	100%

mendations in fact do make a considerable difference. Moreover, among buyers who recall that their agents made specific recommendations, the purchase rate is considerably higher (66 percent) than among those who do not have such recollections (51 percent).

Only 52 percent of the consumers surveyed (and 55 percent of those who bought) received specific recommendations as to how much life insurance should be purchased. Unlike recommendations made as to type of insurance, however, the purchase rate does not vary according to whether recommendations are made on how much should be purchased.

Helpfulness of the Agent. Consumers in the buyer-nonbuyer survey were asked whether they found their agents helpful in explaining various areas of life insurance. The results in table 11-8 show that the more helpful the agent, the higher the purchase rate. Across all the areas of difficulty, the purchase rate is 75 percent or better if the agent is recalled as having been very helpful; at the other extreme, the purchase rate ranges from 21 percent to 32 percent if the agent is viewed as not helpful.

After the Purchase: Measures of Satisfaction. How satisfied are consumers with the information they receive from agents and companies?

Table 11-8
Agent Helpfulness as a Determinant of Purchase Rate

Helpfulness of Agent	Purchase Rate			
	Life Insurance Terminology	Determining Money's Worth	Determining Amount to Buy	Determining Type to Buy
Very helpful	76%	77%	75%	77%
Somewhat helpful	58	58	57	54
Not helpful	30	32	31	21

Nearly half of the consumers surveyed were satisfied with the information, and another 36 percent were very satisfied. As table 11–9 shows, the purchase rate has a strong positive relationship to how satisfied the consumer is with the information he/she receives in the course of meeting with the agent. Among those who were very satisfied, the purchase rate was 78 percent; among those who were very dissatisfied, the purchase rate was 21 percent.

To further assess satisfaction with the sales process, those consumers who actually purchased policies were asked about their understanding of their new policies, whether they felt they received their money's worth, and their overall satisfaction with their recent purchases. The level of understanding claimed by these recent buyers is high: eighty-seven percent of the consumers believed that they understand the provisions of their policies at least fairly well. Similarly, eight in ten of the buyers felt that they received their money's worth, and more than nine in ten expressed satisfaction with their purchases.

Perhaps a better measure of satisfaction with the performance of the agent is whether the buyer is willing to purchase from the same life insurance agent again. Seven in ten buyers indicated that they would. Interestingly, three in ten *non-buyers* expressed willingness to purchase life insurance from the agents with whom they had their recent sales interviews.

A number of factors have strong influences on whether the consumer is willing to buy again from the same agent. Consumers who are programmed are much more likely to be willing to purchase again from the agent than are those who are not programmed. Similarly, the strength of the consumer's prior relationship with the agent and whether the agent reviewed the policy with the consumer at delivery significantly affect whether the consumer is willing to purchase again from the same agent.

These findings about life insurance consumer's view of the personal selling process strongly support using an information-intensive sales approach: Agents who provide objective information to the consumer, who review various alternatives, and who convey the sense that they are trying to tailor a life insurance program to meet the consumer's needs are more successful than those who do not.

Table 11–9
Consumer Satisfaction Relative to Purchase Rate

Consumer Satisfaction	All Households	Purchase Rate
Very satisfied	36%	78%
Satisfied	43	55
Dissatisfied	11	24
Very dissatisfied	5	21
Total	100%	

Keeping the Sale

The selling job of the life insurance company is not over even when the contract is signed. For any extended or permanent policy, it generally takes two years of premium payments to cover the administrative costs of a new policy.

The extent to which policies remain in force is called the *persistency rate;* the extent to which they do not is the *lapse rate.* The persistency problem for life insurance companies is large, and it has been the subject of many studies (for example, LIMRA 1975). These studies, relating information supplied on policy applications to persistency rates, consistently show relationships between persistency and factors such as the age and income of the prospect, the agent's tenure, and whether the prospect has bought previously from the same agent or company. Many of these factors are controllable through careful selection of prospects by agents.

The agent's role in persistency goes beyond prospect selection, however. There is an adage that persistency is made at the point of sale. In an effort to provide useful information for improving persistency rates, LIMRA conducted a two-part study to test that saying (LIMRA 1979).

Four companies (three from the United States and one from Canada) participated in this project. These companies sent questionnaires to a random sample of individuals who had purchased policies over the previous eight months. The questionnaire assessed policyowners' attitudes during and after their experiences in the purchase process. Follow-up data on the persistency of the policies were collected between seventeen and twenty-seven months after the sale.

Components of Persistency

Precontact Factors. As has been found in previous studies, the higher the policyowner's age or income and the longer the agent's tenure, the less likely the policy is to lapse. In addition, sales to prospects who personally, or whose family, had made previous purchases from the same agents or companies are less likely to lapse than are other sales. Most of these factors are best controlled through selection of prospects by agents.

Sales Process Factors. The motivation of the buyer at the time of the initial meeting with the agent influences persistency.

Lapse rates are 50 percent greater among buyers who report that they had not intended to discuss life insurance before the first meeting than among those who had. For insurance agents, this suggests that if the purpose of the initial interview is to discuss something other than life insurance (for example, disability income coverage), the agent should suggest when the meeting arrangements are being made that the prospect's life insurance program be reviewed as well.

Once the agent and the prospective client are face-to-face, the agent's behavior is related to the likelihood of the prospect to buy a policy, to keep the policy, and to consider making a future purchase.

The relationship between the agent's behavior and likelihood of making a sale is demonstrated in the section discussing buyers and nonbuyers. As for keeping the sale, table 11–10 shows that policyowners' perceptions of the informational and interpersonal style of the agent are closely related to policy persistency. The table shows that sales to prospects who think that their agents are being open and honest, are suggesting the right type and amount of insurance, and are avoiding high pressure are likely to stay on the books. The relatively small number of poor ratings of agents in table 11–10 also suggests that agents need to have a fairly thorough knowledge of their product and need to be able to convey that knowledge in a courteous and businesslike fashion in order to even make a sale initially.

(The limited number of poor ratings may also reflect response bias. That is, one might expect that a policyowner who is disstisfied with his/her policy, agent, or company would be less likely than satisfied buyers would be to cooperate by responding to a questionnaire. Comparisons available from two companies show an 18 percent lapse rate among nonrespondents versus a 10 percent lapse rate for respondents.)

The buyer-nonbuyer study shows that there is limited competition for sales from the same life insurance prospect; however, it is interesting to note that the lapse rate among policyowners whose agents *are not* aware of the competition is almost twice that among those whose agents *are* aware of the competition.

Table 11–10
Percent of Policies that Lapsed within Policyowners' Ratings of the Quality of Their Agents' Sales Presentations

	Rating of Agents			
	Excellent	*Good*	*Fair*	*Poor*
Being courteous and businesslike	8%	10%	14%	—
Having thorough knowledge of life insurance	9	9	11	—
Avoiding complex and technical language about life insurance	9	9	16	—
Describing policies openly and honestly	8	9	13	22%
Helping select right amount of coverage	8	9	14	19
Helping select right type of coverage	8	9	16	20
Avoiding high pressure	8	9	11	27

—Indicates too few cases for reliable analysis.

Agent Awareness According to Policyowner	Percent Lapsed	Percent of Total
Aware of competition	7%	53%
Unaware of competition	13	35
Unknown	11	12
Total		100%

There are two possible reasons for this difference. First, agents who are aware of competition are more likely to compare or to be asked to compare products during the sales process. When the agent makes a direct and thorough comparison of policies for the prospect, the policyowner is most likely to understand the policy differences, select the preferred policy, and be convinced that it is a good choice. Second, agents who are aware of competitors are more motivated to be thorough and to ensure that prospects understand the features of their policies than are agents who do not know of the competition. Ensuring that the prospect has a good understanding of the policy's characteristics is in itself related to persistency. Specifically, policyowners who have good understanding of the terms, options, and provisions of their policies have fewer lapses (8 percent) than do those who do not have such perceptions (13 percent). As the figures below indicate, choices made on the basis of policy characteristics have the best persistency. However, characteristics of the selling agent, and in a few cases the competing agent, are also reasons for choosing one policy over another.

Reason for Policy Choice	Percent Lapsed	Percent of Total
Characteristics of policy	7%	36%
Characteristics of selling agent	10	53
Characteristics of company	14	4
Characteristics of competing agent	—	2
Total		100%

—indicates too few cases for reliable analysis

This reinforces the importance of the role that agent characteristics and behavior (good *and* bad) play in policy sales and persistency.

Postsale Factors. The dissatisfaction of policyowners who are not willing to purchase from the same agent or company is also reflected in poor persistency. As shown below, these policyowners are about three times as likely to drop their policies as are those who are willing to make another purchase from the agent or the company.

	Percent Lapsed		
	Yes	No	Not Sure
Willing to purchase from same agent again	8%	22%	10%
Willing to purchase from same company again	8	25	10

These findings are consistent with a precontact factor: the greater likelihood of repeat buyers (apparently satisfied customers) than of first-time buyers to continue making their policy premium payments.

Another factor in postsale satisfaction is policyowner service, measured in terms of the presence of a servicing agent. As can be seen below, there is little difference in persistency between policies that are serviced by the selling agent and those serviced by a different agent; however, orphan policies (policies without servicing agents) have lapse rates 9 or 10 percent points higher than do policies that are being serviced.

	Percent Lapsed	Percent of Total
Selling agent still servicing	19%	89%
Servicing agent other than selling agent	20	6
Orphan policy (no agent)	29	5
Total		100%

In other words, having the selling agent available for policy service is not nearly as important as having *some* agent available for servicing. Service is a selling point for most agents and, if it is promised, it is expected. If it is not delivered, the policyowner may become dissatisfied and may terminate any relationship with the selling company.

In summary, this study clearly demonstrates that the adage, persistency is made at the point of sale, is quite accurate. The prospective client's intentions before the initial interview, perception of the agent's informational and interpersonal style, and satisfaction with service are related not only to making sales but also to keeping them.

Conclusion

A majority of the public views the knowledge, information, and advice that an agent provides as a vital part of the insurance sales process. This perception, combined with the low level of knowledge and shopping for life insurance among prospective buyers, makes the agent a pervasive influence in the insurance sales process.

Some of the ways in which an agent or salesperson may improve the likelihood of making a sale include assessing the prospect's needs and selling products to meet those needs rather than just pushing a product, making product comparisons, and making recommendations. In addition, it is clear that the informational and interpersonal approaches used by the agent are critical to the sale, to the willingness to consider future sales, and to the ongoing patronage of the company by continuing premium payments in subsequent years. It is expected that these dynamics play an important role in the sale of all types of products involving a salesperson, from clothing to cars and from furniture to financial services. However, the emphasis placed on the informational versus interpersonal approach may vary with the complexity of the product.

Note

1. The Life Insurance Marketing and Research Association is an insurance trade association based in Farmington, Connecticut. Started by a handful of companies in 1916, the association's membership now comprises companies that have nearly 90 percent of the life insurance in force in the United States and Canada. In addition, LIMRA has nearly three hundred member companies located in fifty-two countries and territories other than the United States and Canada.

One of LIMRA's primary functions is to conduct research that assists the chief marketing officer and marketing staff of its member companies. Toward this end, LIMRA maintains active programs of research in four primary areas: consumer and organizational research, financial research, manpower and market research, and agent selection research.

References

American Council of Life Insurance (1979, 1981, 1982). Public attitude surveys. Washington, D.C.

Life Insurance Marketing and Research Association (1975). *Persistency and Conservation Measures.* Hartford, Conn.

Life Insurance Marketing and Research Association (1979). *Buyer-Initiated Sales and the Agency System.* Hartford, Conn.

Life Insurance Marketing and Research Association (1981). *The Opportunity to Buy in 1980.* Hartford, Conn.

Life Insurance Marketing and Research Association (1978). *A Profile of Life Insurance Ownership in the U.S.* Hartford, Conn.

Life Insurance Marketing and Research Association and American Council of Life Insurance (1982). *Consumer Experiences in the Marketplace, Volume 1: Buyers and Nonbuyers in the Sales Process.* Hartford, Conn.

12 Consumer Scripts for Insurance Salesperson Behavior in Sales Encounters

Thomas W. Leigh and
Arno J. Rethans

Recently, considerable interest has developed in abstract knowledge structures or *schemata* (Bobrow and Norman 1975; Ortony 1978; Rumelhart 1980; Schank and Abelson 1977; Taylor and Crocker 1980). These schemata are perceived to be the building blocks of cognition in the process of interpreting sensory data, retrieving information from memory, organizing actions, determining goals and subgoals, and generally guiding the flow of information in the system (Rumelhart 1980).

One simple form of schemata is the script, which embodies knowledge of stereotyped event sequences (Abelson 1980). More precisely, a script is a schematic "structure that describes appropriate sequences of events in a particular context" (Schank and Abelson 1977). The script concept is suggested to have broad application and has been applied in such areas as artificial intelligence (Abelson 1981); cognitive science (Schank and Abelson 1977); cognitive, social, developmental, and clinical psychology (Rumelhart 1980; Abelson 1976; den Uyl and van Oostendorp 1980; Tomkins 1978); and, more recently, in marketing (Bozinoff 1982; Calder 1978; Rethans and Taylor 1982; Leigh and Rethans 1983).

More recently, scripts and script theory have been proposed as a possible approach for generating hypotheses within the contingency framework for analyzing effectiveness in sales interactions (Weitz 1981). Sales personnel and customers, it is proposed, possess contingency selling and buying scripts that guide their respective thinking and behavior in sales interactions. This proposition provided the rationale for this chapter. More specifically, the primary purpose of this chapter is to report the results of two studies designed to measure consumers' script norms for salesperson and customer behaviors in life-insurance sales encounters.

The establishment of these script norms is the first requirement of a research program designed to examine the applicability of script theory to the analysis of behavior in sales encounters. That is, it must be shown that when customers and/or sales personnel are asked to describe sales encounter activities and behaviors they agree on characters, props, and actions (Bower, Black, and Turner 1979). Once established, the existence of normative

223

scripts among salespersons and/or customers would suggest alternative research methodologies to investigate buyer/seller interactions, possibly breaking the methodological logjam that has limited the number of empirical investigations in the area. In addition, the existence of these scripts would have important implications for both sales training and consumer education.

Theoretical Framework

Abelson proposed the cognitive script as the basis for an alternative theory of social cognition to the then predominant views. He defined script to mean "a coherent sequence of events expected by an individual, involving him either as a participant or as an observer" (Abelson 1976, p. 33). More recent definitions have included "[a script is] a structure that describes appropriate sequences of events in a particular context" (Schank and Abelson 1977) and "[a script is] a hypothesized cognitive structure that when activated organizes comprehension of event-based situations" (Abelson 1981).

Script theory postulates that, upon activation, scripts, which have been stored in memory, are used to direct behavior. This activation is believed to occur automatically as a function of the situational context. For example, upon entering a restaurant, a *restaurant* script would be activated and begin to guide behavior. The script would contain a standard sequence of typical activities in a restaurant from the point of view of the customer. It may include such activities as talking to the hostess, being shown to a table, reading the menu, reading the wine list, and so forth. The script would also include standard roles, objects, ordinary conditions for entering upon the activity, a standard sequence of scenes or actions wherein one action enables the next, and some normal results from performing the activity successfully. All this information contained in the script aids the restaurant goer in understanding, planning, and executing conventional activities.

Thus scripts are perceived as playing a dual role. First, they guide comprehension and inference-making (Gibbs and Tenney 1980; McCartney and Nelson 1981; Nottenberg and Shoben 1980). Second, since they are formed on the basis of repeated episodes of a particular event sequence, scripts direct behavior. Empirical evidence supporting both the inference function and the structuring function is growing steadily (Bower, Black, and Turner 1979; den Uyl and van Oostendorp 1980; Nottenburg and Shoben 1980).

The relevancy of the script notion to the analysis of sales encounters is intuitively appealing. Salespersons are repeatedly exposed to selling situations through both sales training discussions and direct experience. Over time, such experiences will lead to the development of fairly sophisticated categorical structures of stereotypic-action sequences or even prototype action plans. Activation or instantiation of a particular sequence is then contingent upon the salesperson's observation and evaluation of the target buyer's actions and reactions. Thus, salespersons are hypothesized to possess contingency selling scripts which guide their behavior in customer interactions. Similarly, target buyers or customers can be expected to have stereotypic-action sequences involving both their own behaviors as well as those of the salesperson for the sales encounter. The degree of sophistication of these buyers' schematic structures is likely to vary considerably. However, script theory would suggest that even inexperienced consumers are likely to hold stereotypic scripts of sales encounters and likely salesperson behaviors. A considerable amount of this stereotypic knowledge may have been acquired indirectly rather than directly. Indirect script acquisition is due to portrayals of the salesman in anecdotes and stories, novels and short stories, stage productions, and the mass media in general (Thompson 1972).

Study Objectives and Design

Abelson (1981) has noted that the first requirement for scripts to play their inference-making and behavior-guiding roles is for the individual to have a stable cognitive representation of a particular script. Therefore, the first objective of the two studies reported here was to establish the existence of script norms for life insurance sales encounters. A second objective was to provide an exploratory assessment of the sensitivity of these script norms to experimental manipulation.

To establish script norms, subjects in Study I were requested to list the actions or behaviors of a typical life insurance salesperson on an initial sales encounter in the agent's office. Furthermore, to provide an exploratory assessment of the sensitivity of script norms to experimental manipulation, two sets of instructions were developed. One set noted that the life insurance agent had received the target customer's name from a casual acquaintance, while the second set noted that the source was a close friend. The specific instructions were as follows:

> You have recently accepted an invitation from an insurance agent to discuss life insurance at his office. The invitation was the result of a phone call after your name was given to the agent by a casual acquaintance. You will receive a free World Atlas for agreeing to the sales meeting. Please write a list of actions or behaviors you would expect from the insurance agent during the initial sales meeting. Start the list with "entering the insurance agent's office" and end it with "leaving the insurance agent's office."

These instructions were adapted from Bower, Black, and Turner (1979) and had been successfully used in prior studies (Rethans and Taylor 1982; Leigh and Rethans (1983). Subjects reported these instructions to be clear and found the task to be easy, not too fatiguing, and neither artificial nor unnatural.

Consistent with the view that sales encounters involve interactive behaviors and therefore require an understanding of one's own expected actions as well as the interacting partner's, Study II sought to establish script norms using an interactive script elicitation methodology (Leigh and Rethans 1983). The instructions in this study allowed the subjects to list actions or behaviors for both the salesperson and the customer. The specific instructions were as follows:

> You have recently accepted an invitation from an insurance agent to discuss life insurance at his office. We are interested in the common actions or behaviors of sales representatives and their customers as they discuss life insurance. Please write a list of actions or behaviors you would expect from the typical insurance agent and the typical customer during an initial sales meeting. Start the list with "entering the insurance agent's office" and end it with "leaving the insurance agent's office." For each action, circle "C" if it is a customer action or "S" if it is a salesperson action. Include about 30 activities or events in the order in which they occur. Please note that several actions for either the customer or salesperson may occur in a row.

Previous results (Leigh and Rethans 1983) had indicated that this procedure provided a more complete specification of the temporal and interactive nature of the script, more specific concrete actions for each participant, and insight into the point of origin of the actions.

University seniors with diverse majors were recruited through a newspaper advertisement. Each subject was paid for participating. Fifty subjects were recruited for Study I, while twenty-four subjects participated in Study II. One subject assigned to the "close friend" manipulation in Study I and one subject in Study II failed to complete the script and had to be dropped from the analyses. Discussions with three local insurance agents had pointed to the relevancy of the life insurance selling situation to the subject pool. Graduating seniors are a prime target of insurance purveyors. Furthermore, 48 percent of the U.S. population under the age of twenty-five is covered by life insurance. Of the study subjects, 31 percent had actually purchased or shopped for life insurance, though the mean rating of these subjects on a seven-point familiarity scale was 3.1.

Analysis of Results

The resulting scripts were edited and tabulated according to the frequency of citation of specific events and actions. As might be expected, each subject mentioned a sample of very common actions or events along with some less common ones, presumably reflecting his/her experiences. Indeed, across subjects there was a continuous gradation of frequency of reporting of particular events. As per Bower, Black, and Turner (1979), we defined the group's script to be those actions or events mentioned by more than some criterion percentage of subjects. Specifically, we selected 25 percent mention as a criterion for inclusion of an action in the group script.

Tables 12-1, 12-2, and 12-3 report for each of the sales encounters the actions mentioned by at least one-fourth of the subjects. The tables also provide some further information about the percent-mention distribution for each of the situations. The items in italics were more popular, falling in the criterion of 40–54 percent mention; actions in bold face were most popular, having been mentioned by more than 55 percent of the consumers. Those actions mentioned by more than 75 percent of the consumers have been indicated in bold letters preceded by an asterisk. The actions are listed in the modal serial order in which they were reported. Since these procedures, though reflective of current practices in cognitive psychology, are somewhat

Table 12–1
Insurance Script: Close Friend Manipulation
(n = 24)

Action or Event	Number of Mentions
Greets customer	9
Shakes customers hand	13
Introduces him-/herself	9
Talks about friend	14
Leads customer to office	9
Engages in small talk	11
Explains benefits/importance of insurance	11
Explains company's policies/types of insurance	14
Asks how can help the customer	8
Explains pluses and minuses of each type	13
Gives customer literature	11
*Asks if you have questions	18
Explains company benefits	8
*Singles out best plan for customer	19
Explains benefits of this plan	11
Quotes price for policy	8
Asks for customer comments	7
Tries to seal the deal	11
Gives atlas to the customer	8
Discusses payment plan	6
Makes appointment for later meeting	6
Thanks customer	11
Gives customer his/her business card	8
Walks customer to the door/out of the office	6
Shakes hands with customer	7

Mean:	14.3	Minimum:	8	
Median:	14.5	Maximum:	19	
Mode:	15.0	Reliability:	.70	

Table 12–2
Insurance Script: Casual Acquaintance Manipulation
(n = 25)

Action or Event	Number of Mentions
Greets customer	15
Shakes hand	8
Introduces him-/herself	8
Offers you a seat	15
Engages in small talk	8
Mentions friend's name	6
Inquires about family	7
Asks customer personal information	9
Inquires about present coverage	8
Asks what type policy interested in	8
Agent makes sales pitch/gives reasons why insurance is important	15
Describes types of coverage available	14
Recommends particular policy	7
Agent stresses insurance is important for family	8
Describes details of one particular policy	12
*Describes the benefits	19
Describes the payment procedure	13
Asks if customer is interested	6
Any questions	8
Answers questions	6
Attempts to get the sale	7
Prepares the paperwork	10
Gives you the atlas	7
Shakes hand	7
Walks you to the door	8
Offers business card	7
Says goodbye	6

Mean:	14.6	Minimum:	8
Median:	15.0	Maximum:	21
Mode:	17.0	Reliability:	.72

arbitrary (Bower et al. 1979), the following statistics are provided: the number of mentions for each action or event included, the mean, median, mode, and range of actions mentioned. Finally, the split-half reliability in the frequency with which the particular actions of the respective scripts were mentioned are reported.

Discussion of Results

The data described in tables 12–1 and 12–2 reveal a high degree of agreement in the basic action language that subjects used to describe the sales encounter. Despite the fact that different sets of judges developed the lexicon

Table 12–3
Interactive Script: Insurance Sales Call
(n = 23)

	Action or Event	Number of Mentions
C	Asks to speak with agent	7
S	**Says hello/greets customer**	15
C	*Says hello/exchange greeting*	11
C	*Sits down in office*	8
S	*Small talk (other than customer-related)*	11
C	Responds to salesperson's small talk	6
S	Overviews company background information	8
S	*Asks about dependents/family/marriage*	9
C	Answers about family/marriage	6
S	*Asks about personal history/background*	9
C	*Responds concerning history/background*	10
S	**States necessity of insurance in your life**	12
S	Asks about your present policies	7
C	*Asks questions about policies/insurance types*	9
S	Asks about type of insurance buyer is interested in	6
C	Answers about type/expresses interest	7
S	**Explains benefits of insurance**	13
S	Gives information	6
S	Highlights advantages of policies	7
C	*Asks about terms/costs*	11
S	*Answers questions*	9
S	Discusses price/payment plans	8
S	Tells you more about options/other insurance	6
S	Asks for interest/commitment	6
S	Reassures customer	7
S	Shows copy of insurance form	7
S	Talks about policy forms/options	7
S	Attempts final close/asks for signature	7
C	Would like to think it over	7
C	Signs forms	6
S	Gives you business card/phone number	6
S	Thanks or reassurance/call me if . . .	8
S	Escorts client to door	7
C	Stands/leaves desk/walks to door	6
S	Shakes hand	7
C	Shakes hand	7

Mean:	27.3	Minimum:	4
Median:	30.0	Maximum:	30
Mode:	30.0	Reliability:	.46

and the scripts of these two exhibits, the similarity of the scripts is very high by any standard. The number of actions included in the scripts is twenty-five and twenty-seven, respectively. The descriptive data are highly similar. Most importantly, the set of actions included in the scripts and their respective modal locations are similar.

This uniformity is further reflected in the low incidence of unique actions or events. Only 17 (out of 344 total actions) and 25 (out of 365 total actions) unique events were identified, respectively. Lastly, the split-half reliabilities within the scripts were .70 and .72, respectively. Thus we conclude that script norms for salesperson behaviors exist for the initial insurance sales encounter and that these basic action norms can be reliably elicited.

In terms of specific actions included in the script, it can be seen that each script includes several phases, or what we might call scenes. The scripts start off with a basic introduction phase consisting of a greeting, handshaking, and personal introduction. The next phase includes small talk, some discussion of the friend mentioned in the experimental instructions, and the offering of a seat or conductance into the salesperson's office. Although the difference between "talks about friend" and "mentions friend's name" turns out to be primarily a coder language difference, the location of the action in the scripts and the fact that twice as many subjects mentioned the word *friend* under the close friend manipulation is interesting. The third phase involves a discussion of insurance types and their benefits/costs as well as the solicitation of information from the customer necessary to assess his/her insurance needs. The fourth phase involves a discussion of a particular policy, which was apparently selected by the agent as suitable. This phase ends with an attempt to close the sale. The final phase represents a leave-taking procedure and some attempt to leave the situation open for future sales encounters. In summary, within the limits that such qualitative data can be interpreted, the scripts seem inherently plausible and seem consistent with the observational results reported by Woodside and Taylor (1978) and Taylor and Woodside (1979) for insurance sales encounters.

Table 12–3 presents the script coded for the interactive script methodology. Consumer and salesperson actions were separately coded in order to reflect the origin of initiation of the action. As with an automobile interaction previously reported (Leigh and Rethans 1983), the number of actions reported tightly concentrated around the maximum number of spaces provided. The origination of actions varied considerably among respondents. For the script as a whole, only thirteen of the thirty-six actions included, or 36 percent, were customer-initiated. For the sample as a whole, the mean number of consumer actions was 40 percent. However, the range of consumer initiated actions at the individual level ranged from 20 percent to 60 percent. The patterns of responses across participants varied considerably. Few individuals consistently followed a simple interaction pattern of consecutively alternating salesperson and customer actions. Most scripts contained strings of either salesperson or customer actions, yet few individuals failed to logically provide an interactive structure in their responses. In sum, the subjects appeared to be reporting, as best they could, their conceptualization of the respective salesperson and customer roles in the situation described. The instructions do not appear to induce either a highly oversimplified interaction pattern or consistent consumer perspective effect.

The degree of agreement in the basic actions remains fairly high, though the script is dominated by actions mentioned either 25 percent or 40 percent of the time. Only three actions reached the 50 percent reporting level or better. These results are consistent with those for the automobile study referred to previously. This reduced commonality is due to the separate coding of consumer and salesperson actions. The number of unique actions mentioned was also higher, at 57 (out of 629 total mentions), than with the noninteractive methodology. As a result, the split-half reliability was somewhat lower, at .46.

Despite these problems, the summary script seems remarkably similar to the two scripts previously discussed. The script follows the same basic phases as the prior scripts and the ordering and location, at least on a qualitative judgment basis, seems similar. The key difference seems to be the more specific role decomposition and the ability to determine the degree of perceived control exerted by each party.

Conclusions and Recommendations for Further Research

Normative expectations held by consumers and salespersons concerning their own actions and those of the respective interacting partner have been posited as key determinants of the course and outcomes of sales encounters (Weitz 1981; Sheth 1975). Very little empirical research has been reported concerning the existence and measurement of such expectations or their impact within the context of a sales interaction. In this chapter we have proposed that cognitive script theory represents a paradigm of potential usefulness in investigations of these buyer-seller expectations. The results of the two studies reported here provide some initial support for this premise. The studies suggest that there is considerable agreement in the basic action language used to describe the insurance sales encounter experience. Each of the studies found considerable agreement on basic actions, behaviors, and events. In addition, the structure of the scripts elicited was quite consistent, both in the actions elicited and their temporal orderings. Furthermore, the studies are consistent with the advocated position that scripts are hierarchically organized with varying levels of abstraction. These scripts were seemingly decomposable into subactions, role expectations, and interaction sequences; the studies are thus encouraging from a structural perspective. Finally, the scripts appear to be consistent with previously reported survey and observational models of buyer-seller interaction (*cf.* Wilson 1978) and face-to-face interaction (*cf.* Duncan and Fiske 1977). However, the methodology remains fluffy in the eyes of critics and perhaps, therefore, limited to the hypothesis generation phase of a research program. Given the apparent ability to measure and develop scripts for buyer-seller contexts, several follow-up research methodologies might be useful as a way to validate these scripts and manipulate them to see if, in fact, deviations from script expectations have specific measurable effects on consumer outcomes measures such as affective reaction or behavioral intention.

A variety of follow-up studies have been performed to validate scripts generated under conditions similar to those reported above. Bower et al. (1979), for example, used scripts in text stories to: (1) investigate their constituent structure into superordinate and subordinate actions; (2) investigate the effect of script relevant material on recall of "missing" actions; (3) test the effect of scripts on recognition speed for text-relevant material; (4) test the effect of scripts on remembering script-ordered and misordered stories; (5) measuring the effect of script expectations on comprehension time; and (6) investigating the effect of deviations from script expectations on remembering. Though many unresolved issues were noted, the results were generally consistent with script theory predictions. Several other studies have pursued similar issues: memory for typical and atypical actions in scripted activities (Graesser et al. 1980); ability to fill in missing script links (Kemper 1982); memory for routine activities (Galambos and Rips 1982); recognition memory for energy-conservation scripts (Bozinoff and Roth 1983); and attitudinal effects of script processing (John and Whitney 1983). Obviously, a program of research into cognitive script theory in the analysis of buyer/seller interactions would benefit from a variety of these methods.

Our immediate interest is on several issues for the life insurance selling context. First, given the full set of scripted and nonscripted actions developed for insurance sales encounters, can we validate in more quantitative terms the existence of normative scripts? Several possible tasks seem relevant to this question:

1. *Reordering tasks.* Given a set of script-relevant actions in random order, will subjects be able to construct scripts similar to those originally developed using the procedures described in this study?
2. *Activity typicality ratings.* Given script-relevant and irrelevant activities or events, will subjects be able to accurately judge the typicality (or commonness) of each action or event for sales situations in general?
3. *Script typicality ratings.* Given alternative scripts constructed using both script relevant and irrelevant actions, will subjects be able to accurately judge the typicality of each respective script?
4. *Fill in the missing links tasks.* Given alternative scripts with specific script-relevant activities or sequences of activities missing (that is, removed from the script), will subjects be able to accurately fill in the missing activity links?
5. *Scene specification or matching tasks.* Given an appropriate script, will subjects be able to consistently divide it into a hierarchical structure of scenes?

Together, these validation tasks would provide a rigorous assessment of the validity of the script norms and script orderings collected using the free elicitation and coding methods described here. The *reordering* task is appropriate to validating the sequential and hierarchical causal structure of the scripts. The *typicality* ratings are designed to confirm recognition and commonness distinguishing script main, secondary, and unique actions. *Fill in the missing links* is useful to validate the script itself; if an activity or event is truly important or central in a sales situation, subjects should be able to recognize that it is missing and accurately return it to the script in the appropriate location. Finally, the *scene specification* task is appropriate to evaluating the hierarchical structuring of scripts into main and subsidiary conceptualizations. As a package, therefore, this set of validation tasks should allow a fairly complete assessment of script theory principles.

Second, and more importantly, it would seem useful to investigate the effect of cognitive scripts on other memorial or perceived outcomes in a sales call. For example, alternative scripts of insurance sales calls could be constructed in such a fashion as to be consistent or inconsistent with normative scripts for the particular situation at hand. These scripts could be alternative lists of actions, story texts based on script actions, or even audio or video tapes of a sales encounter. Subjects could be asked to read, listen to, or watch these sales encounters and respond to a battery of questions concerning the sales representative, his/her company, attitude toward insurance, and likelihood of purchase. Alternatively, recall of script relevant and irrelevant activities could be measured.

A final area for empirical research concerns situational effects on script activities: Do different starting conditions prior to a sales call, or even during the initial scenes of a sales call, directly affect cognitive scripts for that particular sales call? These effects could seemingly be measured in a variety of ways: free elicitation of alternative scripts under different situational contexts; construction of appropriate scripts from randomly ordered sets of actions; or, rating the importance or time allocation assigned to various script activities. If cognitive scripts represent a valid psychological construct relevant to sales calls, then such scripts should be experimentally sensitive to situational manipulations.

Implications for Sales Management

Assuming this additional research confirms the role of cognitive scripts in guiding the understanding and behaviors of consumers and agents in sales encounters such as life insurance, then the implications for both customer prospecting and sales training should be considerable. For example, it may be that a significant portion of the potential customer base for life insurance products holds negative expectations concerning insurance sales interviews or insurance agents, either in general or for a specific type or company. These expectations may be rooted in specific activities or events and may be triggered by advertising or other promotional approaches. A consumer or group of consumers holding such expectations may be less likely to agree to an insurance interview. Or, having recognized the need for life insurance, they might agree only if the initial contact matches mental stereotypes and/or scripts considered appropriate for the situation. Development of script expectations would seem to be an effective and efficient method of describing consumers' mental images of sales interactions. This information may in turn be used to design effective communication campaigns.

Description of consumer scripts for sales encounters is, of course, not sufficient. The area of research most related to practical application concerns sales effectiveness once a sales encounter has been broached. The literature in personal selling has noted that the outcomes achieved in a sales encounter are dyadic. That is, sales effectiveness is "moderated or dependent upon characteristics of both the salesperson and the customer" (Weitz 1981, p. 88). Similarity between the customer and agent on some personal interest topic, such as interest in golf, has been a common effectiveness dimension investigated in life insurance studies. Cognitive script approaches have the potential to widen and deepen such research. For example, a considerable portion of a given consumer's expectations for an insurance sales encounter may be shared with other consumers. From a cognitive script perspective, this would suggest that there may be a number of activities or events, or even highly specific actions, which consumers normatively expect to occur in insurance sales encounters. One example might be the small talk phase of the sales interview noted in this discussion. Another might be that many consumers expect the insurance agent to narrow the discussion down to a specific policy. If these and the many other inferences possible from the scripts hold, then the implications are obvious. Management should train sales personnel to meet these specific normative expectations. Of course, there may also be merit to purposely performing in such a manner as to violate, or disconfirm, the existing script. For example, there has been research that suggests that deviation from expectations leads to increased attention, evaluation, and remembrance of informaton presented in interpersonal interactions. Doing something different from the norm in a sales encounter would seemingly stimulate the prospect. However, the consequences of specific activities or events on sales effectiveness may be either positive or negative. Empirical work designed to investigate such effects would, therefore, seem to be both theoretically and practically worthwhile. Training programs for insurance agents and other sales personnel could then be designed to reflect these findings. Perhaps the most useful benefit of this research program is its focus on *specific* activities and events rather than attitudes, moods, and personality. Sales personnel can be instructed specifically in how to behave in order to meet the needs and expectations of their customers. Thus the sales encounter should become more effective.

References

Abelson, Robert P. (1976). "Script Processing in Attitude Formation and Decision Making." In J. Carroll and J. Payne (eds.), *Cognition and Social Behavior*. Hillsdale, N.J.: Lawrence Erlbaum. Pp. 33–45.

Abelson, Robert P. (1981). "Psychological Status of the Script Concept." *American Psychologist* 36, 7, 715–729.

Bower, Gordon H.; John B. Black; and Terrence J. Turner. (1975). "Scripts in Memory for Text." *Cognitive Psychology* 11, 177–220.

Bozinoff, Lorne. (1982). "A Script Theoretic Approach to Information Processing." In A. Mitchell (ed.), *Advances in Consumer Research* 9. Ann Arbor, Mich.: Association for Consumer Research. Pp. 481–486.

Bozinoff, Lorne, and Victor J. Roth. (1983). "Recognition Memory for Script Activities: An Energy Conservation Application." In Alice Tybout and Richard Bagozzi (eds.), *Advances in Consumer Research*, Vol. 10. Ann Arbor, Mich.: Association for Consumer Research. Pp. 655–660.

Calder, Bobby J. (1978). "Cognitive Response, Imagery and Scripts: What Is the Cognitive Basis of Attitude?" In H. Keith Hunt (ed.), *Advances in Consumer Research*, Vol. 5. Ann Arbor, Mich.: Association for Consumer Research. Pp. 630–634.

Duncan, Jr., Starkey, and Donald W. Fiske. (1977). *Face-to-Face Interaction: Research, Methods and Theory*. Hillsdale, N.J.: Lawrence Erlbaum Associates.

Galambos, James A., and Lance J. Rips. (1982). "Memory for Routines." *Journal of Verbal Learning and Verbal Behavior* 21, 206–281.

Gibbs, Raymond W. and Yvette J. Tenney. (1980). "The Concept of Scripts in Understanding Stories." *Journal of Psycholinguistic Research* 9, 3, 275–284.

Graesser, Arthur C.; Sallie E. Gordon; and John D. Sawyer. (1980). "Recognition Memory for Typical and Atypical Actions in Scripted Activities: Tests of a Script Pointer and Tag Hypothesis." *Journal of Verbal Learning and Verbal Behavior* 18, 319–322.

John, George, and John C. Whitney. (1983). "An Empirical Investigation of Attitudinal Effects of Script Processing." In Alice Tybout and Richard Bagozzi (eds.), *Advances in Consumer Research*, Vol. 10. Ann Arbor, Mich.: Association for Consumer Research. Pp. 661–666.

Kemper, Susan. (1982). "Filling in the Missing Links." *Journal of Verbal Learning and Verbal Behavior* 21, 99–107.

Leigh, Thomas W., and Arno J. Rethans. (1983). "Experiences with Script Elicitation within Consumer Decision Making Contexts." In Alice Tybout and Richard Bagozzi (eds.), *Advances in Consumer Research*, Vol. 10. Ann Arbor, Mich.: Association for Consumer Research. Pp. 667–672.

McCartney, Kathleen, and Katherine Nelson. (1981). "Children's Use of Scripts in Story Recall." *Discourse Processes* 4, 59–70.

Nottenburg, Gail, and Edward J. Shoben. (1980). "Scripts as Linear Order." *Journal of Expermental Social Psychology* 16, 329–347.

Rethans, Arno J., and Jack L. Taylor. (1982). "A Script Theoretic Analysis of Consumer Decision Making." In Bruce J. Walker et al. (eds.) *An Assessment of Marketing Thought and Practice*. American Marketing Association: Proceedings of the Educator's Conference. Pp. 71–75.

Rumelhart, David E. (1980). "Schemata: The Building Blocks of Cognition." In R.J. Spiro et al. (eds.), *Theoretical Issues in Reading Comprehension: Perspectives from Cognitive Psychology, Linguistics, Artificial Intelligence and Education*. Hillsdale, N.J.: Lawrence Erlbaum Associates.

Schank, Roger C., and Robert P. Abelson. (1977). *Scripts, Plans, Goals and Understanding*. Hillsdale, N.J.: Lawrence Erlbaum Associates.

Sheth, Jagdish N. (1975). "Buyer-Seller Interaction: A Framework." *Proceedings of the Association for Consumer Research* (Winter), 382–386.

Taylor, James L., and Arch G. Woodside. (1979). "An Examination of the Structure of Buying-Selling Interactions among Insurance Agents and Prospective Customers." In Jerry C. Olson (ed.), *Advances in Consumer Research*, Vol. 7. Ann Arbor, Mich.: Association for Consumer Research. Pp. 387–392.

Thompson, Donald L. (1972). "Stereotype of the Salesman." *Harvard Business Review* (January-February), 20–161.

den Uyl, Martijn, and Herre van Oostendorp. (1980). "The Use of Scripts in Text Comprehension." *Poetics* 9, 275–294.

Weitz, Barton A. (1981). "Effectiveness in Sales Interactions: A Contingency Framework." *Journal of Marketing* 45 (Winter):85–103.

Wilson, David T. (1978). "Dyadic Interactions: Some Conceptualizations." In Thomas V. Bonoma and Gerald Zaltman (eds.), *Organizational Buying Behavior*. Chicago: American Marketing Association. Pp. 78–90.

Woodside, Arch G., and James L. Taylor. (1978). "Observations of Buyer and Seller Transactions." In Keith H. Hunt (ed.), *Advances in Consumer Research*, Vol. 5. Ann Arbor, Mich.: Association for Consumer Research. Pp. 643–652.

13 The Job Satisfaction-Job Performance Relationship: A Preliminary Analysis for Insurance Salespeople

Ben M. Enis and
George H. Lucas, Jr.

The question of why some salespeople are high producers and others fail to ever achieve adequate levels of productivity has long interested academicians and practitioners alike. Information about this topic can strongly influence how tasks are distributed and the way in which employees are compensated. Drawing from several theories available in the management discipline, this chapter attempts to shed some light on the relationships between the component parts of salesperson satisfaction, individual influencing factors, and the level of productivity that salespeople attain. A model of the salesperson performance-salesperson satisfaction relationships is developed and tested using recursive path analysis on data made available from a major national insurance firm.

Literature Review

An examination of the literature reveals three basic schools of thought in the satisfaction-performance area. First, the human relations movement, including the two-factor theory of motivation (Herzberg, Mausner, and Snyderman, 1959), proposes that satisfaction with the motivator aspects of the job influences job performance. Job performance was seen as affecting hygiene factors.

This perspective was rivaled by a second approach that saw satisfaction and performance as independent variables (Scott 1962; Davis, England, and Lofquist 1968). These two perspectives were followed by an approach influenced by Porter and Lawler (1968) which had job satisfaction as a result of, rather than a cause of, job performance. This third viewpoint is similar to that taken by Walker, Churchill, and Ford (1977), and Bagozzi (1980) in the sales management literature.

After evaluating the literature and empirical research on the relationship between job satisfaction and job performance, two points can be made. First, there is little agreement over what type of relationship, if any, exists. Second, the relationship between the two variables appears to be very complex if it exists at all. Lucas (1983) contains a more complete assessment of this literature.

Questions have been raised about the methodology used in studies that support two-factor theory. The research provided by those who contend that the theory is not correct has involved some misinterpretations of the concepts, jobs which may not provide true motivators, and an occasional misinterpretation of results. Thus the degree of support for both proponents and opponents of the theory is less than adequate.

Researchers in the school that saw moderators as limiting the satisfaction-performance relationship and the work of Porter and Lawler (1968) have indicated that the associations are more complex than was previously believed. Research in the consistency theory area (Korman 1976), introduced another variable, task-specific self-esteem, for consideration in evaluating job situations. Based on a review of the research, there appears to be a need for the analysis of higher-level jobs using some aspects of the two-factor theory and evaluating other variables that appear to affect the job satisfaction-job performance relationships.

The Proposed Model

The model presented in figure 13-1 was developed from the literature in the satisfaction-performance area. The influence of the two-factor theory is apparent in the framework. The model is richer than Herzberg's basic formulation in that perspectives from other relevant areas have been incorporated to make the model more appropriate for individuals in sales positions. Differences in the backgrounds of salespeople is accounted for by the inclusion of several demographic variables. The model has also been influenced by the work of Korman (1976), Inkson (1978), and Lopez (1982) in the consistency theory area. Performance and satisfaction are seen as being related in a somewhat more complex manner than was the case with the two-factor theory.

An approach that has been justified in the literature (Lopez 1982) segments job satisfaction into two distinct variables, intrinsic job satisfaction and extrinsic job satisfaction. Walker, Churchill, and Ford (1977), Porter and Lawler (1968) and Baggozi (1980) all identify intrinsic and extrinsic measures of satisfaction in their models.

The perspective taken on satisfaction for this study is similar to that stated in the two-factor theory. *Extrinsic satisfaction* is seen as an attitude

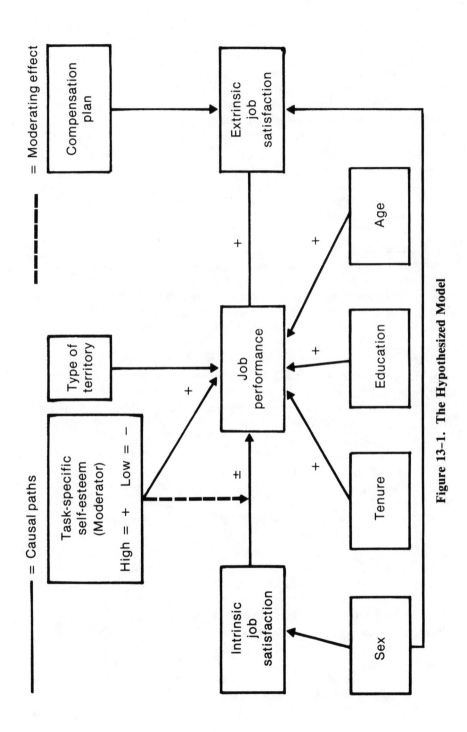

Figure 13–1. The Hypothesized Model

that refers to a reduction in the drive to attain additional quantities of job factors to basic needs. *Intrinsic satisfaction* is viewed as an attitude that refers to an enhancement of the desire to increase the amount obtained of higher-level need factors. Extrinsic satisfaction factors are supplied by other individuals and the organization, while intrinsic satisfaction is derived from the job by the employee himself/herself. While the attitudes are formed in similar ways, postulated effects differentiate the two variables. Intrinsic satisfaction is hypothesized to have an impact on one's drive or motivation to perform, while extrinsic satisfaction is hypothesized to affect decisions related to absenteeism and turnover.

Relationships between Components

Some research on the relationship between the background of salespeople and various aspects of their satisfaction and performance has produced consistent findings. Other topics are still controversial. In many studies, researchers have not controlled for the job type and job level of subjects in the samples. The variety in the types of organizations and jobs involved may help account for the inconsistency in the findings.

Tenure. One variable that has been shown to be positively affected by the amount of time the employee has spent in the position is job performance (Cravens and Woodruff 1973; Beswick and Cravens 1977). With each day the salesperson spends on the job comes increased experience, and in many instances an advanced level of knowledge, which can positively affect the sales level achieved.

1. Increased tenure will have a positive impact on sales representatives' job performance.

Age. Studies by Weaver (1969) and Cotham (1969) have also shown that salespeople's age is significantly correlated with job performance; this variable is closely tied to tenure. As with time on the job, time in life provides individuals with knowledge that can be used to increase job performance. There are certainly practical limits to which this relationship can be taken, as often older salespeople move into retirement or substantially decrease their selling activities. The strength of this relationship may be subject to question (Lamont and Lundstrom 1977), but the impact that age has on job performance is hypothesized to be in the positive direction.

2. Increasing age of the individuals will have a positive influence on the sales representatives' job performance.

Education. Research has indicated that, for salespeople, with increasing levels of education comes a higher level of job performance (Cotham 1969; Weaver 1969). Formal education can aid in developing the knowledge the person brings to the job and enhance the learning that transpires once that individual is employed. This is especially true for salespeople in more technical fields. While there is some evidence that the relationship is not a strong one (Lamont and Lundstrom 1977), education level is hypothesized to have a positive influence on job performance.

3. Increased formal education will have a positive influence on sales representatives' job performance.

Sex. Whether men or women perform better in a sales position and how gender relates to both intrinsic and extrinsic job satisfaction are topics of great importance in the sales management area. Unfortunately, these issues have not been studied in great depth. Research comparing men and women on various aspects of their performance has produced conflicting results (Swan and Futrell 1978; Busch and Bush 1978). There does not, at this point, appear to be a direct relationship between gender and job performance. With regard to job satisfaction, Shapiro and Stern (1975), Weaver (1974), Busch and Bush (1978) found women in professional occupations to be less satisfied than men on both intrinsic and extrinsic variables. Based on the available research, it is hypothesized that men are more satisfied than women on both satisfaction variables.

4. Women will be less satisfied than men on intrinsic job satisfaction.
5. Women will be less satisfied than men on extrinsic job satisfaction.

Task-Specific Self-Esteem. Korman (1968), introduced consistency theory when he put forth the idea that workers will strive to produce in a manner consistent with their own perception of their ability to perform the task. Research on the theory by Greenhaus and Gadin (1974) and Bagozzi (in the sales management area) (1980), has shown one particular aspect of self-esteem, task-specific, to have a significant impact on job performance. Based on this research, the model hypothesized the following relationship:

6. Increasing levels of task-specific self-esteem will have a positive influence on sales representatives' job performance.

The Satisfaction-Performance Relationship. The proposed model goes beyond the basic two-factor theory and considers the perspective that Korman's (1971) consistency theory puts forth regarding the relationship between satisfaction and performance. Recent research by Inkson (1978) and

Lopez (1982) has shown self-esteem, and in particular task-specific self-esteem, to be an effective moderating variable for the intrinsic job satisfaction-job performance relationship. While much of the research has been correlational, the indication is that when task-specific self-esteem is high there is a positive relationship between intrinsic job satisfaction and job performance. When task-specific self-esteem is low the relationship is in the opposite direction. Thus, task-specific self-esteem has been shown to be a moderator variable in the relationship between the two other variables. Incorporating this perspective into the model based on the constructs of the two-factor theory results in the following hypotheses:

7. When the task-specific self-esteem of sales representatives is high, intrinsic job satisfaction will have a positive effect on job performance.
8. When the task-specific self-esteem of sales representatives is low, intrinsic job satisfaction will have a negative effect on job performance.

There is more agreement in the literature on the relationship between job performance and extrinsic job satisfaction. A large majority of the research has job performance influencing extrinsic job satisfaction. This relationship is stronger when the compensation program in use ties rewards to performance (Lawler 1971). While extrinsic satisfaction does not have a direct impact on job performance, it is still an important concern for sales managers because the variable has been shown to have a strong influence on turnover and absenteeism. Both of these outcomes can have an impact on future job performance.

9. Increased sales performance will have a positive influence on satisfaction with extrinsic aspects of the job (that is, pay, benefits, working conditions, and so forth).

Actual levels of these job factors are not the important issues in studies of this type. The fact that pay, benefits, autonomy, and so forth, are in reality high or low is not the chief concern. It is the *perceived* level of, and the satisfaction with, these variables that will have an impact on the hypothesized relationships (Hackman and Lawler 1971).

Basis of Compensation. Research indicates that an important consideration when evaluating extrinsic job satisfaction in general (and satisfaction with pay in particular) is what type of reward system is utilized by the company (Lawler 1971; Cherrington, Reitz, and Scott 1971). When a compensation plan that ties extrinsic rewards directly to performance (straight commission) is used, satisfaction with pay has been found to be higher than when other methods are used.

10. Extrinsic job satisfaction will be higher under a straight commission plan than when compensation is based on factors other than sales performance.

Territory Potential. The model is designed to be applicable for all selling situations. One important factor that can affect the performance of individuals in many outside sales positions is the potential of the salesperson's territory. For insurance sales, this may be a lesser consideration as there are no true boundaries; agents are essentially self-employed. In an effort to develop a broad model based solely on the number of potential customers available, it is hypothesized that salespeople with urban and suburban territories will have larger sales figures than those in rural territories. This relationship will not be examined in the present study.

11. Sales performance will be higher for individuals having urban and suburban, as opposed to rural, territories.

Methodology

The proposed model was preliminarily tested using survey data collected by a large national insurance firm. The sample used for this phase of the study is composed of 1071 insurance agents who provided responses to a survey instrument that could be matched with performance data from the company's records.

The sample used for the present study is not without limitations. Respondents were all employed in a particular firm in a particular industry. The organization is thus a large company providing an intangible product to its customers. These features have an impact on the external validity of the findings obtained from this research. Whether or not the results can be applied to other insurance firms and other types of sales organizations is an important consideration. A comprehensive nationwide data base of this magnitude is, however, very rare in research of this type.

The actual data collection was not conducted by us. The list of items included in the instrument had to be taken as a given. While future research efforts may strive for greater depth in addressing particular constructs, we believe that the questionnaire adequately measured the topics involved. The job performance measure used in the present study was the agent's combined net premium for 1981. This figure, while representing both new and repeat business, was determined by the firm's top management to be the most accurate representation of an individual's overall job performance. At this stage of theory development, it is believed that the advantages of the sample far outweigh any limitations. A more complete presentation of methodological issues is contained in Lucas (1983).

Sample Accuracy

In research efforts involving data collection through sampling, an important consideration is whether the group who responded to the instrument is different in some systematic manner from those members of the sample who chose not to respond. Discrepancies between the two groups can introduce bias, which often has a major impact on the external validity of the findings.

Of the 4000 questionnaires distributed to agents, 1916 were returned in a useable form for a 47.9 percent response rate. Very little can be said about the characteristics of the nonrespondents except for a statement from company sources that these agents probably tended to be older and had been with the company for a longer period of time. Thus readers should be aware of possible bias.

A second aspect of nonresponse can be addressed in greater depth. Of the respondents, 1071 (55.9 percent) elected to provide an identifying contract number (providers), and 845 chose not to provide this information (nonproviders). The absence of the contract number excluded the nonproviders from the evaluation of the model due to the unavailability of job performance information for these unidentified agents. Data on all other variables were available, and thus the providers and nonproviders were comparable on several dimensions. Based on the comparison of personal history information, the nonproviders tend to be: female, with the company more than five years, and on the Potential Commission Advance Plan (a variation of the Straight Commission Plan). A comparison of the two groups on the three scales using the *t*-test indicated that the nonproviders were less satisfied on both the intrinsic and extrinsic job variables ($p < .01$). No significant difference was found for the task-specific self-esteem scale.

In considering these findings one might rightly assume that individuals who are more satisfied intrinsically, as well as extrinsically, would have a greater likelihood of responding to their company's request for information. While the differences were not large, they were statistically significant, and this fact should be kept in mind when analyzing the results.

The providers from this point on are considered to be the sample; they were randomly divided into two groups for cross-validation purposes. The full tested model was run for both groups and resulted in identical paths remaining in the revised equations for both groups. Least-squared solutions were found for the regression of job-performance on intrinsic satisfaction, task-specific self-esteem and tenure, and extrinsic satisfaction of job performance. Only small deviations were noted between the resulting path coefficients and standard errors for the two groups. A Chow test (1960) was conducted to determine if the differences between the two groups was statistically significant. Results from this evaluation indicated no significant difference between the two groups on either of the equations ($p > .25$). On the basis of these findings, the two random segments were reunited for the remainder of the data analysis.

Path Analysis

The statistics are presented in terms of path coefficients. These figures are identified through obtaining the least-squared solution for the regressions of the dependent variables (effects) on the explanatory variables (causes) (Kerlinger and Pedhazur 1973). Wright (1934) assessed on the interpretation of path coefficients by viewing the statistic as the portion of the standard deviation of the effect variable accounted for by the causal variable when all other factors are held constant.

There are nine variables included in the tested model: intrinsic job satisfaction, task-specific self-esteem, job performance, sex, tenure, education, age, compensation plan, and extrinsic job satisfaction. In determining which paths to evaluate, theory must be the overriding decision criterion. The data should be used to test existing theory rather than as a blind search to develop new theories (Kerlinger and Pedhazur 1973). In an effort to be as rigorous as possible, we required that path coefficients surpass two standards to be considered supportive of the model in the present analysis. The standardized coefficient must be twice its standard error and greater than .05 in size to be considered supportive of the hypothesis and remain the model.

In considering the findings, several points must be reinforced. The results from a path analysis can only be considered as a test of the a priori explanatory scheme of the model. The technique is only capable of determining if the data is consistent with this model. Kerlinger and Pedhazur (1973) stressed that no proof of causal relationships is provided by recursive path analysis. True tests of causation can only be performed using time series data and statistical techniques. The present method can substantiate or disprove the theoretically developed system of relationships. Any statements regarding causation refer only to a weak causal ordering among variables. True causation can only be assessed through measures at various points in time.

Hypothesis Evaluation

The amount of time a salesperson has spent on a particular job was hypothesized to have a positive influence on workers' job performance. Results indicate support for this position. A path coefficient of .309 was identified for the relationship with a standard error of only .035 (table 13-1). The removal of all unsubstantiated paths from the equation had no impact on the path coefficient and reduced the standard error slightly to .029. Based on these results, hypothesis 1 was supported.

According to hypothesis 2, an agent's age should have a positive influence on his/her level of sales performance. Age was not found to have a significant relationship with job performance. The data analysis resulted in a very small path coefficient ($P = .005$) and a comparatively large standard error ($s.e. = .035$). Table 13-2 shows that there was a strong correlation between the age and tenure variables ($r = .577$). Such a high partial correlation can be one indication of the presence of multicollinearity in the equation. Further analysis provided additional evidence that the multicollinearity was influencing the results.

Dropping the age variable increases the risk of creating specification bias. Given the nature of the data, the strength of the relationships, and the relative importance of the variables in an explanatory sense, the decision was made to delete the path from age to job performance. Tenure appears to be a suitable surrogate for the age variable since it represents abilities acquired through time—in this instance, time on the job.

The findings from the present data did not support the proposition that salespeople who had higher levels of formal education perform at higher levels (hypothesis 3). A path coefficient of only 0.30 with a standard error

Table 13-1
Path Coefficients for Both Tested and Revised Models

Dependent Variable (Effect)	Independent Variable (Cause)	Tested Model Path Coefficient	Tested Model Standard Error	Revised Model Path Coefficient	Revised Model Standard Error
Intrinsic job satisfaction	Sex	− .022	.098	—	—
Job performance	Task-specific self-esteem	.093	.030	.093	.030
	Intrinsic job satisfaction	.117	.030	.114	.030
	Age	.005	.035	—	—
	Tenure	.309	.035	.309	.029
	Education	.030	.029	—	—
Extrinsic job satisfaction	Job performance	.160	.031	.150	.030
	Compensation plan:				
	C_a	− .035	.094	—	—
	C_b	− .029	.072	—	—
	Sex	− .031	.100	—	—

Table 13-2
Correlations between Variables in the Model

	Job Performance	Intrinsic Job Satisfaction	Extrinsic Job Satisfaction	Age	Tenure	Education	CP_a	CP_b	Sex
Intrinsic job satisfaction	.140								
Extrinsic job satisfaction	.150	.363							
Age	.186	−.022	−.036						
Tenure	.325	.004	.017	.577					
Education	−.018	−.102	−.067	−.036	−.100				
Compensation plan									
CP_a (a = Commission)	.025	−.044	−.018	.351	.311	.006			
CP_b (b = PCAP)	.193	−.035	.014	.125	.386	−.047	−.475		
Sex (l = Male)	.115	−.022	−.018	.073	.175	.062	.034	.162	
Task-specific self-esteem	.176	.271	.139	.069	.172	−.058	.041	.087	.056

nearly equal in magnitude (.029) was produced from the analysis. Because of these insignificant results, the education variable was removed from the job performance equation.

The two hypotheses relating to gender proposed that men would be more intrinsically satisfied (hypothesis 4) and extrinsically satisfied (hypothesis 5) than women. Coding the variable 1 = male and 0 = female, the path coefficients obtained from the analysis were $-.022$ and $-.031$, respectively. On the basis of these findings neither hypothesis was supported, and, in fact, the indication was that the female agents were insignificantly more satisfied on both variables than were the men. Caution should be exercised in considering the paths from gender to the two satisfaction components, because nearly 90 percent of the sample was male.

On the basis of early research in the consistency theory area, it was hypothesized that increasing levels of task-specific self-esteem would have a positive influence on sales representatives' job performance (hypothesis 6). The results presented in table 13–1 indicate that the path coefficient obtained for this relationship in the tested model was .093 with a standard error of .030. Removing age and education as causal influences of job performance had no impact on either of these figures. Based on the two criteria used to evaluate path coefficients, there was support for the hypothesis that task-specific self-esteem influences job performance.

On the basis of recent research in consistency theory, it was hypothesized that task-specific self-esteem would moderate the intrinsic job satisfaction-job performance relationship. The path was proposed as being positive when task-specific self-esteem (TSSE) was high (hypothesis 7), and negative when TSSE was at low levels (hypothesis 8). The results indicated support for the first proposition ($P = .114$), but a lack of evidence in favor of the later one ($P = .108$). A Chow (1960) test produced results ($p < .01$) indicating no difference between the two groups segmented at the mean TSSE level of 7.74 on a 9.0 point scale. Due to the lack of support for the moderating influence of TSSE, the sample was reunited to obtain a value for the intrinsic job satisfaction-job performance relationship. A path coefficient of .117 was obtained, indicating support for the presence of this important relationship in the model.

Hypothesis 9 addressed the relationship between job performance and extrinsic job satisfaction. The results contained in table 13–1 indicate the presence of a path coefficient of .160 with a standard error of .031 for the two variables in the tested model. The removal of the non-significant dummy variables representing compensation plan and agent's sex resulted in a slight decrease in both figures to .150 and .030, respectively. On the basis of these results, there was support for hypothesis 9.

The final tested hypothesis (10) proposed that extrinsic job satisfaction would be higher the closer one's compensation was tied to job performance.

Two dummy variables were used due to the three forms of compensation. The results indicated that the type of compensation failed to affect the agents' level of extrinsic job satisfaction ($CP_a = -.035$, $CP_b = -.029$).

Model Performance

The evaluation of the size of path coefficients and their relative magnitude in comparison to their respective standard errors can shed light on the appropriateness of individual paths in the model. This analysis, however, offers little indication concerning the performance of the model itself. Two aspects that can be used to evaluate the model are (1) the R^2 values from the least-squared solutions to the regressions of the effect variables on the causes and (2) the precision with which the model reproduces the original correlation matrix for the variables in the system. The latter has often been omitted from path-analysis marketing studies.

An examination of the percent of deviation in the two remaining effect variables (job performance and extrinsic job satisfaction) that has been explained by the causal or independent variables indicated that there were unmeasured exogenous variables not included in the model. Task-specific self-esteem, intrinsic job satisfaction, and tenure were found to account for slightly over 13 percent of the variability in job performance ($F = 54.4$; $p < .01$). Job performance, the sole remaining causal variable in the equation with extrinsic job satisfaction as the effect variable, explained only slightly over 2 percent of the variability in extrinsic job satisfaction ($F = 24.8$; $p < .01$). These R^2 figures are not particularly high; however, values in this range are fairly common in path-analysis marketing studies (Churchill and Moschis 1979). Duncan (1975) stated that while the unexplained percent of variation is of concern in evaluating causal models, frameworks should not be rejected on the basis of low R^2 values alone. This aspect of the model's performance, however, must be kept in mind in evaluating the various paths and the completeness of the explanatory power of the framework.

The reconstruction of the original matrix of the correlations between model variables provides an indication as to what information was lost in an effort to develop a more economical model. Kerlinger and Pedhazur (1973) stated that if discrepancies are small between the original and reconstructed matrices (in the area of .05), the deletion of paths not included in the revised model can be considered justified. Table 13–3 contains a comparison of the observed and reconstructed correlations between the variables included in the model. Minor yet important discrepancies are noted for the following variable pairs: task-specific self-esteem–job performance (.083); tenure–extrinsic job satisfaction (.116); and task-specific self-esteem–extrinsic job satisfaction (.113). These results indicate the potential for indirect effects

Table 13-3

Comparison of Observed Correlations and Correlations Reconstructed from Revised Model

Correlation	Observed	Reconstructed
r_{17} (IJS–JP)	.140	.114
r_{37} (Ten–JP)	.325	.309
r_{67} (TSSE–JP)	.176	.093
r_{19} (IJS–EJS)	.363	.021
r_{39} (Ten–EJS)	− .067	.049
r_{69} (TSSE–EJS)	.139	.026
r_{79} (JP–EJS)	.150	.150

Note: IJS = intrinsic job satisfaction; JP = job performance; TSSE = task-specific self-esteem; EJS = extrinsic job satisfaction; Ten = Tenure.

in the TSSE–job performance relationship, and a direct effect between both tenure and TSSE and job performance.

A major limitation of the revised model was in the reconstruction of the correlation between intrinsic job satisfaction and extrinsic job satisfaction (discrepency = .342). The observed correlation of .363 (table 13-2) was one of the highest between any two variables in the model. An indirect effect (.021) was not adequate to explain the relationship. Potential ways of enhancing the models performance are identified in the discussion that follows. These limitations of the revised model must be kept in mind when considering the discussion of the results obtained.

In summary, analysis of the tested model indicated that much of what had been proposed was supported by the data. Intrinsic job satisfaction was supported as an influence on job performance, which in turn had a positive path to extrinsic job satisfaction. Thus the basic vein of the model remains intact. Gender was not found to influence either satisfaction variable. Both age and tenure, for different reasons, were removed as influences on job performance. Form of compensation was not found to have an impact on extrinsic job satisfaction. While the path from task-specific self-esteem to job performance was supported, the role of TSSE as a moderator variable has been deleted. The model itself has shown strong performance in some areas; however, its explanation of extrinsic job satisfaction, and, in particular, intrinsic job satisfaction's relationship with that variable, was a major weakness.

Discussion and Implications

The results from the path analysis of the tested model produced some reinforcement of existing theories of the satisfaction-performance relationship.

There were, however, some findings that contradict previous theory and research. Some of these discrepancies can be addressed based on the specific nature of the data utilized in the present study. Others raise issues that can be dealt with only through future research efforts. The focus of this section is the discussion of the important issues and the assessment of the implications of the present findings for individuals involved in motivating, and studying the motivation of, salespeople.

The Revised Model

As a result of the data analysis, a revised model is presented in figure 13-2. Looking first at the personal history variables, we see that the amount of time an individual has spent on the specific job has by far the most substantial impact on job performance. In an industry such as insurance sales, which depends extensively on repeat business, the development of a customer base over time can have a substantial impact on an agent's performance figures. The tenure variable also represents knowledge, both in terms of product and customer, much of which can only be gained through time on the job.

For the present study, the results failed to show a significant effect for the agents' age on job performance. An explanation for the low path coefficient was the high correlation between the age and tenure variables. The presence of multicollinearity is a potential problem for studies involving many job positions as time in life and time on the job tend to increase in a parallel fashion. Due to the stronger level of association between tenure and job performance, age was removed from the revised model. Education, hypothesized as a strong cause of positive results, was identified as being a nonsignificant influence. In other fields, or even in other insurance surveys, this influence might be found to be equal to or greater than that of job tenure. Based on the results from the present study, education was not included in the revised model.

The two hypotheses involving agents' gender (4 and 5) were both found not to hold for the present study. In fact, women were even slightly more satisfied than men on both the intrinsic and extrinsic dimensions of the job. The percentage of female agents contained in the present study was small (10.2 percent); however, their sheer numbers (109 respondents) may support the results. Perhaps meaningful changes have taken place due to the great strides made by women in the labor force during the 1970s and early 1980s. While there may still be instances in which women are less satisfied than men intrinsically and/or extrinsically, this was not true for the members of the present sample.

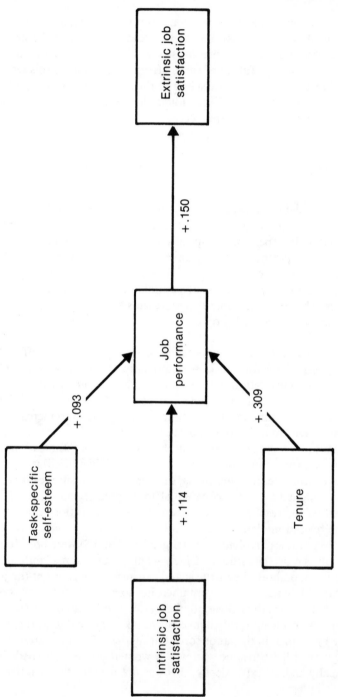

Figure 13-2. The Revised Model

With regard to the role of task-specific self-esteem as a component of consistency theory, the results were mixed. As hypothesis 6 stated (Korman 1968; Bagozzi 1980), a salesperson's feeling of competency in performing important aspects of their task did have a positive impact on his/her job performance. The results support the proposition that when an individual perceives him-/herself to be capable, the tendency is to perform at a level consistent with this positive self-image. Agents who see themselves as lacking in key areas will tend to perform at levels consistent with these feelings. The task-specific self-esteem path to job performance was supported and it remains in the revised model.

More recent research in the consistency theory area (Inkson 1978; and Lopez 1982) led to the position stated in hypotheses 7 and 8 that the task-specific self-esteem variable would moderate the intrinsic job satisfaction-job performance relationship. This aspect of the theory was not supported by the data. Splitting the agents at the mean level of the task-specific self-esteem variable into high and low groups did not have a significant impact on the path coefficients for the intrinsic job satisfaction-job performance relationship. An aspect of the present data set that may have affected this section of the model was the high mean rating of the agents on the task-specific self-esteem scale. The mean value of 7.74 on the nine-point scale indicates that the agents possessed a relatively high self-image of their abilities. Even those salespeople in the low-image group had an average score of 6.01. Studies which show a greater variability on this dimension may produce a negative path coefficient for salespeople in the low esteem group. Based on the results from the present study, however, the moderating influence of task-specific self-esteem was not supported, and thus this aspect was not included in the revised model.

Due to the evidence that task-specific self-esteem did not serve as as moderator, the sample was reunited to examine the extent of the impact of intrinsic job satisfaction on job performance. In support of Herzberg's two-factor theory, a significant and meaningful path coefficient was obtained for the relationship. The results were also found to support the theory's contention that job performance has an impact on extrinsic job satisfaction. The nature of the work itself was identified as being important not just from the perspective of having satisfied workers but also as an influence on the productivity of the employees. Of the three proposed influences, only job performance was found to have an impact on a salesperson's satisfaction with extrinsic job outcomes. Extrinsic job satisfaction has been identified as a major determinant in the decision to go to work for or remain with a particular company. The relationships between the two satisfaction variables and job performance are thus important issues influencing the continued viability of a sales organization. On the basis of the results obtained, this integral part of the model remains intact in the revised version.

Agents' basis of compensation was not found to have any appreciable or significant impact on their satisfaction with extrinsic aspects of the job. The research setting provided three compensation plans which were coded into two dummy variables. The largest segment of the sample (53.3 percent) was under the Potential Commission Advance Plan. This plan was a derivation of the Straight Commission Plan. More recent hires were compensated using the salaried Training Allowance Plan (27.5 percent of the sample). Agents under this plan were being shifted over time to a commission pay structure. Nearly all other agents (16.5 percent) had their salaries tied directly to job performance under the Straight Commission Plan. The fact that no difference in extrinsic job satisfaction was found between agents under the various plans may be due to the present setting where nearly all agents had their pay tied to their performance in some fashion. Studies involving salespeople permanently on salary and commission plans would represent a more meaningful test of the impact that the form of compensation plan has on extrinsic job satisfaction.

Considering the overall model, the results also provide mixed signals. The basic core of this model, with its roots in two-factor theory, was supported by the path analysis. Despite this support, the percentage of variance explained in the effect variables by the causal variables in the model was not large. Such results indicate that there are unmeasured exogenous variables that were having an impact on job performance and extrinsic job satisfaction. Before a greater understanding of the processes involved can be realized, these additional variables must be identified.

It has been previously stressed that theory must precede, as opposed to being an output from, the path analysis process. A meaningful analysis can only be performed when the proposed paths are the result of theory rather than a search for significance. With these warnings clearly in mind, an attempt was made to determine if the R^2 value for the extrinsic job satisfaction variable could be enhanced through direct effects from the intrinsic job satisfaction, task-specific self-esteem, and tenure variables. Insignificant path coefficients were found for tenure ($P = -.024$) and task-specific self esteem ($P = .032$). A significant direct effect was identified for the path from intrinsic satisfaction to extrinsic satisfaction ($P = .339$; $s.e. = .030$). The inclusion of this new path increased the R^2 value from .02 to .14. While including paths identified in this manner in the revised model is not justified, doing so may provide some additional insight for future researchers in this area.

The above-cited activity also improved the model's performance on the second aspect of its evaluation, the reconstruction of the correlation matrix. Table 13-3 shows that with regard to job performance, the direct effects from intrinsic job satisfaction and tenure provided acceptable reconstruction. Other indirect effects were apparently present in the task-specific self-esteem-job performance relationship. An examination of the paths leading to extrinsic job satisfaction indicated that only the direct effect from job performance resulted in an adequate reconstruction. Indirect effects from intrinsic job satisfaction, tenure, and task-specific self-esteem do not result in acceptable reconstructed values. The exploratory look at direct paths from these exogenous variables to extrinsic job satisfaction resulted in nearly perfect correlation reconstruction for intrinsic job satisfaction-extrinsic job satisfaction (reconstructed r = .369). This provided additional support for a direct effect between the two variables.

Overall, much of the hypothesized model has been supported by the data. The basic underpinnings of the two-factor theory were upheld. Paths from intrinsic job satisfaction to job performance and job performance to extrinsic job satisfaction were supported and remain in the revised model. The direct impact of task-specific self-esteem on job performance was found to be significant, although its influence as a moderator variable in sales situations remains subject to question. The only path from a demographic variable supported by the data was between tenure and sales performance. At this point, the importance of the form of compensation in determining extrinsic job satisfaction is still unclear.

In the development of the model, it was stated that the processes involved are more complex than the two-factor theory implied. On the basis of the R^2 values obtained and the several discrepancies in the reproduction of the correlation matrix, it is clear that the revised model does not contain all the relationships involved. The revised model is a foundation for future research efforts. More questions were raised by the present study than were answered.

Directions for Future Research

As with most empirical studies at this stage of development in the sales management area, the results obtained here represent one step in a long process. Much work remains to be done, and many questions must be answered. These answers will raise yet more questions. This section attempts to provide some guidelines for future research endeavors.

Efforts to examine job satisfaction as the single cause, or result, of job performance show a lack of understanding of the complexities of work in general and personal selling in particular. Additional efforts must be made to increase the level of understanding of the relationships between the variables involved in this many-faceted process.

A major limitation of this study, and any study that involves the collection of data at one point in time, is that only weak causal orderings can be addressed. Future studies need to collect data at well-thought-out intervals and should apply in-depth analysis available for time series data. Only through this process can causal orderings between variables be proven.

This model or others assessing the relationship between intrinsic job satisfaction, job performance, and extrinsic job satisfaction, needs to be tested on industries and companies outside the insurance field. Other settings might provide more meaningful comparisons between salaried and straight commissions salespeople. Highly technical industries will also provide a better assessment of the impact of the formal education variable on sales performance. Other research settings may also involve individuals with greater variability in their task-specific self-esteem.

Future studies should involve individuals who are still employed by *and* salespeople who have left the organization. The homogeneity of the present sample in this respect resulted in less variability in the measures of variables and may have decreased the model's explanatory power.

A key aspect of the model that needs further study is the relationship between intrinsic job satisfaction and extrinsic job satisfaction. Additional research involving these variables needs to be done before an understanding of the processes involved can be achieved.

The final, and perhaps most important, suggestion for future research endeavors is the identification of additional variables that will result in the explanation of a larger percentage of the variability in the effect variables. In particular, sales ability needs definition in ways that can be operationally measured.

The true worth of this study can be assessed mainly through its contribution to research. In the next section some preliminary directions for the practice of sales management derived from the present study will be identified. These implications are *preliminary* and are, in fact, dependent on the performance of additional research of the type outlined above.

Implications for Sales Managers

The process of improving salespeople's performance levels is a critical aspect of the sales management function. Sales figures for the region, district, and entire company are nothing more than the sum total of the results from each individual salesperson. Clearly the abilities to hire, train, motivate, and retain quality people are major reflections on the success of the sales management process. Answers to the questions of how best to perform these functions are not provided here. The results from the present study do provide some tentative guidance for practitioners in these areas.

The results reflecting on the relationship between intrinsic job satisfaction and job performance indicated the importance of structuring sales positions so that they will provide important and meaningful work for the employees. Efforts at improving this aspect of sales jobs must be done with a consideration of the difference between job enlargement (more tasks) and job enrichment (more meaningful tasks). Sales positions, as with all other occupations, can never be without mundane tasks. Paperwork will always prove to be less than appealing for creative salespeople. Intrinsic satisfaction can be increased by involving the salespeople to a greater degree in the planning process and showing people how the information provided contributes to the success of the organization.

Providing salespeople with a feeling of competency was also shown to have an impact on sales performance. One way to enhance a person's self-image is to provide them with the training that teaches them how to do it. Reinforcement of an individual's good performance in key aspects of the sales job can also have an impact on the person's task-specific self-esteem, which can influence how successful s/he is.

Tenure was found to have the largest impact on job performance. Keeping quality people in the organization for long periods of time has often been recognized as a key to the success of a company. Greater understanding of the relationship between extrinsic job satisfaction and turnover could provide assistance in this area. The identification of this area as a priority item in many organizations and current studies should provide additional insight into this area.

The relationship between formal education and job performance again shows that there are numerous jobs for which high qualifications on this aspect of a person's background have been established as perhaps unnecessary. This is a feature of the recruiting process, which can be studied by examining company records.

The non-significance of the gender variable as an influence on both intrinsic and extrinsic job satisfaction again shows that women and men are achieving equality in the sales force. Numerous companies have made moving qualified saleswomen into management a top priority.

Which factors affect the satisfaction level of salespeople with the extrinsic aspects of the job in general, and pay in particular, is a question that cannot be answered from the present study. A salesperson's performance level was found to be an influence, but this factor explained a surprisingly small portion of the variability in extrinsic job satisfaction. This appears to be a key area for firms to investigate both through monitoring present employee attitudes and carefully conducting exit interviews.

These guidelines are presented in an attempt to form a bridge between theory and practice in the sales management area. The tentative nature of these comments must be stressed. Previously outlined limitations of the research upon which these implications were developed should be kept in mind when considering the relevance of these comments for a particular sales situation.

References

Arnold, H.J. (1982). "Moderator Variables. A Clarification of Conceptual, Analytic, and Psychometric Issues." *Organizational Behavior and Human Performance* 29:143–174.

Asher, H.B. (1976). *Causal Modeling.* London: Sage Publications.

Baggozi, R. (1980). "Performance and Satisfaction in an Industrial Sales Force: An Examination of Their Antecedents and Simultaneity." *Journal of Marketing Research* 44:65–77.

Beswick, C., and D.W. Cravens (1977). "A Multistage Decision Model for Sales Force Management." *Journal of Marketing Research* 14:135–144.

Busch, P., and R.F. Bush (1978). "Women Contrasted to Men in the Industrial Salesforce: Job Satisfaction, Values, Role Clarity, Performance, and Propensity to Leave." *Journal of Marketing Research* 15:438–448.

Cherrington, D.J.; H.J. Reitz; and W.E. Scott, Jr. (1971). "Effects of Contingent and Noncontingent Reward on the Relationship Between Satisfaction and Task Peformance." *Journal of Applied Psychology* 55:531–536.

Chow, G.C. (1960). "Tests of Equality Between Sets of Coefficients in Two Linear Regressions." *Econometrica* 28:591–605.

Churchill, G.A., Jr., and G.P. Moschis (1979). "Television and Interpersonal Influences on Adolescent Consumer Learning." *Journal of Consumer Research,* 6, pp. 23–35.

Cotham, J.C. (1969). "Using Personal History Information in Retail Salesman Selection." *Journal of Retailing* 45:31–38.

Cravens, D.W., and R.B. Woodruff (1973). "An Approach for Determining Criteria of Sales Performance." *Journal of Applied Psychology* 57:240–247.

Davis, R.; G. England; and L. Lofquist (1968). *A Theory of Work Adjustment: A Revision.* Minneapolis: University of Minnesota, Industrial Relations Center.

Deshpande, R., and G. Zaltman (1982). "Factors Affecting the Use of Marketing Research Information: A Path Analysis." *Journal of Marketing Research* 19:14–31.

Duncan, O.D. (1975). *Introduction to Structural Equation Models.* New York: Academic Press.

Fisher, C.D. (1980). "On the Dubious Wisdom of Expecting Job Satisfaction to Correlate with Performance." *Academy of Mangement Review* 5:607–612.

Greenhaus, J., and I.J. Gadin (1974). "Self-Esteem, Performance, and Job Satisfaction: Some Tests of a Theory." *Journal of Applied Psychology* 59:722–726.

Hackman, J., and E. Lawler (1971). "Employee Reactions to Job Characteristics." *Journal of Applied Psychology* 55:259–286.

Herzberg, F.; B. Mausner; R. Peterson; and D. Capwell (1957). Job Attitudes: A Review of Research and Opinion. Pittsburgh: Psychological Service of Pittsburgh.

Herzberg, F.; B. Mausner; and B. Synderman (1959). *The Motivation to Work,* 2nd ed. New York: Wiley.

Inkson, J.H. (1978). "Self-Esteem as a Moderator of the Relationship Between Job Performance and Job Satisfaction." *Journal of Applied Psychology* 63:243–247.

Kerlinger, F.N., and E.J. Pedhazur (1973). *Multiple Regression in Behavioral Research.* New York: Holt, Rinehart and Winston.

King, N. (1970). "Clarification and Evaluation of the Two-Factor Theory of Job Satisfaction." *Psychological Bulletin* 74:18–31.

Korman, A.K. (1971). "Expectancies as Determinants of Performance." *Journal of Applied Psychology* 55, 218–222.

———. (1976). "Hypothesis of Work Behavior Revisited and an Extension." *Academy of Management Review* 1:50–63.

Lamont, L.M., and W.J. Lundstrom (1977). Identifying Successful Industrial Salesmen by Personality and Personal Characteristics." *Journal of Marketing Research* 14:517–529.

Lawler, E., III (1971). *Pay and Organizational Effectiveness: A Psychological View.* New York: McGraw-Hill.

Lopez, E.M. (1982). "A Test of the Self-Consistency Theory of the Job Performance-Job Satisfaction Relationship." *Academy of Management Journal* 25:335–348.

Lucas, G.H., Jr. (1983). "An Assessment of the Job Satisfaction-Job Performance Relationship: An Analysis for Insurance Salespeople." Unpublished Ph.D. dissertation, University of Missouri-Columbia.

Maslow, A. (1943). "A Theory of Human Motivation." *Psychological Review* 50:370–396.

Mobley, W.H.; R.W. Griffeth; and B.M. Meglino (1979). "Review and Conceptual Analysis of the Employee Turnover Process." *Psychological Bulletin* 86:493–523.

Porter, L., and E. Lawler, III (1968). *Managerial Attitudes and Performance.* Homewood, Ill.: Dorsey Press.

Scott, W.G. (1962). *Human Relations in Management: A Behavioral Science Approach.* New York: McGraw-Hill.

Swan, J.E., and C.J. Futrell (1978). "Men Versus Women in Industrial Sales: A Performance Gap." *Industrial Marketing Management* 8:360–364.

Walker, O., Jr.; G. Churchill, Jr.; and N. Ford (1977). "Motivation and Performance in Industrial Selling: Present Knowledge and Needed Research." *Journal of Marketing Research* 14:156–168.

Weaver, C.N. (1969). "An Empirical Study to Aid the Selection of Retail Clerks." *Journal of Retailing* 45:22–26.

Whitsett, D.A., and E.K. Winslow (1967). "An Analysis of Studies Critical of the Motivator-Hygiene Theory." *Personnel Psychology* 20:391–415.

Wright, S. (1934). "The Method of Path Coefficients." *The Annals of Mathematical Statistics* 5:161–215.

14

The Impact of Interpersonal Attraction on Salesperson Effectiveness

Robert W. Chestnut and
Jacob Jacoby

Financial services "are an unpleasant experience for many consumers . . . involving abstract concepts that most people don't understand."
—Ad Forum 1983

The financial industry, in all its various components—banks, savings and loan associations, insurance companies, brokerage houses, and so forth—has long suffered from one major disadvantage. The service provided is in most cases so complex as to be totally beyond the average consumer's understanding. Consumer reaction is predictable. As noted in the quotation above, for the consumer finance is an unpleasant business.

The industry realizes this and has coped in the only way possible outside of attempting to educate major segments of the population: It has introduced a cost-efficient buffer, the salesperson. Our stockbroker informs us of market conditions; our bank branch manager helps us fill in our mortgage or loan application; and our insurance agent provides solutions and, as necessary, upgrades our policy to meet our changing requirements. All of these professionals act to sell us on a particular service, but in the process they educate us regarding the decision. Each helps us manage a domain of complexity which might otherwise overload and thus frustrate our decision-making capabilities and purchase intentions.

One question raised by the salesperson's role is striking. When we decide on a particular financial service, what exactly do we buy—the salesperson or the service? The economist would say that, of course, we buy the service (that is, the product communicated by the salesperson). Its utilities can be stated in dollar and cents terms and, given a state of "perfect information," comparisons can be made on an objective basis so as to maximize our financial return at a minimum of risk.

The psychologist would advance a somewhat different point of view. In a decision context for which few of us really have the ability to implement an economic analysis, it is by far more natural to turn to a quantity or aspect of the purchase environment that we can evaluate: the salesperson.

Given recent changes in the structure of the financial industry, it seems likely that in the future we will have increasing numbers of such salespeople to turn to. Competition in this industry is increasing and with it has come a new intensity of marketing effort. Sears, for example, which currently has just a few test sites, is now embarked on a program that will see over four hundred financial service centers in operation by the late 1980s. Heavy emphasis is placed on the staff supporting these centers and management is keenly aware of the cost of attracting and maintaining a high quality sales staff. "The interface between broker and client is what makes our difference—and that's up to us." (Robert M. Gardiner, Chairman of the Dean Witter Financial Services Group, *New York Times*, May 11, 1983.)

Just how important is the salesperson in the purchase of a complex financial service? This chapter briefly reviews the literature on the salesperson as a separate source of purchase information, concentrating on the attribute of liking or attraction. Next we describe an experiment that pits the informational component of the purchase against the personal component of the salesperson.

Salespeople as Sources of Information

Commercial messages have well-defined points of origin. In fact, this is one of the formal defining characteristics of advertising. From salespeople conversing with their clients to television spots on familiar brands, the source of a communication is known and acts as a potential influence on its audience. "When a communicator presents a view on an issue, the message itself is a primary source of information, but so are the communicator's attributes . . ." (Eagly and Himmelfarb 1978, p. 518.)

In examining the attributes of a source or salesperson, theory does not focus on the attribute per se but on the consumer's reaction to the attribute and the information derived therefrom. Two broad types of consumer derived information are hypothesized. Consumers tend to process the attributes of a salesperson in order to make judgments of credibility or attractiveness (McGuire 1969). This information, rather than the specifics of a salesperson's experience, appearance, or training, is used to guide the purchase outcome.

This chapter focuses on source attractiveness. Both common sense and theory argue for the proposition that attractive or liked salespeople are more persuasive. Advertisers, for example, have long recognized this fact in their selection of spokespeople. The importance of interpersonal attraction and the information it conveys is observed in many different situations and finds empirical support in a number of now-classic experiments (Brock 1965; Berscheid 1966; Byrne 1971).

Beyond the general proposition, however, there is a surprising lack of detail and agreement. Studies on source attractiveness continue, but they do not appear to have gained momentum. "Unfortunately, the relationship between attraction to source (like-dislike, friendly feelings, etc.) and attitude change has received scant attention, especially when compared with the vast output of literature linking respect and trust factors to attitude change." (Simons, Berkowitz, and Moyer 1970, p. 9.) In a review of the "reliable" effects in persuasion (Ronis et al. 1977), attraction is still described to be important but thought to be inadequately understood.

Research in the consumer setting tends to address a special form of interpersonal attraction. It is the attraction or identification that results from people's being similar to one another. Early studies in marketing (Evans 1963; Gadel 1964) establish this emphasis with a correlational analysis of sales performance. Salespeople who were demographically similar to their customers were found to be more successful.

Brock (1965) provided one of the first systematic tests of such similarity. Consumers were observed in the process of buying paints. Similarity was manipulated by having a salesperson claim to be in a similar/dissimilar product-usage situation (the "I just bought some for my house" approach). Claims of similarity in this study were found to influence both the acceptance of message and the actual purchase behavior.

Subsequent studies, which either replicated or elaborated upon the experiment by Brock (Woodside and Davenport 1974; Riordan, Oliver, and Donnelly 1977), confirm the effect. What is happening? Clearly, similarity information is assisting the prospect to reach certain judgments or conclusions. Customers accept the paint recommendation, for example, because a similar usage of paint implies a certain amount of information relevance. The assumption is that attraction/similarity is of persuasive value in so far as it implies a new level of trust or credibility. This is often referred to as the "instrumental value" of similarity information: ". . . the recipient changes toward the position of a communicator to the extent he perceives that he shares with the communicator an attribute *pertinent* [emphasis added] to the dimension along which change is advocated." (Brock 1965, p. 653.)

Before we accept this as the only effect at work, however, there is a second potential influence of similarity information. Strangely, in discussing interpersonal attraction and its influence on purchase, we have yet to raise the basic concept of liking versus disliking. There has been a tendency for consumer research to focus exclusively on the rational model of humans where only pertinent attributes are of interest. What of the irrational and emotional model of people in which non-pertinent attributes play a role?

Social psychology has long posited a model in which similarity information of a non-pertinent character acts to create internal states of affect or liking (Byrne 1971). It is no accident that the words *alike* and *like* share the same root meaning. Does this liking in turn lead to persuasion and purchase?

An Experiment on Information Acquisition Behavior

An experiment (see Chestnut, 1977 for further detail) was conducted to systematically vary the attraction response to different salespeople on the basis of non-pertinent attributes, that is, attributes not directly or logically related to a particular salesperson's ability to provide a better or worse product. The dependent measure of interest was that of pre-purchase information acquisition behavior. The general hypothesis was that attraction to a salesperson would lead to a greater probability of requesting information from that salesperson. Given a "bounded rational" (Newell and Simon 1972) approach to the human decision-making process, this would also imply a greater market-share result for the liked salesperson.

What follows, in brief, is a description of the procedure. The method used in the experiment was a behavioral process tracing technique administered by an IBM 5100 microcomputer (for a general description of such techniques see Jacoby, Chestnut, and Fisher 1978; for a specific description of this experiment, see Chestnut and Jacoby 1982).

The experiment was in three parts. In all, ninety-six college undergraduates were tested in a one-on-one, personal interview format implemented both orally and by a microcomputer television monitor hook-up. Upon entering the test room, subjects were seated in front of a television monitor linked to a microcomputer programmed for the storage and sequential display of product information. They were told that the purpose of the study was to recreate the conditions of buying a life insurance policy. A pre-task questionnarie was administered after which subjects were introduced to the purchase task by a 1400-word buyer's guide designed to acquaint them with the properties or types of information that would later be made available.

The second part of the experiment began with the turning on of the computer system and an explanation of its information storage and display device capacities. The first items of information displayed by the computer were complete descriptions of purportedly real agents who had provided policy information to the interviewer for purposes of the study. In actuality, these agents were hypothetical. These descriptions were prefaced with the cover story that such personal details were an attempt to recreate the natural situation in which the subject might actually meet and buy from these agents. Checks throughout the experiment showed that subjects fully believed the explanation provided.

Four such agents were described sequentially. These descriptions included a name and a series of general opinion statements. This constituted the attraction manipulation, with names pretested and selected so as to produce different levels of initial attraction (from high to low levels) and opinions manipulated to have different degrees of similarity to those expressed earlier by the subject tested.

With liking of agent established, the experiment proceeded by having subjects verbally request, item-by-item, policy information stored in a 4 (agent) by 36 (property or type of policy information) matrix. For example, a subject might request an item of information from Ed (Agent C2) on annual premium (Policy Information R12) and receive displayed on the television monitor the value or item of information: "$149.38" (C2,R12).

After each subject acquired those values that s/he deemed necessary to the purchase decision, this subject indicated a choice of policy by naming the agent from whom s/he would most likely buy. A third and final part of the experiment went on to assess a variety of post-purchase subjective states and to debrief the subject as to the true interests of the experiment.

It is important to note that the information matrix was programmed into the computer in such a way that agents were fully counterbalanced across the "facts." That is, each agent represented all possible sets of policy information. In analysis, this allows for a comparison of the magnitude or effect size of attraction (the salesperson) versus information (the service) in the direction of search behavior and, by implication, purchase.

The Findings

Results are summarized in two parts. The first considers the overall characteristics of the information acquisition behavior exhibited in the process of selecting a complex financial service. The second presents the comparison of salesperson to service.

No subject selected a policy without acquiring any items of information. However, of the 144 items of information available, the maximum number of items any one subject acquired was 86, or 59.7 percent of the potential load. Repeat selections of the same value were low (less than 1 per subject). On average, subjects accessed 27 different items of information, examined 5 out of 8 policy options (each agent had information on two types of policy), and considered 11 of the 36 properties. This represents attention to only 18.8 percent of the 144 items of information, 62.5 percent of the available policies, and 30.6 percent of the available properties. Mean start-to-finish decision time was 508 seconds. It is clear from these results that subjects set a priority in the coverage of selected aspects of their decision environment.

The hypothesis on interpersonal attraction was strongly supported. Subjects devoted more of their acquisition behavior to liked than disliked agents, regardless of the policy sold by that agent. An ANOVA on the four levels of attraction significant at $p < .001$. Mean values acquired per agent decreased in a significant and linear manner from most- to least-liked agent: 8.94; 7.59; 6.18; and 4.51.

The comparison of effect size is interesting. Policy information itself does exert a significant influence ($p < .001$) in directing search. As the economist would predict, finding something useful tends to make one explore that utility in more depth. However, compared to that of attraction, the strength of this effect is nowhere near as powerful. An Omega-squared estimate (Winer 1971, p. 42) shows that information explains only 15.85 percent of the variance in search, while attraction of liking as produced by non-pertinent attributes results in an explanation of 38.47 percent of search.

Purchase behavior follows in line with this finding. The most-liked agent produces a market share of over 40 percent, significantly different from the expected level of performance at 25 percent ($p < .05$). All other agents are at or below the expected level of market performance.

Implications

In addition to their rational beliefs, our prospective customers have feelings: liking/disliking reactions to the various commercial entities and sources of information in their environment. Although of little instrumental value when viewed in an objective, product-related sense, these feelings are extremely powerful in guiding the consumer's information accessing and choice behavior.

The present experiment suggests the following causal links: Non-pertinent attributes of salesperson or source of information lead to liking versus disliking which leads to bias in depth of search toward most-liked salespeole or sources and this finally, leads to a tendency to eventually purchase the policy from the most-liked salesperson. The last link is tenuous and needs to be explored at subsequent stages of information processing but is nevertheless a striking implication for the design of sales strategies.

One possible explanation of this chain is as follows. Financial decision making is a complex and unpleasant domain for the consumer because it overloads with information at a level well beyond that of average comprehension abilities. The result is a search process, established by the consumer in interaction with his/her environment, which sets strict boundaries on the information to be acquired. As suggested by Chestnut and Jacoby (1983), the potential values thus excluded from the decision process become a strong factor in determining the outcome of purchase.

Much like the non-durable marketing strategist, the financial service strategist needs to strive for inclusions in the evoked set of considered information. This means an advertising strategy and a sales force geared to produce liking and therefore acceptability in the eyes of the consumer.

References

Berscheid, Ellen (1966). "Opinion Change and Communicator-Communicatee Similarity and Dissimilarity." *Journal of Personality and Social Psychology* 4, 670–680.

Brock, Timothy C. (1965). "Communicator-Recipient Similarity and Decision Change." *Journal of Personality and Social Psychology* 1, 650–654.

Byrne, Donn (1971). *The Attraction Paradigm.* New York: Academic Press.

Chestnut, Robert W. Information acquisition in life insurance policy selection: Monitoring the impact of product beliefs, affect toward agent, and external memory. Unpublished doctoral dissertation, Purdue University, 1977.

Chestnut, Robert W., and Jacoby, Jacob (1982). "Source Attractiveness and External Memory in a Computer-Aided Purchase Task." *Columbia University Working Paper.*

Chestnut, Robert W., and Jacoby, Jacob (1983). "Behavioral Process Research: Concept and Application in Consumer Decision Making." In *Decision Making: An Interdisciplinary Inquiry*, Gerardo Ungson & Daniel Braunstein (eds.). Boston: Kent Publishing, pp. 232–248.

Eagly, Alice H., and Himmelfarb, Samuel (1978). "Attitudes and Opinions." *Annual Review of Psychology* 29, 517–554.

Evans, Franklin B. (1963). "Selling as a Dyadic-Relationship—A New Approach." *The American Behavioral Scientist* 6, 76–79.

Gadel, M.S. (1964). "Concentration by Salesmen on Congenial Prospects." *Journal of Marketing* 28, 64–66.

Jacoby, Jacob; Chestnut, R.W.; and Fisher, W. (1978). "Simulating Nondurable Purchase: Individual Differences and Information Acquisition Behavior." *Journal of Marketing Research* 15, 532–544.

McGuire, William J. (1969). "Nature of Attitudes and Attitude Change." In *Handbook of Social Psychology*, vol. 3, G. Lindzey and E. Aronson (eds.). Reading, Mass.: Addison-Wesley.

Newell, A., and Simon, H.A. (1972). *Human Problem Solving.* Englewood Cliffs, N.J.: Prentice-Hall.

Riordan, E.A.; Oliver, R.L.; and Donnelly, J.H. (1977). "The Unsold Prospect: Dyadic and Attitudinal Determinants." *Journal of Marketing Research* 14, 530–537.

Ronis, D.L.; Baumgardner, M.H.; Leippe, M.R.; Cacioppo, J.T.; and Greenwald, A.G. (1977). "In Search of Reliable Persuasion Effects:

I. A Computer-Controlled Procedure for Studying Persuasion." *Journal of Personality and Social Psychology* 35, 548–569.

Simons, Herbert W.; Berkowitz, Nancy N.; and Moyer, R. John (1970). "Similarity, Credibility, and Attitude Change: A Review and Theory." *Psychological Bulletin* 73, 1–16.

Winer, Benjamin J. (1971). *Statistical Principles in Experimental Design.* New York: McGraw-Hill.

Woodside, Arch G., and Davenport, James W. (1974). "The Effect of Salesman Similarity and Expertise on Consumer Purchasing Behavior." *Journal of Marketing Research* 11, 198–202.

15 Improving Retail Selling: A Corporate Cultures Perspective

Ben M. Enis and
Lawrence B. Chonko

Multiple choice: The current status of retail selling is:

1. abysmal
2. benighted
3. contemptible
4. duplicitous
5. enervated
6. all of the above

Most knowledgeable observers would choose "all of the above"—not as an accurate description of all salespeople, all stores, or even all companies, but sufficiently general to warrant careful consideration.

Much is known about personal selling and about retailing organizations. The purpose of this chapter is to integrate and synthesize these two streams of knowledge to improve personal selling in retailing organizations. The discussion is divided into three major sections.

First, our general model of the selling process is offered to structure thinking and guide discussion about specific problems in retail selling. Second, this examination demonstrates the need for a common foundation upon which solutions can be erected, and the current work in corporate cultures is suggested as a possible foundation. Third, research needed to operationalize corporate cultures concepts in retail settings is discussed.

Examining Retail Selling with a Personal Selling Model

In an earlier work (Enis and Chonko 1978), we proposed a comprehensive model of the elements of the selling process and their interrelationships, as depicted in figure 15-1. At the risk of redundancy, this model is interpreted in its entirety in retailing terms in order to demonstrate the complex, interactive nature of the problem of improving retail selling.

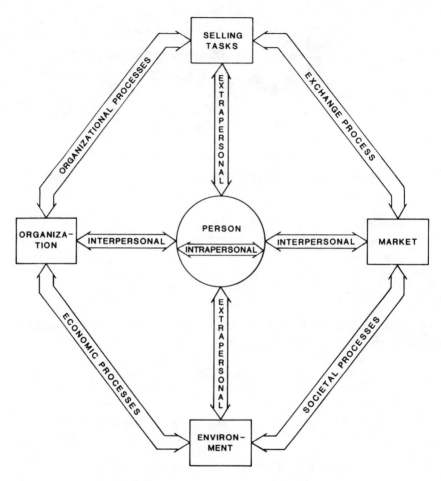

Source: Enis and Chonko, 1978.

Figure 15-1. A Personal Selling Model

Elements of the Model

Salesperson. The central focus is upon the individual retail salesperson sta-
tioned on the floor, behind the register, or on the telephone bank. Other
aspects of the selling situation are viewed in relation to the salesperson.
Ideally, this person is enthusiastic, energetic, knowledgeable about the company and its products, empathetic to customer desires, and motivated to a
mutually satisfactory resolution of the sales encounter.

Unfortunately, reality in retail selling today is far from ideal. Salespeople are apathetic rather than aggressive, abrasive rather than empathetic, ig-

norant of merchandise, and indolent of manner. Not all, but too many, are simply "doin' time."

The Market. The selling encounter occurs in the market. At any one time, the individual buyers in the store or other sales situation are the focal point. Collectively, these buyers and potential buyers constitute the target market that the salesperson should aim to please. Ideally, the market is well understood by salesperson and/or company so that the right products are offered at the right time, place and price.

In reality, the right products are too often out of stock or were never ordered in the first place; and the salesperson seldom probes to determine the buyer's real needs. Perhaps a substitute product would do, maybe even a more profitable one. Surely other purchases could be suggested while the buyer is in the store. If the alert salesperson attempts to satisfy the buyer by ordering the product from the warehouse or another branch store, this effort will probably consume all profit on the transaction. Moreover, the salesperson rarely is consulted about, let alone volunteers, information about the market.

The Company. The salesperson is associated with an organization that supplies the products that s/he offers to customers in the target market. The company may be a single store, a multistore corporation, or a mail-order firm. Ideally, this is a well-structured and -staffed organization which follows a carefully conceived and vigorously implemented marketing plan.

Again, reality is often quite different. The retail organization frequently operates in reactive fashion: Salespeople are added as conditions warrant, perhaps with little initial training, and they are seldom enrolled in a comprehensive development program. Training most often focuses upon register operation, prevention of shoplifting, credit-card checking, and other control issues. Rarely is the salesperson trained in selling techniques.

The Selling Environment. The target market of individual buyers usually constitutes only a small proportion of the people in the selling environment. Some are potential buyers; many are not. All may be affected by sales transactions to which they are not parties: for example, air, noise and water pollution; increased economic activity. In addition, there are physical (buildings, streets, climate) and institutional (businesses, schools, hospitals) features of the environment. Ideally, the salesperson, aided by his/her organization, understands the selling environment, particularly the roles played by various people.

In reality, most salespeople ignore the environment. Their task responsibilities are completely divorced from the larger environmental context. It is as if they cease being human beings when they come to work. They are automatons doing an isolated job, not functioning as members of their society.

The Selling Task. To sell products to the target market, the company sets forth specific responsibilities of the salesperson. Ideally, these duties are reasonable, clearly understood, supported with adequate resources, and so forth. Once again, reality is often quite different: duties are demeaning, instructions are not clear, resources are not adequate, and so forth.

Personal Relationships

These five elements of the model are related. Ideally, these relationships coordinate the activities associated with the elements by processes, shown in figure 15—1 as double-ended arrows. The model postulates three personal relationships: intrapersonal, interpersonal, and extrapersonal.

Intrapersonal. These are the individual characteristics (capabilities, traits, attitudes, constructs) of the salesperson that are used in personal selling. Though terminology varies, one classic set of intrapersonal characteristics is emphathy and ego-drive (Meyer and Greenburg 1963). The salesperson perceives the buyer's desires and is motivated to satisfy them. By whatever terminology, the fact is that too few retail salespeople utilize their intrapersonal characteristics in ways that lead to effective sales performance. This is essentially a failure of motivation.

Interpersonal. These relationships involve contacts with other people in the performance of selling tasks. Of course, the salesperson has contacts with buyers and potential buyers. Less obvious, but no less important, are the salesperson's contacts with other people in the company: supervisors, credit personnel, stockpeople, display arrangers, and other salespeople.

Ideally, these contacts are conducted with cheerful efficiency and mutual respect. The salesperson is, in a very real sense, the personal linkage between these two groups of people who are essential to the company's welfare. In fact, these relationships are too often impersonal at best and not infrequently are so poorly handled as to actually threaten the company's welfare. Poor interpersonal relationships are essentially manifestations of communications failure.

Extrapersonal. Here the relationships are roles: contractual and/or customary activities to be performed. In contrast to interpersonal roles—how people *do* relate to each other—extrapersonal roles denote how these relationships *should* be conducted to achieve company objectives. Extrapersonal relationships therefore are qualities of a particular sales position rather than of a particular individual. The salesperson plays many roles in performing the selling task: counselor to the buyer, company representative, complaint handler, money collector, package-wrapper, and others. In addition, s/he plays roles in the informal organization of the company. Society sees the salesperson in many roles: spouse, parent, citizen, consumer, and so forth; each of these roles has expectations, responsibilities, norms, rewards.

Ideally, the company specifies these aspects of the roles that it assigns to its salespeople. Through training, coaching, and example, the salesperson is consciously taught how to effectively perform his/her roles. Needless to say, reality is frequently quite different, leading to role ambiguity and conflict. This is essentially a failure of leadership.

Process Relationships

Not only does the salesperson have relationships with each of the other elements of the selling situation; these elements are also related to each other. As figure 15-1 shows, four such relationships are relevant to a thorough examination of the selling situation.

Organizational Processes. The salesperson is employed by an organization that buys, ships, stores, price-marks, stocks, packages, and delivers the products that the salesperson sells; other organizational personnel also perform many other activities. Several processes are involved. Most of the list above would be classified as part of the logistics process; there are also financial, personnel, merchandising, accounting, security, maintenance, legal, and public relations processes.

Ideally, the activities of these processes are coordinated, and the salesperson has at least a general knowledge of them. But, too often in the salesperson's eyes, logistics is a mystery, merchandising a hindrance, security an adversary, and personnel an impenetrable bureaucracy. The salesperson neither understands these processes nor comprehends his/her role(s) in them.

Exchange Processes. The relationship between the selling task and the buyer in the market constitutes the exchange relationship, which hopefully culminates in a sales transaction. Flows of all of the 4 Ps—product, promotion, place (distribution), and price—must be completed.

Ideally, the salesperson is the catalyst for this completion. S/he demonstrates the product, provides information about its care and use, arranges delivery, and explains the terms of sale. In practice, sales are too often lost because the salesperson fails to complete one or more of the essential flows, preferring instead to passively react to the buyer's statements and actions. Even when the buyer persists and closes the sale, a residue of bitterness between them may cloud future exchanges.

Economic Processes. The organization for which the salesperson works is one of a number that constitute the economic aspect of the environment. There are two basic economic processes by which these organizations interact: competition and regulation.

Ideally, the salesperson understands these processes and is motivated to compete effectively within the regulatory framework of the society. But the salesperson too often is indifferent to sales lost to competitors and unaware that the company may be liable for the consequnces of his/her statements and actions. The buyer is perceived as a nuisance to which the competitor is welcomed; company policies and regulations are circumvented or ignored.

Societal Processes. Finally, exchange transactions take place within the larger society, a part of the environment. There are demographic, structural, and normative aspects of any given society; these interact in complex fashion to produce the characteristics and values that constitute the society.

Ideally, the salesperson understands these processes and believes that his/her work contributes positively to them. Too often, reality, is quite different. Salespeople feel alienated. They do not see the contribution their work makes and consequently exert little effort.

Summary. The problems in retail selling are too numerous, too complex, and too interrelated to be solved piecemeal. A comprehensive model was used to guide the examination of the retail selling situation to conclusively make this point. The thesis of this chapter is that a comprehensive approach is required to improve retail selling. The recent work in corporate cultures may provide the foundation for such an approach.

Corporate Cultures in Retailing

In their best-selling *In Search of Excellence*, Peters and Waterman (1982) contend that companies considered excellent do not manage only the traditional strategy, structure, and systems, but also four soft S's: staff, style, skills, and shared values. Deal and Kennedy (1982), who acknowledge Peters as "the intellectual and spiritual godfather" of their work, use the term *corporate culture* to describe this additional managerial emphasis. Specifically, corporate culture connotes the integrated pattern of corporate behavior, a cohesion of values, myths, heroes, and symbols which describes "the way we do things around here."

Peters and Waterman list the following retailers among "50 top performing companies": Avon, Bloomingdale's, Disney Productions, K Mart, Marriott Corp., McDonald's, Neiman-Marcus, Tupperware and Wal-Mart. Deal and Kennedy mention Avon, L.L. Bean, Bloomingdale's, Mary Kay

Cosmetics, McDonald's, Sears, and Tupperware. Others (Berry 1983; Ouchi 1981; Pascale and Athos 1981) also include 1776 Restaurants, Cohoes (specialty store), Dayton-Hudson Corp. (Dayton's, Hudson's, Target, Mervyn's, and B. Dalton Bookseller), and Jewel Tea Co.

Anecdotes

Here are a few illustrative comments, synthesized in no particular order from the works listed above.

McDonald's theme for years has been Quality, Service, Cleanliness, Value (OSCV). Since the early days of the organization, all of its stores have been regularly measured on their performance in these categories. Consistent failure to meet McDonald's high QSCV standards can get store managers fired or cause loss of a franchise.

Mary Kay Cosmetics stages lavish, multimillion-dollar seminars. At these sales meetings, classes are conducted and the hundreds of Mary Kay salespeople learn something. But the main attraction is awards nights. Salespeople parade across the stage in bright red jackets, telling stories about how they personally achieved success, just like Mary Kay herself.

Disney Productions has a special language. The employees out front are cast members and the personnel department is casting. Working with the public is being on stage. Customers are Guests—upper-case "G". New employees are brought into the culture early. Everyone has to attend Disney University and pass Traditions I. Disney expects the new CM [cast member] to know something about the company, its history and success, its management style, and how each division relates to others (Operations, Resorts, Food and Beverage, Marketing, Finance, Merchandising, Entertainment, and so forth) and how each division relates to the show.

Cohoes is a specialty store in Cohoes, New York. Despite a sales staff of more than three hundred people (three to four times the staffing of a suburban department store), Cohoes has been making after-tax profits of 6 percent. Shopping Cohoes can surprise a customer. It is not just the sheer number of salespeople, or even their relentless enthusiasm; it is also their dedication to the shopper. Salespeople have just one responsibility at the store: service. Cashiers total the bill, and wrappers wrap the packages; managers make exchanges, and there is a credit applications lady at the front door. No salesperson says, "That's not my department." Salespeople can travel anywhere, selling everything.

Wal-Mart, with over 26,000 employees, grew during the 1970s from $45 million in sales to $1.6 billion, from 18 stores to over 500 by 1984. Sam Walton, or "Mr. Sam" as he is called in the company, is the driving force behind this success. Walton stories have become legends. Mr. Sam, quite simply, cares about his people, referring to them as associates, not employees; and he listens to them. "The key is to get out into the store and listen to what the associates have to say," he says. "It's terribly important for everyone to get involved. Our best ideas come from clerks and stockboys."

Concepts and Principles

The preceding anecdotes illustrate fundamental principles of corporate culture. As noted, Peters and Waterman use the "McKinsey 7S" framework in their work. These concepts have meaning for retailing.

Strategy connotes the manager's need for a charted course of action, the practice of good time-management, and the allocation of scarce resources over time to meet the identified goals and objectives of the organization. In retailing, this involves buying plans, employee training budgets, scheduling of work assignments, and so forth.

Structure refers to the way a firm is organized—centralized or decentralized, line/staff relationships, hierarchy of responsibilities. Often the organization chart of the store indicates the formal organization structure.

Systems include procedures, reports, routine processes, policies, complaint handling, and rewards. In retailing, examples include hiring procedures, sales reports by item and line, security policies, and vacation assignments.

Staff is the demographic description of important personnel categories within the organization. (The anecdotal examples above of referring to salespeople as associates or as cast members are illustrative.)

Style is the characterization of the behavior of key managers in achieving the organization's goals within the cultural context of the store. Mr. Walton cares about his people; the griddle is never clean enough at McDonald's.

Skills represent the company's willingness to spend money to adequately train each employee: Mary Kay's seminars, Disney's Traditions I, and McDonald's Hamburger University are examples.

Shared values have a significant meaning, since these are the guiding philosophies of employees' actions: Sears' "quality at a good price," McDonald's QSCV, Cohoes' dedication to the shopper are illustrations.

Deal and Kennedy present essentially the same concepts in somewhat different terms. Their list follows.

Business environment is the particular reality faced by a given company in the marketplace, depending on its products, competitors, customers, technologies, government influences, and so forth. The environment in which a company operates determines what it must do to be successful.

Thus Avon and Mary Kay must develop hard-driving sales forces, Disney must put on a show, and Wal-Mart must carefully manage costs.

Values are the basic concepts and beliefs of an organization, the heart of its culture: Wal-Mart's concern for employees, McDonald's QSCV, and Bloomingdale's commitment to experimentation and inter-departmental competition.

Heroes personify the culture's values and as such provide tangible role models for employees to follow: Ray Kroc, Sam Walton, Mary Kay Ash, Walt Disney typify this aspect of corporate culture.

Rites and rituals are the programs of day-to-day life in the company, from mundane routines like McDonald's continual cleaning to extravagant ceremonies like Mary Kay's seminars.

The cultural network is the informal carrier of the corporate values and heroic mythology: "Walton's is one in which stories have become legends . . . ." Our favorite is one in which Mr. Walton's pilot landing the private plane conveyed him to his next store visit in a vacant field so that Mr. Sam could flag down a Wal-Mart truck in order to chat with the driver.

Similar discussions, with relatively minor variations in terminology, are offered by Pascale and Athos (1981) who use the McKinsey 7-S framework and by Ouchi (1981) who employs the catchy term *theory Z*. These authors tend to use Japanese examples and do not emphasize retailing situations, but the concepts and principles of corporate culture are clearly illustrated. Corporate culture is a real phenomenon; understanding it can be quite useful to retail managers, particularly in improving retail selling performance.

This review of corporate anecdotes, concepts, and principles is by no means complete. Its purpose is rather to demonstrate that, in contrast to the generally bleak selling situations faced by most retail organizations, some have managed to instill enthusiasm, pride, loyalty, and energy into their salespeople and all of their employees.

This fact has classic good-news-and-bad-news aspects. It suggests that the development of a proper organizational culture can go a long way toward solving the retail selling problem. But retail managers and scholars really do not know how to do that—yet. Implementation of an excellent, or at least a better, corporate culture in a given organization poses interesting challenges for the manager and the scholar.

Managerial and Research Challenges

Three basic questions frame these challenges:

1. What is the ideal culture for a given retailer?
2. What is the current culture?
3. How does the retailer improve toward the ideal?

These questions can be explored from both managerial and research perspectives.

The Ideal Retail Culture

Peters and Waterman (1982) suggest that eight attributes characterize the managements of outstanding companies: (1) a bias toward action, (2) simple form and lean staff, (3) continued contact with customers, (4) productivity improvement via people, (5) operational autonomy to encourage entrepreneurship, (6) stress on one key business value, (7) emphasis on doing what they know best, and (8) simultaneous loose-tight controls.

In retailing, Bloomingdale's is famous for continuous experimentation with floor layouts and merchandise assortments, and Tupperware has weekly rallies to motivate salespeople. Ray Kroc is quoted as contending that less is more in the case of corporate management; Sam Walton believes in the "empty headquarters rule." Both Kroc and Walton are also famous for visiting their stores continually to talk with customers and employees. These visits not only keep them in touch with customers, but also familiarizes them with employee ideas and suggestions for improvements. McDonald's franchising arrangements, Bloomingdale's boutiques, Mary Kay's independent agents and Wal-Mart's store-manager authority are examples of autonomy which promotes entrepreneurship. The key business values of Sears, McDonald's, Mary Kay, and Disney should by now be familiar to the reader. By sticking to what they know best and allowing autonomy while adhering strongly to the central values, these retailers qualify for the title of excellent companies. Most managers in retailing would agree that the appellation is apt.

This evidence, however compelling, is anecdotal. Researchers might well be interested in going beyond Peters and Waterman's designation of excellence in terms of company reputation for performance and innovation plus six general measures of "financial superiority." The other corporate cultures authors are even less methodologically precise in their definitions of excellence.

Two research approaches might be useful here. The first is clinical: careful study of recognized excellent companies with a view toward validating/modifying the eight criteria. An alternative approach would be deductive rather than inductive: establishment of operational criteria of excellence and using these to identify top performers.

The Enis and Chonko model of personal selling could be used to guide research of either type. The intrapersonal, interpersonal, and extrapersonal characteristics of top-performing salespeople could be identified. We believe that these traits might be measured in the following terms:

intrapersonal—determinants of motivation, for example, attitudes

interpersonal—communications skills

extrapersonal—role perceptions

Comprehension of the four processes, and the salesperson's relationships to them, would involve measures of information processing by salespeople to guide subsequent training.

Alternatively, it might be interesting to attempt to operationalize such constructs as the following:

feeling a part of the team—an intrapersonal trait

being close to the customer—interpersonal

common understanding of one basic value—extrapersonal

These ideas have tremendous popular appeal but have not been scientifically validated. Both inductive and deductive measures would be confounded by the facts of the company's culture and by the individual salesperson's perceptions of that culture, so the research would have to be more comprehensive and rigorous than previous studies of the what-makes-a-good-salesperson type.

Current Retailing Culture

Peters and Waterman do not explicitly discuss the assessment of corporate culture, although they provide many examples. But diagnostic procedures are suggested by Deal and Kennedy: (1) study the physical setting, (2) read what the company says about itself (annual reports, quarterly statements, press releases, comments to financial analysts), (3) test how the company greets strangers, (4) interview company people, (5) observe how people spend their time, (6) understand the career path progressions of employees, (7) determine how long people stay in jobs, particularly middle-management tenure, (8) look at the content of what is being discussed or written, and (9) pay particular attention to the anecdotes and stories that pass through the cultural network. Retailing examples from excellent companies would be redundant; to cite less-than-excellent organizations impolitic. This point itself says something relevant to retailers: Few manage excellent companies.

Nevertheless, the Deal and Kennedy suggestions could guide managerial examination of retail selling (and other areas). Again, we contend that our selling process model could improve the comprehensiveness, consistency, and communicability of such an examination. Even a systematic verbal review of the factors mentioned by Deal and Kennedy as they relate to the elements, relationships, and processes specified in the model might be beneficial—both in terms of understanding salespersons' views of the company culture and perhaps in beginning to shape that culture in positive ways.

The researcher's role here would be to add structure and rigor to such examinations. The selling process model suggests a number of possibilities: There are potential role conflicts (sales enhancer versus credit checker, selling items that the salesperson cannot afford to buy), managerial trade-offs (the value of additional training in hopes of reducing turnover, more full-time salespeople at higher salaries and benefits versus more part-timers who are likely to be less productive), information overloads (the salesperson is supposed to know merchandise, company policies, point-of-sale (POS) operations, competitors' actions, directions to the restrooms, and so forth), and problems of sales force training and motivation (Why should workers earning the minimum hourly wage sell aggressively? How can functional illiterates be trained to operate POS equipment?).

More precisely, we hypothesize that the three relationships in the model can be regarded in the traditional organizational behavior terms of behavioral antecedents, moderators, and outcomes as follows:

Antecedents	Moderators	Outcomes
Interpersonal		
Management style		
Organizational climate		Attitudes/Behavior
Leadership	Interpersonal	Job satisfaction
Managerial behavior	Education	Productivity
	Age	Stress
Extrapersonal	Personality	Turnover
Role conflict	Experience	Absenteeism
Role ambiguity	Career orientation	Effort
Variety		Grievances
Autonomy		Sacrifice
Feedback		
Identity		
Significance		

We are convinced that these issues must be addressed within the context of corporate culture. Perhaps retailing researchers need to study the anthropologists' methodologies. The popular writings on corporate culture hardly provide sufficient scientific foundations for rigorous analysis.

Improving Retailing Management and Research

These are propitious times for retailing. Economic conditions seem to be improving, the computer promises to raise productivity, and the regulatory climate appears less restrictive. But these positive notes will be more than offset in many companies by the dismal performance of the salesforce, unless improvements are also made here.

This chapter is a preliminary survey which attempts to integrate two sets of literature and experience: personal selling and retail organization. Consequently, conclusions on retail selling improvement must be tentative. One seems clear: Productive selling in any field involves considerable investment for recruiting, training, motivating, and supervising. Retailers who have made this investment—for example, Brooks Brothers, Disney, McDonald's, Cohoes—enjoy enviable reputations for personal sales and service. Conversely, other successful retailers—notably Wal-Mart, K-Mart, and the L.L. Bean Catalogue operation—deliberately downplay personal selling. In the middle are stores that do little recruiting and training, pay their clerks the minimum wage, and watch them almost like criminals yet expect professional sales performance. Our strong suspicion is that this middle-of-the-road approach correlates with negative sales productivity. We speculate that more and more retailers will be forced to choose between adequate investment to develop professional sales people and a deliberate emphasis upon self-service. Perhaps the rapid growth of automatic teller machines in banks and the increasingly popular self-service gasoline pumps are harbingers here.

The corporate culture concept appears to offer significant possibilities for improving retail selling, particularly if it is applied comprehensively and systematically. We believe that our model, or a similar construct (*cf.* Bagozzi 1978; Walker, Churchill, and Ford 1977), could guide such an application.

The key factor in attaining this improvement will be implementation. The importance of implementation is increasingly recognized in corporate strategy (Keichel 1982). Given the lack of specific procedures for improving corporate culture in any business and the severity of problems in selling, retailing managers must be particularly sensitive to implementation issues. The work of Management Analysis Center, Inc. (MAC) (Stonich 1982; Uttal 1983) might prove useful in this regard. MAC suggests that implementation of any strategy must consider the interrelationships among four sets of factors: organization structure and management processes (roughly analogous to McKinsey's "hard S's") and human resources and culture (approximately the "soft S's").

Effective implementation of improved retail selling performance using the corporate culture concept can be facilitated, in our opinion, by more and better contact and interaction between retail managers and researchers.

It is suggested that managers do more research or at least cooperate more with researchers. Many academics are concept and methodology rich but data poor.

In the same spirit, academics need to be closer to management issues and constraints. Research can be relevant and decision-facilitating without sacrificing rigor and scientific validity. This will require creativity and realism in research design, which can come only from better understanding of actual retailing management situations, particularly in retail selling.

Conclusions

We believe that retail selling can and should be improved. There are many problems, as a comprehensive examination has demonstrated. Consequently, a comprehensive approach is needed. The corporate culture concept may provide the foundation. Some retailers have generally-acknowledged excellence in their salesforces and, not coincidentally, in other areas of their operations. Their cultures are offered in explanation for this excellence.

The challenge to retailing managers and researchers, therefore, is to understand the cultural traits that nurture excellence and implement (develop, change, augment) these traits in other retailing companies. This challenge is formidable, particularly in improving retail selling, but it can and must be met.

We hope that this chapter begins to meet the challenge by cataloging the issues in retail selling, reviewing the corporate culture concept in retailing terms, and raising questions about the implementation of excellent cultures in retailing. We do not offer final answers but rather attempt to frame a useful dialogue on these points. Our purpose is to provide a catalyst discussion and research—to improve retail selling.

References

Bagozzi, Richard P. (1978). "Salesforce Performance and Satisfaction as a Function of Individual Difference, Interpersonal, and Situational Factors." *Journal of Marketing Research* 15 (November):517–531.

Berry, Leonard L. (1983). "The Effects of the Marketing Concept on American Business." *Proceedings of the Marketing Concept Workshop*. Chicago: American Marketing Association, forthcoming.

Deal, T.E., and A.A. Kennedy (1982). *Corporate Cultures: The Rites and Rituals of Corporate Life*. Reading, Mass.: Addison-Wesley.

Enis, B.M., and L.B. Chonko (1978). "A Review of Personal Selling: Implications for Managers and Researchers." *Review of Marketing 1978*. Chicago: American Marketing Association, pp. 276–302.

Keichel, W.W. III (1982). "Corporate Strategy under Fire." *Fortune* 107 (November 15):84-85.

Ouchi, W.G. (1981). *Theory Z: How American Business Can Meet the Japanese Challenge*. Reading, Mass.: Addison-Wesley.

Pascale, R.T., and A.G. Athos (1981).*The Art of Japanese Management: Applications for American Executives*. New York: Simon and Schuster.

Peters, T.J., and R.H. Waterman, Jr. (1982). *In Search of Excellence: Lessons from America's Best-Run Companies*. New York: Harper & Row.

Stonich, P.J., ed. (1982). *Implementing Strategy: Making Strategy Happen*. Cambridge, Mass.: Ballinger Publishing.

Uttal, Bro (1983), "The Corporate Culture Vultures," 108 *Fortune* (October 17):66-72.

Walker, O.C.; Gilbert A. Churchill, Jr.; and Neil M. Ford (1977). "Motivation and Performance in Industrial Selling: Present Knowledge and Needed Research." *Journal of Marketing Research* 14 (May):156-168.

16 Issues in Retail Selling: A Panel Discussion

To sharpen the focus on the issues facing retailing practitioners, a panel of six leading retail executives was included as part of the conference. These executives were from a wide range of retail organizations and provided considerable insight into the personal selling problems facing retailers in the 1980s. The panel consisted of:

C. Samuel Craig, New York University (Moderator)

Jay F. Hundley, Assistant Director, Corporate Personnel, J.C. Penney Co.

Stanley R. Jaffee, General Merchandise Manager, Brooks Brothers

Robert L. Koch, Vice President of Personnel, Bally of Switzerland

Donald Merritt, Senior Vice President, Human Resources, Saks Fifth Avenue

Larry J.B. Robinson, Chairman of the Board, Robinson Jewelers

Harmon Tobler, President & C.E.O., Joseph Magnin

Following is an edited transcript of the panel discussion:

SAM CRAIG: I'd like to start with a quote from an article by Isadore Barmash that appeared in the March 15, 1983 *New York Times:* ". . . The biggest problem in retailing today is the salespeople . . ." I'd like to use this as a point of departure and ask each of the panelists in turn how they're dealing with this concern. We'll start with Jay.

JAY HUNDLEY: The biggest problem in retailing may not be with the salespeople but with the managers. As an industry, we have not done an awful lot to investigate, to analyze, what it is that encourages people to go into the selling field. We know there are differences between those who sell and those who clerk, but it's difficult—at least for J.C. Penney—to differentiate between them. In order to separate out the successful salesperson from the unsuccessful salesperson, we need to look at the qualities that make a salesperson successful, which we have not done up to this point.

We are asking ourselves, "Are we providing the right staffing, that is, the right quantity of staffing?" Some interesting studies within our own company would indicate that we're putting selling people on the floor when the customers aren't there and letting them leave when shoppers come in!

Also, I think we have to look at our motivational systems. Within the industry, we have never agreed on whether commissioned selling—incentive selling, perhaps better said—or straight salary is a better way to both serve the customer and remunerate the employee. We need to analyze that. It might vary from organization to organization based on the particular organization's culture.

Finally, I think we must provide more training. We have not invested a great deal of resources in training, in either product knowledge or basic selling skills.

STAN JAFFEE: We have one-on-one selling in our stores; we're probably one of the few companies left in America that has that. We spend a great deal of time getting product information to our salespeople. We have product continuity so that the training lasts for a long period of time. We have salespeople continuity. We feel that they stay with us because the money they take home is the best that they can get in the industry. That way, they can afford to be professional salespeople when they work at Brooks Brothers. We also feel that no matter how good the salespeople are, if the proper merchandise in the right size and in the right color is not readily available, they can't do good jobs. This becomes our problem and our responsibility.

We are constantly working to improve the average sale and to make the customer's life easier by having a one-stop shopping experience as opposed to an ordeal.

BOB KOCH: There are four variables that I think we in the retail industry should consider: measuring, monitoring, managing, and motivating. Concentration of those efforts in the first-line supervisor who in smaller stores such as ours involves focusing on the store manager. There is a need for a specific regime cf training, to develop not only the pragmatic skills involved in selling a pair of shoes or in servicing a customer, but also the specifics of what a manager does outside of those disciplines required to manage the achievement of all tasks in his or her store.

I also believe we do not focus enough attention on the individual salesperson's performance. We accept mediocre performance, for a variety of reasons, most of which revolve around the quality of the population interested in jobs offered on that level. As a result, we not only accept lower performance standards, but also begin to fleet up people from that population into management positions and these people are not as well prepared as they should be.

Finally, we have to change the ways in which we believe motivation is operating within a store; part of that is improving the visibility of performance measurement and looking at the individual in terms of the facts of his/her performance. If researchers would spend some time thinking about those kinds of projects and providing some specific information, it would help overcome some of those problems.

DON MERRITT: Well, I agree with all of the above. It is pretty hard to argue with all the things that we should be looking at and all the things we should be doing. For me, it's a point of view that deals with funding, with the ability to flex budgets and dollars behind all this commitment; because otherwise it's academic. I think we talk a good game; our selling associates know that we talk a good game because we're in the good talking game business. Just ask any of our customers. If we in fact believe that training is important, and if we in fact believe that assessment is important and that it should be fair and equitable, and if we believe in incentives—be they commission or non-commission—then what are we doing about it? Are we taking people off the floor and committing time and energy to quality instruction? If we are, are we funding in a very forward way or are we just telling the general manager we believe in training? We want productivity, but are we willing to invest in the dollars to make it really possible?

Organizations have to stop treating selling associates as clericals because as long as we treat them as clericals, that's what they'll be. You walk into a specialty store, and maybe it's also true of many other stores, and you are looking at a selling associate who writes a book of $400,000-$800,000. If we could manifest the same kind of attention and treatment to that new selling associate and try to better understand how Mary or John is able to have a clientele, maintain and leverage that big book even in difficult economic climate, then I think we might be in a better position to deal with selling. I don't know if we should treat all selling associates the same. Still, I think attention to care and feeding sometimes gets pushed off to the side.

So, for me, the issue is one of funding; it's one of commitment; it's putting your money where your mouth is. Selling today can be as exciting as we want to make it. We need to put selling back into a very valued and esteemed position. But that requires an enlightened management and a point of view that seeks to tap the intellect of the selling associate. Until we are able to do that, most of us retailers are going to have a rough time of it.

LARRY ROBINSON: I think that the subject we are talking about is of enormous importance to the national economy, to our companies, and to us as individuals. Today economists are talking about retailers leading the country out of recession. While we see some moderately favorable statistics along that line, nobody knows if we are going to make it. I think that one enormous opportunity in that respect that is also an opportunity to improve bottom line in a highly competitive environment awash with excess retail space is to improve sales productivity. From my experience and observations, I think that while American retailing may be in the twentieth century in our use of management information systems and computers, we are in the sixteenth century when it comes to our human resources management, particularly with regard to our salespeople.

The most striking experience that I've had recently in this regard occurred in a store that's part of one of the companies represented here—a beautifully designed store in an excellent location, with very costly construction, expensive merchandise, and good advertising. I've had some very good experiences in that store in the past. But this time I saw a shirt I wanted, picked it up, walked over to a salesperson, and asked if I could buy it. There were two salespeople behind the counter, and I stood there as they argued about which one would not have to wait on me. The person whom I approached said to the other: "I took the last one, you take this one." Well, I had to make a plane and I knew that I couldn't last through the whole discussion, so I regretfully put the shirt back on the counter and left to go to the airport.

Some interesting buzz words have come into vogue in American business in the last few years: corporate culture and Japanese management. I don't think that either concept provides ready answers for people in our business, but they do help us raise some of the right questions and give us a more focused framework for our thinking. I happen to be in the jewelry business where, if you want to survive, you really have to know how to sell. If you are going to do business, you have to have salespeople in whom customers have confidence; thus we have been forced in my company to focus on the consequences being addressed here. We have seventy-four stores, and we must put a great deal of care in selecting people, training them, and motivating them. What do corporate culture or Japanese management have to do with that? First, salespeople have to know what their job is. The person behind the counter where I went to buy the shirt really has to want to make sales, to know why it is important for the company, in order to be motivated to make the sale. If they really understand what your company is all about in subjectives—how they can do well, what their job assignment is, what they can do to progress—and more importantly, if they can truly share in decision making—then I think you begin to move toward salespeople who'll want to make the sale of the shirt rather than fight over not making it.

It is very hard to develop a corporate culture that forces that kind of attitude, whether it be with salespeople, accounting clerks, or any other part of your company. As you know, the Nordstrom Company is a very interesting example of the point that I am making: the company selects people using thoughtful kinds of testing and, above all, training people so that they know exactly what they can and have to do to move up the ladder. I think this can make an enormous difference in terms of productivity, profitability, return on investment, success of the kinds of companies represented here, and your own personal success. I think that the chances of accomplishing worthwhile progress are as great in the kinds of subject matters discussed here as anywhere else in our business.

It's time that retailers began to catch up in our human resources management to make the kind of progress that we have in our use of computers in inventory control and in automating our clerical functions. It's a wonderful opportunity for the next decade.

HARMON TOBLER: My background covers quite a broad spectrum, since I have been in both department stores and now in a specialty store operation. Prior to either of those I was, for fifteen years, in a very small store operation; ten of those fifteen years were spent in personal selling. So I think I have had some opportunity to look at selling from various perspectives.

I agree that in retailing today there is a lot of lip service given to selling; but I believe there is a great difference in opinion as to what the customer really expects in terms of selling, or even if s/he wants selling. Many people say that selling is very important but they don't really mean it. I can remember a few years ago reading a speech given to the May Company by Dave Babcock, in which he said that for the past several years this organization has been talking about how important selling is and, at the very same time, has been getting its profits from reductions in sales personnel and in training. I think there is still a lot of that going on. When I left the department store business, where my primary responsibility was developing a professional sales approach in the total corporate structure, I imagined that going to a specialty store would be easy. Yet in a specialty store I find basically the same problems: budgets, priorities, and productivity.

It's a chicken-and-egg situation: If you can develop professional salespeople, then there is no question about it, you can build volume; if you can fund training programs that will bring them productivity long enough to accomplish that, then you will get the result.

I am convinced that the number one thing that we must continue to strive for in retailing is to teach our people to think in terms of what the customers' needs are, what they're really looking for; to understand the customer, to talk to the customer in a more effective way than most of us do. I believe that the average kind of selling is really based on presenting solutions before anyone understands the need of the customer; continually pushing at the customer with solutions without understanding those needs. In one of my stores, I recently talked to a customer who was standing near a selection of handbags and I said to her: "You shop at Joseph Magnin often?'' She said ''I used to. It used to be my store, but not anymore.'' I immediately went on to describe the merchandise content and explained some of the places we've been and where we are going, and so forth, and she cut me off and said ''Merchandise isn't my problem. It's the way your people sell, that's my problem! My store is next door.'' Then I introduced myself and asked if she would tell me a little bit about what she meant, and she said ''I am a busy executive woman''—and that's who we call our customer, you see—''I have little time to shop. I don't like being placed in a fitting room and left, or being placed in a fitting room to buy a dress and then have the salesperson continually feed me dresses. I expect what I get from next door.'' I happen to know a little bit about the store next door; unfortunately they do more volume in half the space than we do in our space. She went on, ''The sales associate knows me, understands my needs, brings me accessories, brings me suggested wardrobes. ''I may go in there for a single item and come out with a $350 purchase or $500 purchase. Your store used to be like that. Right here, in this store, I used to be a customer, but no longer.''

I believe we all have the opportunity to have customers beat a path to our doors if we can rise above the mediocrity in selling that exists in the retailing industry today. There are a few stores that are really doing more than a lot of lip service. I know that there are many smaller stores that may be doing better but I am talking about the larger stores; I include ourselves in them, even though we may be doing more than others. We still have a tremendous way to go. I think it is an immense opportunity but I don't think we'll ever get there, as has been mention earlier, by just talking about it. It's going to take up-front investment, commitment on the part of management, and management understanding of the sales associates and what they need: But the primary goal is understanding of the customers and what they need. Only then can a program be tailored for the salespeople.

SAM CRAIG: Many of Harmon's comments have suggested a number of areas dealing with recruitment, selection, training, motivation, compensation, and finally evaluation of the sales associate. What we might do next is address a few of those issues in turn, basically discussing what it is you've tried, what has worked, and what has not. Let's first focus on the areas of recruiting and selection. What kinds of things are you doing to recruit and select better people so that you start with better material out on the sales floor?

BOB KOCH: There are methods and there are methods. In terms of recruitment today, most is being done by people who are not very sophisticated or well trained to perform that function. Consequently, you are going to get the result of this lack of understanding. So, we have taken two hundred years of experience in our industry, determined the characteristics of those people who have been extraordinarily successful selling in this industry, and created a device which we use to train our people to select the best people from a range of applicants.

Several years ago I wrote an article about the selection of salespeople using not qualitative but quantitative measures. It's very difficult to do this, but the results are comparatively extraordinary. There are very simple methods to train the untrained person to recruit and select from among a pool of applicants, many of whom are unacceptable, but for a variety of reasons are hired.

JAY HUNDLEY: I think at the moment what most retailers do is not recruit, but employ. They put out a sign that says "We are hiring." If you walk in the door and profess some interest in selling, that makes you a pretty good candidate. If you have some previous experience in selling, that makes you an even better candidate. Selling skill is defined as just having spent some time in a store. Yet there are selection devices that can be used and that have demonstrated themselves on a limited scale to be successful in screening out people lacking the characteristics that we find in the more successful selling people in our stores. Our use of those devices is still in a test stage, that is to say, we have used them in a few stores; but I do think it is something that retailers, if they can afford to, obviously should use.

LARRY ROBINSON: I agree. I think it is very worthwhile to try to find some kind of testing that's appropriate for your needs, even if it has less than perfect ability to predict performance; at least you may reduce the unknown somewhat and improve the opportunity for success. As I am sure you know, there are a number of different tests available, several of which are inexpensive to administer and very quick. They may help you to screen out people who really don't have what's necessary to do a good selling job.

A very large national chain asked me to come in a few weeks ago and consult. I said I couldn't do that, but that I would come for a lunch and talk about human resources management. They wanted magic answers on some of these issues. We talked for about twenty minutes and then I asked "What are you doing to screen sales people?" The answer was that they were doing nothing. Local store managers recruited and made hiring decisions, without being trained in this activity. We build beautiful stores and invest millions in inventory and advertising and then at the important moment of making the sale, if the salespeople can't sell, it doesn't happen.

Three things—testing, educating the people who do the hiring in how to hire, how to interview, what to look for, what to say, and getting good headquarters people out, at least on a sporadic basis, who are knowledgeable in the area of screening, so they can reinforce what's done in the field and keep on teaching—can improve human resources management. In our company, teaching is paramount and never stops, maybe because of turnover, maybe because of people changing jobs, maye because we're all so busy. Retailing is such a fast paced business that it's sometimes difficult to get people to focus on screening people.

SAM CRAIG: After we've gotten that person with high potential as a sales associate, the next key is to train them. Don, I know that Saks is doing quite a bit with training; do you find it to be effective in increasing productivity? Have you seen good results from your training activities? Maybe some of the other panelists want to comment on what they're doing to help train people effectively.

DON MERRITT: Before I comment on training, I'd like to follow up on the earlier comments. I don't believe in any Dr. Strangelove testing devices. Personnel people do not hire the sales associates. It's the line manager who makes that decision. Our job in personnel is to facilitate. All of us would like to think that we could go out and find this bevy of qualified people. You know and I know that that's not exactly the case. For us, one of the basic answers to that question—not that we have magic pills or prescriptions—is that the person has to be interviewed with an understanding as to the requirements of the position. Often, if you look at why John or Sally ended up in that department, it's because it was just a mass screening without any application to the skills or the level of skill related to that department. Yet selling eggs is very different than selling in our salon. The ability to understand some of those requirements, and the mix of the fellowship of associates in that department and how they will be brought into that environment, is important.

In terms of training, one of these days we ought to stop talking about training and do it! That may require some research, some coming together between academia and the business world.

QUESTION FROM THE FLOOR: I may have a wrong conception, and I don't live in New York City, but my perception is that the average retail salesperson doesn't make a lot of money.

DON MERRITT: Where do you live?

QUESTIONER: I live in Columbus, Ohio.

DON MERRITT: Maybe in Columbus, Ohio, they don't make much money.

QUESTIONER: Okay, that was a premise, but let me ask you a question. Has there been much experimentation with the level of pay? What I am wondering is, is pay a problem in attracting good people? Do some retailers refuse to pay those people more than minimum wage and then wonder why they leave?

STAN JAFFEE: I am sure that generally speaking, in retailing the small specialist pays much more than the large department store. S/he gets much better quality help. Nordstrom happens to be one of the highest paying department stores in the field. They demand a lot of their people and they get a lot from their people; they get it voluntarily because their people are brought to a professional level. As you go around the country with us—we have thirty-seven stores, coast-to-coast—we look at our competition as the specialist all over and we examine what makes them great. What makes them great is that they have a small, strong, well informed, interested sales staff that we try to pattern ourselves after, and pay is an important part of that.

QUESTIONER: I think that's important. My point is that it obviously works with small stores, but is it more adaptable for high quality mid-level stores than for large stores?

BOB KOCH: It's an interesting question, and I would suggest that the entry-level wage rate is really irrelevant, except when you get into a highly labor-intensive area. There's a sparse amount of information available on the subject. However, in the areas where we have spent some time looking at these things, it seems that even in those areas where you'll have a shoe salesperson earning a significant income selling shoes, you are not necessarily getting the kinds of qualities that you would want in the broadest sense. Sure, you can point to individual cases and identify people who can make it in any organization. But, in the main, looking at that normal curve, you're getting the same people that J.C. Penney is attracting. Remember, when we talk about this, we talk about a given point in time, and the specific time when you recruit will determine the quality of the applicant you're going to get. So it is difficult to equate a specific pay system with the quality you are going to attract. Sure, if you pay more, you're obviously going to get a better quality candidate. But even among that range of better quality there may not be the individual that you want.

LARRY ROBINSON: Our experience shows something different, namely, that the quality of sales effort sometimes tends to be more a function of corporate culture than of pay. Pay is very important, but my own experience indicates that there is much less of a relationship between pay and sales results than many of us would expect. I would wager—and it would be interesting to research—that if you talked to a sample of salespeople in retail stores and asked why they were in that store, many would tell you something along the lines of, "I like the people here." It's not going to be the pay. I believe that if you can develop an atmosphere of mutual caring, teamwork, and understanding of objectives among your people—whether they be bank tellers or salespeople—you'll have a much better opportunity of providing high quality service than when those circumstances don't prevail.

QUESTIONER: What you have to do is combine the two.

LARRY ROBINSON: Then you'll be successful.

QUESTION FROM THE FLOOR: I've done one study at the Emporium in northern California which seems to go along with what you said. I would guess the leverage in a store is really not in training the sales associates but in training what at the Emporium are called department sales managers, the first level supervisors. I think the first level supervisor is the person who is really going to create a lot of the atmosphere that you are talking about. I mean that the first level supervisor can do a tremendous amount to increase the productivity of salespeople. I believe that person is probably more important than pay.

LARRY ROBINSON: I agree. S/he becomes a role model in a corporate culture. S/he can become what the sociologist studying corporate culture call a "priest."

HARMON TOBLER: But the corporate culture has a great deal to do with how that first level supervisor operates and how important s/he is in the scheme of things; that corporate culture really determines what the attitude is about selling, and what the attitude is about the sales associate. We've talked here about $40,000-a-year shoe salespeople, but I think it is important to note that there are a tremendous number of salespeople operating in retail stores across America who work for $3.50, $4.00, and $4.50 an hour. You have those who make money, and there is an opportunity for making money based on productivity, but there's no magic in saying "We're going to pay somebody $20,000 a year." Sooner or later that has to relate to productivity, or you can't continue to pay the person.

I'll give you just a little run-down on an approach that I used prior to taking on my present responsibilities. It was a total process, starting with recruitment and selection going all the way through to follow-up service with a customer: about a five-step program. In the recruitment part of our program, we said we really were interested in people who have a desire to become professional sellers. We advertised in our major communities, "We will train you to be a professional seller. Opportunities of earning in a range of . . ." We got, from one ad, 150 to 250 applicants; these were screened by line managers. We didn't screen with personnel, other than their giving us training and guidelines on how to do it. Out of 150, we ended up with about 75 applicants who would be interviewed by five line managers who were given and who understood a set of criteria that we were looking for. Those five interviewed every one of the 75 in a round-robin interview and then voted on and selected those candidates that they felt were most likely to succeed. In order to qualify for the program, interviewees had to get four yesses out of five. Those people who succeeded with the four yesses were interviewed by three other line managers. I was explaining this to a consultant on recruiting and he said, "God, you really hate those people don't you, to give them 8 interviews in a day." Inerestingly, we found that the most successful of the candidates we selected were usually people who had not been in retailing before, who had never sold in a store—schoolteachers, secretaries—but they had desire.

The second part of our program, once the selection of candidates took place, was to train. We gave them seven full days without any in-the-field work, and then a half-day a week for another week, where they spent a half-day in classroom training and a half-day working in the departments. Within three months, even though we were hiring them on a base pay ($3.50/hr.) plus commission, they were making $12,000 to $14,000 dollars a year. But they had a lot of help. The third step in the program was a goal-setting process. We sat down and let them develop their goals and talk about them. We gave them norms of what's possible, what's expected, and what might be reached through the practice of certain principles, and so forth. For the first ninety days, the floor manager and the department sales manager met with each of those people on an individual basis, reviewed their accomplishments, gave rewards, and so forth. That dropped off to a monthly and then to a quarterly review.

In other words, there are millions of people out in the communities who will and can be productive sellers if they are sold on the idea of becoming professionals. People want to be professionals. And I have a belief that you do well that which you enjoy, and you enjoy that which you do well. You can take either side of that equation and make it work.

DON MERRITT: Just to follow up on that, I think we seduce ourselves to disappointment when we ask the selling associate, or the department manager or any of us, to be professional. We are looking for the best professional person because we have that standard, "We are the best." It's like this: You get your camera rolling and they are walking down a corridor where there are beautiful flowers and beautiful paneling and it all looks professional; this is great. This is the pre-selection process. Then we open the door and we put them in there; we have that professional person who has bought into professionalism. Then we close the door behind them. And there are people out there saying "Wait a minute. You want me to be professional! Look at this jungle." There are people still out there waiting in certain stores, waiting to be professional, because we haven't followed up. We haven't reinforced the behavior. We haven't committed the necessary time, dollars, energy, and education to reflect that level of professionalism. It's not being modeled by the department manager or by the store manager. We talk about corporate culture! If in fact it is not being reinforced on a day-to-day basis in their environment, then I think we are really kidding ourselves and we're back to lip service.

HARMON TOBLER: Of course, I think that is what is happening today in the good specialty store. They're doing consistently a lot of what we're talking about, and that's their reason for being.

Just one additional point concerning what salespeople do, how they become professional, and how we manage them: The problem in many department stores is that the god of the store is merchandising. A sales manager is a second, third, or in some cases, a fourth-class citizen. If you're in the selling end of the business, there's a "Don't talk to me" attitude because we are after, and we promote, and we support *merchants.* That attitude reaches all the way down to the salesperson. If the person who manages salespeople is treated as a second-class citizen, if all the priorities of management are directed toward whether that particular god is in the right place, whether the aisle is placed right or whether the colors are selected right, if that's the only thing that's given attention when senior management (and all the way through management) comes into the store, then that becomes the priority of the store manager and all the people in the store. I think that's a major disease in retailing that is only slowly being overcome.

SAM CRAIG: One thing that some of the discussion seems to indicate is that there is a lack of information about the best method of compensating or motivating. We have here an audience that includes a lot of research academics. What each of you might do is briefly indicate one or two things on which you'd like to see some research done to help you improve the effectiveness of retail sales associates.

JAY HUNDLEY: It is perplexing to us at J.C. Penney that we cannot find a consistent correlation between successful selling and pay. People here have cited Nordstrom. To our knowledge, Nordstrom is almost 100 percent on incentive pay, not only at the selling associate level, but all the way up the management ranks. They have been terribly successful in the Northwest and down the West Coast. By the same token, there are some equally successful retailers around the country who demonstrate productivity as good as Nordstrom's using straight dollars.

MEMBER OF THE AUDIENCE: *Low* straight dollars?

JAY HUNDLEY: Yes, low straight salary. We have 1700 stores and if you want to refer to the quality of customer service, we can show you stores side by side in which the quality of service to the customer is radically different. We would like very much to have anyone do research on how, and where, and for how long incentive pay systems change the behavior of selling associates and in what way it changes their behavior. We are running our own tests at the moment in order to try and ascertain that. With 1700 stores, it's fairly easy to build a number of experiments. It is a key question because, at the moment, salary cost constraints tend to drive wages to the minimum and tend to condition whom you can employ in a store.

STAN JAFFEE: I think the most beneficial research would tell us what it takes to make department store selling, which includes a lot of employees, an important profession. We do a lot of things such as calling salespeople "sales associates," make movies for them, and so on; but do we really do what it takes to bring selling in the stores up to a professional level?

BOB KOCH: Let me give you a little analogy. Suppose this were a football field and I were a defensive end. All of a sudden I see a pass coming from the offense; what is my initial response? To catch the ball and run like crazy for that goal, despite the fact there is a thundering herd of 260-pound animals out there to clobber me. Why? Behavioral science has known why for a long time—our society has conditioned us to enthusiastically respond to situations and circumstances that will provide the recognition we all want and need. Thus, there are four conditions that operate to create this motivation and sustain its momentum. (1) There is going to be a recognition of my achievement. I will be recognized by friends and people whom I don't know. (2) There is a record of the accomplishment. (3) There is a potential for a lucrative pro-ball contract, or, if I'm a pro player, a better contract next time. (4) There is the roar of the crowd. Now, all of those things we can replicate in a business environment, except that we have a problem with the roar of the crowd. But that problem is not insurmountable. If we create communicative devices that will generate specific kinds of internalization of my desire, to achieve more of these recognitions and rewards, are we not then able to achieve a greater result?

As researchers, in what ways would you: (1) measure, and (2) reward the kinds of motivations that you think are necessary to achieve the intent of such a management system? We have experimented with a variety of these things fairly successfully. I think it's got to start with recruitment obviously. Then we have to conduct some effective training—not the kinds of things we currently do. Then we have to be able to evaluate that individual. Sandy Dornbush, from Stanford, in *The Nature of Power and Authority,* indicates what effects one can get with a very good evaluative device in various organizational settings. The same thing is true, I think, in the retailing area. But a conventional kind of performance appraisal is not enough—and again, performance appraisal fails in the United States for a variety of reasons—but the facts of the performance in terms of the ability to perform to produce those facts are the keys to effective performance appraisal. Finally, we need to link all of that to compensation and to incentive compensation that is directly connected in the mind of the individual to performance. Researchers who came up with those kinds of things would find that we would have a very, very receptive ear.

DON MERRITT: It might be interesting for us to understand better what happens by throwing a net over some selling associates in any of our organizations. They are customers. I've always wondered what happens to these customers when they put on the badge of selling associate; there is a distinct change in their behavior. As customers, they know exactly how they like to be treated. Yet yesterday's customer who today comes into those four walls as a salesperson acts very differently. As customers, they can moan and groan about the very things that we're trying to correct and fix among our sales people.

It would also be interesting to look at a group who were all basically happy with their environment, their salaries, and their compensation, and to compare their expectations as related to service with the expectations of those who were not. What makes that difference? That might help us—whether in our training, orientation, modeling, or reinforcement—to understand and to deal better with the issue. Another interesting research area might be the impact of creating a value system anchored to the environment that they work in. I am not talking about basic one-to-one hygiene, really looking at ferreting out what makes that selling associate proud. But what in the environment—management, systems, store planning efforts in terms of lighting, the carpets, the walls, the access—impacts the selling associate in his/her relationship with the customer?

LARRY ROBINSON: My experience teaches me that retailing research has concentrated too much on stock turn and not enough on people turn. In many cases, it's likely that the easiest way to improve stock turn is by increasing sales. I think a major opportunity in research, then, is to transfer some ideas from the social and behavioral sciences to retailing. It's a task of going back to Mayo, Rothlisberger and the bank wiring room at G.E. in 1938, the work of Skinner, Rieseman, Freud, and others. We've quantified retail operating results to a fare-thee-well. While there are further opportunities in that area, the great possibilities concern people.

HARMON TOBLER: I think you have been given a pretty good agenda for research already. I'd like to just state a couple of biases I have in this regard. First, with respect to the question of commission versus hourly compensation, I personally believe that the question begs the issue; it is not the key issue at all. I have strong belief that professionalism and fulfillment are the critical issues. In medicine for instance, there are professionals and there are quacks, and I believe that the difference has to do with the amount and quality of service that they render to their fellow human beings.

I think that's also the critical issue in selling. If we can somehow—through our corporate culture, our understanding of the customer and his/her needs—insure that the salesperson experiences the fulfillment of making a contribution, then salespeople will perform and produce to such an extent that they will be well rewarded, regardless of whether it's by salary or by commission. I don't know if that can be translated into a research opportunity, but I firmly believe that fulfillment and making a contribution to your fellow human beings are possible in this business of selling. I believe that today hundreds and thousands of people in America are being sold wrong things for the wrong reasons, and commission selling contributes to that, as do spiffs, and all the methods that retailers use to push goods on the public that they really don't need or want. Yet people have a great number of needs, and the reason we sell them what they don't want is that we don't take the time to understand what it is they do want, on an individual basis, and to give them that. Once we teach salespeople how to do that, they'll love the business and will make tremendous contributions.

QUESTION FROM THE FLOOR: Considering that if we do this kind of research we will have your ear, could we have your help? Could we use your stores as laboratories? We have a lot of sophisticated techniques and we can do the background reading, but we don't have access to real data. Can we have access to compensation data? Can we interview your salespeople and your first line supervisors? If we can do that, I think we can provide some of these things for you. We are technique-rich but data-poor. If we can have your help, I think we can strike a bargain.

QUESTION FROM THE FLOOR: There seems to be an inconsistency between what I see and what you see in the store, and I have charge cards in three of the stores represented on the panel. What I see when I go into one of your stores is not professional salespersons. Instead, I see minimum-wage, part-time seasonals. Half the time they're floaters, and they've generally been there less than a year and don't intend to stay.

BOB KOCH: You are not talking about Bally. We can't get rid of some of our people.

QUESTIONER: I'm talking about stores like Macy's and Federated in cities like San Francisco and Seattle. My wife and I do our shopping on the weekend and you don't have the professional people on the floor, though there are a lot of people in the store. I understand problems connected with that. I don't seen the kinds of sales representatives that you are talking about, except in men's suits or carpeting or something like that.

BOB KOCH: That, I think, is what we have been describing all afternoon. Unfortunately, we are not able to attract, in all cases, a range of people who would meet the criteria that you're describing. Consequently, we do the best we can with what we have. Don't misunderstand me; these are not bad people. They may not be as acutely atuned to the selling techniques that we would like them to display, and therefore we train them, motivate them,

and do whatever we can to elevate their level of interest, their professionalism, their product knowledge, and their techniques of interpersonal
relationships. It's very difficult to answer your question. When you have a
50 percent turnover in the retail industry on the average, or when you get into Brooks Brothers, J. Magnin, Robinson's, Saks, or Bally, it's not as easy
to see the kinds of turnover that you're talking about. The people in those
stores are generally a better level of retail salespersons than can be seen in
most other stores. We are not saying that we're satisfied with that. We
believe we have good people, but we are also saying that there are better
people, and that distributed among the range of that population are some
people who are not as good as we would like them to be.

HARMON TOBLER: I would like to say, in fairness to companies like
Macy's and other department stores, there are a goodly number of fine
quality, turned on, professional salespeople; but there are not in that total
number enough so that your wife or you get the impact when they shop in
those stores. But they have some very fine professional people. The problem
with all of us is we don't have all of them that way; that is partly due to the
economics of productivity. Some stores, I would assume, like Brooks
Brothers, have been able to accomplish this without going to short-hour
scheduling. You are of little importance to a person's livelihood if he or she
is getting only eight hours a week; you can't live much on eight hours a week
so that really becomes just a place to pick up some extra money. I think
that's one of the key problems.

STAN JAFFEE: Also, while you're referring to department store
trends, I'd like to point out that we see more and more supermarket merchandising. They have terrific salespeople; they call it a chrome rack. You
can't find anyone else to ask a question or to sell to you. I had that experience myself last Saturday while I was shoppng with my wife, who was
looking for a top and bottom garment in a department store. She found one
part of the outfit but nobody to ask for the other, except two salesladies
behind a formica island who were busy wrapping packages.

HARMON TOBLER: Of course, I think that's really the problem we're
facing. We talk about Nordstrom's: They've got an approach, and it's a
very fine one, but nobody has been more successful than Macy's California.
Their approach involves eliminating salespeople, putting efforts into merchandising, into the way goods are presented, and so forth. I don't think
they have to take a back seat to anyone in their success pattern, and that
suggests, "Hey, are salespeople all that important?"

DON MERRITT: Well, I will risk leaving these gentlemen and joining
you all out there, because I think your observation is right on. I think when
we look at short-hours staffing, we look at it as a necessary investment to

cover our regulars. We look at it from a standpoint of what minimal invest-ment of time, energy, training, supervision, over weekends or on nights or early mornings versus viewing it as a part of the total resources available in the store. I don't think we do a good job in terms of really investing as we do in the full-time regular. We don't commit to it. It's like a chicken one day and feathers the next. I think we need to reevaluate how we maximize our total resources.

JACK JACOBY: The problem seems to vary as a function of the prod-uct. I would imagine that Larry, especially with the kind of product sold in jewelry stores, and to a certain extent Stan, considering the kinds of clothing sold in Brooks Brothers probably need a higher level of selling sophistication. This, then, leads to two questions especially for those two gentlemen. First, what are you doing now, and are you happy with this ap-proach? Second, what things are you not happy with in your current ap-proach to recruiting, training, and motivating your sales force?

LARRY ROBINSON: Well, Brooks hasn't had an opening for five years.

STAN JAFFEE: We are very fortunate. We usually have waiting lists of people, probably from some of the other stores, who are waiting to come to work. We are happy with the people we're getting.

MEMBER OF THE AUDIENCE: I would just like to get back to a comment made earlier, with which I personally agree: that we are losing some of the focus on who it is we are trying to train in the business. The focus has shifted in the wrong direction. We need to train the managers of the salespeople. If you ask, "What is making the customers turn off?" Well, customers are not looking for somebody who has all the knowledge about the product. They are getting turned off by salespeople who are rude, who don't service them at all. Most customers would feel very comfortable with somebody who went the extra mile and said, "I don't know, but I'll try to get the answer; let me get somebody who can get you the answer," rather than knowing all the answers right away. The focus has to be on the man-agement of the salespeople, not training the salespeople.

BOB KOCH: You're absolutely correct. However, although your point is intrinsically related, I don't think that we were addressing the variables sur-rounding how you achieve that. Still you cannot and should not expect the line manager to develop the salespeople. That has to be done by the staff people in the corporate environment. Once you have that package put to-gether, then you train him/her to use these tools with these people. That is not as easily done as it is said.

SAM CRAIG: What I would like to do is to give each of the panelists an opportunity to comment on any aspect of the topic that hasn't been covered or that they feel is important.

HARMON TOBLER: Well, I would just say that in this whole area of selling today I believe that the retail industry, especially at the department store level, on a scale of one to ten, we're still somewhere between a two and a three in where we have to go in the area of selling. There is a greater realization of that today than there has been in the past. I think that the recession has made a great impact on retailers in terms of the importance of selling in our business, but I think there is a long, long way to go and we need a lot of help. I, for one, have no question that without that help, as tough as it's been already, we couldn't possibly make it.

LARRY ROBINSON: I agree. The country is awash with excess retail space, as indicated by sales-per-square-foot figures, and retailing is even more competitive than ever. Many retailers are not achieving satisfactory returns on investment. The greatest opportunity in this situation, then would be to focus on opportunities to improve sales productivity. That's where the chances are very great to do things in retailing that benefit the economy as a whole, individual companies, and you as individuals.

DON MERRITT: I think that we've hit on a lot of different topics and, at the risk of being redundant, I think one of the critical roles of management (we've known about it for a long time) is how we model the expectations, be it service or productivity issues. Unless we can become a more enlightened management and let that message be very clearly demonstrated to our selling associates, until we create that colony, if you will, of self-support, a consistent standard that's reinforced, we're really kidding ourselves. I don't think it's necessarily just compensation; I don't think it's just benefits; I don't think it's just the environment of the store. I think it's all these things. But, most important, I think it's the signals we give about what we expect: Do we expect it and do we reinforce it? Do we do something about it? When we walk through a store and we see a selling associate chewing gum, or leaning on a counter, or doing nothing, do we say to ourselves "Gee, if that's the department manager, it's sure hard to find good help these days." Or, do we really get involved? Do we confront? I think we have to learn how to be better, more constructive confronters. I think our selling associates will respect us if we respect them and if we're consistent.

BOB KOCH: I would sum up by saying, first of all, that we must define the problem. Productivity—it's a buzz word that's been around for a few years now—is not what everyone in this room is sitting here thinking it is. Productivity, as defined by macroeconomists, is the result of dividing output by input. We in the retail business rely upon the industrial engineering equation, which simply inverts that equation and divides the input variables by the output to come up with another number which we call productivity. Based on research with the National Commission on Productivity, that is wrong. Productivity is not the result of the equation. Productivity is the relationship of each variable of input, one to another, and their combined relationship to that which is produced. We now use those equations and rely upon them to take an after-the-fact measurement, believing that this is going to help us achieve a better result. But there's another mathematical equation that we have to develop and use. We would rely upon that information to help us further.

STAN JAFFEE: We've talked about raising the level of professionalism and getting more professional people into selling, but there's one variable that we didn't discuss: Our industry is open eighty some hours a week, including Saturdays, Sundays, and nights, and it does not offer high pay even at its optimum. How do you attract young people, at a professional level, to work in an industry like that, as opposed to a corporate setting where they work five days a week in set hours? Everyone wants to go to a corporate setup; that's easy. To get them on the line is the problem that's facing us, and that's where we need help.

About the Contributors

Donald W. Barclay is currently a doctoral candidate in marketing at the Graduate School of Business Administration, the University of Michigan. He completed his B.Sc. at Bishop's University in 1968 and his M.B.A. at McMaster University in 1970 where he was awarded the Matthew S. Litvak Gold Medal. Mr. Barclay worked for the following seven years with IBM Canada Ltd., Data Processing Division, where he held various sales and national account management positions. From 1977–1981, he was Assistant Professor and from 1979–1981 he was also assistant dean, Undergraduate Programme in the Faculty of Business Administration at Memorial University, St. John's, Newfoundland. His work with Professor Michael J. Ryan at the University of Michigan has resulted in an article in the *Association for Consumer Research Proceedings* (1982) and together they are currently working on a study of industrial buying behavior sponsored by the National Association of Fleet Administrators.

John T. Cacioppo is an associate professor of psychology at the University of Iowa. He received his B.S. from the University of Missouri-Columbia in 1973 and his M.A. in 1975 and Ph.D. in 1977 from Ohio State University. Professor Cacioppo is co-author or editor of three books with Richard Petty: *Attitudes and Persuasion: Classic and Contemporary Approaches; Perspectives in Cardiovascular Psychophysiology;* and *Social Psychophysiology: A Sourcebook.* Professor Cacioppo is currently on the advisory board of the *Journal of Consumer Research* and serves on the editorial boards of three other journals. His empirical work centers on the cognitive and physiological foundations of attitudinal processes and has been published in journals such as the *Journal of Personality and Social Psychology, Psychophysiology, Personality and Social Psychology Bulletin*, and the *Journal of Consumer Research.*

Robert W. Chestnut is senior vice president and director of research at Advertising Research Foundation (ARF). Dr. Chestnut came to ARF in January 1983. Prior to that time, he had served as an assistant professor of business at the Graduate School of Business, Columbia University, and as a professor of economic psychology at Tilburg University in the Netherlands (1981 visiting appointment). He earned an M.S. and Ph.D. in consumer/social psychology from Purdue University (1977) and has published extensively in marketing and advertising research. Since 1978, Dr. Chestnut has been active as a consultant and expert witness in matters concerning advertising and has testified on behalf of the industry before the U.S. Senate, the FTC, and the International Trade Commission. In addition to his council responsibilities, he is in charge of ARF's focus on new technology and its implications for both advertising and advertising research.

Lawrence B. Chonko is an assistant professor in the Department of Marketing at Texas Tech University, Lubbock, Texas. Professor Chonko completed his B.A. (1973) at Lehigh University and his M.B.A. (1975) and Ph.D. (1978) from the University of Houston. His research interests include personal selling, sales management, and marketing management; his most recent empirical work involves an examination of ethical behaviors in the marketing management profession. Professor Chonko's recent publications have appeared in journals such as the *Academy of Management Journal*, the *Journal of Personal Selling and Sales Management*, the *Journal of Purchasing and Materials Management*, and *Psychological Reports*.

Robert B. Cialdini is a professor in the Department of Psychology, Arizona State University, Tempe, Arizona. He received his Ph.D. in Social Psychology from the University of North Carolina. Portions of his chapter were adapted from his book, *Instant Influence* (Wm. Morrow & Co., forthcoming).

Terry Deutscher is an associate professor in the Department of Business Administration at the University of Western Ontario, London, Canada, where he is currently serving as director of research. Prior to his arrival at Western, Professor Deutscher taught at Ohio State and Cornell. He has a chemical engineering degree from the University of Alberta, and an M.B.A. and Ph.D. degrees from Stanford University. Besides his research interest in sales force management, Professor Deutscher conducts research on marketing management issues. His publications have appeared in such journals as *Industrial Marketing Management, Journal of Marketing Research,* and *Business Quarterly*.

Ben M. Enis is a professor of marketing at the University of Southern California. He received his Ph.D. from Louisana State University in 1967. Dr. Enis's outstanding teaching abilities have been recognized in three separate awards presented by the College of Business Administration Alumni Association, the Faculty Senate of the University of Houston, and by the M.B.A. Students Association of the University of Missouri.

Dr. Enis has written five textbooks, including *Marketing Principles, The Marketing Research Process*, and *Personal Selling*. He has also edited several anthologies, including *Marketing Classics, Marketing Is Everybody's Business*, and *Review of Marketing 1982*. In addition, he has contributed research papers to a number of marketing and retailing journals. He serves as section editor (Marketing Programs) for the *Journal of Marketing* and on the Editorial Review Boards of several other academic journals.

James M. Hunt is an assistant professor on the faculty of the Department of Marketing, Temple University, Philadelphia. Previously, Professor Hunt held a visiting appointment in the Marketing Department at the University of Florida, Gainesville. His bachelor degree work was completed in economics at Virginia Polytechnic Institute in 1965. Professor Hunt later received a masters degree in business administration from the University of Dayton, where he taught until 1974. Professor Hunt completed his education at the University of Cincinnati, receiving his Ph. D. in marketing in 1981. Professor Hunt's teaching and research interests lie in the area of consumer decision making, with particular emphasis on the subject causal inference making. Currently, he is involved in a program of research dealing with attributional processing and persuasion.

Elizabeth J. Johnston-O'Connor received her B.A. from St. Bonaventure University and earned an M.A. and Ph.D. in social psychology from the University of Rochester. Previously a human resources consultant for Xerox Corporation, she joined LIMRA in 1980 and was named scientist for consumer and organizational research in 1983. Professor Johnston-O'Connor has written many articles for insurance and psychology-related publications and has co-authored a book entitled *Management Dynamics* with Grace M. Reale. She is an adjunct professor at St. Joseph College (Connecticut), and a member of the American Psychological Association and the American Marketing Association.

Jerome B. Kernan is professor of behavioral analysis and a fellow of the graduate school at the University of Cincinnati, where he also directs the M.S. and Ph.D. programs in the Department of Marketing. Prior to his appointment at Cincinnati (1967), he worked at the Graduate School of Business, University of Texas at Austin. A graduate of the University of Illinois (M.S., 1959; Ph.D., 1962), Kernan also has done post-doctoral work at Carnegie-Mellon University (1962) and the University of Kansas (1963), both sponsored by the Ford Foundation. His publications, which include six books and scores of articles, have reflected his principal research interest—consumer psychology—and his efforts have been supported with grants from the American Association of Advertising Agencies Educational Foundation and the George A. Ramlose Foundation. In addition to consulting, he has been active for a number of years in the American Marketing Association, American Psychological Association (Division 23), and the Association for Consumer Research, for which he served as president in 1978.

Lawrence M. Lamont is a professor of commerce at Washington and Lee University. He received his B.S., M.B.A., and Ph.D. degrees from the

University of Michigan. Dr. Lamont was on the teaching faculty of the University of Colorado prior to his position at Washington and Lee. He has published numerous articles in marketing journals, including the *Journal of Marketing Research*, and serves as a consultant and expert witness to several firms.

Thomas W. Leigh is an assistant professor in the Department of Marketing at the Pennsylvania State University, University Park. Professor Leigh received a B.S. in Economics and an M.B.A. from Southern Illinois University. He completed the D.B.A. in Marketing in 1980 at Indiana University, Bloomington. Immediately prior to beginning the doctoral program at Indiana University, he taught for six years at Lincoln Land Community College in Springfield, Illinois. During the latter two of these years, he served as Business Division Chairman. Professor Leigh's research interests focus on marketing communications issues. He is currently involved in work with nonverbal communications in sales encounters, cognitive script analysis of industrial purchasing processes, sales encounters, and negotiations, and impression formation processes in industrial sales encounters.

George H. Lucas, Jr., is an assistant professor in the Department of Marketing at Texas A&M University, College Station. Prior to graduate work, he was actively involved in sales as a representative for both American Hospital Supply Corporation and Pitney Bowes Corporation. Upon completing a doctoral program with an emphasis in the sales management area, he received his Ph.D. in business administration from the University of Missouri-Columbia in 1983. His research and teaching interests lie in the personal selling, sales management, and buyer-seller dyad areas. Professor Lucas is presently involved with the development of selling strategies for technological advancements as an assistant research scientist for the Institute for Ventures in New Technologies (INVENT) at Texas A&M. He also serves on the Faculty Advisory Board of the Center for Retailing Studies at TAMU. The hypothesized model of the job satisfaction-job performance relationship contained in his chapter is presently being tested by Dr. Lucas in a national retail chain.

William J. Lundstrom is chairman and professor of marketing at Old Dominion University. He earned his B.S. from Purdue University, M.B.A. from Indiana University, and D.B.A. from the University of Colorado. He has served on the faculties of Indiana University, California State University at Fullerton, Southern Methodist University, and the University of Mississippi. His publications include articles in the *Journal of Marketing Research, Journal of Marketing, Journal of Advertising,* and *Journal of Business Research* among others. He is on the editorial board of two marketing journals and serves as a consultant to consumer and industrial firms.

Robert J. O'Connor works in the Consumer and Organizational Research Unit at LIMRA (Life Insurance Marketing and Research Association). His recent projects have included a major study on consumer experiences in the life insurance marketplace and a study of small business insurance in the United States. He is now working on a survey of people who have had life insurance death claims experience and an extensive study of the baby boom generation. He is also engaged in a study of life insurance ownership in Canada.

Before joining LIMRA, Dr. O'Connor was with the American Council of Life Insurance, where he directed several large-scale surveys of public opinion, including annual studies of the general public's attitudes toward health insurance, disability insurance, and government involvement in the health care system.

He has a Ph.D. in political science from Stanford University; he did his undergraduate work at the University of California, Riverside. Dr. O'Connor taught at Georgetown University for several years before entering the world of insurance-related research.

Richard E. Petty is an associate professor of psychology at the University of Missouri-Columbia. He received his B.A. from the University of Virginia in 1973 and his M.A. in 1975 and Ph.D. in 1977 from Ohio State University. Professor Petty is co-author or editor of three books with John Cacioppo: *Attitudes and Persuasion: Classic and Contemporary Approaches; Perspectives in Cardiovascular Psychophysiology;* and *Social Psychophysiology: A Sourcebook.* He is also co-editor (with Thomas Ostrom and Timothy Brock) of *Cognitive Responses in Persuasion.* Professor Petty is currently associate editor of the *Personality and Social Psychology Bulletin* and serves on the editorial board of three other journals. His empirical work focuses broadly on social influence processes in individuals and groups and has been published in a number of professional journals.

Peter H. Reingen is an associate professor in the Department of Marketing at Arizona State University, Tempe. Professor Reingen was previously at the University of Houston, University of South Carolina, and Iona College. He completed his formal education at the University of Cincinnati, receiving a Ph.D. in business administration in 1974. Professor Reingen's research interests lie in the areas of persuasion and interpersonal influence. His present research examines interpersonal influence on consumer brand choices with social network techniques. His publications have appeared in the *Journal of Marketing Research, Journal of Consumer Research,* and *Journal of Applied Psychology*, among others.

Arno J. Rethans is an assistant professor in the Marketing Department at the Pennsylvania State University, University Park. Professor Rethans's current research interests center around the application of script theory to the understanding of consumer and industrial buyer purchasing processes. Some of his work on script theory has been presented at the national conferences of the American Marketing Association and the Association for Consumer Research.

Adrian B. Ryans is a professor of business administration at the School of Business Administration, University of Western Ontario, London, Canada. Professor Ryans was previously on the faculty of the Graduate School of Business, Stanford University, from 1975 to 1981. Professor Ryans has a B.AS. from the University of Waterloo, and M.B.A. and Ph.D. degrees from Stanford University. His current research and teaching interests lie in the areas of sales force management and marketing strategy. Recent publications have appeared in such journals as the *Journal of Marketing Research,* the *Journal of Consumer Research,* and *Organizational Behavior and Human Performance.*

David Schumann is a Ph.D. candidate in social psychology at the University of Missouri-Columbia. He received his B.A. from the University of Arizona in 1971 and his M.C. from Arizona State University in 1975. His current research interest focuses on consumer response to advertisements and has been published in the *Journal of Consumer Research.*

Michael F. Smith is an assistant professor in the Department of Marketing at Temple University, Philadelphia. Professor Smith completed his B.A. and M.A. degrees at Wayne State University in 1976. Professor Smith recently received his D.B.A. in Marketing from Indiana University, Bloomington. Professor Smith's teaching and research expertise lie in the areas of retailing and marketing channels. His present research focuses on the retailing of services and the study of interorganizational conflict in marketing channels. His recent publications have appeared in several American Marketing Association special conference proceedings.

Barton A. Weitz is an associate professor of marketing at the Wharton School of the University of Pennsylvania. Professor Weitz received his M.B.A. and Ph.D. in Business Administration from Stanford University and a B.S. in Electrical Engineering from the Massachusetts Institute of Technology. Prior to his appointment at Wharton, Dr. Weitz was an associate professor of marketing at the UCLA Graduate School of Management. Professor Weitz has completed a number of projects on personal selling effectiveness and salesforce management issues. His research in these areas has appeared in journals such as *Journal of Marketing Research, Journal of Marketing, Journal of Consumer Research,* and *Administrative*

Science Quarterly. Presently, Professor Weitz is engaged in projects concerning salesforce compensation, the management of independent representatives, and the development of sales training programs. He presently serves on the editorial boards of the *Journal of Marketing Research, Journal of Marketing,* and the *Journal of Personal Selling and Sales Force Management* and is the section editor for a special *Journal of Marketing Research* issues on Competition in Marketing. In addition, he has co-authored two textbooks: *Selling: Principles and Methods* and *Strategic Marketing: Making and Implementing Decisions.*

Arch G. Woodside is a professor of marketing at the University of South Carolina. He is the editor of the *Journal of Business Research.* Arch is President of Division 23, Consumer Psychology, American Psychological Association. He received his Ph.D. from Pennsylvania State University. He co-edited *Buyer-Seller Interactions: Empirical Research and Normative Issues* with Peter Reingen in 1981.

William G. Zikmund is a professor of marketing at Oklahoma State University. He holds a B.S. from the University of Colorado, a M.B.A. from Southern Illinois University, and the D.B.A. from the University of Colorado. His articles have appeared in the *Journal of Marketing* and other marketing and psychological journals. His current scholarly activities involve the writing and publication of texts in marketing research and marketing management.

Walter H. Zultowski, assistant vice president, Research Division, is responsible for all primary consumer behavior research on life insurance and related financial products at LIMRA and directs the staff involved in this function. The author of numerous articles in both professional journals and insurance publications, Dr. Zultowski joined LIMRA in 1978. He was appointed director for economic and consumer research in 1980 and was named to his present position in 1982. A graduate of Hartwick College, he received his M.A. from Wake Forest University and was awarded his Ph.D. from the College of Business Administration at the University of Tennessee. Dr. Zultowski is a member of the American Marketing Association, the Association for Consumer Research, and the American Psychological Association. He also serves as an adjunct faculty member at the University of Hartford's Barney School of Business where he teaches graduate courses in consumer behavior and marketing research.

About the Editors

Jacob Jacoby, a psychologist by training, is Merchants Council Professor of Marketing and Director of New York University's Institute of Retail Management. He is a past president of both the Association for Consumer Research and the Division of Consumer Psychology (Division 23) of the American Psychological Association. Among other honors, he received the American Marketing Association's 1978 Maynard Award for the article in the *Journal of Marketing* that made the most significant contribution to marketing thought during that year.

Professor Jacoby has served on the editorial boards of the *Journal of Marketing Research* and *Journal of Consumer Research* and has reviewed for numerous other journals and government agencies. Professor Jacoby has also served as a consultant or conducted research for various clients in government (for example, the U.S. Senate, Department of Justice, FDA, FTC) and industry (for example, American Home Products Corp.; the American Association of Advertising Agencies; Bristol Myers; E.I. Du-Pont; Firestone Tire and Rubber; GAF; General Electric; the Grocery Manufacturers of America; McCormick & Co.; The Million Dollar Round Table; The National Football League; Pillsbury; Procter & Gamble; The Proprietary Association; and Standard Oil of California).

C. Samuel Craig is an associate professor of marketing at New York University's Graduate School of Business Administration. Professor Craig received a B.A. from Westminster College, an M.S. from the University of Rhode Island, and a Ph.D. from the Ohio State University. He has taught at the Ohio State University, College of Administrative Sciences, and Cornell University, Graduate School of Business and Public Administration. Professor Craig has done considerable work in the areas of advertising, assessing communication effectiveness, the diffusion of innovation, and marketing of energy conservation. His research on these areas has appeared in journals such as the *Journal of Marketing, Journal of Marketing Research, Journal of Consumer Research, Journal of Applied Psychology,* and *Journal of Energy and Development.* He has co-authored two books: *Consumer Behavior: An Information Processing Perspective,* and *International Marketing Research,* and is on the editorial boards of the *Journal of Marketing Research* and the *Journal of Retailing.*

Members of IRM Industry Councils

National Advisory Council

Francis C. Rooney
Chairman of the Board,
Melville Corporation;
Council Chairman

William P. Arnold
Chairman and Chief
Executive Officer,
Associated Dry Goods

Robert J. Suslow
Chairman of the Board,
Batus Retail Division

Waldo Burnside
Vice Chairman and Chief
Operating Officer,
Carter Hawley Hale Stores

George L. Lawson, Jr.
Vice President, Corporate
Development, Dayton Hudson
Corporation

Michael J. Boyle
Executive Vice President,
Specialty Retailing,
General Mills Corporation

James M. Tait
President, Household Merchandising

Stewart Turley
Chairman of the Board, Jack
Eckerd Corporation

Alvin Lubetkin
Vice Chairman and Chief
Executive Officer, Oshman's
Sporting Goods

Donald V. Seibert
Chairman of the Board,
J.C. Penney Company

Herbert H. Schiff
Chairman of the Board,
SCOA Industries

Merchants Council

Frank Armsworthy
Vice Chairman, Saks Fifth
Avenue; Council Chairman

John Burden III
Chairman, Abraham & Strauss

Robin Farkas
Chairman, Executive Committee,
Alexander's, Inc.

John S. Burke, Jr.
Chairman of the Board,
B. Altman & Company

Nicholas A. Gallopo
Partner, Arthur Andersen & Co.

Lee Abraham
Chairman of the Board, Associated
Merchandising Corporation

Bamberger's

James S. Schoff, Jr.
President, Bloomingdale's

Wilmer Bresee
Chairman of the Board, Bresee's
Oneonta Department Store

Frank T. Reilly
President, Brooks Brothers

James O. Marrs
Senior Vice President of Retail
Development, Brown Shoe Company

315

Werner J. Kaplan
President, Certified Creations

Samuel S. Gross
Partner, Ernst & Whinney

Gimbel's

William Tobin
President, Kaufmann's

Lane Bryant, Inc.

Frank Watson
*Vice Chairman, Lord
& Taylor*

Arthur Reiner
*President, Macy's
New York*

Montgomery Ward & Company

Herbert Solomon
*Chairman of the Board,
Ohrbach's, Inc.*

Irwin Cohen
Partner, Touche Ross & Co.

Edward J. Seward
*Vice President, Administration,
Wallach's, Inc.*

PERSONAL SELLING

Theory, Research, and Practice

edited by

JACOB JACOBY and C. SAMUEL CRAIG

For too long, retailing researchers and professionals have struggled with the question most basic to their business: how can the salesperson influence the customer to buy? **Personal Selling** addresses this issue head on. This edited volume integrates the findings of leading psychologists and marketing experts with the insights of top executives from J.C. Penney, Brooks Brothers, and Saks Fifth Avenue to provide a cogent, fresh solution.

The contributors understand the necessity of improving personal selling—of transforming mere clerking into selling—in order to enhance employee productivity and, thereby, profitability. With a broad variety of expertise, they explore the distinct routes to persuasion, the relationship between the consumer's feeling about the salesperson and his decision to buy, and such pervasive influence principles as consistency and scarcity. They illustrate how to use behavioral science theory to diagnose problems in closing, and provide a summary of seventeen basic closing techniques. A closer look at the insurance industry, in particular, reveals the relationship of job satisfaction to job performance, and the variables that influence a successful sale and the persistency of a sale. Finally, the contributors discuss corporate culture and its importance in establishing a personal selling style.

Personal Selling offers a range of practical knowledge that goes a long way toward solving the biggest problem in retailing today—improving the productivity of the salesperson.